ISLAMIC CROSSPOLLINATIONS

Interactions in the Medieval Middle East

edited by

Anna Akasoy, James E. Montgomery,
and Peter E. Pormann

Gibb Memorial Trust
2007

Published by

The E. J. W. Gibb Memorial Trust

ISBN 978 0 906094 55 6

A CIP record for this book is available from the British Library

Further details of the E. J. Gibb Memorial Trust and its publications
are available at the Trust's website

www.gibbtrust.org

Printed in Great Britain by
Short Run Press
Exeter

Contents

List of Contributors

ANNA A. AKASOY
Departmental Lecturer, Oriental Institute, Pusey Lane, Oxford OX1 2LE
anna.akasoy@orinst.ox.ac.uk

ELIZABETH K. FOWDEN
Research Fellow, Centre for Greek and Roman Antiquity, National Research Foundation, 48 Vas. Konstantinou, 116 35 Athens, Greece
ekfowden@hlk.forthnet.gr

GARTH FOWDEN
Research Professor, Centre for Greek and Roman Antiquity, National Research Foundation, 48 Vas. Konstantinou, 116 35 Athens, Greece
gfowden@eie.gr

DEBORAH HOWARD
Professor of Architectural History, St John's College, Cambridge CB2 1TP
djh1000@hermes.cam.ac.uk

JOHN MARENBON
Senior Research Fellow, Trinity College, Cambridge CB2 1TQ
jm258@cam.ac.uk

JAMES E. MONTGOMERY
Professor of Classical Arabic, Trinity Hall, Cambridge CB2 1TJ
jem33@cam.ac.uk

DAVID NICOLLE
Visiting Research Fellow, Institute of Medieval Studies, Nottingham University; 67 Maplewell Road, Woodhouse Eaves, Leics. LE12 8RG
david.c.nicolle@btinternet.com

PETER E. PORMANN
Welllcome Trust Assistant Professor, Department of Classics & Ancient History, University of Warwick, Coventry CV4 7AL
p.e.pormann@warwick.ac.uk

ULRICH RUDOLPH
Orientalisches Seminar, Universität Zürich, Wiesenstrasse 7-9, CH-8008 Zürich
u.rudolph@access.unizh.ch

Preface

James E. Montgomery

Islam as a series of cultural, intellectual, and religious ventures appears in the popular imagination as a monolithic entity. Many scholars of a traditional bent have tended to describe it in essentialist terms, whilst many Muslims themselves promote their construction of a pure and unadulterated Islamic past, to which they strive to return by purging foreign or unauthentic elements from their religion. Next to these attempts, another more traditional view sees in linear and teleological terms any relationships of influence which obtained between the Islamic and the non-Islamic worlds. In the case of the Greek philosophical, scientific and intellectual heritage, for example, knowledge was thus transmitted from Alexandria to Baghdad to Toledo.

The present volume challenges the exclusivity, and at times the applicability, of both these myths of the development of Islamic cultures. To do justice to the complexity of structures within which the Muslim Middle Ages unfolded, customary approaches to the questions of interaction and influence are expanded through a novel concept, that of crosspollination. Instead of telling *the* story of the transmission of Western works from Greece via Islam into the Latin world, a number of case studies highlight the plurality of encounters between Islam and other adjacent cultures. Of course, to achieve this, these studies take advantage of a variety of approaches and paradigms traditionally used to explore and account for these processes. What is distinct, I think, is that, through their concentrations on the complexities and multiplicities of the phenomena which they study, they reveal that there is occasion for a new dimension to our conceptualisations, that afforded by the notion of crosspollination. This notion is itself the subject of a lengthy study in the final contribution to the volume, one which attempts to situate it with regard to a number of other prevalent paradigms and approaches.

Yet, this is, in many ways, an unusual book. Its unusualness may even make it unique. It does not present the reader with the theories or the thinking of a specific school or the concerted arguments of a research group or even with a rigid and closely argued methodological coherence, but with the varied results of a process, a process of reflection which began in earnest in the course of the year 2003. Thus, the reader can expect to discern in the articles collected in this volume a variety, at times even a variance, of approaches to the study of the phenomena of the cultural interface as it was played out in some moments in the histories of Muslim societies over some seven centuries. After all, individuals, societies, traditions, and cultures do not follow any rules when they interact (contrary to what some taxonomists may wish to maintain). The activities are often spontaneous, and the results unforeseen (or better: unforeseeable). If they are characterised at all, they are characterised by the sense of the possible, by the urgency of the contingent, by the pressure of the moment. In this sense the volume is inchoate and messy. In a deep sense which I find very appealing, the messiness of the volume (in terms of the cornucopia of approach, rather than of its impeccable scholarship) reflects the messiness of the phenomena studied. In order to appreciate why this is so, the reader has a right to expect an explanation. Which is what this Preface attempts to provide.

Inchoateness is not tantamount to incoherence. There are several foci around which the contributions to this volume revolve, in the considerations of which they cohere. The most obvious is the chronological. The Editors have chosen to replicate the chronology of the Colloquium, in so far as they were able. Thus Elizabeth Key Fowden's article, 'The Lamp and the Wine Flask: Early Muslim Interest in Christian Monasticism,' 1–28, is a bold survey of some three centuries of interface, which takes as its point of departure the pre-Islamic Hijaz and culminates in the early third/ninth century with the scintillating verse of Abū Nuwās. Garth Fowden's appreciation of Quṣayr ʿAmra, 'Greek Myth and Arabic Poetry at Quṣyar ʿAmra,' 29–45, takes us to the days of the late Umayyad dynasty and the poetry of al-Walīd II ibn Yazīd, while Anna Akasoy's wise charting of 'The Influence of the Arabic Tradition of Falconry and Hunting on Western Europe,' 46–64, takes up her story in the last decades of the reign of the Banū Umayya in the second/eighth century and traces the filament of falconry through some six centuries to the Sicilian court of Frederick II Hohenstaufen. Ulrich Rudolph's subtle interest, in his 'The Pre-Socratics in Arabic Philosophical Pseuepigrapha,' 65–75, is most firmly in the third/ninth century of the ʿAbbāsids and the first efflorescence of that astounding phenomenon which has come to be known as the Greek-Arabic translation movement, itself one of the tributaries for a true high point of pre-modern Islamic civilisations, the medical tradition. It is this tradition which, in his 'Islamic Medicine Crosspollinated: A Multilingual and Multiconfessional Maze,' 76–93, Peter E. Pormann studies with erudition, placing the developments of the third/ninth century and the experiments of the fourth/tenth century most firmly in its manifold contexts: pre-Islamic Arabian, Hippocratic and Galenic, Alexandrian and Syriac. And note the ambitious sweep of his survey, features too of Akasoy's and Elizabeth Fowden's studies. Chronological ambition is the hallmark also of David Nicolle's survey of types of weaponry and armour, from four civilisations: 'Byzantine, Western European, Islamic and Central Asian Influence in the Field of Arms and Armour from the Seventh to the Fourteenth Century AD,' 94–118. In her 'Memories of Egypt in Medieval Venice,' 119–34, Deborah Howard reveals how important Alexandria was to Venice in the *Serenissima*'s emergence as culturally as well as fiscally autonomous, while it is to the thirteenth and fourteenth centuries of the Latin Middle Ages and the early Renaissance which John Marenbon turns in his revivification of a radically reinterpreted notion of Latin Averroism.

These contributions, then, range across some seven to eight centuries of crosspollinatory phenomena, their chronologies steady but not monotonous. My own study, 'Islamic Crosspollinations' eschews chronology for a paradigmatic approach, considering how other scholars in previous studies have responded to the challenges of writing about and reflecting on the cultural contact zone.

Another focus around which many of these studies cohere is the interstices of 'donation' and 'reception'. In such cases of 'donation' or 'reception', the authors do not restrict themselves to a taxonomy of what was donated and by whom, or what was received, from whom and by whom, but rather try to think through the implicatures, the ramifications and the complexities of the processes involved.

Most studies in this volume take as their methodological points of departure a version of the 'influence' paradigm. In my own study, I am very critical of this approach, for the restraint which it imposes on both the material and the researcher. I was encouraged in my critique of 'influence' by the observation that the contributors to this volume do not apply 'influence' in isolation, but temper it, or extend it, usually through the idea of 'crosspollination', with the result that the paradigm of 'influence' can almost be said to rise, Phoenix-like, from the ashes of its philological resting-place. Thus Akasoy and Pormann use 'influence' as a thread to chart their way through some dense labyrinths. In Akasoy's establishment of the 'court' as an archetype we have the opportunity for considering other courtly features beyond the cynegetic in terms of polygenesis, whilst the iatric creativity of the Muslim physicians shines bright against the background of the traditions by which Pormann shows they were influenced. For David Nicolle, 'influence' is synonymous with 'cultural contact'; for Elizabeth Key Fowden, Christianity represents an 'anxiety of influence' in the sense established by Harold Bloom and applied by Maria Rosa Menocal to Dante's vision of Islam; while for John Marenbon, the 'influence' of Averroism is that of a philosophically creative misprision. Appropriation is the paradigm which best describes the approaches of Ulrich Rudolph and Deborah Howard, in the first instance a pseud-epigraphical appropriation, in the second a communal one, played out over time. And it is the aesthetic and emotional meaning of the 'influence' of the Greek artistic and mythical traditions on the Umayyad builder of the hunting lodge in the Jordanian desert, al-Walīd II, which Garth Fowden sets out to analyse. That these analyses are not trammelled by the constraints of 'influence' may be due, in no little part, to the addition to the mix of the notion of 'crosspollination'.

The second explanation which the reader may rightfully expect is an account of how I think we arrived at this volume of essays. In the course of 2003, I came across Lenn E. Goodman's *Jewish and Islamic Philosophy: Crosspollinations in the Classic Age*, Edinburgh, 1999. I was intrigued as much by his notion of 'crosspollination' as I was by the brilliance and philosophical acumen which he so capably displays in his studies of the Jewish, Islamic and European philosophical traditions. Thanks to the generosity of the Degree Committee of the Faculty of Oriental Studies of the University of Cambridge, who are the managers of the William Wright Studentship, I was able to contemplate an exploration of this concept through the medium of a Colloquium.

I was heartened in my serendipity by a further coincidence – the Centre for Research in the Social Sciences and Humanities (CRASSH), at the University of Cambridge, was in the second of a two-year series of events, conferences and projects, devoted to study of the concept of 'migration', and its then Director, Professor Ludmilla Jordanova, had advertised CRASSH's intention to concentrate a large part of the year's activities on the 'migration of ideas'. This provided me with the fortunate opportunity of testing the viability of 'crosspollination' against the much more firmly established paradigm of 'migration'. These occurrences, then, planted the seeds of the Colloquium.

Having decided on my conceptual framework, I next proceeded to remind myself that as someone interested in the history of ideas I needed to venture beyond the ambit of my interests, to remember that ideas do not live in a vacuum, and so I extended the focus of the Colloquium to include weaponry, art and architecture, social practices and customs. Finally, only too aware that the study of the pre-modern Islamic world and that of Medieval Europe are sadly conducted in isolation rather than in unison, I was pleased to include, by Professor Rosemond McKitterick of the University of Cambridge, a presentation on early Medieval Europe, by way of comparison and reminder.

Let me furnish, then, a summary of the Colloquium programme.

After a welcome address, on Friday, 23 January, Elizabeth Key Fowden spoke on 'Early Muslim Interest in Christian Monks and Holy Places', followed by Garth Fowden, 'Greek Myth and Arabic Poetry at Quṣayr ʿAmra', Peter E. Pormann, 'Medical Care in the Hospitals of Baghdad in the Early Tenth Century', Peter Adamson, 'Physics or Metaphysics? The Eternity of the World Debate in Early Arabic Philosophy',[1] Ulrich Rudolph, 'The Presocratics in Arabic Philosophical Pseuepigrapha', and Tony Street, 'Al-Fārābī, Avicenna and the Averroist Interpretation of the Modal Syllogistic'.

The following day began with David Nicolle's paper, 'Byzantine, Islamic, Central Asian and Western European Influences in the Field of Arms and Armour from the Seventh to the Fourteenth Century AD', followed by Jeremy Johns, 'From Heterosis to Hybrid Sterility: Some Contradictory Case Studies of Crosspollination from Norman Sicily', Deborah Howard, 'Memories of Egypt in Medieval Venice', Anna Akasoy, 'The Influence of the Arabic Tradition of Falconry and Hunting on European Culture', John Marenbon, 'Latin Averroism', and Rosmaond McKitterick, 'Travelling Ideas in Early Medieval Europe'.[2]

The impact which the Colloqium had on me did not stop with the departure of the participants. We had, of course, agreed to attempt a volume of articles arising out of our meeting, but the seriousness with which my colleagues had taken the notion of 'crosspollination' and the richness of their presentations convinced me that there was indeed something of a bright future in store for it. And it set me to thinking about the plethora of works which discuss some aspect or feature or moment of Islam's long and illustrious history of 'in-between-ness', when viewed from a Eurocentric perspective: in between Late Antiquity and the Renaissance of the Twelfth Century. As my contributors submitted their contributions to the present volume, and as I read them, I began constructively to enter into what has been for me a most fruitful and rewarding dialogue with them. The result of this dialogue is my own contribution to the volume, 'Islamic Crosspollinations', an attempt both to make some sense of the problems encountered in studying these phenomena in the specific context of Islam, to tie together the articles in the volume and to promote 'crosspollination' as an approach to this study. It is therefore the culmination of the responses to my original invitation to colleagues and would not have been possible without their learning and generosity. That they are not responsible for what I have done with their suggestions, ideas and approaches is a trope familiar from many a preface. In this case, it applies in a very real sense.

Let me iterate, however, that in my contribution to this volume (I hope) and whether in an organisational or an editorial capacity, my interpretations of crosspollinatory processes are in no sense intended to be hegemonic or prescriptive. As I have tried to show in this Preface and in the end-notes to my article, some of my fellow contributors elect to continue *credibly, profitably* and *fruitfully* with the other paradigms or approaches surveyed in the first half of my study. All the while, my own thinking on the question of 'crosspollinations' has been inspired by their researches: that it is not always consonant with their approaches is simply an indication of how profoundly my thinking on these issues has been influenced by their work.

Of course, there may well be some who grow impatient with this refusal on my part to present a united front, to impose *one* method, to trumpet *one* methodology. To them, I can only reply that the one thing which 'crosspollination' as an approach precludes and militates against is precisely such a reduction of the plurivocal to the monotonous.

I must also add that it has been my great good fortune to work on the editing of this volume with two very fine young scholars: Anna Akasoy and Peter E. Pormann. At a very dark time in November of 2005, it seemed that the volume was moribund, and would be consigned to oblivion. With bold alacrity they stepped forward and volunteered to see the project through. Anna has worked tirelessly on the electronic preparation of the contributions and has been wonderfully resolute in her insistence that the volume must work as a whole, while Peter has been generous with his skilled eye for the lapsus machinae or the editorial divagation and he prepared the index. They also championed the project with various institutions before the Trustees of the Gibb Memorial Trust kindly agreed to accept it for publication in their series. At a time when the academic monograph is being imperilled by publishers and libraries alike, despite the relentless devotion to it on the part of academic promotion committees, tenure-review committees and public funding bodies, the continued promotion by the Gibb Trust of what is now, sadly, an almost out-moded tradition of academic publishing is a rare contribution to the community.

Notes

1 The substance of his presentation has appeared in his monograph: P. Adamson, *Al-Kindi* (New York, 2006).

2 The material was drawn in part from her monograph, *History and Memory in the Carolingian World* (Cambridge, 2004).

Abbreviations

ArScPh	*Arabic Sciences and Philosophy*
BEO	*Bulletin d'Études Orientales*
BJMES	*British Journal of Middle Eastern Studies*
BSOAS	*Bulletin of the School of Oriental and African Studies*
DOP	*Dumbarton Oaks Papers*
EI^2	*Encyclopaedia of Islam*, New edition (Leiden 1960-).
GAL	Carl Brockelmann, *Geschichte der arabischen Litteratur*, 2. ed., 2 + 3 vols., (Leiden, 1937–1946)
IJMES	*International Journal of Middle Eastern Studies*
IC	*Islamic Culture*
IOS	*Israel Oriental Studies*
JAL	*Journal of Arabic Literature*
JAOS	*Journal of the American Oriental Society*
JIS	*Journal of Islamic Studies*
JNES	*Journal of Near Eastern Studies*
JRAS	*Journal of the Royal Asiatic Society*
JSAI	*Jerusalem Studies in Arabic and Islam*
JSS	*Journal of Semitic Studies*
MIDEO	*Mélanges de l'Institut Dominicain d'Études Orientales*
MW	*Muslim World*
REI	*Revue des Études Islamiques*
SI	*Studia Islamica*
ZDMG	*Zeitschrift der Deutschen Morgenländischen Gesellschaft*
ZGAIW	*Zeitschrift für die Geschichte der Arabisch-Islamischen Wissenschaften*

List of Illustrations

Chapter 2 - Garth Fowden

Chapter 6 - David Nicolle

Chapter 7 - Deborah Howard

1

The Lamp and the Wine Flask: Early Muslim Interest in Christian Monasticism[1]

Elizabeth Key Fowden

Aramaic monasticism on the way from the Hijaz

The famous story of the Christian monk Baḥīrā, first attested in the eighth century, was carefully designed to take the hearer back to the very earliest origins of Islam. Baḥīrā was a Syrian monk who emerged from his cell to question the young Muhammad as he passed by in a caravan of traders from the Hijaz. The monk was so used to seeing Arab merchants pass his cell that he never took any notice of them, until this particular year when he divined that there was someone special travelling with the caravan. What struck him were various physical marks that were described in his holy books and that he discerned on the boy – including the seal of prophethood.

The framework of the Baḥīrā story is in fact so plausible that it could be true, though it is usually assumed that it is not. It appears in a very early Muslim source, the *Life of the Prophet* by Ibn Isḥāq, who was born in Medina about the year 85/704.[2] Baḥīrā is painted by Ibn Isḥāq as a fixed point and an authority. 'A monk had always occupied that cell', he writes. 'He gained his knowledge from a book that was in the cell, so they allege, handed down from generation to generation.' It is the ancient topos of scripture kept in a holy place, guarded by a holy man.

For Muslims, the story offered that necessary symbolic moment in a prophetic career, the first recognition by an authoritative representative of an earlier tradition.[3] With this nod toward the past, the momentum of the *Sīra* moves steadily forward, staking out a context for the Muslim revelation. Ibn Isḥāq's design was apologetical, as he was knitting together a Muslim history in an environment of awareness of other, older and related religious traditions. Baḥīrā emerges later as a 'character in the drama of inter-religious controversy'[4] when the Muslim legend is embraced by Christian authors and made to serve their own polemical purposes.

There is, of course, a long, scholarly tradition dedicated to searching in the Syriac and Christian Aramaic literary tradition for the background of Islam.[5] It is not my purpose here to reopen the debate over whether the Christianity presented in the Qurʾān reflects Chalcedonian, Monophysite or Nestorian doctrine, or that of some other late antique sect. I shall focus instead on the evidence on the ground and build toward suggestions of how the material circumstances would have informed early Islamic views of Christianity, and monasticism in particular.[6] One advantage we have today over early twentieth century scholars working mainly from literary evidence is the tremendous increase in material evidence for Syria and Jordan in the sixth to eighth centuries. Unusually for early Islam, which is so desperately short of material remains, it is archaeology, quite as much as philology, that seems to offer us a new angle on, or at least a fuller contexualisation of, the Muslim Baḥīrā story and much of what it stands for. The archaeological evidence is particularly helpful in two areas: first, in presenting a clearer picture of the aesthetic richness early Muslims encountered in churches and monasteries in these areas, and secondly, in adding to our growing knowledge of a strong presence of an Aramaic Christianity that would have allowed Arabs in the sixth to eighth centuries an easier entrance into the Christian world. It should now be possible to situate the traditional studies of Christian influence and perhaps even reveal further areas in which monastic culture stimulated Arab Muslim culture. My specific aim here is to look at ways in which Muslims responded to the continuing presence of monks and monasteries in early Islamic society.

Baḥīrā is a good place to begin since according to Ibn Isḥāq he was said to have lived in a cell at Buṣrā near what is now Syria's southern border with Jordan. We do not need to take this topographical detail literally – Buṣrā seems to have denoted, in shorthand, the Hijazi merchants' northerly horizon.[7] At Buṣrā they exchanged their goods and other dealers forwarded them.

In this region both Greek and Aramaic were used, though to what extent and in what contexts they overlapped is still somewhat unclear. After the recent austerely philological re-investigation of the Qurʾān's Aramaic heritage by Christoph Luxenberg,[8] one cannot help being particularly intrigued by archaeological investigations of the Aramaic as well as Greek Christian communities in the region through which the caravans would have travelled to Buṣrā, by way of what is now northern Jordan. It is a landscape now being cultivated, or built over, to saturation point – hence the spate of discoveries.[9] Buṣrā too has been the object of much recent archaeological work.

One thing we already knew from our texts is that Buṣrā at this period had a bishop loyal to the emperor's Church and the Council of Chalcedon, and another bishop who was opposed, one of the so-called Monophysites.[10] So it is a fair assumption that a similar division characterised the thickly settled countryside south of Buṣrā through which the trade routes ran and the Hijazi caravans slowly plodded. Nonetheless, both Greek and Aramaic seem to have been used by both Christian communities; and in general it is hard if not impossible to tell a Chalcedonian from an anti-Chalcedonian church, unless an inscription refers to a bishop whose allegiance is attested in other sources.

All this will have been fine print for most if not all the Hijazis. What will undoubtedly, though, have struck them forcibly was two things, neither of which we were very much aware of until recently. Firstly, the way in which these wealthy, closely-spaced agricultural settlements were literally bursting with church buildings, many of which were built in or around 600, or a little later under the Persian occupation, or even later under the Umayyads, who ruled the Islamic Empire from 661–750. This was an area where both the economy and the Church were doing very well. Secondly, the Hijazis will have found all this Christian activity relatively accessible, because so much of it was conducted in Aramaic, which appears to have been the favoured language of international commerce and was presumably easier for them to learn than Greek.

These two points help provide a more vivid setting for Qurʾānic perceptions of monasticism. To illustrate this profoundly Christianised countryside we may take just one site out of several possibilities, namely Riḥāb, a small village on the road from Jerash to Buṣrā. In his survey *The Christian Communities of Palestine*, published in 1995, Robert Schick listed eight churches at Riḥāb, dated between 534 and 635; only one of them is dated before 594. So the Persians clearly did not stop the local Christians from building. It is now clear that the armies of Islam did not either. Excavations done by Jordanian archaeologists from 1991 onwards have revealed 28 churches at the latest count – including what is said to be a late fourth century cathedral, a monastery dated 623 and another from the Umayyad period, and churches dated by inscriptions from 534 to 686, the bulk of them belonging to the mid-seventh century.[11] In this environment the slow-travelling cameleers and their customers, who came back year after year, were dependent on local innkeepers and dealers. And monasteries commonly served as hostels and taverns, a subject to which I shall return.[12] Many inhabitants of the area bore Arabic names, as one can see from the mosaics of Mādabā, and undoubtedly spoke Arabic as well as Aramaic.[13] Even a minimum of social intercourse would have taught the Hijazis quite a lot about their hosts, and their all-pervasive faith.

This linguistic semiticism is in fact the second point I want to emphasise. It is now firmly underlined by the fascinating publication of their excavations at Khirbat al-Samrāʾ by Jean-Baptiste Humbert and Alain Desreumaux in 1998. Khirbat al-Samrāʾ lies directly on the Via Nova Traiana, southeast of Jerash. One might just as easily have chosen it rather than Riḥāb to illustrate the region's profound Christianisation, and at Khirbat al-Samrāʾ it is also just as clear as at Riḥāb that Christianity maintained itself vigorously long after the Umayyad period – it was no desert spring bloom to shrivel with the harsher sun of May. What is particularly remarkable about Khirbat al-Samrāʾ, though, is the extraordinary new impetus its publication has now given to the study of Christian Melkite Aramaic. We now have 821 unmistakably Christian gravestones marked with crosses. Thirty-five are inscribed in Greek. Another eighty-five are in the local variety of Aramaic known as Christian Melkite Aramaic, the language used – as the name Melkite suggests – by Christians loyal to the imperial Church of Chalcedon, a grouping traditionally thought of as Greek-speaking and urban, cast adrift in a countryside given over to Monophysitism. Other discoveries, for example of manuscripts in this same language, have accumulated since Desreumaux began his researches in 1978. We have a whole new cultural zone revealed to us, of wealthy Chalcedonian villages in northern Jordan that continued to flourish under the caliphate as well. In fact, it seems that much of what we now call Jordan was Melkite, which opens up a new perspective on the sources of knowledge about Christianity that were available to our Hijazi traders.

Contact with monks was not, of course, limited to those who travelled north from the

Hijaz. Monasticism had taken root in Arabia, most notably in the Najrān area, and also appears to have gained a foothold in the Persian Gulf, where archaeological discoveries confirm our limited literary evidence for a Christian presence, and links to the monastic culture of Mesopotamia.[14] Our Greek and Syriac sources suggest that monks were largely responsible for the Christianisation of the Arabs, especially the pastoral Arabs. Sozomen describes how long before the reign of Theodosius II (408–450) the Arabs began to convert: 'they became familiar with faith in Christ through their encounters with the priests and monks who lived close to them, virtuous men and wonder-workers, who were living a contemplative life in the neighbouring desert'.[15] In the mid-fifth century Christianised Arabs in Palestine pitched their tents around a church founded for them by the abbot Euthymius at some distance from his monastery.[16]

Two Syriac hagiographies survive that recount the Christianising activities of Aḥūdemmeh and Marūtā, both missionaries among the Arabs of Mesopotamia in the sixth century.[17] The success of their missions owed much to the way in which they accomodated the material needs that sprang from the landscape. Marūtā, for example, turned his attention to those who traversed the Middle Euphrates region, especially the Arab pastoralists.[18] He tapped a water source, imported monks and built a magnificent monastery in the countryside near an important route between Takrīt and ʿĀqūla (future Kūfa). Shelter, food and drink welcomed the traveller, who once inside would also behold the impressive architecture and its adornment, perhaps even witness a service. At least some of the monks' outward spiritual life would have been visible to the casual visitor to the monastery church – major feasts provided opportunity for that. The veneration of saints through their relics and icons would have been one of the most striking visual memories of a monastic sojourn. The patron saint of Marūtā's monastery was Saint Sergius, already by that time esteemed as a miracle-worker among Arabs of the region.[19] The openness of these monasteries to visitors should dispel the view that monks in late antique West Asia were secluded.[20]

In addition to these more rural communities, the monasteries of Ḥīra near the Euphrates in central Mesopotamia were especially renowned, and al-Ḥīra's inhabitants were noted for their use of both Arabic and Aramaic, though culturally Aramaicised.[21] Here we see how in a more urbanised area too monasteries had been woven into the social fabric of the pre-Islamic Arab tribes. Services in monastic churches and great feasts in particular provided a context for social gatherings and display. The beauty of their decoration is often commented on, and likened to the starry sky. We see the development of what could be called the tribal church or monastery, an establishment under the patronage of a particular tribal group. The fourteenth century al-ʿUmarī cites the following passage recorded by the tenth century al-Iṣfahānī:

> Three groups of Yamanite Christians used to compete with one another in the construction of *biyaʿ* (churches) with attention to their decoration and the beauty of their structures: the house of al-Mundhir in Ḥīra, and Ghassān in al-Shām, and Banū al-Ḥārith ibn Kaʿb, the Ḥārithids in Najrān. Their *diyārāt* (monasteries), which were exceedingly high, were located in places that abounded with trees, gardens and streamlets. They used to have the furnishings of these structures made of gold and silver and their curtains of brocade. In their walls they had mosaics and in their ceilings gold.[22]

It is worth noting here that *biya*ʿ is made to cover a wide spectrum of religious arrangements that co-existed in late antiquity, continuing well into the medieval period.[23] Many times *biya*ʿ and *dayr* seem to be used interchangeably. Another description – possibly by Hishām ibn al-Kalbī – that is preserved in ʿUmarī concerns the last Lakhmid king at the monastery of Hind the Younger:

> And it was related that al-Nuʿmān used to pray in it and receive communion; that he hung in its chapel (*haykal*) five hundred lamps made of gold and silver. Their oil during feast days [was] oils of lily and of willow and others there were similar to these. And the wood he used to buy [for censing in the chapel] consisted of Indian aloes and of ambergris, in quantities that defy description.[24]

The light-flooded monastery had found a place in the Arab Christian social fabric and it quite naturally became a common image in Muslim portrayals of Christianity. What, above all, caught the Arabs' imagination, to judge from early evocations of monks in Arabic poetry and prose, as well as the Qurʾān, was not so much the panoply of Christian parishes, dioceses, Councils and Fathers, but a single evocative sight – the ascetic in his cell, with his book and his lamp, already a beloved theme in pre-Islamic poetry.

In his best known poem, the sixth century Imruʾ al-Qays had compared the light of a threatening storm with 'the lamps of a hermit (*rāhib*) who has been generous with oil on the twisted wicks'.[25] Or he sang thus of his beloved: 'In the evening she lights up the darkness as though she were the light in the place where the hermit (*rāhib*) does his eventide devotions'.[26] Ascetics were so much part of the scenery that Imruʾ al-Qays could exclaim that 'the stars were like lanterns/lamps (*maṣābīḥ ruhbān*) lit by monks guiding returning travellers'.[27]

Muslim tradition explains the use of lamps in Muslim holy places through the mediating figure of Tamīm al-Dārī. According to various traditions, Tamīm was a Christian from Palestine who converted to Islam and became a companion of the Prophet.[28] He is said to have been a monk, as well as a wine merchant, a description that evokes the close association in early Muslim sources of monasteries with wine, as will be explored later.[29] He is also considered to have been responsible for introducing Muhammad to the use of the oil lamp, which was thereafter employed in the mosque at Medina. The person of Tamīm brings the monk, wine and the lamp neatly together and tempts one to understand him as a merging of early Muslim stereotypes, a distillation of the most salient features of Christian monasticism that will be put to new uses in Islamic culture.

The lamp is, of course, the centrepiece of the celebrated Light Verse:[30]

> God is the Light of the heavens and the earth; the likeness of His Light is as a niche wherein is a lamp – the lamp in a glass, the glass as it were a glittering star – kindled from a Blessed Tree, an olive that is neither of the East nor of the West whose oil wellnigh would shine, even if no fire touched it; Light upon Light; God guides to His Light whom He wills. And God strikes similitudes for men, and God has knowledge of everything.

It is not necessary to locate this image in a specific place; it can be said to belong naturally to the environment of late antique holy places, both Jewish and Christian.[31] On the Christian background, G. Böwering has observed that 'the light verse occupies the pivotal point of a Qurʾānic passage that clearly refers to forms of early Christian worship'.[32]

As we have already seen, *bayt* commonly indicated a monastery. In the verses immediately following the Light Verse we read:

> In temples (*buyūt*) God has allowed to be raised up and His Name to be commemorated therein, therein glorifying Him in the mornings and the evenings, are men whom neither commerce nor trafficking diverts from the remembrance of God.

That these men are monks is suggested by the association of monks with commerce that is found elsewhere in the Qurʾān, for example at Sura 9:34 (further discussed below), where some monks are explicitly censured as those who 'consume the goods of the people with vanity'. I suggest that we understand the appearance of *buyūt* directly after the Light Verse, combined with the mention of men who glorify God in the morning and evening and 'whom neither commerce nor trafficking diverts from the remembrance of God', as a localisation of the un-localised divine light so powerfully evoked in the immediately preceding Light Verse.

Rejection

To accuse one's opponent of theological or ritual corruption was hardly a new tactic – it had long been used by Jews and Christians against each other. In the Muslim tradition it appears already in the Qurʾān where, for example, Christians are accused of compromising the unity of God (*shirk*), variously understood as associationism, idolatry or polytheism. Christians committed *shirk*, for instance, when they perverted the divine message as conveyed by the Prophet Jesus. Monks in particular are condemned for allowing themselves to become associated with the One God, to be held up as the Christians' masters. Closely linked with this accusation is the claim that monks exploit those who honour them and lead them astray. The larger context for the monks who consume people's goods is:

> The Jews say, 'Ezra is the Son of God'; the Christians say, 'The Messiah is the Son of God.' That is the utterance of their mouths, conforming with the unbelievers before them. God assail them! How they are perverted! They have taken their learned men and their monks as lords in place of God, and the Messiah, Mary's son – and they were commanded to serve but One God; there is no god but He; glory be to Him, above that which they associate.
>
> ...
>
> O believers, many of the learned men and monks indeed consume the goods of the people in vanity and bar from God's way.[33]

In this passage, monks are mentioned in the same breath as Jesus, Mary's son, as objects of misguided association with God. The accusation that monks were taken as lords apart from God reflects two intertwined developments in late antiquity: the rise of saint cult and the expansion of monasticism.[34] Monks who are taken 'as lords apart from God' can be understood as the holy men to whom people appealed for succour. Ultimate blame fell on those who could not see through the monk to God – *they* are the Christian associators; but deeply implicated in the accusation are also the monks themselves, who also maintained the cult of saints in the monasteries that either housed a living saint or preserved the relics and icons in which the saint's presence and power was thought to reside. Monks had come to 'consume the goods of the people in vanity and bar from God's way' by their involvement in the cult establishment that had grown so large and so wealthy, a trend that had begun already in the fifth century. Future chastisement is promised in the following line for 'those who treasure up gold and silver and do not expend them in the way of God'. One may recall the warnings of the fifth century Syriac writer Isaac of Antioch, who in his scathing censure of the development of the pilgrimage centre built around the pillar of Symeon the Elder in Syria observed that the monks 'have deserted the (spiritual) heights and have plumbed the depths with their many grandiose building activities'.[35] 'The sun blushed to see monks who had turned into merchants'.[36]

The Qur'ānic condemnation of monks was further developed in a story that appears already in the second century of the Muslim era. Here it is explained that a handful of true followers of Jesus were driven into exile by the majority of Christians who had strayed into *shirk* and falsified the scriptures to accommodate their perverted beliefs. These few exiles became monks – some stylites, others wandering ascetics, and a third group coenobites. As time went on some members of the Christian associators who had falsified scripture *also* adopted the monastic way of life, but their tainted theology assured their failure to live it properly. The proof came when the original, true monks learned of Muhammad's teaching and embraced Islam.

This story – related in versions by Muqātil ibn Sulaymān (d. 150/767), al-Ṭabarī (d. 310/923), drawing on Muḥammad ibn Sa'd (d. 230/845), and al-Tirmidhī (d. *c.*320/938) – contains both views of monks, as perverters of Jesus' teaching on the one hand and as true followers of Jesus and Muhammad on the other.[37] The Muslim writers used it in their exegesis of another Qur'ānic passage, the much-discussed mention of monkery at Sura 57:27:

> And we put in the hearts of those who followed Jesus, compassion and mercy, and the monastic state (*rahbāniyya*); they instituted the same only out of a desire to please God (we did not prescribe it to them). Yet they observed not the same as it ought truly to have been observed. And we gave unto such of them as believed, their reward; but many of them have been doers of evil.[38]

There are two schools of thought that part ways over whether 'we put' should have three direct objects – compassion, mercy and the monastic state – or just two, leaving the monastic state to go with the following verb ('instituted'), producing in Arberry's translation, for example: 'We set in the hearts of those who followed him [Jesus] tenderness and mercy. And monasticism they invented'. If we follow the first interpretation, monasticism bears a divine seal; if the latter, it is a human invention.[39] What immediately precedes and follows the troublesome passage is also highly suggestive in the context of early Islamic ideas about monks and their calling. Preceding it is God's statement 'We sent Jesus, son of Mary, and gave unto him the Gospel', so that monasticism (whether a divine or human idea) is presented in the Qur'ān as one of the fundamental features of Christianity, after Jesus and the Gospel. This is borne out repeatedly in both Qur'ānic and other early Islamic portrayals of monks as representatives of Christianity. What follows, namely, that the intention was good, but in practice the monastic vocation was not lived properly, is absolutely crucial to early Islam's mixed view of monasticism.

Absorption

Like Christ's Forerunner John the Baptist, monks were meant to fade into the background once the true protagonist appeared on the scene. Such is the role given to all good monks in Islamic tradition from the Qurʾān onwards: they uphold the true monotheist tradition until the next phase of revelation in the guise of Muhammad. In the last passage I will consider, from the Sura of the Table, we read:

> Thou wilt surely find the nearest of them in love to the believers are those who say, 'We are Christians'; that, because some of them are priests and monks, and they wax not proud, and when they hear what has been sent down to the Messenger, thou seest their eyes overflow with tears because of the truth they recognize.'[40]

Muslim exegetes have understood these priests and monks who 'wax not proud' but weep at the coming of Muhammad to have included Baḥīrā, and a few other 'true' monks (though none of them is identified by name in the Qurʾān). In Muqātil ibn Sulaymān, Ṭabarī and Tirmidhī we see the development of the idea, already mentioned, that those faithful followers of Jesus' teaching were pushed to the fringes by the majority of so-called Christians, who perverted true belief and became guilty of *shirk*. Commenting on the good monks and priests in Sura 5:82, who 'wax not proud' but weep at the truth God has sent down, Muqātil explains that these were the few true disciples of Jesus, those who dwellt in cells (*ṣawāmiʿ*) and included among their number the monk Baḥīrā. These fringe groups scattered to become either stylites, wanderers or dwellers in 'monasteries (*duyūr*) in the desert' sustained by wells and gardens.[41]

Perhaps there were indeed, as the Muslim tradition asserts, some such figures who were open to the expectation of a new prophet, to bring hope to the melancholy Christian world wracked by fratricidal Christological strife. The 'good monk' is he who recognises the truth of Muhammad's message, whether he lived to learn of the new revelation or whether, as in some accounts, he was a sort of Muslim before Muhammad (not unlike the Christians before Christ, including Plato, Aristotle and even Aristophanes, who can still today be seen on church walls in the Balkans and Greece). On the authority of Wahb ibn Munabbih al-Yamānī, Ibn Isḥāq relates the story of Faymiyūn, the epitome of the 'good monk'[42].

A Syrian holy man who would not have been out of place in John of Ephesus' *Lives of the Eastern Saints* or the *Pratum spirituale* of John Moschus, Faymiyūn withers sacred palm trees by his prostrations and prayers, heals the sick and curses a noxious snake that creeps up on him while he is praying in the desert solitude. Mobbed by seekers of cures, he is forced by his holiness to keep to the road. While walking with Ṣāliḥ,[43] a persistent disciple, Faymiyūn is abducted by an Arab caravan, which then sells him as a slave in Najrān. There Faymiyūn continues his ascetic life. 'One night Faymiyūn stood up in a hut his master had allotted to him, praying, when the whole hut was filled with light as if from a lamp, until it was completely illuminated but without the presence of any lamp'.[44] The Najranis are converted, though 'afterwards they suffered the same misfortune [or "innovations"] which befell their co-religionists in every land' – a sentiment echoing Sura 57:27.[45] Faymiyūn's devotions attract another disciple, ʿAbdallāh ibn al-Thāmir, who 'began to sit with him and listen until he became a Muslim and acknowledged the unity of God and worshipped Him'.[46] Healing the sick of Najrān in the name of the One God, ʿAbdallāh eventually falls foul of the king, who kills him by his own hand. Years later, in the reign of ʿUmar I, ʿAbdallāh's grave is opened and the words 'Allāh is my Lord' are found inscribed on his ring.

The descriptions of Faymiyūn and ʿAbdallāh are intended to show how the prayerful devotion of these miracle-working holy men points toward Muhammad's revelation. As in the portrayal of other Christians who had a cameo role to play in the formation of Islam, their holy book possesses a prophetic authority. We see this in the many versions of Muhammad's encounter with the monk Baḥīrā, who consulted his books to confirm the signs of the boy's unique future.[47] The truth of Baḥīrā's discernment was confirmed by Khadīja's cousin Waraqa ibn Nawfal, who is described as a 'Christian who had studied the scriptures and was a scholar'[48] and knew that a 'prophet would arise among this people [the Quraysh]'.[49]

Ibn Isḥāq also recorded the story about Zayd ibn ʿAmr, who did not attach himself to any religion of the day, but lived according to principles of purity, abstention from idolatry and humility before God. Ibn Isḥāq recounts that Zayd left Mecca in order to wander in search of the religion of Abraham,

> questioning monks and rabbis – he says – until he had traversed Mosul and the whole of Mesopotamia; then he went through the whole of Syria until he came to a monk at Mayfaʿa in the Balqāʾ [that is, central Jordan]. This man, it is alleged, was well instructed in Christianity. He asked him about...the religion of Abraham, and the monk replied, 'You are seeking a religion to which no one today can guide you, but the time of a prophet who will come forth from your own country which you have just left has drawn near. He will be sent with...the religion of Abraham, so stick to it, for he is about to be sent now and this is his time'.[50]

What is of interest for our purposes is not whether this eighth century account preserves traces of a pre-Islamic monotheism, the religion of Abraham, but rather the way in which the tradition takes for granted the place of pre-Islamic monks as preserves of wisdom.[51]

At Ibn Isḥāq's Mayfaʿa, now known as Umm al-Raṣāṣ, there is still today a tall tower, thought to have been used as a hermit's cell.[52] Mayfaʿa stood in the same region crossed by many trade routes that forms the backdrop of the Muslim Baḥīrā legend. In the ninth century al-Jāḥiẓ linked Baḥīrā to exactly this cultural environment and, specifically, to 'the monk who served Salmān al-Fārisī', another seeker of the true religion who, like Zayd, was told by a monk to return to Arabia after being disappointed in Mesopotamia and Syria.[53] This was the brand of monk Muslims were urged to esteem, not the latter-day disputatious Christians familiar to early ʿAbbāsid Muslim polemicists.[54]

These 'good monks' were not meant to be a permanent feature of the religious landscape. The continuing existence of monks after the coming of Islam was a sign of waywardness. Logically, they should have converted. Considered obsolete at best and willful perverters of the truth at worst, nonetheless the Christian monks kept alive, even developed their spiritual traditions, and did not cease to attract the interest of Muslims. The 'Muslims before Muhammad' had their uses, though, as they offered a bridge to Muslim ideas of holiness: for instance, the shrine of Saint Sergius at Tarīm in the Hadramawt region of Yemen could be embraced as a Muslim holy place if Sergius were to be understood to have been a pre-Islamic warner like Hūd who (unlike Sergius) is named in the Qurʾān and whose grave was, and is, after all, only 87 km away from Tarīm.[55] This brings us to the question of how the place and understanding of Christian holy men and holy places, including monasteries, were transformed by Muslims to meet the needs of emergent Islamic society.

Transformation

True to the Qurʾānic ambivalence about monks, their habitations were a source of both attraction and repulsion for early Muslims. Large tracts of the Muslim Empire – Mesopotamia, Syria and Palestine, as well as Egypt – were still highly Christianised societies in which monasteries continued as religious, but also educational and social centres. A look at the involvement of monasteries in the region's economic life in the seventh to tenth centuries shows monastic gardens and fields producing surplus, including wine, oil, fruits and vegetables, and monastic camel trains playing a role in the local economy, perhaps reaching even further afield. Muslim interaction with monasteries was as varied as the functions monasteries served.

As we have seen, one way of responding to Christianity was to absorb their holy men, and the same process applied also to holy places. In the early decades of Muslim rule we see Muslims praying in churches, or perhaps praying like Christians in mosques.[56] The eventual take-over of some holy sites is quite well attested and has been often discussed: it is enough just to mention Hama, Damascus and the Ḥaram al-Sharīf in Jerusalem as examples of the absorption and development of pre-existing holy places (though in the case of Jerusalem, the holy place was not functioning as such when taken over as a Muslim sanctuary). A less-often discussed example – fully published in 1996 – which involves a shared saint, a shrine, a monastery, a mosque and a *madīna* is the great pilgrimage city of al-Ruṣāfa in the Syrian steppe.

Al-Ruṣāfa was the centre of the cult of Saint Sergius, who began as a soldier martyr in the early fourth century CE and whose fame as miracle worker made him the favourite of Christian Arabs both before and after the conquests. By the sixth century the Sergius cult had spread across West Asia, with dozens of churches and monasteries dedicated to his memory, including one monastery back at Riḥāb dated to 623.

In a manner characteristic of Umayyad efforts to manifest authority through architectural display, the Caliph Hishām ibn ʿAbd al-Malik, who reigned from 724–743, associated himself with the saint and his tremendous influence among the region's Arabs by building at al-Ruṣāfa not just a residential complex, a *madīna* made up of at least three *quṣūr*, or residential complexes, surrounded by gardens and enclosures outside the massive city walls, but also a monumental mosque that adjoined the Christian complex inside. The latter included an imposing fifth century basilica in whose northeast corner was the shrine that housed the saint's silver sarcophagus.

To the south of the basilica was a baptistry with stunning mosaic pavement and, quite possibly, al-Ruṣāfa's famous monastery. The north side of the shrine communicated directly with a spacious courtyard onto which the mosque also opened, through a door cut in the *qibla* wall – that is, the one denoting the direction of prayer – in order to facilitate direct access to the courtyard and thence the shrine. The positioning of the mosque may of course imply some hope that Sergius' worshippers would be attracted to Islam; but on balance it seems to be the saint who retained the advantage, since the main mosque was built at his shrine rather than close to Hishām's residence outside the walls – and normally the *dār al-imāra* and the Friday mosque went closely together. Instead, Hishām and his court had to ride to the mosque and enter the essentially Christian old city. How Muslims participated in the cult of Saint Sergius is left to our imagination – the architecture suggests at the very least participation in processions and litanies that would have taken place in the shared courtyard. Just a few steps further took you into the saint's shrine.

In 1225 Yāqūt wrote of al-Ruṣāfa:

> 'I myself have seen this monastery and it is one of the wonders of the world as regards its beauty and its architecture. I believe that Hishām built his *madīna* next to this monastery and that it existed before the *madīna*. There are monks in it and religious men. It stands in the middle of the city of Ruṣāfa'.[57]

It is difficult to get around Yāqūt's explanation that Hishām built his residential compounds outside al-Ruṣāfa's walls because he wanted to be near the monastery and the city's famous saint.[58] Without diminishing the devotion Hishām may have felt for Sergius, certainly his prominent marking of the Muslim presence at the saint's pilgrimage centre suggests the caliph's interest in not only the spiritual, but also the social and political dimensions of Sergius' popularity that could be used to reinforce his own authority. Al-Ruṣāfa was, after all, one of the major pilgrimage sites in the East – it was a place of convergence for the region's many different peoples and for that reason had already been cultivated by the Roman emperors Anastasius and Justinian, the Sasanian Shah Khusrau II and Rome's allies, the Christian Ghassanid Arabs as well. Hishām was entering into a long-established network of regional relationships that were reinforced at al-Ruṣāfa.[59]

Building at or near the site of a Christian holy place or monastery was not unique to Hishām. There are numerous examples of Umayyad *quṣūr* that reoccupied monastic sites. This further corroborates the socio-economic role played by monasteries, since the remoteness combined with access to routes and natural resources that a monastery required were also sought by the Umayyad elites who found in these places both refuge and a means of surveying the tribes on whose support their rule depended.[60] Monasteries were bound up with trade, hospitality and, inevitably, political relations. What al-Ruṣāfa offers is a frame of reference for similar encounters glimpsed at other shrines and monasteries under Umayyad rule.

Saint Sergius was a celebrated miracle-worker whose healing powers would have drawn Muslim as well as Christian visitors to al-Ruṣāfa, where we can imagine the shrine and monastery were closely associated. Care of physical infirmity was in any case among the concerns of monasteries and Christians were among the best-known doctors in the Umayyad and ʿAbbāsid period. Whether monastic libraries were the source of the various Greek medical texts that were translated into Arabic is a question that cannot be satisfactorily answered at present. The hospital-type services performed by monasteries can, though, be glimpsed in, for example, the still unpublished discussion between the monk of Bēth Ḥālē and a Muslim emir.

This emir should most probably be identified with ʿAbd al-Malik's son Maslama, a general and governor whose career spanned the period from 86/705 to his retirement to northern Syria in 114/732, six years before his death in 121/738.[61] For a cure for an unnamed affliction, the emir had resorted to the monastery of Bēth Ḥālē, which would appear to have been built in the mid-seventh century near al-Ḥīra, famous for its salubrious climate.[62] This account is one of several that alert us to the role of monasteries as hostels and the home of doctors and healers.[63] Whether or not the text records an actual event is of less interest than the details of the encounter, since in order for the text to have been at all convincing, these must have been deemed within the realm of the possible.

The emir is versed in both Christian scripture and the Qurʾān, but claims that 'we do not accept all your Books'.[64] 'Even Muhammad our prophet said about the inhabitants of the monasteries and the mountain dwellers that they will enjoy the kingdom'.[65] During his sojourn, the emir is allowed to witness the monks' rites 'performed at the appropriate seven times',[66] further textual confirmation that Muslims had occasion to observe Christian practices not only from afar as in public processions, but also in more intimate settings. The emir's reported reactions too are of a more general interest: awe at the frequency and devotion of the monks' prayers, repulsion from their reverencing of the cross, icons and relics – highlighting the more widespread worry about saint cult expressed by Muslims elsewhere.[67]

Curiosity about the healing powers of monks and their saints' relics might attract visitors to a monastery, but so might a library. Mālik ibn Dīnār al-Sāmī (d. 130/747–8) described a visit he paid to a monastery in order to borrow a book.[68] He claims to have done this during the time of al-Ḥajjāj, the Umayyad governor of Iraq from 73–95/692–714. Mālik was a preacher and ascetic, who flourished in late seventh/early eighth century Basra and numbered among his teachers the traditionists and mystics Anas ibn Mālik, Ibn Sīrīn, al-Ḥasan al-Baṣrī and Rābiʿa al-ʿAdawiyya. Though he left no written work, a multitude of sayings and anecdotes have attached to him.[69] In one account, Mālik was reported to have conversed about ascetic practices with a monk whom he encountered on a mountain. The latter, surprised to be met with such questions, inquired whether he was not a follower of the Qurʾān. Mālik (who earned his daily bread from copying the Holy Book) replied that he was indeed, but that that should not stop him from sitting at the feet of the Christian ascetic.[70] That monasteries in Syria and Mesopotamia preserved Hellenic learning is widely acknowledged, although our sources are not often explicit about the libraries where books were found to study and translate. Dayr Qunnā roughly 90 kilometres south of Baghdad, close to the Tigris' left bank, was the site of one monastic centre of learning that is known to have played a role in the philosophical circles of early tenth century Baghdad. For example, al-Fārābī's teacher, Mattā ibn Yūnus, had studied and taught at Dayr Qunnā.[71]

Perhaps above all, monasteries were perceived as oases removed from the physical and social constraints of urban life. The shade of their courtyards and green of their gardens attracted visitors, Christian and Muslim. The great early ʿAbbāsid poet Abū Nuwās (*c*.140–*c*.200/*c*.757–*c*.815) evokes the pleasures of pilgrimage to a monastery of Saint Sergius, possibly that near ʿĀna on the Euphrates, even comparing it to the great Meccan hajj, while a tenth century poet Abū 'l-Naṣr al-Baṣrī records his fascination with a statue in an unspecified monastery dedicated to the same saint.[72] The polychrome mosaics and architectural variety that continually come to light through excavation in Syria and Jordan reinforce the point that in the early Islamic caliphate, churches and monasteries were some of the most impressively constructed and adorned buildings, whose impact especially on Umayyad architectural experimentation cannot have been insignificant. Monastic culture would leave some impression on later aesthetics too, as the ʿAbbāsid elite continued to order silver drinking cups decorated with monkish vignettes and had scenes of lamp-lit churches filled with monks at prayer painted on the walls of their residences.[73]

Part of the allure of monasteries for Muslims was precisely the architecture and its decoration. As a passing remark from a Muslim in the tenth century *Book of Strangers*, we read 'when I was a boy in Syria I went into a Christian church to see things in it that I had heard praised'.[74] This reputation is well illustrated by a visit reportedly made by al-Mutawakkil, the ʿAbbāsid caliph who reigned between 847 and 861. On a visit to the region of Homs, the caliph requested to 'walk around in all the monks' churches'. 'So he took my hand', the narrator relates, 'and proceeded to explore the churches and monasteries at length, looking at their marvellous pictures and splendid accessories and seeing the young monks and daughters of priests with faces like moons on branches strut about in porticos and courtyards.'

We should not be surprised that a monastic church was reported to be among the wall paintings adorning an ʿAbbāsid residence at Sāmarrāʾ, capital of the caliphate from 836–*c*.892.[75] One visitor to the al-Mukhtār palace at Sāmarrāʾ left a written record of the painting he saw there: 'One of [the paintings] was of a church with monks in it, and the best was of the priests who officiate at night.' He goes on in verse:

> We never saw anything like the splendour of the al-Mukhtār,
> nor anything like the painting of the night priest.[76]

Presumably, the painting struck the viewer because it depicted the generous use of lamps in churches during night-time offices. Of all church decorations, lamps were the most evocative.

> I was sleepless in the monastery of al-Māṭirūn,
> as if I were guarding the stars,
> that travel at the end of the night.
> Sirius passed by,
> looking like churches hung with lamps.[77]

The luxuriously decorated monastery of Dayr Murrān in the foothills of Jabal Qaysūn overlooking the Ghūṭa oasis of Damascus was another favourite haunt of caliphs and notables – Umayyad, but also ʿAbbāsid.[78] Al-Walīd I is said to have died there. It is hard to believe that the more festive and social dimensions for which we have evidence mainly in the pre-Islamic and ʿAbbāsid periods did not also exist under the Umayyads, especially given their relish for *la dolce vita*.

Most Muslim literary reflection on monasteries does not come, as we might expect, from Muslim-Christian polemical texts where dialogue was commonly set at a monastery. Rather, our more extensive descriptions of monasteries appear in collections of poetry – either of wine songs, or in the genre known as the *diyārāt*, poetry anthologies organised round the theme of monasteries that had become something of a fashion by the tenth century.[79] The genealogist and historian Hishām al-Kalbī (*c*.120–*c*.204/*c*.737–*c*.819), who was born, studied and died in al-Kūfa, cited among his sources the archives of the *biyaʿ* of al-Ḥīra, the most important Christian Arab centre in the Middle Euphrates region.[80] Though his work devoted to the churches and monasteries of al-Ḥīra has not survived, it was mined by later writers such as Abū 'l-Faraj al-Iṣfahānī (d. 967), who also wrote a *Book of Monasteries* (*Kitāb al-diyārāt*), which suffered the same fate as Hishām's.[81] The only such work to have survived intact is by al-Shābushtī (d. 998 in Fusṭāṭ).[82] Another text, the previously-mentioned *Book of Strangers* (*Kitāb adab al-ghurabāʾ*, attributed to al-Iṣfahānī), is a compilation of Arabic graffiti, linked together by a common theme of nostalgia. In it monasteries, as places haunted by travellers, pilgrims and monks, all people who have to some degree uprooted themselves from their accustomed place, provide the backdrop for scenes of tourism, drinking and sexual encounter.[83]

In the *diyārāt* literature, descriptions of monasteries – their silver vessels, luxurious vestments and colourful mosaics – serve as an ornate frame round the poems, while the poems too are sometimes inspired by monastic images. In both cases the material may in part have been invented, or at least exaggerated, though based on true-to-life settings. What is of interest to us, though, is not what exactly went on, but instead the double role monasteries came to play in early Islamic culture – they were both real places that continued to offer a venue for social encounter as they had in pre-Islamic times; and at the same time they provided raw material to feed the Arabic poet's imagination.[84]

Muslim encounters with the Christian milieu continued as the wine song (*khamriyya*) developed.[85] The on-going fertilisation of Bacchic poetry by Christian symbolism encountered at monasteries should be understood as part of the role Christians and Christianity continued to play in literary culture well into the tenth century – a point made recently by Hilary Kilpatrick with reference to *diyārāt* literature, which served a plurality of purposes.[86]

The *khamriyyāt* and *diyārāt* overlap in their sources of inspiration and neither is exhausted by the theme of monks and drunks. Monasteries attracted pederasts and gluttons too. A thirteenth century Arabic cookery book even recommends a meatless version of the luxurious Persian dish *bazmāward* as it was prepared in monasteries.[87] This aromatic dish was a favourite among the Umayyad elite and would no doubt have been included in the feasts served at the elegant residential compounds that spread out amidst the gardens and monasteries of al-Ḥīra and environs, a traditional meeting place of Arab, Persian and Christian culture.

Al-Ḥīra, along with neighbouring al-Kūfa, was also the mother of the wine song – the Christian poet ʿAdī ibn Zayd, belonged to this courtly milieu and was well acquainted with the area's monasteries and their Bacchic potential, while Ḥassān ibn Thābit (who later converted to Islam) and al-Akhṭal were also influenced by the literary trends of al-Ḥīra.[88] While staying in al-Kūfa, the poet Jaḥẓa (224–324/839–936) was invited to visit Dayr Ḥanna, a celebrated monastery near al-Ḥīra.

> This is the time to visit [explained his host], in the spring; while the gardens are in full bloom, and the pools are yet standing after the rain. The steppe is near at hand...and we shall not fail to hear the purest Arabic borne on the air to our ears...' We found the Dayr indeed a beautiful building, [confirms the poet] encompassed by its gardens, with the river of al-Ḥīra... flowing near by. So there our tents were pitched. And the monks came out bringing us such

> gifts and favours as they had. As we sat there eating and drinking there passed by us a lovely youth,...carrying one of the Christians' holy books.[89]

This description can stand in for many similar vignettes. We may most profitably understand it as a distillation of what monasteries had come by the early ʿAbbāsid period to represent in the Muslim literary imagination: places of sensual beauty and ease, where food, wine, sacred books and sexual titillation converged.

The celebrated wine songs of Walīd ibn Yazīd – heir apparent from 724–743 and briefly caliph from 743–744 – benefited from the many levels of inspiration that monasteries (we assume inadvertently) provided poets. Besides offering a congenial setting, monasteries were also an example of a living tradition rooted in a ritualised and symbolic conception of the world. That Walīd met with his drinking companions in a monastery in Damascus' Ghūṭa oasis and play-acted at taking communion and reverencing the cross, as he describes in one poem, may or may not be true. But it certainly *could* have happened and his use of Syriac liturgical language reflects at the very least a minimal knowledge of the Aramaic Christianity that Walīd could transform to create his poems of love and wine. In another poem, Walīd longs to become the cross kissed by a young girl he espied at a church.[90]

A mischievous interplay between the themes of love and wine poetry on the one hand, and images drawn from Christianity and Islam on the other, is also pronounced in the poems of the early ʿAbbāsid master, Abū Nuwās.[91] In his imagery and language inspired by Christian tradition, Abū Nuwās goes beyond using monasteries and monks as a backdrop for his revelry, or plundering them for aesthetic raw materials, as is more typical of the *diyārāt*. His love of paradox and jarring juxtaposition, and in particular his relish for using the physical to transport the auditor or reader to the metaphysical, are literary traits also prominent in Eastern, especially Syriac Christian writings.[92] Christian symbols lent themselves naturally to reuse and transformation in the hands of such an inventive and thoughtful poet. It is conventional to refer to Abū Nuwās' use of Christian imagery as 'irreligious', 'blasphemous', or at least 'irreverent' and 'ironic'. And no doubt it came across that way to many auditors or readers, as it still does today. But irony and irreverence do not necessarily make one irreligious; in Abū Nuwās' verses the ironic and the glib go hand in hand with playful seriousness.

Another, more positive and productive level would appear to exist which, to my mind, displays the deepest variety of crosspollination: Abū Nuwās absorbed images and symbols from an inherited tradition and then used them to think within the context of a new, developing tradition. The poetry of Abū Nuwās offers us a glimpse of that very personal process of spiritual and intellectual crosspollination that we lack in, say, the more conventionally 'religious' literature. To illustrate this I will briefly comment on two poems from the *dīwān* of Abū Nuwās, both of which employ language and imagery from the Qurʾān and Christian tradition.

The first begins with the poet's recollection of a youthful symposium and ends with a prayer for divine forgiveness.[93] He works within the formal sequence of *khamriyyāt* – prologue on the drinking company; the inn-keeper; the wine; the symposium; epilogue on the poet's repentance – but makes selective re-use of seemingly familiar Qurʾānic and Christian language and imagery to undermine the religious conventions and even force the auditor or reader to rethink the range of their meaning.

Abū Nuwās begins in the first line by describing his fellow revellers as 'lamps in the darkness' (*maṣābīḥ al-dujā*), thereby evoking from the outset, I would suggest, a monastic ambience by this allusion to the well-known image of the monk's lamp-lit cell. This is effected by his choice of the word *miṣbāḥ* (pl. *maṣābīḥ*), which appears in the celebrated Light Verse as a lamp in a niche wherein the divine light shines, and whose monastic overtones I have discussed earlier. At the same time by likening his drinking companions to monks/containers of divine light he sets up an extended playful parallelism in which his 'monks' are greeted by an anchoress-taverner (lines 7–8), refered to as heir to 'monastic idol-worshippers', and, one assumes, pursue their bibulous devotions in her house of idolatry, the classic setting for drinking parties. The young men's own idol, of course, is wine and sensual pleasure. Once by line 21 the wine is brought – 'when mixed with clear rain-water it is like a network of pearls on a ruby brocade' – it is refered to by the word *muzijat* (Qurʾānic *mizāj*), an Arabic term for wine derived from Syriac *mzāgā*, the term for eucharistic wine mixed with water still in use at the time.[94] Their enjoyment of the drink, lutenist and gardens is interrupted not, as elsewhere, by the monastery bells, but here by morning birdsong (line 29).[95] That disruption brings the poet to remorse.

The shape of the poem can be said to echo the cycle of ecstasy followed by contrition that is as characteristic of the monk's experience as it is of the reveller's, while in both cases (though not within the confines of this poem) the cycle commonly repeats itself.[96] James Montgomery rightly describes the poem as a 'religious *khamriyya* which has many points in common with *zuhdiyya* [poems of repentance]'.[97] I would argue that the sentiments of these two genres overlap in the experience, or at least the creative imagination, of Abū Nuwās, who discerned the metaphysical resonance of a physical symbol that in turn engendered a heightened appreciation of sensual beauty and pleasure in material things. The physical symbol performs an anagogic role that leads to the recognition of the ephemerality of the sensual. One could even say that the *khamriyyāt* lead naturally to the *zuhdiyyāt* in a dynamic and ever-repeating process rather than a linear development.

The second poem – formally a courtly *ghazal*, or love poem – displays a more intense use of Christian symbolism for a new purpose; it is a transfer of symbolic charge from one religious context into the poet's world, and may be prefaced with the comment by Andras Hamori that 'imagery with transcendental associations creates in the wine songs a sense of something like a rival religion'.[98]

1. My body is racked with sickness, worn out by exhaustion: my heart smarts with a pain searing like a blazing fire!
2. For I have fallen in love with a darling whom I cannot mention without the water of my eye<s> bursting forth in streams.
3. The full moon is his face and the sun his brow. To the gazelle belong his eye<s> and his breast.
4. Wearing the *zunnār*, he walks to his church; his god is the Son, so he said, and the Cross.
5. O I wish I were the priest or the metropolitan of his Church! No, I wish that I were the Gospel and the Scriptures for him!
6. No, I wish that I were a Eucharist which he is given or the chalice from which he drinks the wine! No, I wish I were the very bubbles <of the wine>!
7. So that I might obtain the benefit of being close to him and my sickness, grief and cares be dispelled![99]

I cannot improve on James Montgomery's analysis of the subversive fusion of *ghazal* tone and *khamriyya* themes, and particularly the poet's exploitation of Qurʾānic echoes and Christian imagery. Commenting on line 6, Montgomery concludes, 'Yet this [the poet's wish to be the bubbles in the blood of Christ] is a further allusion to one of the highpoints of the Arab erotic experience, the imbibing of the beloved's saliva which is as potent and sweet as wine. Proximity (= intercourse) may be what the Muslim Abū Nuwās yearns for: but for him to possess this Christian, he wishes to become the very body and blood of Christ Himself, a sacramental presence which is, ultimately, essentially Arab, being a conventional metaphor for a kiss'.[100] But I would protest that what is described here is not, as Montgomery claims, the 'debunking of the Christian tradition'. Instead it shows the creative transformation of pre-existing symbols, by merging them with Arabic poetic conventions into something new and potent. I would imagine it has little to do with contemporary Christianity.

It has been suggested that the question of whether the poetic fashion for delight in profanity that was initiated by Abū Nuwās was sincere – or whether that poet's sexual proclivities are in fact reflected in his writings – is irrelevant. Instead, these poems represent a 'well-constructed literary game'.[101] One could conclude the same about the *diyārāt*, but in both cases one must still ask, as James Montgomery does, 'what social reasons, if any, could have led to such a literary game proving so popular?'

The *diyārāt* as a genre represent one response to the past that reflects in part the encyclopaedic tendencies of the tenth century and can be understood as efforts to digest and control the inheritance of the Islamic Empire. Like geographical works, the *diyārāt* describe many places that still existed and could be visited, while at the same time there is an antiquarian dimension as well. To what extent is it important that they described places whose original purpose was religious and Christian?

A key to answering this question may be that these collections appear to have flourished as a Muslim genre. This was, I suggest, because the literary interest in monasteries that was initiated by Hishām al-Kalbī, a contemporary of Abū Nuwās, represents yet another way in which the Christian tradition was absorbed and made usable in Islamic society. It took a genius like Abū Nuwās to do more than treat monasteries as archival sources or stage sets, but instead to master the inheritance by transforming it. We can fairly conjecture that the attitude of most Muslims is reflected in what we have examined in the Qurʾān, Ibn Isḥāq and later writers: figures in Christian history were best viewed as paving the way to Muhammad.[102] Muslims were free to salvage what was useful from Christian culture both before and after Muhammad as long as the mortal threat of *shirk* was avoided. Even Abū Nuwās distances himself from *shirk*, the one sin God will not forgive.[103] He uses the idea of *shirk* to contemplate the meaning of idolatry as established by conventional Islam. With it he seems to be thinking through – with the playful self-knowledge of a Socrates – other possible definitions of transgression and of devotion.

We may seem, at this point, a long way from the sober Baḥīrā and the vigilant 'Muslims before Muhammad', whose memories were, though, very much alive among at least some Christian and Muslim contemporaries of Akhṭal, Walīd and Abū Nuwās. What I should emphasise is the coexistence and overlapping of the three general ways of encountering the monastic tradition that I have been discussing – rejection, absorption and transformation.

The monastic milieu bore many fruits. Arabic poets transformed images and symbols snatched from monasteries for their own use. One is even tempted to wonder whether, say, Walīd or Abū Nuwās was aware of the Christian use of wine imagery for spiritual instruction. The seventh century Isaac the Syrian, born about the time of the Hijra, describes how the ascetic will become 'drunk on [the sweetness of God] as on wine; his limbs will relax, his mind will stand still and his heart will follow God as a captive'.[104] The imagery would no doubt have appealed.

Of course, the question of direct influence of Christian ascetical ideas and practices on early Islamic thought has often been posed. The nature of such crosspollination was so individual – and evidence for it so tangled in the web of legend – that scholars have been forced into making tabulations of similar practices or sweeping claims about some shared oriental mentality, neither of which are ultimately very satisfying. In an effort to complement these studies, I have attempted something different here by looking at some ways not overtly theological – though many derived from religious sources – in which Christian monastic culture nourished Arab Muslim culture.

The relatively pervasive presence of monks and monasteries in the areas taken over by Muslims does not necessarily imply that the Christian monastic tradition was a prominent feature of every Muslim's identity, or that most Muslims had visited a monastery or met a monk. Having assembled the disparate evidence presented here, though, what strikes me is the inventiveness with which Muslim writers drew on the wide-ranging monastic culture they encountered – either directly or indirectly – as a spiritual provocation or an aesthetic source.

***

I shall conclude with the theme of ephemerality and repentance. The true monk is one who lives a life of repentance, and it was this quality among others that presumably made pre-Islamic ascetics worth absorbing into Muslim history. One repentant pre-Islamic figure whose story became part of Islamic culture was the Lakhmid sovereign Nuʿmān I (*c*.400–*c*.418), the ruler of early fifth century al-Ḥīra. Nuʿmān was the builder of al-Khawarnaq, a fabled residence in the vicinity of the Lakhmid capital. The story of al-Khawarnaq and its lord, and of its association with the famous Sasanian hunter-monarch Bahram Gūr (420–438) – who as a boy had been placed under Nuʿmān's tutelage – became the stuff of legend in Arabic and later Persian literature.[105] The story is related by the eighth century writer Hishām ibn al-Kalbī, who recounts that:

> Nuʿmān was sitting one spring day in his audience chamber at al-Khawarnaq and looked down at...the gardens, date-palms, orchards, and canals adjoining it, on his western side, and down at the Euphrates on his eastern side... He exclaimed to his vizier [as our source puts it], 'Have you ever seen the like of this view?' The vizier replied, 'No; if only it were to last!' 'What then endures?' the king asked. 'That which is with God in the next world.' The king asked, 'How can *that* be attained?' 'By your abandoning this present world, by devoting yourself to God and by seeking that which is laid up with Him.' So the king renounced his kingdom that very night; he put on coarse garments and left secretly in flight, without anybody knowing.[106]

The Umayyads are said to have enjoyed the pleasures afforded by al-Khawarnaq and its surroundings. It was in many ways a precursor to the residential complexes, or *quṣūr* they would later build for themselves.[107] After his victory near al-Kūfa in the autumn of 690/71 or 691/72, ʿAbd al-Malik, the father of Hishām, ordered a banquet to be prepared at al-Khawarnaq and amidst the feasting sighed, commenting to his companions on the fleeting nature of man and all his efforts.[108]

Some four decades after his father's celebrated banquet, Hishām received a delegation from Iraq at his court at al-Ruṣāfa. The group included the eloquent orator and transmitter of poetry, Khālid ibn Ṣafwān ibn al-Ahtam. After being shown in, Khālid invoked God's blessings on the caliph and proceeded to recite the story of al-Khawarnaq and its lord. When Khālid had finished, the lord of al-Ruṣāfa – his beard and turban moist with tears – had them all dismissed and shut himself up in his palace. One of Hishām's courtiers chastised the orator for his indelicate choice of subject, but Khālid responded that he had resolved never to sit with a king without speaking to him of God.[109]

It was not so great a leap from Nuʿmān's gesture to the life of the good Christian monk, and thence to the 'Muslims before Muhammad'. Al-Khawarnaq was not a monastery, but its appeal lay in a similar contrast it embodied between the passing happiness of man and the lasting bliss sought by him – a poignant contrast appreciated both before and after the coming of Islam. The Qurʾān leaves no doubt concerning the dangers awaiting those who 'treasure up gold and silver and do not spend them in the way of God'.

In early Islamic society, monasteries contributed to the on-going struggle to understand what it meant to spend 'in the way of God'. The safest path, but perhaps not the only path if the tendencies of some early Islamic poetry are any indication, avoided monastic sensuality and turned instead to the lonely cell and ancient books of the hermit 'who has been generous with the oil on the twisted wicks'.

Notes

1 I would like to thank Aziz Al-Azmeh, who organised the Colloquium on Islam and Late Antiquity at the Central European University, Budapest (January 2003), on which occasion some of the ideas presented here were first aired. The kind invitation from James Montgomery to participate in the Islamic Crosspollinations colloquium at Cambridge University (January 2004) offered me the opportunity to develop my treatment of the subject. I have also enjoyed the criticism of Garth Fowden throughout the gestation of this article, as well as the detailed comments of Barbara Roggema on its final version. Editions and translations frequently cited are as follows: Abū 'l-Faraj al-Iṣfahānī (attributed), *Kitāb adab al-ghurabāʾ*, ed. S. al-D. al-Munajjid (Beirut, 1972); trans. P. Crone and S. Moreh, *The Book of Strangers: Medieval Arabic Graffiti on the Theme of Nostalgia* (Princeton, 2000); Ibn Isḥāq, *Sīrat rasūl Allāh*, ed. F. Wüstenfeld (Göttingen, 1858–60); trans. A. Guillaume, *The Life of Muhammad* (Oxford, 1955); *The Koran Interpreted*, trans. A.J. Arberry (London, 1955); Abū Jaʿfar Muḥammad ibn Jarīr al-Ṭabarī, *Taʾrīkh al-rusul wa'l-mulūk*, ed. M.J. de Goeje et al. (Leiden, 1879–1901); English translation edited by E. Yar-Shater, *The History of al-Ṭabarī* (Albany, 1985–).

2 The earliest appearance of the legend is in Ibn Hishām's redaction of Ibn Isḥāq, *Sīrat rasūl Allāh*, i/1, 115–17; trans. 79–81 (as in n. 1). Christian authors from the ninth century onward adapted the Muslim legend to promote and develop the claim that Muhammad received the teachings of the Qurʾān from a Christian monk, variously known as Sergius or Baḥīrā. A critical edition

of the Syriac and Arabic Christian recensions of the legend is under preparation by Barbara Roggema, *The Legend of Sergius Baḥīrā: Eastern Christian Apologetics and Apocalyptic in Response to Islam* (Leiden, forthcoming). For discussion of the Christian legends, see S. Gero, 'The Legend of the Monk Baḥīrā, the Cult of the Cross and Iconoclasm', in P. Canivet and J.-P. Rey-Coquais (eds.), *La Syrie de Byzance à l'Islam VIIe–VIIIe siècles* (Damascus, 1992), 47–58; S. Griffith, 'Muḥammad and the Monk Baḥīrā: Reflections on a Syriac and Arabic Text from Early Abbasid Times', *Oriens Christianus*, 79 (1995), 146–74; B. Roggema, 'The Legend of Sergius-Baḥīrā: Some Remarks on its Origin in the East and its Traces in the West', in K. Ciggar and H. Teule (eds.), *East and West in the Crusaders States: Contexts – Contacts – Confrontations* (Leuven, 1999), 107–23, esp. n. 1 for bibliography on Muslim sources for the legend; B. Roggema, 'A Christian Reading of the Qur'an: the Legend of Sergius-Baḥīrā and its Use of Qur'an and Sīra', in D. Thomas (ed.), *Syrian Christians under Islam: the First Thousand Years* (Leiden, 2001), 57–73. I would like to thank Barbara Roggema for her correspondence with regard to the Sergius-Baḥīrā legend.

3 Parallel motifs have been traced in the Baḥīrā legend and the life of Jesus: for example, Muhammad is said by Ibn Isḥāq to have been twelve at the time he met the monk, the same age as Jesus when he disputed with the doctors in the Jerusalem temple. For a discussion of this and other parallels, see the bibliography in Roggema, *East and West* (as in n. 2), 107 n. 1; Gero, 'Legend of the Monk Baḥīrā' (as in n. 2), 48, nn. 5 and 6.

4 Griffith, 'Muḥammad and the Monk Baḥīrā' (as in n. 2), 153.

5 One such study with far-reaching impact is T. Andrae, 'Der Ursprung des Islams und das Christentum', *Kyrkohistorisk Årskrift*, 23 (1923), 149–206; 24 (1924) 213–92; 25 (1925) 45–112. See also, M. Smith, *Studies in Early Mysticism in the Near and Middle East* (London, 1931), esp. 101–52; O. Livne-Kafri, 'Early Muslim Ascetics and the World of Christian Monasticism', *JSAI*, 20 (1996), 105–29. A shortcoming of Livne-Kafri's important collection of scattered material is the absence of any chronological analysis of the sources cited. M. Morony, *Iraq after the Muslim Conquest* (Princeton, 1984), 445–66, remains the best synthesis of Muslim belief and practice set against the diverse inherited culture of Iraq. On the Christian context as a 'generative point' for Islam, see G. Böwering, 'The Light Verse: Qur'ānic Text and sūfī Interpretation', *Oriens*, 36 (2001), 144. For a sensitive overview of the problem of 'influence' between Christianity and Islam, see S. Seppälä, *In Speechless Ecstasy: Expression and Interpretation of Mystical Experience in Classical Syriac and Sufi Literature* (Helsinki, 2003), 310–15; and for a stimulating discussion of encounters between ṣūfī and yogic traditions that attempts to avoid what the author calls 'essentialist dichotomies', in other words, assertions of what is the 'source' and what the 'derivative', see C.W. Ernst, 'Situating Sufism and Yoga', *JRAS*, 15 (2005), 15–43.

6 For a general exposition of this approach, see R. Hoyland, *Seeing Islam as Others Saw it: a Survey and Evaluation of Christian, Jewish and Zoroastrian Writings on Early Islam* (Princeton, 1997), 34: 'Much effort has been expended in the past on highlighting the similarities and parallels between the literatures of the different communities of the Middle East, especially traits common to Judaism and Islam, but often with a view to ascertaining origins and establishing borrowing. Before such judgements can be made, greater consideration would have to be accorded to the ways in which information was transmitted and to the affects of a shared physical and cultural environment'; and n. 8, citing J. Wansbrough, *The Sectarian Milieu: Content and Composition of Islamic Salvation History* (Oxford, 1978), 51–4. Particularly succinct is the latter's assessment: 'Required is some means of determining the origin or native habitat of "universal" theologoumena' (54), though it is of utmost importance to recognise that 'native habitat' need not be understood as a cloying mother from whom the offspring can never detach itself and develop.

7 Ibn Isḥāq, *Sīra* (as in n. 1), 102.

8 C. Luxenberg, *Die syro-aramäische Lesart des Koran: Ein Beitrag zur Entschlüsselung der Koransprache* (Berlin, 2000), with the critical review by F. De Blois in *Journal of Qur'ānic Studies*, 5 (2003), 92–7,

and A. Neuwirth, 'Qurʾān and History – a Disputed Relationship. Some Reflections on Qurʾanic History and History in the Qurʾān', *Journal of Qurʾānic Studies*, 5 (2003), 7–10.

9 For a report of archaeological work, see ʿA. al-Ḥuṣān, 'Al-Natāʾij al-awwaliyya li'l-tanqībāt al-athariyya fī 'l-Mafraq mā bayna al-aʿwām 1991–2001', *Annual of the Department of Antiquities in Jordan*, 45 (2001), 5–13.

10 On sees, both Chalcedonian and anti-Chalcedonian, east of the Jordan, see G. Fedalto, *Hierarchia ecclesiastica orientalis* (Padua, 1988), 744–53, 1032–46; G. Troupeau, 'Églises et chrétiens dans l'Orient musulman', in J.-M. Mayeur et al. (eds.), *Histoire du christianisme des origines à nos jours*, iv (Paris, 1993), 440–41 (maps).

11 See al-Ḥuṣān, 'Al-Natāʾij al-awwaliyya' (as in n. 9), 5–13, for dated churches: 534 (repaired 582), 544, 594, 604, 611, 620, 621, 623, 624, 635, 636, 638 (Syriac inscription), 663, 686.

12 On the pervasiveness of monks in Syrian society, see A. Vööbus, *History of Asceticism in the Syrian Orient* (Louvain, 1960), ii, 316–26 and ii, 362–5, on the importance of hospitality in the Syrian monastic tradition; ii, 372–3 on monasteries as hospitals.

13 R. Contini, 'Il Hawrān preislamico. Ipotesi di storia linguistica', *Felix Ravenna*, 133–34 (1987) [1990], 65–6, concludes that, unlike the rest of Syria, the area from the Ḥawrān southwards was linguistically Arabised before the conquest and that Aramaic did serve as a vehicle for communication among Arabophone peoples, especially for commerce. Epigraphical evidence from Mādabā attests the pattern according to which, in urban areas, epigraphy was in Greek, while Aramaic predominated in rural areas. Even amidst Mādabā's Greek inscriptions, though, signs of spoken Aramaic are preserved: see the brief discussion of this area in R. Hoyland, 'Language and Identity: The Twin Histories of Arabic and Aramaic (and: Why Did Aramaic Succeed Where Greek Failed?)', *Scripta Classica Israelica*, 23 (2004), 187 with n. 17.

14 G.R.D. King, 'A Nestorian Monastic Settlement on the Island of Sīr Banī Yās, Abu Dhabi: A Preliminary Report', *BSOAS*, 60 (1997), 221–35 with bibliography; H. Bin Seray, 'The Arabian Gulf in Syriac Sources', *New Arabian Studies*, 4 (1997), 205–32 and D. Potts, *The Arabian Gulf in Antiquity* (Oxford, 1992), ii, 124. Reference to a 'monk in his secluded cell on high (*ustwān*), where the vulture round his nest doth fly' appears in verses attributed to the Yemeni poet Dhū Jadan, suggesting at least a familiarity with the ascetic phenomenon of stylitism in South Arabia: Ibn Isḥāq, *Sīra* (as in n. 1), 26–7; trans. 19.

15 Sozomen, *Historia ecclesiastica*, ed. J. Bidez (Berlin, 1960), vi, 38, 14. Many of the scattered references to encounters with monks tend to portray the pre-Islamic Arabs as plunderers tamed only by monkish miracles: e.g. Cyril of Scythopolis, *Vita Euthymii*, ed. E. Schwartz (Leipzig, 1939), 51; John Moschus, *Pratum spirituale*, *Patrologia Graeca* (hereafter: *PG*), lxxxvii, col. 155. Occasionally we find accounts not without a touch of humour, such as the story of some Monophysite Arabs who met a bald-headed mime who, fleeing the law, had taken to the countryside. Both his appearance and his presence in the 'desert' persuaded the Arabs that he was a monk, so they compelled him to celebrate the liturgy for them: Leontius of Jerusalem, *Contra monophysitas*, *PG*, lxxxvi, col. 1900–1.

16 Cyril of Scythopolis, *Vita Euthymii* (as in previous note), 15.

17 Denha, *Histoires d'Ahoudemmeh et de Marouta, métropolitains jacobites de Tagrit et de l'Orient (VIe et VIIe siècles)*, ed. and trans. F. Nau (Patrologia Orientalis, 3/1; Paris 1909), 7–51. At 22, the biographer provides the interesting comment that Aḥūdemmeh found the language of the pastoral Arabs difficult. For a discussion of these texts, see E.K. Fowden, *The Barbarian Plain: Saint Sergius between Rome and Iran* (Berkeley, 1999), 121–6.

18 Denha, *Histoires d'Ahoudemmeh* (as in previous n.), 85–9.

19 On Saint Sergius, see above 10–11.

20 See, for example, the misrepresentation of late antique monasteries by J. Berkey, *The Formation of Islam: Religion and Society in the Near East, 600-1800* (Cambridge, 2003), 154: 'Sufis were not monks isolated in remote areas behind imposing monastic walls'. This statement is odd given

the same author's insistence that pre-existing religious traditions and the cultural context should be seen as the background to ascetic developments in Islam, on his following page, for example.

21 I. Toral-Niehoff, 'The *ʿIbād* in al-Ḥīra: An Arab Christian Community in Late Antique Iraq', Proceedings of the conference *Koran in Context* (Berlin, 2004), forthcoming.

22 The account is preserved by Ibn Faḍl Allāh al-ʿUmarī, *Masālik al-abṣār*, ed. A. Zakī Pasha (Cairo, 1924), i, 309, citing al-Iṣfahānī as his source; and also by al-Bakrī, *Muʿjam mā istaʿjam*, ed. M. al-Saqqā (Cairo, 1945–51), ii, 603, s.v. Dayr Najrān; Yāqūt, *Muʿjam al-buldān* (Beirut, 1955–57), ii, 538, s.v. Dayr al-Najrān. See I. Shahîd, *Byzantium and the Arabs in the Sixth Century* (Washington D.C., 2002), ii/1, 160–63 for translation and discussion of the texts. Noteworthy are the sources and modern bibliography noted in Shahîd, *Byzantium and the Arabs*, ii/1, 164–219, a long listing and discussion of monasteries the author believes to have been associated with pre-Islamic Arabs.

23 A comparative, historical study of the terms *bīʿa* and *dayr*, including also *ṣawmaʿa*, *kanīsa* and *haykal*, would be a great service. As a start, see Shahîd, *Byzantium and the Arabs*, ii/1, 172, where he briefly discusses the 'interchangeability' of the two terms *bīʿa/biyaʿ* and *dayr/diyārāt* both in general and with specific reference to a passage describing al-Ḥīra's famous Dayr Hind, which like all monasteries contained at least one church, and was located within the loosely built settlement of al-Ḥīra: Bakrī, *Muʿjam* (as in n. 22), ii, 606–7.

24 ʿUmarī, *Masālik al-abṣār* (as in n. 22), i, 309. For translation and discussion of this passage, see Shahîd, *Byzantium and the Arabs* (as in n. 22), ii/1, 163–4.

25 Imruʾ al-Qays, *Muʿallaqa*, ll. 71–2, ed. and trans. A. Jones, *Early Arabic Poetry* (Reading, 1996), ii, 82–3. On this and other poetic allusions to monks and Christianity, see J.S. Trimingham, *Christianity among the Arabs in Pre-Islamic Times* (London, 1979), 245–8.

26 Imruʾ al-Qays, *Muʿallaqa*, l. 39, ed. and trans. Jones, ii, 69–70 (as in n. 25).

27 Imruʾ al-Qays, *Diwān*, cited by A. el-Tayib in A.F.L. Beeston et al. (eds.), *Arabic Literature to the End of the Umayyad Period* (Cambridge, 1983), 48.

28 M. Lecker, 'Tamīm al-Dārī', *EI*[2] and D. Cook, 'Tamīm al-Dārī', *BSOAS*, 61 (1998), 20–28.

29 According to G. Levi della Vida, 'Tamīm al-Dārī', *EI*[1], al-Nawawī derives his name from al-Dayrī, from convent (*dayr*). J.D. McAuliffe, *Qurʾānic Christians: an Analysis of Classical and Modern Exegesis* (Cambridge, 1991), 243, n. 14, questions the source for his identification as a monk, but for present purposes the association of monk with wine merchant in this influential early personality is of greater interest than the historical veracity of the identification with a particular figure. Tamīm al-Dārī is discussed by C. Clermont-Ganneau in his paradigmatic contextualisation of a lamp, originally from the mosque of ʿUmar in Jerusalem, acquired by the Louvre: 'La lampe et l'olivier dans le Coran', *Revue de l'histoire des religions*, 81 (1920), 213–59, esp. 247–50.

30 24:35–7; trans. ii, 50–51 (as in n. 1).

31 On lighting in late antique synagogues as background for the Light Verse, see F.B. Flood, 'Light in Stone. The Commemoration of the Prophet in Umayyad Architecture', in J. Johns (ed.), *Bayt al-Maqdis: Jerusalem and Early Islam* (Oxford, 1999), esp. 329–39. See the comments regarding the Christian background of these lines in R. Bell, *A Commentary on the Qurʾān*, ed. C.E. Bosworth and M.E.J. Richardson (Manchester, 1991), i, 600–3; and R. Blachère, *Le Coran* (Paris, 1950), iii, 1011–5.

32 Böwering, 'Light Verse' (as in n. 5), 116.

33 9:30–31, 34; trans. i, 210–11 (as in n. 1), with adjustments after R. Paret's German translation, *Der Koran* (Stuttgart, [7]1996), 135; with R. Paret, *Der Koran: Kommentar und Konkordanz* (Stuttgart [5]1993), 201.

34 On Christianity as *shirk*, see the discussion in G.R. Hawting, *The Idea of Idolatry and the Emergence of Islam: From Polemic to History* (Cambridge, 1999), 82–5.

35 *Homiliae S. Isaaci Syri Antiocheni*, ed. P. Bedjan (Paris, 1903), i, 29; trans. S. Brock, 'Early Syrian Asceticism', *Numen*, 20 (1973), 17. Vööbus, *History of Asceticism* (as in n. 12), ii, 145–58, discusses

opposition to developments within coenobitic life that included, among other dangers, property ownership, architectural display and agricultural exploitation.

36 *Homiliae S. Isaaci Syri Antiocheni*, i, 41; trans. Brock, 17 (as in previous n.). Also S. Isaaci Antiocheni doctoris, *Opera omnia*, ed. G. Bickell (Giessen, 1877), ii, 146 and ii, 332.

37 Muqātil ibn Sulaymān, *Tafsīr al-Qurʾān*, MS Istanbul, Ahmet III 74, ii f.185a; al-Ṭabarī, *Jāmiʿ al-bayān ʿan taʾwīl āy al-Qurʾān* (Beirut: Dār al-Fikr, 1984), xxvii, 238; al-Ḥakīm al-Tirmidhī, *Nawādir al-uṣūl* (Istanbul, 1877), 10–11. For an analysis of these texts, see S. Sviri, 'Wa-Rahbānīyatan ibtadaʿūhā: An Analysis of Traditions Concerning the Origin and Evaluation of Christian Monasticism', *JSAI*, 13 (1990), 201–8; and also McAuliffe, *Qurʾānic Christians* (as in n. 29), 263–6.

38 57:27; trans. A.J. Wensinck, 'Rahbāniyya', *EI*².

39 For discussion of the problem, see E. Beck, 'Das christliche Mönchtum im Koran', *Studia Orientalia*, 13 (Helsinki, 1946), 17–29, who understands *rahbāniyya* as one of three objects. Beck reviews earlier modern readings and concentrates particularly on grammatical problems raised in this passage. Also, L. Massignon, *Essai sur les origins du lexique technique de la mystique musulmane* (Paris, 1968), 145–53; Sviri, 'Wa-Rahbānīyatan ibtadaʿūhā' (as in n. 37), 195–208; and McAuliffe, *Qurʾānic Christians* (as in n. 29), 263–84, a detailed discussion of commentaries on 57:27, beginning with al-Ṭabarī. None of these primarily text-based discussions is much concerned to place the passage in a wider historical context.

40 5:82–3; trans. (as in n. 1), i, 141.

41 For translation and discussion, see Sviri, 'Wa-Rahbānīyatan ibtadaʿūhā' (as in n. 37), 205–6 with n. 28. The Kufan Maymūn ibn Mihrān (b. 40/660–61), an influential *faqīh* and administrator for ʿAbd al-Malik and later Umayyads, espoused the view that even pious monks were damned, being non-Muslims: al-Qushayrī, *Taʾrīkh Raqqa*, ed. T. al-Nāʾdānī (Damascus, n.d.), 27, cited by J. van Ess, *Theologie und Gesellschaft im 2. und 3. Jahrhundert Hidschra: Eine Geschichte des religiösen Denkens im frühen Islam* (Berlin, 1991), i, 20 with n. 4. See Sviri, 'Wa-Rahbānīyatan ibtadaʿūhā' (as in n. 37), 199–201 for two further anti-monastic sources from the Umayyad period.

42 Ibn Isḥāq, *Sīra*, 20–22 and 23–4 (trans. 14–16 and 16–17) (as in n. 1) on his disciple ʿAbdallāh ibn al-Thāmir; also recorded in al-Ṭabarī, *Taʾrīkh*, i, 920–23 (as in n. 1) (English translation [as in n. 1]: *The Sasanids, the Byzantines, the Lakhmids, and Yemen*, trans. C.E. Bosworth [The History of al-Ṭabarī, 5; Albany, NY, 1999], 195–9) and 923–5 (trans. Bosworth, 199–202 with n. 487 on the name Faymiyūn; n. 490 on Wahb; n. 501 on Muḥammad ibn Kaʿb as a source; and nn. 491–505 for commentary on the story of Faymiyūn and his disciple). On the influence of the Syrian holy man literary model on the representation of Faymiyūn, see J. Tubach, 'Die Anfänge des Christentums in Südarabien. Eine christliche Legende syrischer Herkunft in Ibn Hišam', *Parole de l'Orient*, 18 (1993), 101–11; and more recently, T. Sizgorich, 'Narrative and Community in Islamic Late Antiquity', *Past and Present*, 185 (2004), 29–31.

43 Ṣāliḥ is a rare name evocative of Qurʾānic associations with the pre-Islamic warner of the Thamūd: see Ṭabarī, *Sasanids*, trans. Bosworth (as in n. 42), 196, n. 492.

44 Ibn Isḥāq, *Sīra*, 22 (trans., 15) (as in n. 1).

45 Ibn Isḥāq, *Sīra*, 22 (trans., 16) (as in n. 1). A nearly identical phrase appears also at 24; see above for similar interpretations of Christians who have strayed from Jesus' teaching.

46 Ibn Isḥāq, *Sīra*, 23 (trans., 16) (as in n. 1).

47 On Baḥīrā, see Ibn Isḥāq, *Sīra*, 115–17 (trans., 79–81); cp. 119–20 (trans., 82) (as in n. 1).

48 Ibn Isḥāq, *Sīra*, 121 (trans., 83) (as in n. 1).

49 Ibn Isḥāq, *Sīra*, 101 (trans., 69) (as in n. 1). C. Robinson, 'Prophecy and Holy Men in Early Islam', in J. Howard-Johnston and P.A. Hayward (eds.), *The Cult of Saints in Late Antiquity and the Early Middle Ages* (Oxford, 1999), 244–6, has reviewed the evidence for the Christianity of Waraqa and is inclined to accept it, with due reserve, rather than view the evidence strictly as a backward projection. On early Muslim views of Waraqa and the relationship between Baḥīrā and Waraqa, see also C.F. Robinson, 'Waraka b. Nawfal', *EI*².

50 Ibn Isḥāq, *Sīra*, 148-9 (trans., 102–3) (as in n. 1). Guillaume mistranslates 'at Mayfaʿa' (no doubt an unfamiliar toponym to him) as 'in the high ground'.

51 For the Mayfaʿa monk and Zayd, see Ibn Isḥāq, *Sīra*, 143–9 (trans., 98–103) (as in n. 1). On the controversy over interpreting the tradition of *ḥanīfiyya* (right belief as opposed to polytheism), see A. Rippin, 'RHMN and the Hanīfs', in W.B. Hallaq and D.P. Little (eds.), *Islamic Studies Presented to Charles J. Adams* (Leiden, 1991), 153–68.

52 M. Piccirillo, 'L'identificazione storica di Umm al-Rasas con Mefaa', in M. Piccirillo and E. Alliata, *Umm al-Rasas - Mayfaʿah 1: Gli scavi del complesso di Santo Stefano* (Jerusalem, 1994), i, 37–46. Vööbus, *History of Asceticism* (as in n. 12), ii, 272–3, esp. nn. 103 and 104, and 164–5, esp. n. 21, discusses evidence from Syriac manuscripts that mention the use of *būrgā* (towers) and abandoned fortifications by hermits; see also Shahîd, *Byzantium and the Arabs* (as in n. 22), ii/1, 188–9; and E.K. Fowden, 'Christian Monasteries and Umayyad Residences in Late Antique Syria', in J.M. Blázquez Martínez and A. González Blanco (eds.), *Sacralidad y arqueología: Homenaje al Prof. Thilo Ulbert al cumplir 65 años* (Antigüedad y cristianismo, 21; Murcia, 2004), 572.

53 Jāḥiẓ, *Kitāb al-radd ʿalā 'l-Naṣārā*, cited in Griffith, 'Muḥammad and the Monk Baḥīrā' (as in n. 2), 155. For the story of Salmān al-Fārisī, see Ibn Isḥāq, *Sīra*, 136–43 (trans., 95–8) (as in n. 1). The Qurʾānic distinction between the good monk and the rapacious one is echoed in the report of Salmān al-Fārisī's experience first with a corrupt Syrian bishop who hoarded his parishioners' gold, followed by a sequence of pious ascetics (including the bishop's successor) in Syria, then in Mosul, Nisibis and Amorium. The last one recommended that Salmān go to Arabia where a prophet of the religion of Abraham was about to arise: Ibn Isḥāq, *Sīra*, 138–9 (trans., 97–8) (as in n. 1).

54 S.H. Griffith, 'The Prophet Muhammad, his Scripture and his Message, According to the Christian Apologies in Arabic and Syriac from the first Abbasid Century', in T. Fahd (ed.), *La vie du Prophète Mahomet* (Paris, 1983), 108.

55 7:63–70/65–72; 11:52–63/50–60; 26:123–40; 46: 20/21. See R.B. Serjeant, 'Haram and Hawtah, the Sacred Enclosure in Arabia', in id., *Studies in Arabian History and Civilisation* (London, 1981), ii, 574–5; Fowden, *Barbarian Plain* (as in n. 17), 179.

56 S. Bashear, 'Qibla Musharriqa and Early Muslim Prayer in Churches', *MW*, 81 (1991), 267–83. In these encounters we glimpse individual efforts to ignore the dangers of *shirk* that shadowed the saints and the forms of worship that had evolved in Christian tradition. The problematic icons, for example, could be covered: this is a solution accepted by al-Barqī (d. 274/887), *al-Maḥāsin* (Najaf, 1964), 507, cited by Bashear, 'Qibla Musharriqa', 280. For a synthetic discussion of direct survivals of pre-Islamic beliefs and practices, and the nature of the many accommodations of such customs in early Islamic Iraq, see Morony, *Iraq* (as in n. 5), 502–6, arguing at 503, for example, that 'Monophysite forms of Christian asceticism were brought by the pastoral Arabs of Iraq who settled in Basra and Kufa. As Muslims, such converts continued to do those things which could be supported by the Qurʾān or by early Islamic pratices in the Hijaz.'

57 Yāqūt, *Muʿjam*, ii, 510 (as in n. 22) (trans. after G. Le Strange, *Palestine under the Moslems* [Boston, 1890], 432).

58 T. Ulbert, *Die Basilika des Heiligen Kreuzes in Resafa-Sergiupolis* (Resafa, 2; Mainz, 1986), 118–27, 144–5; also T. Ulbert, *Die Kreuzfahrerzeitliche Silberschatz aus Resafa-Sergiupolis* (Resafa, 3; Mainz, 1990), 3. Al-Ruṣāfa's largest basilica, located in the southeast corner of the walled city and housing the shrine of Saint Sergius, has been known as Basilica A and, mistakenly, as the Basilica of the Holy Cross. The German archaeologists now refer to it as the Great Basilica and Hishām's construction as the Great Mosque.

59 Fowden, *Barbarian Plain* (as in n. 17), 174–83.

60 See Fowden, 'Christian Monasteries' (as in n. 52), 565–81. At Qasṭal in the Balqāʾ there appears to have been another Umayyad *qaṣr* that co-existed with a monastery: G. Bisheh, 'Two Umayyad Mosaic Floors from Qastal', *Studium Biblicum Franciscanum. Liber Annuus*, 50 (2000) 437.

61 In 98–99/717–18, he besieged Constantinople, which may have boosted his notoriety among eastern Christians, making a date in the 720s the most likely date for the disputation. This text has been recently commented upon by Hoyland, *Seeing Islam* (as in n. 6), 465–72, and S. Griffith, 'Disputing with Islam in Syriac: the Case of the Monk of Bêt Halê and a Muslim Emir', *Hugoye*, 3 (2000), 1–22.

62 J.M. Fiey, *Assyrie chrétienne: Contribution à l'étude de l'histoire et de la géographie ecclésiastiques et monastiques du nord de l'Iraq* (Beirut, 1965–68), iii, 204, 223; Griffith, 'Disputing with Islam' (as in n. 61), 7; Hoyland, *Seeing Islam* (as in n. 6), 465, considers a monastery near Mosul a possible alternative.

63 Cp. a vizier who was cured at a monastery where he had stopped to recover from an illness while travelling to Diyarbakır, and fell into conversation with a monk: in Griffith, 'The Monk in the Emir's *majlis*: Reflections on a Popular Genre of Christian Literary Apologetics in Arabic in the Early Islamic Period', in H. Lazarus-Yafeh et al. (eds.), *The Majlis: Interreligious Encounters in Medieval Islam* (Wiesbaden, 1999), 50. H. Kilpatrick, 'Monasteries through Muslim Eyes: The *diyārāt* Books', in D. Thomas (ed.), *Christians at the Heart of Islamic Rule: Church Life and Scholarship in ʿAbbasid Iraq* (Leiden, 2003), 27, cites other examples of monasteries known for their medicinal resources, notably springs or earth with healing properties. I am grateful to Hilary Kilpatrick for sending offprints of her work.

64 Trans. Hoyland, *Seeing Islam* (as in n. 6), 467. By the early ʿAbbāsid period, the monastery – as well as the *majlis* – had become an established setting for descriptions of theological disputations between Christian monks and Muslims. On this subject see the work of Griffith, esp. 'The Monk in the Emir's *majlis*' (as in n. 63), 13–65.

65 Trans. Griffith, 'Disputing with Islam' (as in n. 61), 11.

66 Tr. Hoyland, *Seeing Islam* (as in n. 6), 466.

67 Hoyland, *Seeing Islam* (as in n. 6), 469–70; Griffith, 'Disputing with Islam' (as in n. 61), 9–12.

68 Abū Nuʿaym al-Iṣfahānī, *Ḥilyat al-awliyāʾ wa-ṭabaqāt al-aṣfiyāʾ* (Cairo, 1932–38), ii, 375, cited in Livne-Kafri, 'Early Muslim Ascetics' (as in n. 5), 108, who draws on an article in Hebrew by S. D. Goitein, 'Isrā'iliyyat', *Tarbiz*, 6 (1934/5), 89–101, 510–22. The references cited in the present article are taken from Livne-Kafri.

69 See Ch. Pellat, 'Mālik b. Dīnār', *EI*^{2} and van Ess, *Theologie und Gesellschaft* (as in n. 21), ii, 91–3.

70 This story was recorded by Abū Nuʿaym al-Iṣfahānī (336–430/948–1038), whose grandfather, a convert to Islam, had been a famous ascetic. Abū Nuʿaym himself travelled widely and studied in Iraq, Hijaz and Khurāsān, and came to be respected as a transmitter of *ḥadīth*, a ṣūfī and the author of an immense collection of the lives and sayings of six-hundred and forty-nine pious figures. Though he begins formally with the four Righteous Caliphs, he is a more or less untapped source of evidence concerning monks in early Islamic circles. Abū Nuʿaym claims that Christian scriptures were a direct influence on Mālik. Abū Nuʿaym al-Iṣfahānī, *Ḥilya* (as in n. 68), ii, 358, 359, 369, 370, 382, 386. Also on Mālik's asceticism, see Goldziher, 'Asceticism and Sufism', in *Introduction to Islamic Theology and Law* (Princeton, 1981), 134.

71 D. Sourdel, 'Dayr Ḳunnā', *EI*^{2}.

72 For Abū Nuwās, see E. Wagner, *Abū Nuwās: Eine Studie zur arabischen Literatur der frühen ʿAbbāsidenzeit* (Wiesbaden, 1965), 111, 197–9; for Abū 'l-Naṣr al-Baṣrī, see B. Farès, *Vision chrétienne et signes musulmans* (Cairo, 1961), 7.

73 B.I. Marschak, *Silberschätze des Orients* (Leipzig, 1986). For illustration and discussion of clay wine jars painted with figures, including a likely monk, found at a palace at Sāmarrāʾ built in 221–5/836–9, see D.S. Rice, 'Deacon or Drink: Some Paintings from Samarra Re-examined', *Arabica*, 5 (1958), 15–32; G. Strohmaier, 'Die bemalten Weingefäße aus Samarra', *Klio*, 63 (1981), 123–30, repr. in id., *Hellas im Islam: Interdisziplinäre Studien zur Ikonographie, Wissenschaft und Religionsgeschichte* (Wiesbaden, 2003), 149–54, interprets the painted figures as wine labels. On wall painting, see below, n. 75.

74 Abū 'l-Faraj al-Iṣfahānī, *Kitāb adab al-ghurabāʾ*, 78 (trans. 70); cp. 36 (trans. 34) (as in n. 1): 'I passed by the church in Edessa on my way to Iraq and, having heard about it, went inside to see it'. See P. Crone and S. Moreh, *The Book of Strangers* (as in n. 1), 15-18 for their discussion of the edition and 146–82 for the work's literary context. References are to al-Munajjid's paragraph numbering and the page number of the translation. H. Kilpatrick, 'On the Difficulty of Knowing Medieval Arab Authors: the Case of Abū l-Faraj and Pseudo-Iṣfahānī', in R.G. Hoyland and P.F. Kennedy (eds.), *Islamic Reflections, Arabic Musings: Studies in Honour of Professor Alan Jones* (Oxford, 2004), 230–42 persuasively defends the attribution to Abū 'l-Faraj against Crone's denial of its genuineness. I thank James Montgomery for sending me a copy of this article.

75 See K.A.C. Creswell, *Early Muslim Architecture* (Oxford, ²1969), ii, 232–42, 265–70. Also, E. Herzfeld, *Die Malereien von Samarra* (Berlin, 1927), 84.

76 *Kitāb adab al-ghurabāʾ*, 25 (trans. 24) (as in n. 1).

77 *Kitāb adab al-ghurabāʾ*, 94 (trans. 84) (as in n. 1).

78 D. Sourdel, 'Dayr Murrān', *EI²*. ʿUmar ibn ʿAbd al-ʿAzīz was buried at another Dayr Murrān (also, confusingly, known as Dayr Samʿān), near Maʿarrat al-Nuʿmān in northern Syria. One wonders where at al-Ruṣāfa Hishām was buried.

79 Modern selections from this literature have been made by E. Sachau, *Vom Klosterbuch des Šâbuštî* (Abhandlungen der Preussischen Akademie der Wissenschaften, Phil.-hist. Klasse, Jahrg. 1919, 10; Berlin, 1919); H. al-Zayyāt, 'Al-diyārāt al-naṣrāniyya fī 'l-Islām', *al-Mashriq*, 36 (1938), 291–418; S. Munajjid, 'Morceaux choisis du livre des moines', *MIDEO*, 3 (1956), 349–58; G. Troupeau, 'Les couvents chrétiens dans la littérature arabe', *La nouvelle du Caire*, 1 (1975), 265–79; K. Zakharia, 'Le moine et l'échanson, ou le *Kitāb al-diyārāt*' d'Al-Shābushtī et ses lecteurs', *BEO*, 53–54 (2001–2), 59–74. For an overview of the Arabic literature on monasteries, see Shahîd, *Byzantium and the Arabs* (as in n. 22), ii/1, 156–64.

80 Al-Ṭabarī, *Taʾrīkh*, i, 770; trans. iv, 150 (as in n. 1). T. Khalidi, *Arabic Historical Thought in the Classical Period* (Cambridge, 1994), 52, translates *biyaʿ* as 'monasteries'; whereas M. Perlmann opts for 'churches' (Ṭabarī, *The Ancient Kingdoms* [The History of al-Ṭabarī, 4; Albany, NY, 1987] 150). I. Shahîd, *Byzantium and the Arabs in the Fourth Century* (Washington D.C., 1984), 354 with n. 14, also takes it as 'churches'.

81 See Shahîd, *Byzantium and the Arabs* (as in n. 22), ii/1, 159–60.

82 Al-Shābushtī, *Kitāb al-diyārāt*, ed. G. ʿAwwād (Baghdad, 1966). On this work, see H. Kilpatrick, 'Representations of Social Intercourse between Muslims and non-Muslims in Some Medieval *adab* Works', in J. Waardenburg (ed.), *Muslim Perceptions of Other Religions: a Historical Survey* (New York, 1999), 217–18.

83 Mention of monasteries is to be found at 27–8 (trans. 26–7); 34–6 (trans. 32–4); 59 (trans. 53); 64–5 (trans. 58–9) (as in n. 1).

84 Whether or not the more exuberant debauchery actually took place in monasteries is impossible to gauge, though one can imagine monks – whose political status was always potentially delicate – would have been put in an impossible situation as their houses were seen as oases by the Muslim elite if not more widely. Words for priest (*qass*), monastery (*bīʿa* and *dayr*) even appeared together in a 'slang phrase for sexual intercourse': see J. Montgomery, 'For the Love of a Christian Boy: A Song by Abū Nuwās', *JAL*, 27 (1996), 124 for the reference. Mosques too might provide similar opportunities, whether actual or fantastical: numerous examples appear in Abū Nuwās' verses and are discussed by G. Schoeler, 'Iblīs in the Poems of Abū Nuwās', in *ZDMG*, 151 (2001), 43–62, 48–9.

85 For the standard survey of the wine song genre, see J.E. Bencheikh, 'Khamriyya', *EI²*.

86 Kilpatrick, 'Monasteries through Muslim Eyes' (as in n. 63), 19–37, esp. 36–7.

87 See 'The Description of Familiar Foods: Kitāb waṣf al-aṭʿima al-muʿtāda', trans. C. Perry in M. Rodinson, A.J. Arberry and C. Perry, *Medieval Arab Cookery* (Totnes, 2001), 448 for recipe.

88 For the contributions of ʿAdī ibn Zayd, Ḥassān ibn Thābit and Akhṭal, see Bencheikh, *EI²*; and

on the latter in particular, see Kilpatrick, 'Representations of Social Intercourse' (as in n. 82), 216-17.

89 ʿUmarī, *Masālik al-ab ār*; trans. in R.W. Hamilton, *Walid and his Friends: An Umayyad Tragedy* (Oxford, 1988), 87–8.

90 Al-Walīd ibn Yazīd, *Dīwān*, ed. Ḥ. ʿAṭwān (Beirut, 1998), 127; trans. R.W. Hamilton, *Walid and his Friends* (as in previous note), 165.

91 A wide range of genres intersect in the work of Abū Nuwās and each scholar comes to his poetry with an interest in different aspects of this unusually subtle poet: see, for example, Wagner, *Abū Nuwās* (as in n. 72); A. Hamori, *On the Art of Medieval Arabic Literature* (Princeton, 1974), chap. 1–4; P.F. Kennedy, *The Wine Song in Classical Arabic Poetry: Abū Nuwās and the Literary Tradition* (Oxford, 1997); and articles cited in this section by J.E. Montgomery (especially his 'Abū Nuwās the Alchoholic', in U. Vermeulen and D. De Smet [eds.], *Philosophy and Arts in the Islamic World* [Leuven, 1998], 19–20, where he reviews the approaches of Hamori and Mattock) and G. Schoeler.

92 See, for example, Seppälä, *In Speechless Ecstasy* (as in n. 5), esp. 86–116, where symbolic language and, in particular, images of drunkenness are discussed.

93 *Dīwān Abī Nuwās*, ed. A. al-Ghazālī (Cairo, 1953), 38–40; trans. J. Montgomery, 'Revelry and Remorse: A Poem of Abū Nuwās', *JAL*, 25 (1994), 117–19. My reading owes much to the illuminating discussion of Qurʾānic references in this poem by James Montgomery, at 123–32, though he should not be held responsible for any excesses on my part.

94 For this derivation Montgomery, 'Revelry and Remorse' (as in n. 93), 127–8, cites the authority of S. Fraenkel, *Die Aramäischen Fremdwörter im Arabischen* (Leiden, 1886), 172.

95 See, for example, Kennedy, *Wine Song* (as in n. 91), 67. A more daring reading would see the antiphonal song of the birds as that of the monks' morning chant – cf. al-Nābigha's likening of the morning chanting at the Church of St. John the Baptist at Damascus to the morning trilling of swallows: al-Nābigha al-Shaybānī, *Dīwān*, ed. A. Nasīm (Cairo, 1932), 53, l. 1; trans. R. Nadler, *Die Umayyadenkalifen im Spiegel ihrer zeitgenössischen Dichter*, doctoral thesis (University of Erlangen-Nürnberg, 1990), 231.

96 The 'metaphysical hang-over' anticipates the next binge: see J. Montgomery, 'Abū Nuwās the Alcoholic' (as in n. 91), 25.

97 Ibid. It is quite natural, rather than 'ironical' – the position of P.F. Kennedy, 'Zuhdiyya', *EI*[2] – that the same poet, the Christian ʿAdī ibn Zayd of al-Ḥīra, was and is considered to be the father of both genres.

98 Hamori, *On the Art of Medieval Arabic Literature* (as in n. 91), 67.

99 *Dīwān Abī Nuwās* (as in n. 93), 333; trans. Montgomery, 'For the Love of a Christian Boy' (as in n. 84), 119.

100 Montgomery, 'For the Love of a Christian Boy' (as in n. 84), 123.

101 J. Scott Meisami, 'Arabic *mujūn* Poetry: The Literary Dimension', in F. De Jong (ed.), *Verse and the Fair Sex: Studies in Arabic Poetry and in the Representation of Women in Arabic Literature* (Utrecht, 1993), 17–18, with reference to *mujūn* poetry, cited with approval in Montgomery, 'For the Love of a Christian Boy' (as in n. 84), 117 with n. 7.

102 The idea that Christian ascetics, our 'good monks', served as paradigms for Muslim heroes, especially *mujāhidūn*, has been discussed recently by T. Sizgorich, 'Narrative and Community' (as in n. 42), 9–42.

103 Schoeler, 'Iblīs in the Poems of Abū Nuwās' (as in n. 84), 55; Kennedy, *Wine Song* (as in n. 91), 225–6.

104 Isaac of Nineveh, *The First Part*, ed. P. Bedjan (Paris, 1909), 337–8, trans. A. Wensinck, *Mystic Treatises by Isaac of Nineveh* (Amsterdam, 1923), 226. Isaac was born in Qaṭar where he first lived as a monk, but spent most of his life in Mesopotamia: see S. Brock, 'Syriac Writers from Beth Qatraye', *ARAM*, 11–12 (1999–2000), 85–9, and id., 'From Qatar to Tokyo, by Way of Mar Saba:

the Translations of Isaac of Beth Qatraye (Isaac the Syrian)', *ARAM*, 11–12 (1999–2000), 475–84. Two extant translations into Arabic from a Greek translation of part of Isaac's writings are dated 885/6 CE: S. Brock, 'Syriac into Greek at Mar Saba: The Translation of St. Isaac the Syrian', in J. Patrich (ed.), *The Sabaite Heritage in the Orthodox Church from the Fifth Century to the Present* (Leuven, 2001), 207. Isaac was by no means unique in his fondness for wine and drunkenness in his writings. Another Iraqi ascetic who flourished in the eighth century, John of Dalyatha, wrote: 'Blessed are those who are drunk by your love, my God, for through their drunkenness in you they have become possessed of madness and they have forgotten the things previously necessary for them': *La collection des lettres de Jean de Dalyatha*, ed. and trans. R. Beulay (PO, 39; Paris, 1978), 326–7, discussed by Seppälä, *In Speechless Ecstasy* (as in n. 5), 146; see also 145 for further examples of this imagery in Isaac and other Syriac writers, and 204–15 on later ṣūfī wine imagery. A.J. Wensinck considered that Isaac had 'one of the first places in the history of sūfism': Wensinck, *Mystic Treatises* (as in n. 104), lvi. See in general his introduction, esp. xlv–lvi; and, also on holy drunkenness, his *Bar Hebraeus's Book of the Dove* (Leiden, 1919), esp. xc–xci. I would like to thank Peter Brown for drawing to my attention some Syriac wine songs written for the Mongol court by Khāmīs bar Qardāhē and translated by David G.K. Taylor of The Oriental Institute, Oxford. One cannot help regretting the loss of the Christian ʿAdī ibn Zayd's wine songs when reading these verses that are striking for their blend of Christian symbolic language and hackneyed *khamriyya* themes, some seven centuries after al-Ḥīra's father of the wine song was active.

105 On the history and legends of al-Khawarnaq, see M. Pantke, *Der arabische Bahrām-Roman: Untersuchungen zur Quellen- und Stoffgeschichte* (Berlin, 1974), 52–68. J. Stetkevych, *The Zephyrs of Najd* (Chicago, 1993), 66–73 discusses Khawarnaq's summing up of the delicate balance between the paradisal and the ephemeral, between the 'contained power' and 'carnal impetuousness' of Khawarnaq's legendary first prince, Bahrām Gūr. (I thank James Montgomery for putting these pages in my way). ʿAdī ibn Zayd makes a glancing reference to the story in one of his poems meditating on the decay of mortal fame: al-Ṭabarī, *Taʾrīkh* (as in n. 1), i, 853–4 (trans. Bosworth [as in n. 42], 81); cf. also al-Iṣfahānī, *Kitāb al-aghānī*, ed. ʿA. Muhannā and S. Jābir, 25 vols. (Beirut, 1992), ii, 131–2.

106 Al-Ṭabarī, *Taʾrīkh* (as in n. 1), i, 853 (trans. Bosworth [as in n. 42], 80–81).

107 Several of these either incorporated elements from former monasteries or were built in close proximity to existing communities: Fowden, 'Christian Monasteries' (as in n. 52), 565–81.

108 Al-Ṭabarī, *Taʾrīkh* (as in n. 1), ii, 819–21 (*The Victory of the Marwanids*, trans. M. Fishbein [The History of al-Ṭabarī, 21; New York, 1990], 195–6). He said: 'How pleasant our life is! If only anything lasted!' and, quoting a well-known line, "Everything new, O Umaymah, goes toward decay; and every man will some day become a has-been"'.

109 Al-Iṣfahānī, *Kitāb al-aghānī* (as in n. 105), ii , 128–32.

2

Greek Myth and Arabic Poetry at Quṣayr ʿAmra

Garth Fowden

Quṣayr ʿAmra is a hunting lodge in the stony desert which covers the eastern Balqāʾ region of Jordan.[1] It lies some 65 km east-southeast of Amman as the crow flies, and 27 km west of the al-Azraq oasis. The site's main feature is an ancient stone bath house whose excellent structural state, including vaulting, has preserved some 450 m^2 of brightly coloured frescoes, one of the most extensive – and geographically remote – sequences of paintings to have survived anywhere in the ancient world.

A number of labels and brief prayers are still to be read on the frescoes, a scattering in Greek, but most in Arabic, including one of the earliest epigraphical occurrences of the term 'Muslim'.[2] But a more specific *terminus post quem* is provided by a painting of six kings labelled in Arabic and Greek – one of them is Roderic the Visigoth, defeated and killed by the Umayyad conquerors of Spain in 711/12.[3] In fact Quṣayr ʿAmra belongs to a group of country residences, or 'desert castles' as they are often rather misleadingly called, which lie scattered across the Syro-Jordanian steppe and desert, and were apparently built by members of the Umayyad dynasty which ruled the Muslim caliphate from Damascus between 661 and 750. That Quṣayr ʿAmra in particular was a princely project is suggested by the portrait of an enthroned prince which dominates the alcove at the focal point of the bath house's main hall.[4]

Between 711 and 750 the only Umayyad princes who lived for substantial periods of time in the Balqāʾ were the caliphs Yazīd II (720–24) and his son al-Walīd II, who ruled for just 15 months in 743–44 but before that had for 19 whole years served as heir apparent to his uncle the Caliph Hishām (724–43). Al-Walīd and Hishām hated each other, and al-Walīd eventually walked out of his uncle's court at al-Ruṣāfa. He settled instead near al-Azraq. A hunting lodge in a wadi whose seasonal water attracted animals and funneled them down towards the pools and thickets of al-Azraq would have fitted neatly into the scheme of al-Walīd's life and entertainments. That it is more likely to have been commissioned by him than by his father, and then abruptly abandoned after al-Walīd's murder in 744, is suggested in the first place by the fact that there is no sign at Quṣayr ʿAmra of the wear and tear which usually afflicted bath houses – alterations and extensions; repainting of frescoes, especially in the hot rooms; abrasion to the well head or deposits of crustaceous lime; and furring of water pipes. But besides being an enthusiastic hunter and, it seems, a considerable hedonist, al-Walīd was also a poet, a musician and a major patron of architecture and the arts.[5] These tastes mesh well with the subjects of the Quṣayr ʿAmra frescoes: hunting scenes, musicians, dancing girls and other decorative women, a sequence of vault panels illustrative of the building trade, personifications of Poetry, History and Inquiry or Philosophy, together with various paintings perhaps romantic or erotic, but hard to decipher.[6]

The artistic genealogy of the Quṣayr ʿAmra paintings is a complicated subject, and nothing I say here will encourage rash judgments. Nonetheless, as a broad generalisation one may say that the atmosphere is Greek. Sometimes the prevalent influence is the so-called 'Byzantine' art of the East Roman Empire, as in the paintings of the six kings or the enthroned prince. At other times it is the 'classical' art of Greek and Roman polytheism, as in the personifications I just mentioned or the paintings of a bathing beauty modelled on Aphrodite[7] or of an amorous couple who seem to recall Aphrodite and Ares.[8] But the predominantly Greek atmosphere is tempered by a distinct if less explicit Iranian element.[9] In this paper I shall confine myself to just one panel, which testifies to awareness of Greek mythological iconography on the part of Quṣayr ʿAmra's creators.

The painting in question (Fig. 1) occupies a sensitive transitional point in the building, in the tympanum above the doorway through which, after taking one's bath, one passed

Fig. 1: Quṣayr ʿAmra, apodyterium, lunette over door into hall. A.J. Jaussen and R. Savignac, Mission archéologique en Arabie (Paris, 1909–22), iii, pl. xlv.

from the apodyterium, the changing room, back into the hall, the bath's main social area. In the upper left part of the composition[10] we see, apparently amidst a landscape of rounded rocks, a pensive and at least partly naked young man – he is visible only from roughly his navel up – resting head on hand while contemplating a long object of irregular shape that slants up and towards the right across the panel's foreground. Quṣayr ʿAmra's discoverer and first student, Alois Musil, thought this object was a shrouded corpse, though he offered no further explanation.[11] On the far left of the composition is to be seen a square cupboard or table with a water jug standing on it. On the right is a palm tree, its trunk clearly distinguishable at the bottom of the panel, and its branches at the top. This element of the composition is best studied in the early photograph taken by the Dominican Père Raphaël Savignac between 1909 and 1912, not long after Musil's visits.

A naked, winged Eros hovers in the upper central area of the lunette and gestures toward the young man, or perhaps rather beckons him. Here is a strong hint that the scene has been borrowed from classical mythology. The subject in question is easy to identify: 'Dionysus discovering Ariadne' asleep on the beach at Naxos, abandoned there by faithless Theseus after she had helped him slay the Minotaur.[12] The god bears the girl off and marries her. It is true that, at Quṣayr ʿAmra, 'Ariadne' herself is missing – unless she is inside the shroud. To this little problem we shall have to return; but first it should be made clear that the whole Dionysiac cycle had been enormously popular, and well understood, in the art of pre-Islamic Syria until well into the sixth century.[13] It is, for example, interesting to note that the mosaicists of the town of Mādabā, south of Amman and one of the nearest substantial settlements to Quṣayr ʿAmra, were still in the sixth century producing images rich in explicit, labelled mythological – including Dionysiac – content.[14] Further to the north, at Jerash, has recently been discovered a house decorated with sixth century Dionysiac mosaics which – most unusually – can be shown to have been still visible under the Umayyads.[15] Al-Shahbāʾ (Philippopolis) in the Ḥawrān in southern Syria and Sarrīn on the Euphrates southwest of Ḥarrān have yielded mosaics depicting the marriage of Dionysus and Ariadne, respectively of the fourth and – according to the latest estimate – the later fifth centuries.[16] As for the specific theme of 'Dionysus discovering Ariadne', an excellent example (Fig. 2) has survived in a third century CE mosaic found in a house at Seleucia near Antioch,[17] and another one, of the late second or early third century, at Beirut.[18] Most of these mosaics were probably not visible by the Umayyad period, let alone widely known; but it is conceivable that others like them were, while portable works – ivories, silver plates and textiles – continued at least until the sixth century to depict the story of Dionysus and Ariadne, and may very well have continued in circulation for centuries after that.[19] Of the familiarity or at least availability to the Arab invaders of Dionysiac imagery there can, then, be no reasonable doubt.

If we take the literary evidence into account as well, we find that in educated Christian circles some acquaintance, however shallow, with Greek mythology continued for a very long time to be thought desirable, even if only in order to grasp the classical allusions in patristic literature. Hence, for example, the mythological scholia on select orations of Gregory of Nazianzus composed in Greek, apparently in Syria in the sixth century, then translated into Syriac by *c.*600. The Syriac version was revised in 623/24 by an anti-Chalcedonian bishop of Edessa exiled on Cyprus, and further tinkered with by the scholar-

Fig. 2: Seleucia, House of Dionysus and Ariadne: Dionysus discovering Ariadne (mosaic, Severan). Antakya Museum. By permission of the Department of Art and Archaeology, Princeton University.

patriarch Athanasius II of Balad who died in 686. Our earliest manuscript of this Syriac version was copied in a monastery near Antioch in 734, and others continued to be produced into the ninth century. The scholia contain numerous references to Dionysus, including his discovery of and marriage to Ariadne.[20]

The next question, of course, is what a Greek mythological image may have *meant* to the Arab patron and his artist who chose to deploy it at the end of the Umayyad period. It is a commonplace that the transmission of Greek images, as they travelled in space, eastwards into Asia for example, or in time, down the centuries into late antiquity and beyond, often had a lot more to do with form than content.[21] Philostratus, the early third century biographer of the first century CE philosopher Apollonius of Tyana, catches this very well when he asserts that Apollonius saw certain tapestries in the royal palace at Babylon, and that these tapestries were decorated with scenes from the myth of Orpheus, 'perhaps out of regard for his peaked cap and breeches, for it cannot be for his music or the songs with which he charmed and soothed others'.[22]

It is conceivable, then, that Ariadne and Dionysus found their way onto the wall at Quṣayr ʿAmra purely and simply because the patron or artist thought the image intriguing and suggestive. We are no longer in a milieu where we can take for granted knowledge of the Greek myths themselves.[23] Even though the artists may well have been Christians, the surviving Christian art of the eighth century no longer embraces mythological themes, while Nonnus' mythological scholia were perhaps perused only by an elite of learned clerics. As for Quṣayr ʿAmra's patron, he was an Arab Muslim. There are, as it happens, a few labels painted on the frescoes in Greek, alongside others in Arabic, but nothing to convince us the patron actually spoke or at least understood Greek.

The problem, though, with any explanation of our painting as a purely formal borrowing from Graeco-Roman art, with strictly aesthetic motives, is that the artist has made a striking innovation: he has omitted – or at least hidden – Ariadne. It would have been perfectly consistent with his patron's taste, as manifest elsewhere at Quṣayr ʿAmra, for him to have rendered Ariadne semi-naked, as was the convention in ancient art, her *chitōn* clinging to her body and emphasizing its sexual allure, or slipping to reveal a single breast or the whole of her torso, while she raises one arm and places her hand behind her head in a conventional gesture indicating sleep but also emphasizing her exposure. There must have been a good reason why this seductive image was foregone at Quṣayr ʿAmra. I would like to suggest that the choice was made in response at once to a major crisis in al-Walīd's life, and to the way in which 'Dionysus discovering Ariadne' had traditionally been used in Graeco-Roman art.

This approach assumes that an Umayyad patron or the artist who worked for him could still have known where a particular image had most characteristically been deployed in the by then far-off pre-Islamic world. But some basic information was not, in fact, very hard to come by, given the image's popularity and the interesting fact that it had been deployed with particular frequency in two specific contexts, namely the more intimate rooms of private dwellings,[24] and on sarcophagi.[25] If some awareness of the first of these preferences had been retained, then it may not be by chance that the image occurs, at Quṣayr ʿAmra, in the apodyterium rather than in the hall used for social gatherings. But what is more suggestive in the present context is the use of the image on sarcophagi – something perhaps more readily apparent to Umayyad observers (given the number of ancient sarcophagi that had survived) than the occurrence of the scene in the decoration of private rooms in houses, most of which had by the eighth century been redecorated, remodelled, demolished or allowed to fall into ruin.

Although Ariadne is represented on sarcophagi, her pose is unmistakably that of a living person, nor is it a particularly relaxed posture for sleep (Fig. 3). Yet the further her body tilted back, the easier it became for the mythologically illiterate to imagine her not just unconscious but as dead as the denizen of the sarcophagus itself. And the more encompassing the folds of her *chitōn*, the more they might suggest a winding sheet. The famous

Fig. 3: Sarcophagus from St-Médard-d'Eyran (Bordeaux): Dionysus discovering Ariadne (220–35 CE). Louvre Museum, Paris.

Vatican sculpture of Ariadne (Fig. 4), a second century CE copy of a Hellenistic original,[26] was after all long mistaken for a dying Cleopatra, and her serpent armband for a real snake.[27] Pope Julius II, who bought her for the Vatican in 1512, had her placed above a fountain whence water plashed into a sarcophagus supported by dolphins.[28] And this was far from being the only reclining Ariadne early moderns insisted on seeing as the tragic, notorious Egyptian queen.[29] At least one sixteenth century bronze copy of the much imitated Vatican statue, by Primaticcio and now in the Louvre, gave it a more markedly recumbent position, as befitted a subject conceived to be not just asleep but dead.[30] And again four centuries later, in Giorgio de Chirico's long series of Ariadne paintings and

Fig. 4: Sleeping Ariadne (second century CE). Vatican Museum.

sculptures, the reclining statue – initially modelled on the Vatican sculpture – sinks into a funereal repose, drained of colour or liveliness (Fig. 5) and more reminiscent now of Bernini's rendering of the Blessed Ludovica Albertoni on her tomb in Rome's San Francesco a Ripa (where de Chirico himself was buried).[31] In the classical iconography, the surprise and concern of Dionysus and his retinue on suddenly discovering Ariadne might strengthen this misinterpretation – or rather, this departure from strict adherence to the literary tradition – and cause the god to be taken as a mourner. The young man in our Quṣayr ʿAmra painting does indeed seem to be preoccupied: his attitude is one of contemplative repose, even grieving, rather than surprise, excitement or erotic arousal.

All of which makes one wonder whether Alois Musil's first intuition was not right, and this is indeed a shrouded corpse. Although an approximately human shape is discernible under the drapes, no head is visible at the right of the composition where one would most

Fig. 5: Giorgio de Chirico, Mélancolie (c.1938–40). Salvador Dalí Museum, Saint Petersburg, Florida. M.R. Taylor, Giorgio de Chirico and the Myth of Ariadne (London, 2002), 146, pl. 34.

naturally expect it.[32] And one begins to wonder about that water jug. With one very odd exception, a sarcophagus found in Alexandria that depicts Ariadne asleep in front of a building, perhaps a temple, rather than on a beach,[33] such a container is never part of the Graeco-Roman iconography of this scene, in which it would indeed have been quite incongruous. But what if it has just been used for washing the corpse?

Al-Walīd was an accomplished poet, whose verses on love and wine are still appreciated in the Arab world.[34] Nobody familiar with his poetry[35] will by now be in any doubt which way my argument is heading. Much of his poetry revolves round his long frustrated and eventually tragically thwarted love for Salmā.[36]

Sometime before al-Walīd became heir apparent in 724 at the age of 15, he had been married to Saʿda, the daughter of Saʿīd ibn Khālid ibn ʿAmr ibn ʿUthmān ibn ʿAffān, a great-grandson in other words of the third caliph, ʿUthmān (644–56). Likewise before his father Yazīd's death, though, he fell desperately in love with Saʿda's sister Salmā. So he divorced Saʿda and asked Saʿīd for his other daughter's hand; but Saʿīd, backed up by Hishām who had now succeeded Yazīd, and was married to another of Saʿīd's daughters, rebuffed al-Walīd in no uncertain terms: 'Do you want me to take you as a stud for both my daughters?'[37] The young prince then busied himself with pining away in verse, but made no practical progress until, on Hishām's death, he himself became caliph. Nobody could say no to him now, and Salmā was duly fetched from al-Madīna to meet al-Walīd in the Balqāʾ where he was continuing, as caliph, to reside, having evidently enjoyed his self-inflicted exile there. The two were married, an event al-Walīd celebrated in ecstatic verse; but seven days later, or forty according to other accounts, Salmā died. Al-Walīd was plunged into a much intenser grief than any he had known before.

> Salmā, you were a garden, and its fruits
> in all their kinds near ripe for harvesting.
> The husbandmen with loving care kept watch,
> nor slept until, when spring had eased their fears,
> its fruits were scattered by the autumn winds.[38]

In another poem al-Walīd speaks of Salmā lying 'imprisoned in a desert grave'.[39]

Al-Walīd's frivolous father had been carried to an early grave by his grief over the death of his beloved singing girl Ḥabāba, an accident for which he himself had been responsible.[40] Al-Walīd too seems to have become almost unbalanced in lamenting Salmā, if we may judge from another poem he must have produced at this time:

> God may yet make me and Salmā one;
> does God not do whatever He wills?
> He'll bring her out and cast her in the earth
> and make her sleep; and look! her robe has slipped.
> And He'll bring me and cast me down on her.
> I'll rouse her, when judgment has been passed,
> and He'll send rain on us abundantly,
> to wash us, so no weariness remains.[41]

In these extraordinary and painful verses, al-Walīd vividly imagines intercourse with Salmā in Paradise, 'when judgment has been passed' and when they have been purified by the rain which, when it falls on parched earth, the Qurʾān itself uses as an image for the resurrection of the dead.[42] Inevitably this poem, with its combination of eroticism and apparent impiety, became a hostage to fortune, and will undoubtedly have been much quoted by the caliph's numerous enemies. A variant version in which it has been transmitted substitutes for the first half of the first verse:

> Why, if only God would cause Salmā to die![43]

This sentiment is incredible on al-Walīd's lips[44] and reads like a substitution for the much more natural

> God may yet make me and Salmā one.

The earliest known transmitter of the variant version died in 806,[45] which is therefore the latest possible date for it – when al-Walīd was still the object of vivid controversy. It makes the four verses straightforwardly and unforgivably vile: al-Walīd prays that Salmā will die so that he will be able to possess her in Paradise. But it also makes the poem far more quotable, by doing away with the need to explain the whole story – the variant beginning immediately suggests the thwarted lover's familiar spite, whereas 'God may yet...' evokes a more complicated prehistory. The variant also renders merely tasteless, rather than ironical,[46] the Qurʾānic allusion in the second half of verse 1: 'does God not do whatever He wills?'[47]

My suggestion, then, is that our painting is al-Walīd's visual memorial to his love for Salmā, a heartbreaking image to be set directly alongside his no less personal and deeply wounded poem.[48] As in the poem, so too in the painting, Eros – Love – leads al-Walīd towards reunification with his beloved. And if we allow ourselves now to read the image in the light of the poem, we can see that al-Walīd is making a no doubt uninformed, but still perspicacious variation on an ancient view, known from sarcophagus reliefs, that Ariadne asleep on her Naxian strand (or for that matter Endymion on Latmus) is a symbolic expression of longing for reawakening from death through the intervention of a god.[49] At Quṣayr ʿAmra, Ariadne is literally, not figuratively, dead, and the god is merely a caliph (God's deputy); but that does not make any less real her promise of joy in Paradise, which in the Muslim understanding of things might mean, specifically, an erotic pleasure she was charged to bestow on a particular individual, our poet-patron.

As must by now be apparent, I am convinced al-Walīd was one of those patrons who knows what he wants and does not hesitate to give instructions to the artists he employs. And it seems to me that, even without knowledge of the original myth, a sensitive and educated person like him could easily have read his own predicament into some depiction he came across of 'Dionysus discovering Ariadne', and – as grieving poet rather than mythographer – have transformed the sleeping figure into a dead woman ready to be buried 'in a desert grave', in the shade of a palm tree.[50] Yet it is not in fact necessary to put all the creative responsibility on al-Walīd. As it happens, there was at least one person in his immediate entourage who could have helped him to arrive at this inspiration, and that was Sālim Abū 'l-ʿAlāʾ, a secretary who had also served Hishām,[51] and indeed composed the letter which apprised al-Walīd of Hishām's death and his own succession.[52] Sālim is known in the history of early Arabic literature as a leading stylist and the editor of a translation from Greek into Arabic of *Letters of Aristotle to Alexander* perhaps originally composed in the sixth century.[53] In him we have a figure close to the very centre of political power, who marks the highest level of Umayyad literary culture, and is likely to have known Quṣayr ʿAmra at first hand. He may even have been involved in the latter phases of its decoration, once al-Walīd became caliph – the panel I have discussed here is not the only one that appears to have been designed after al-Walīd's accession.[54] Sālim offers a valuable guarantee that the interpretation of the apodyterium panel as a conscious derivative of 'Dionysus discovering Ariadne' cannot be dismissed as in principle implausible. He knew both the Greek tradition in itself and, presumably, how to adapt it to the taste of his patron.[54a]

To conclude: through my discussion of the Quṣayr ʿAmra painting I have tried to convey two basic points, one about the general cultural receptivity of the Umayyad elite, and another, which I still need to elaborate a bit, about what one might call the possibilities of mutuality in cultural transfers or crosspollinations.

With regard to receptivity, it was recognised long ago that Umayyad art was exceptionally eclectic in its inspiration, reflecting a considerable curiosity about the cultural traditions of the vast territories conquered by the Islamic armies, even defunct ones directly accessible only through archaeology, such as the Nabatean and the Palmyrene.[55] Interest in the art of the pre-Islamic Arab world might, of course, claim some sanction in the Qurʾān's repeated references – albeit for the sake of a dire moral warning – to the pre-Islamic people of Thamūd and the rock-hewn monuments they left behind them.[56] By contrast, Quṣayr ʿAmra's receptivity to Greek mythological imagery cannot by any stretch of the imagination claim Qurʾānic inspiration. At first sight it seems like a new departure. But once we have linked 'Dionysus discovering Ariadne' with al-Walīd's love poetry to Salmā, it is tempting to wonder how distinctive to al-Walīd this particular form of cultural receptivity may in fact have been. After all, the surviving images must still have been numerous, if we judge from what has come down to our own times. And al-Walīd cannot have been the only love-lorn Arab capable of seeing his emotion reflected in them. It is a pity this encounter does not show up more often in our sources, though one may recall, for example, Aws ibn Thaʿlaba al-Taymī, a noted leader of the Arabs in Khurāsān, who declaimed before the Caliph Yazīd I (680–83) some verses about a sculpture of two young women which had impressed him when he was passing through Palmyra.[57] At much the same time we find the so-called ʿUdhrī poets, who specialised in yearning mournfully after women who were in one way or another out of reach, and in swearing eternal fidelity even beyond the grave.[58] Though he is much less chaste, there is a certain element of this style in al-Walīd himself,[59] and it is unlikely that such spirits would have been less moved than he was by the mythological images they saw around them. 'Classical art and the Byzantine beholder' is a theme which has been much investigated of late;[60] but about 'Classical art and the Muslim beholder', if Quṣayr ʿAmra is anything to go by, there is a great deal more to be said.

As for the mutuality of cultural transfers, or what Nasser Rabbat has recently called 'the dialogic dimension of Umayyad art':[61] it is increasingly recognised that even politically and militarily subject peoples, the conquered who do not write the history books, may be more than just recipients of cultural goods from the conqueror. They too may be donors. For example, the seeping of native ways of thought and expression into the Greek and

Roman literary and artistic culture of Ptolemaic and Roman Egypt has been receiving growing attention.[62] This mutual transfer of cultural goods is what we may also call, in the looser sense used by historians rather than botanists, crosspollination. Although Horace famously remarked of the Greeks that, even when conquered, they led the savage victor captive,[63] not all such transferences are so easily traceable in the historical record. But even when they have been written out of the grand scheme of the clash and merging of civilisations, they can occasionally be shown at work in the individual mind, in which *cordons sanitaires* are less easily constructed, or at least maintained, than in the relations of peoples and nations. Hence my concentration on al-Walīd, who for three reasons offers a particularly illuminating case study in the history of Graeco-Arabica: firstly he was the absolute lord of what had until recently been some of the most culturally vigorous areas of the Greek world; second he was both a poet and a patron of architecture and art; and third he was so open-minded, or at least indifferent to Islam, that he went down in Muslim tradition as a *zindīq*, a heretic.[64]

There is a fourth factor, too, that endows al-Walīd's probable creation, Quṣayr ʿAmra, with absorbing interest, and that is the difficulty of determining who, here, is the conqueror, and who the conquered. The enthroned Muslim prince in the hall, and near him the portrait of the six kings, among them not just Roderic the Visigoth but also Qayṣar and Kisrā, the rulers of East Rome and Iran, seem to point to the conventional political narrative of Arab triumph; yet the artistic and iconographic analysis of Quṣayr ʿAmra suggests a triumph of the Greeks. It is almost as if al-Walīd were setting out to create an icon of crosspollination. And in doing so, he and his artists were surely aware that the Greek tradition they were working with presented itself to them under a double aspect. There was the art of the Christian East Roman Empire, as reflected in the portrait of the enthroned prince and in the six kings panel. This was a contemporary idiom whose adoption signified engagement with a living civilisation and an empire which, however battered, still existed and continued to enjoy great cultural prestige. But there was also the art of the classical and polytheistic past. Here the conventions were defunct and knowledge of their signification hard to come by.

Astonishingly, al-Walīd undertook to resuscitate them; and he was helped in this attempt by his visual rather than literary approach to the originals. We can only guess what his secretary Sālim may have told him about what they had once been thought to signify; but even if that was not very much, al-Walīd will have speculated about the general drift of the story on the basis of the image alone, and then added his own preoccupations. All of a sudden, there was new wine in old skins; the old images were exposed there on the bath house wall in a new interpretation, and daily acquired fresh resonances in the mind of their beholders, in a way like the statues of the two ladies of Palmyra, but more powerfully, because at Quṣayr ʿAmra 'Dionysus discovering Ariadne' has been reconceived in the wake of al-Walīd's tumultuous and ultimately tragic emotional involvement with Salmā. This erotic charge breathes entirely new life into an image which is still recognisably a rendering of the Greek myth (itself highly erotic). It seems to me, then, entirely proper that the editors of the indispensable *Lexicon iconographicum mythologiae classicae* should have included the Quṣayr ʿAmra fresco in their vast compendium of classical imagery. Significantly, they have placed it in the lemma on 'Eros',[65] for Eros is indeed the one figure in our fresco which has survived the process of transmission entirely unscathed. But it ought to have been referred to under the entries 'Ariadne' and 'Dionysus' as well.

When it was transmuted by the same mind that conceived the poem 'God may yet make me and Salmā one', our image of 'Dionysus discovering Ariadne' did not cease to be Greek; but it conveyed a new and indeed powerful charge in its adopted Arab milieu. This is one face of what was in fact a double crosspollination effected by al-Walīd at Quṣayr ʿAmra. The other face has more to do with genre than with 'ethnic' tradition. At the same time as the lover expresses himself in paint, he writes a poem too, in which not only is the same emotion at work, but the same aspiration for unity in death is stated. The two artifacts, the painting and the poem, explain and reinforce each other, as interlinked expressions of the overwhelming grief evoked in al-Walīd by the sight of Salmā as she was laid to rest in her desert grave.

Notes

1 For the most recent account, see G. Fowden, *Quṣayr ʿAmra: Art and the Umayyad Elite in Late Antique Syria* (Berkeley, 2004).

2 R.G. Hoyland, 'The Content and Context of Early Arabic Inscriptions', *JSAI*, 21 (1997), 87.

3 Fowden, *Quṣayr ʿAmra* (as in n. 1), 197–226.

4 Ibid., 115–41.

5 The best biography is Ḥ. ʿAṭwān, *Al-Walīd ibn Yazīd: ʿArḍ wa-naqd* (Beirut, 1981); cf. also R. Hamilton, *Walid and his Friends: an Umayyad Tragedy* (Oxford, 1988).

6 For the fullest available sequence of colour photographs see M. Almagro, L. Caballero, J. Zozaya and A. Almagro, *Qusayr 'Amra: Residencia y baños omeyas en el desierto de Jordania* (Granada, ²2002).

7 Fowden, *Quṣayr ʿAmra* (as in n. 1), 227–47.

8 Below, n. 50.

9 The evidence is summarised in Fowden, *Quṣayr ʿAmra* (as in n. 1), 291–310.

10 Illustrated and most recently discussed by L. Winkler-Horacek, 'Dionysos in Quṣayr ʿAmra – ein hellenistisches Bildmotiv im Frühislam', *Damaszener Mitteilungen*, 10 (1998), 261–90. For an excellent early photograph see A.J. Jaussen and R. Savignac, *Mission archéologique en Arabie*, 3 vols. (Paris, 1909–22), iii, pl. xlv (my fig. 1); for a colour photograph see Almagro et al., *Qusayr 'Amra* (as in n. 6), 92, fig. 64. See also now C. Vibert-Guigue and G. Bisheh, *Les peintures de Qusayr 'Amra: Un bain omeyyade dans la bâdiya jordanienne* (Beirut, 2007) pls 64a, 105, 107c, 133a.

11 A. Musil, *Ḳ^{u}ṣejr 'amra und andere Schlösser östlich von Moab: Topographischer Reisebericht* (Sitzungsberichte der Kaiserlichen Akademie der Wissenschaften in Wien, Philosophisch-historische Klasse, 144,7; Vienna, 1902), 39; see also J. von Karabacek, 'Datierung und Bestimmung des Baues', in A. Musil et al., *Ḳuṣejr ʿAmra* (Vienna, 1907), i, 232: 'an der halbverhüllten Leiche der Gattin trauert der von dem Todesengel... abgewehrte Gatte'. Jaussen and Savignac, *Mission archéologique* (as in n. 10), iii, 91, found the funerary explanation improbable in the context of a bath house, and thought they discerned two bodies lying side by side, while admitting that no head was visible. Almagro et al., *Qusayr 'Amra* (as in n. 6), 86 suspect erotic content.

12 Winkler-Horacek, 'Dionysos in Quṣayr ʿAmra' (as in n. 10).

13 E.g. C. Augé and P. Linant de Bellefonds, in *Lexicon iconographicum mythologiae classicae* (Zurich, 1981–99), iii/1, 514–31, esp. 524–6; P. Baumann, 'Götter und Helden im Dienst der Repräsentation: Mythologische Themen auf spätantiken Mosaiken im Heiligen Land', *Antike Welt*, 34/2 (2003), 165–70; G.W. Bowersock, *Mosaics as History: The Near East from Late Antiquity to Islam* (Cambridge, MA, 2006).

14 M. Piccirillo, *The Mosaics of Jordan* , ed. P.M. Bikai and T.A. Dailey (Amman, 1993), 25–6, 69, 76–7. For Ariadne at Madaba see *Lexicon iconographicum* (as in n. 13), iii/1, 525, no. 117.

15 I. Z'ubi, P.-L. Gatier, M. Piccirillo and J. Seigne, 'Note sur une mosaïque à scène bachique dans un palais d'époque byzantine à Jérash', *Studium Biblicum Franciscanum: Liber annuus*, 44 (1994), 539–46. The mosaics were eventually deliberately disfigured, a practice apparently confined to the Umayyad period: cf. R. Schick, *The Christian Communities of Palestine from Byzantine to Islamic Rule: a Historical and Archaeological Study* (Princeton, 1995), 207–9. (This discovery invalidates Schick's assertion, 205, that no secular buildings suffered 'iconoclast' damage.)

16 Al-Shahbāʾ: *Lexicon iconographicum* (as in n. 13), iii/1, 525, no. 114. Sarrīn: G. Brands, 'Anmerkungen zu spätantiken Bodenmosaiken aus Nordsyrien', *Jahrbuch für Antike und Christentum*, 45 (2002), 131–2. Note also the Triumph of Dionysus and Ariadne on a mosaic from Jerash in Jordan: H. Joyce, 'A Mosaic from Gerasa in Orange, Texas, and Berlin', *Mitteilungen des Deutschen Archaeologischen Instituts, Römische Abteilung*, 87 (1980), 309 and pl. 103.

17 *Lexicon iconographicum* (as in n. 13), iii/1, 525, no. 111, iii/2, 415.

18 M.H. Chéhab, *Mosaiques du Liban* (Paris, 1957), 11–14 and pls. ii–iii.

19 E.g. *Lexicon iconographicum* (as in n. 13), iii/1, 525–8, nos 112, 115–16, 118–21, 123–4, 127–8, 135–7.

20 For an edition, English translation and extensive discussion of the Syriac version see S. Brock, *The Syriac Version of the Pseudo-Nonnos Mythological Scholia* (Cambridge, 1971). A similar work, derived from the Greek version and itself in Greek, has been attributed to Cosmas of Jerusalem (b. Damascus mid-670s, d. early 750s). But it may belong to the tenth century: A. Kazhdan, in collaboration with L.F. Sherry and C. Angelidi, *A History of Byzantine Literature (650–850)* (Athens, 1999), 118–24. See also the many mentions of Dionysus, often of considerable visual suggestiveness, in the probably late sixth-/early seventh-century Syriac version of Ps.-Callisthenes's Alexander Romance: 1.6,12,30,35,46; 3.7 (ed. E.A. Wallis Budge, *The History of Alexander the Great, being the Syriac version ... of the Pseudo-Callisthenes* [Cambridge, 1889]). For further background on non-theological Greek learning in the early Islamic period, especially in the Edessa region, see L.I. Conrad, 'Varietas Syriaca: Secular and Scientific Culture in the Christian Communities of Syria after the Arab Conquest', in G.J. Reinink and A.C. Klugkist (eds.), *After Bardaisan: Studies on Continuity and Change in Syriac Christianity in Honour of Professor Han J.W. Drijvers* (Leuven, 1999), 85–105.

21 J. Boardman, *Classical Art in Eastern Translation* (Oxford, 1993); G. Dagron, *Constantinople imaginaire: Études sur le recueil des Patria* (Paris, 1984), 133; J.D. Breckenridge, *The Numismatic Iconography of Justinian II (685–695, 705–711 A.D.)* (New York, 1959), 56–9.

22 Philostratus, *The Life of Apollonius of Tyana* (*Vita Apollonii*), trans. F.C. Conybeare (The Loeb Classical Library, 16–17; Cambridge, MA, 1912), i, 25.

23 On a growing preference, already long before Islam, for free deployment of mythological imagery primarily to reflect the patron's circumstances rather than to evoke narratives with which Christians were anyway less and less familiar, see e.g. P. Zanker, 'Phädras Trauer und Hippolytos' Bildung: Zu einem Sarkophag im Thermenmuseum', in F. de Angelis and S. Muth (eds.), *Im Spiegel des Mythos: Bilderwelt und Lebenswelt* (Wiesbaden, 1999), 142, concluding 'daß die Mythen oft nicht als narrative Einheit zum allegorischen Vergleich dienten. Vielmehr wurden nur bestimmte Eigenschaften und Verhaltensweisen der mythischen Gestalten auf die Verstorbenen bzw. ihre Angehörigen bezogen. Eine bestimmte Situation konnte dabei sogar gegen den narrativen Kontext umgedeutet werden.' Also Baumann, 'Götter und Helden' (as in n. 13), 165: 'Der tradierte literarische Stoff rückte in den Hintergrund... Der ins Bild gesetzte Mythos wurde der angemessenen und standesgemäßen Repräsentation der vermögenden Oberschicht verfügbar gemacht und diente letzlich als Vorwand, die von ihr beanspruchten Werte und Einstellungen, wie Status, Bildung, Reichtum und Freigebigkeit, aufzuzeigen.'

24 S. Muth, *Erleben von Raum – Leben im Raum: Zur Funktion mythologischer Mosaikbilder in der römisch-kaiserzeitlichen Wohnarchitektur* (Heidelberg, 1998), 255, 259 n. 1051; and cf. 213 on the image's

eroticism. Catullus 64 (see the edition and commentary in D.F.S. Thomson, *Catullus* [Toronto, 1997] 150–64, 386–443) has the coverlet on Peleus' and Thetis' marriage bed decorated with depictions of Ariadne abandoned on Naxos, and the approaching Dionysus. (My thanks to Pavlos Sfyroeras for this reference.)

25 M.-L. Bernhard in *Lexicon iconographicum* (as in n. 13), iii/1, 1063–64.

26 *Lexicon iconographicum* (as in n. 13), iii/1, 1062, no. 118.

27 F. Haskell and N. Penny, *Taste and the Antique: the Lure of Classical Sculpture 1500–1900* (New Haven, 1981, corrected reprint 1982), 184–7; A. Wilton and I. Bignamini (eds.), *Grand Tour: the Lure of Italy in the Eighteenth Century* (London, 1996), 246–7, 256.

28 A. Michaelis, 'Geschichte des Statuenhofes im Vaticanischen Belvedere', *Jahrbuch des Kaiserlich Deutschen Archäologischen Instituts*, 5 (1890), 20.

29 C. Laviosa, 'L'Arianna addormentata del Museo Archeologico di Firenze', *Archeologia classica*, 10 (1958), 164–71.

30 W. Müller, 'Zur schlafenden Ariadne des Vatikan', *Mitteilungen des Deutschen Archaeologischen Instituts, Römische Abteilung*, 53 (1938), 169–70.

31 M.R. Taylor (ed.), *Giorgio de Chirico and the Myth of Ariadne* (London, 2002), passim, esp. 141–2.

32 This was recognised, already, by the artist who made the facsimiles for the original Vienna publication of Quṣayr ʿAmra: A.L. Mielich, 'Die Aufnahme der Malereien', in A. Musil et al., *Ḳuṣejr ʿAmra* (as in n. 11), i, 192. Winkler-Horacek, 'Dionysos in Quṣayr ʿAmra' (as in n. 10), 267–8, also acknowledges the problem, but in practice ignores it. Although Jaussen and Savignac, *Mission archéologique* (as in n. 10), iii, 91, thought they discerned *two* bodies lying side by side, we more probably have to do with a rather loosely fitting shroud.

33 F. Matz, *Die dionysischen Sarkophage* (Berlin, 1968–75), 401–3, no. 228 and pl. 250: Matz lists this piece under the 'Sonderformen' of 'Dionysus discovering Ariadne'. The combination of the building, a ship, and Ariadne on a sort of pedestal, is an extraordinary anticipation of de Chirico. Another rare element in the iconography that Quṣayr ʿAmra nevertheless picks up (or duplicates by chance) is the palm tree. See the fourth century CE painting from a house at Sabratha in Libya: R. Ling, *Roman Painting* (Cambridge, 1991), 191, fig. 209.

34 ʿAṭwān, *Al-Walīd* (as in n. 5), esp. 210–64.

35 Edited by 1) F. Gabrieli, 'Al-Walīd ibn Yazīd, il califfo e il poeta', *RSO*, 15 (1934), 1–64 (with variants and additions in D. Derenk, *Leben und Dichtung des Omaiyadenkalifen al-Walīd ibn Yazīd: Ein quellenkritischer Beitrag* [Freiburg im Breisgau, 1974], 10–26); 2) Ḥ. ʿAṭwān, *Shiʿr al-Walīd ibn Yazīd* (Amman, 1979; repr. Beirut, 1998 with different pagination).

36 The story is told and the poetry discussed by ʿAṭwān, *Al-Walīd* (as in n. 5), 70–89; cf. also Hamilton, *Walid and his Friends* (as in n. 5), 103–8, 147–9.

37 Al-Haytham ibn ʿAdī in al-Balādhurī, *Ansāb al-ashrāf*, ed. Derenk, *Leben und Dichtung* (as in n. 35), 4.

38 Al-Walīd ibn Yazīd, no. 56 (Gabrieli) = 55 (ʿAṭwān) (as in n. 35), freely trans. Hamilton, *Walid and his Friends* (as in n. 5), 148, and cf. R. Blachère, *Analecta* (Damascus, 1975), 396; Derenk, *Leben und Dichtung* (as in n. 35), 117.

39 Al-Walīd ibn Yazīd, no. 29 (Gabrieli) = 25 (ʿAṭwān) (as in n. 35), trans. Hamilton, *Walid and his Friends* (as in n. 5), 148-9, and Derenk, *Leben und Dichtung* (as in n. 35), 116.

40 Abū 'l-Faraj al-Iṣfahānī, *Kitāb al-aghānī*, ed. ʿA. Muhannā and S. Jābir, 25 vols. (Beirut, 1992), xv, 139–40.

41
laʿalla 'llāha yajmaʿunī bi-salmā — *alaysa 'llāhu yafʿalu mā yashāʾu*
fa-yukhrijuhā fa-yaṭraḥuhā bi-arḍin — *wa-yurqiduhā wa-qad saqaṭa 'l-ridāʾu*
wa-yaʾtī bī wa-yaṭraḥunī ʿalayhā — *fa-uwqiẓuhā wa-qad quḍiya 'l-qaḍāʾu*
wa-yursilu dīmatan saḥḥan ʿalaynā — *fa-yaghsilunā fa-lā yabqā 'l-ʿanāʾu*

Al-Walīd ibn Yazīd transmitted by Abū 'l-Yaqẓān Suḥaym ibn Ḥafṣ (d. 806) to al-Balādhurī, *Ansāb al-ashrāf*, ed. Derenk, *Leben und Dichtung* (as in n. 35), 18, but in line 1 following Ibn ʿAbd Rabbih, *Al-ʿIqd al-farīd* (ed. A. Amīn, A. al-Zayn and I. al-Abyarı, 7 vols. [Cairo 1940–49]), iv, 151 (for minor variants see N. Abbott, *Studies in Arabic Literary Papyri* [Chicago, 1957–72] iii, 80–81) in reading *laʿalla allāha yajmaʿunī bi-salmā* instead of al-Balādhurī's *alā layta al-ilāha yuḥīnu salmā*, for reasons given below. Gabrieli follows the *ʿIqd*; on ʿAṭwān see below, n. 47. My thanks to James Montgomery for helping me with this piece, though he is not responsible for the critical choices I have made.

42 Qurʾān 7:57; 30:19, 48–50; 35:9; 43:11; 50:11. The prayer that rain may fall on a loved one's grave has been a durable *topos* in Arabic laments and funerary poetry, from the earliest times through to the modern period: A. Jones, *Early Arabic Poetry* (Reading, 1992–96), i, 114–17; W. Diem and M. Schöller, *The Living and the Dead in Islam: Studies in Arabic Epitaphs* (Wiesbaden, 2004), i, 1, 231, 402; ii, 185–8, 338-44, 370–73, 408–9; M. Sharon, *Corpus inscriptionum arabicarum Palaestinae* (Leiden, 1997–), i, 1–2, an inscription of AH 1295 which also deploys the theme of gratification bestowed on the righteous in Paradise by young women and youths. Evidently al-Walīd is playing with the conventions of funerary poetry or even epigraphy, and perhaps with the conventional idea that the deceased will be joined with the Prophet or some other holy person: Diem, *The Living and the Dead*, i, 447–558, especially 467–71 on the verb *j-m-ʿ* (used by al-Walīd), and 469 for a third-century AH letter expressing a desire to be joined with the female addressee in Paradise. For an erotic poem remarkably parallel to al-Walīd's, see *Dīwān ʿUmar ibn Abī Rabīʿa* (d. 712/721CE) (Beirut, 1978), 388, trans. J.E. Montgomery and J.N. Mattock, 'The Metaphysical ʿUmar?', *JAL*, 20 (1989), 19.

43 See above, n. 41.

44 Cf. al-Walīd ibn Yazīd, no. 64 (Gabrieli) = 66 (ʿAṭwān) (as in n. 35), trans. Hamilton, *Walid and his Friends* (as in n. 5), 168, and R. Jacobi, 'Zur Ġazalpoesie des Walīd ibn Yazīd', in W. Heinrichs and G. Schoeler (eds.), *Festschrift Ewald Wagner zum 65. Geburtstag* (Beirut, 1994), ii, 145–61, begging Salmā never to die.

45 See above, n. 41.

46 Cf. al-Walīd ibn Yazīd, no. 36 (Gabrieli) = 32 (ʿAṭwān) (as in n. 35), and P.F. Kennedy, *The Wine Song in Classical Arabic Poetry: Abū Nuwās and the Literary Tradition* (Oxford, 1997), 27 (with translation).

47 Qurʾān 3:40; 14:27; 22:14, 18. I reject the long-standing view in the Arab world that this poem is not by al-Walīd. Its unbalanced tone reflects his devastation at Salmā's unexpected death. It may be that the poem was excluded from Khalīl Mardam's Damascus 1937 reissue of Gabrieli's edition (see above n. 35) (cf. Abbott, *Studies* [as in n. 41], iii, 91 n. 96, 102–3) out of mere prudery; but ʿAṭwān, *Al-Walīd* (as in n. 5), 260, and in his edition of the *Dīwān* (as in n. 35), 147–8, offers actual arguments, none of which convince. For example, Abū ʾl-Yaqẓān (see above, n. 41), is deemed hostile to al-Walīd by ʿAṭwān; yet Ibn al-Nadīm, *Kitāb al-fihrist* (ed. R. Tajaddud, Tehran, 1971), 107, trans. B. Dodge (New York, 1970), 204, accounts him 'trustworthy', while even if he did (as here suggested) change the poem's first phrase, the rest may still be genuine. ʿAṭwān, who in general prefers the historians' testimony to the philologists' because the latter tend to 'improve' the text (cf. introduction to his edition, 8–9), prints only al-Balādhurī's version, relegating the *ʿIqd*'s reading to his apparatus and not broaching the possibility that it is authentic. He also gives excessive weight to a story about an encounter between the philologist al-Aṣmaʿī (d. 828) and an anonymous Arab of the desert, who recited a poem closely related but by no means identical to al-Walīd's – for ʿAṭwān, this is reason enough to question al-Walīd's authorship of 'God may yet make me and Salmā one', when in fact it has simply been plagiarised. (A ninth -century papyrus version of this anecdote – which ʿAṭwān quotes from al-Nawājī [d. 1455] – had already been published by Abbott, *Studies* [as in n. 41], iii, 79 [and comment, 95], herself under the mistaken impression [107] that the story was previously unknown.) Note that the Last Judgment motif, and the idea that lovers ought to die together, also occur in al-Walīd's no. 64

(Gabrieli), which ʿAṭwān prints without disquiet as his no. 66 (for translations see n. 44 above). This too, al-Balādhurī derived from Abū 'l-Yaqẓān.

48 Winkler-Horacek's recent extensive discussion of this painting, 'Dionysos in Quṣayr ʿAmra' (as in n. 10), not only recognises the allusion to 'Dionysus discovering Ariadne', but also (like G. Macchiarella, 'Sull'iconografia dei simboli del potere tra Bisanzio, la Persia e l'Islam', in *Convegno internazionale La Persia e Bisanzio (Roma, 14–18 ottobre 2002)* [Rome, 2004], 611–13; cf. Fowden, *Quṣayr ʿAmra* [as in n. 1], 265 n. 62) argues for Dionysiac references elsewhere at Quṣayr ʿAmra. He discusses al-Walīd's Dionysiac character, especially his love of wine. But he rejects Musil's view that 'Ariadne' is dead, and does not investigate al-Walīd's relationship with Salmā.

49 On Ariadne as an allegory of salvation see R. Turcan, *Les sarcophages romains à représentations dionysiaques: Essai de chronologie et d'histoire religieuse* (Paris, 1966), 510–23. On Endymion see H. Gabelmann, *Lexicon iconographicum* (as in n. 13), iii/1, 727–8, 742.

50 The painting on the apodyterium's east wall, just opposite the tympanum panel here discussed, shows a young, nude man and a young, half-nude woman looking at each other, the woman seen frontally, the man from behind. Between them, underneath the window they flank, seems to have been depicted a reclining baby: A. Musil et al., *Ḳuṣejr ʿAmra* (as in n. 11), ii, pl. xxxv; Jaussen and Savignac, *Mission archéologique* (as in n. 10), iii, pls. xlvi–xlvii.1; M. Almagro et al., *Qusayr ʿAmra* (as in n. 6), 86 and 92, fig. 65; Vibert-Guigue and Bisheh, *Peintures* (as in n. 10) pls 64b, 106, 133a. This image too derives from the Greek. This image too derives from the Greek mythological tradition: compare the sexually extremely suggestive fourth-century mosaic of Aphrodite and Ares at al-Shahbāʾ (Philippopolis), illustrated and discussed by Janine Balty, *Mosaïques antiques de Syrie* (Brussels, 1977), 58–65, and ead., *Mosaïques antiques du Proche-Orient: Chronologie, iconographie, interprétation* (Paris, 1995), 342, pl. x. In this particular case the figures are clearly labelled; but even without any knowledge of the scene's specific mythological reference, al-Walīd could have adopted it as an image of his desire for the living Salmā (and for a child by her, for which cf. his poem no. 56 [Gabrieli] = 55 [ʿAṭwān] [as in n. 35], quoted above, p. 36) to set alongside the nearby image of his grief for the dead Salmā. Note that the same house at al-Shahbāʾ also contained a mosaic of the marriage of Dionysus and Ariadne: see above, n. 16.

51 Al-Jahshiyārī, *Kitāb al-wuzarāʾ wa'l-kuttāb*, ed. M. al-Saqqāʾ, I. al-Abyārī and ʿA. Shalabī (Cairo, 1938), 59, 65; trans. J. Latz, *Das Buch der Wezire und Staatssekretäre von Ibn 'Abdūs al-Ğahšiyārī: Anfänge und Umaiyadenzeit*, doctoral thesis (University of Bonn, 1958).

52 I. ʿAbbās, *ʿAbd al-Ḥamīd ibn Yaḥyā al-Kātib wa-mā tabaqqā min rasāʾilihi wa-rasāʾil Sālim Abī 'l-ʿAlāʾ* (Amman, 1988), 30.

53 Ibn al-Nadīm, *Kitāb al-fihrist* (as in n. 47), 131, trans. Dodge (as in n. 47), 257–8, implying the translation circulated under Sālim's name in the late tenth century but that Ibn al-Nadīm assumed it was really made by assistants, probably because Sālim's name did not sound Christian like those of most translators. A file of Arabic documents relating to Alexander, now edited for the first time in its entirety by M. Maróth, *The Correspondence between Aristotle and Alexander the Great: an Anonymous Greek Novel in Letters in Arabic Translation* (Piliscsaba, 2006), may be more or less identical with Sālim's *Letters*. A colophon in the two main manuscripts (Maróth, 133 [Arabic], trans. M. Grignaschi, 'Le roman épistolaire classique conservé dans la version arabe de Sālim Abū-l-ʿAlāʾ', *Le muséon* 80 [1967], 216–17), reveals that by AH 491/1097 CE at the latest (Grignaschi wrongly gives 471) this Alexander-file was circulating without its editor's name, which is nowhere mentioned.

54 See e.g. Fowden, *Quṣayr ʿAmra* (as in n. 1), 174–96, 227–47.

54a If Sālim's *Letters of Aristotle to Alexander* are indeed substantially preserved in the Alexander-file mentioned above, n. 53, then we have proof of Sālim's skill at rendering unfamiliar Greek mythological references in the ps.-Aristotelian *De mundo* in ways comprehensible to Arabs: Fowden, *Quṣayr ʿAmra* (as in n. 1), 262. It is certain he did not adopt these renderings (Tower of

Babel and Sibyl in place of Aloadae and Delphi respectively) from the intermediate Syriac translation, which is faithful to the Greek: see V. Ryssel, *Über den textkritischen Werth der syrischen Übersetzungen griechischer Klassiker* (Leipzig, 1880–81), i, 7–8 (on *De mundo* 391a[11]), 46 (on 395b[29]); S.M. Stern, 'The Arabic Translations of the Pseudo-Aristotelian Treatise De mundo', *Le muséon*, 77 (1964), 194 (repr. F. Sezgin [ed.], *Pseudo-Aristotelica Preserved in Arabic Translation* [Frankfurt am Main, 2000], 248).

55 E.g. D. Schlumberger, 'Les fouilles de Qasr el-Heir el-Gharbi (1936–1938): Rapport préliminaire', *Syria*, 20 (1939), 359–60; Fowden, *Quṣayr ʿAmra* (as in n. 1), 291–324.

56 Qurʾān 7:74, 26:149, 29:38, 89:9.

57 E.g. Hishām ibn Kalbī in al-Balādhurī, *Kitāb futūḥ al-buldān*, ed. M.J. de Goeje (Leiden, 1863–66), 355.

58 E. Wagner, *Grundzüge der klassischen arabischen Dichtung* (Darmstadt, 1987–88), ii, 68–77.

59 Al-Walīd ibn Yazīd, no. 42 (Gabrieli) = 34 (ʿAṭwān) (as in n. 35), with Abbott, *Studies* (as in n. 41), iii, 94 n. 136; Jacobi, 'Ġazalpoesie' (as in n. 44), 158–60.

60 See e.g. S. Bassett, *The Urban Image of Late Antique Constantinople* (Cambridge, 2004).

61 N. Rabbatt, 'The Dialogic Dimension of Umayyad Art', *Res*, 43 (2003), 79–94.

62 G. Fowden, *The Egyptian Hermes: a Historical Approach to the Late Pagan Mind* (Cambridge, 1986; corrected reprint Princeton, 1993); M.S. Venit, *Monumental Tombs of Ancient Alexandria: the Theater of the Dead* (Cambridge, 2002); S.A. Stephens, *Seeing Double: Intercultural Poetics in Ptolemaic Alexandria* (Berkeley, 2003).

63 Horace, *Epistulae* 2, 1, 156, (ed. D.R. Shackleton Bailey, *Q. Horati Flacci Opera* [Stuttgart, [3]1995], 297).

64 On this see, most recently, J.M.F. van Reeth, 'Die Transfiguration Walīd b. Yazīds', in S. Leder with H. Kilpatrick, B. Martel-Thoumian and H. Schönig (eds.), *Studies in Arabic and Islam: Proceedings of the 19th Congress, Union Européenne des Arabisants et Islamisants, Halle 1998* (Leuven, 2002), 501–11.

65 *Lexicon iconographicum* (as in n. 13), iii/1, 948, no. 90 = iii/2, 675, no. 90.

3

The Influence of the Arabic Tradition of Falconry and Hunting on Western Europe

Anna Akasoy

Introduction

The most important medieval Arabic treatise on falconry, the so-called "work of Adham and Ghiṭrīf", begins in one of its two versions with an account of the reason for its composition:

> Al-Ḥajjāj ibn Khaythama said: We took this book on hunting animals out of the library of (the Caliph) al-Rashīd and showed it to al-Ghiṭrīf ibn Qudāma al-Ghassānī, who was in charge of the hunting animals of (the Caliphs) Hishām and al-Walīd. Al-Ghiṭrīf recognised the book and said: Muʿādh ibn Muslim added anecdotes about the kings and Persian emperors to it, and when Michael son of Leon, a Byzantine nobleman, learned about (the Caliph) al-Mahdī's passion for hunting, he gave him a book about birds of prey which belonged to his ancestors. Al-Mahdī ordered Adham ibn Muḥriz al-Bāhilī to be present, from whom he had heard anecdotes of the Arabs about birds of prey. He commissioned him to compose a book which includes the treatises of the learned men from among the Persians and the Turks, from the Greek philosophers, and what the Arabs had learned from experience. So he composed this book.[1]

This short episode reflects some of the aspects which are crucial for medieval Arabic literature on falconry and which will be discussed in this article: the intercultural character of falconry in the Middle Ages, the significance of science within this tradition, and the institution where both falconry was cultivated as a practice and as a science. A definition of the transmission of falconry from the pre-Islamic Middle East to the Umayyad and ʿAbbāsid courts and finally into medieval Christian Europe as a crosspollination enables us to grasp the manifold layers of this process. The variety of the sources testifies to this complexity as well as to the significance of falconry among medieval elites in East and West. There are also several elements (such as the aspects mentioned above) which recur throughout the different phases of this transmission.

Since it might not be immediately evident why one should pick a highly specialised field such as falconry as an example of intercultural relations in the Middle Ages, I will begin my discussion with a brief sketch of the diversity of the historico-cultural backgrounds of falconry in the Middle East and Central Asia. I will then give an overview of the variety of sources which reflect the importance of falconry in medieval Islamic societies. In the main part I will elaborate on one particular aspect of falconry which is crucial for the Arabic influence on the Western European tradition, namely scientific treatises on falconry, above all of medical contents. In order to illustrate both the Arabic tradition and its transmission to the West I will use as examples the most important Arabic text on falconry, the "work of Adham and Ghiṭrīf", and a Latin translation of an Arabic treatise produced at the court of Frederick II, the *Moamin*. In the last part I will deal with the conditions of the transmission of this particular corpus of Arabic literature into Western Europe. Although I will focus in my contribution on falcons (representing the various kinds of birds of prey used for hunting) and on falconry, much of what I discuss applies to hunting in general.

Historical and cultural backgrounds

In the mythological traditions of many of the peoples who inhabited the regions which came to form the lands of the Islamic empires in the Middle Ages, birds of prey played a major role. A well-known case is ancient Egypt where Horus is one of the most important and powerful gods.[2] The son of Osiris and Isis appears in the shape of a falcon or a falcon-headed man. As a sky god his eyes represent the sun and the moon, and as a sun god he wears a disk on his head. Horus' fight against Seth, murderer of his father Osiris and representative of disorder, is a key feature of ancient Egyptian mythology and has political as well as cosmic implications.

In the north-eastern part of what would become the Islamic world are the lands of origin of the Turkic peoples.[3] In the early days of their civilisation, their subsistence was based on hunting which determined their social structures as well as their mythologies. They may even be described as followers of a "hunters' religion". Here too, birds of prey – falcons, hawks, and eagles – range among the most distinguished mythological animals. Male heroes, for instance, can transform into birds of prey. Furthermore, in one of the Central Asian myths of creation an eagle and a raven lead to the creation of mankind itself.[4] These complex connections are reflected in the etymologies of some bird names: two of the names for falcons used in several Islamic languages, *togan* and *togril*, are thought to stem from the same Turkish root, *tog-* = to be born.[5] Furthermore, some of the Central Asian tribes were named after birds of prey, and military and political leaders had names which referred to birds of prey, such as Togrilbeg (d. 1063), the founder of the Seljuk Sultanate in Persia and Iraq.

Such myths of Central Asian origin were preserved throughout and after the Islamisation of these Turkic peoples and sometimes combined with Islamic narrative traditions. In the *Book of Dede Korkut* for example, an oral composition from the fifteenth century, the mystic Hacı Bektaş fights a certain Hacı Tuğrul who has not only the name, but also the form of a bird of prey.[6]

What all these mythological traditions concerning birds of prey have in common is the presentation of these animals as proud, powerful, and independent. It is not by coincidence that these characteristics were attributed to birds of prey. Hawks, the *captatores* or *accipitres* in Frederick's *De arte venandi cum avibus*, are majestic birds which chase their prey without mercy until they catch and kill it; proper falcons fly high in the air and kill their prey by stooping down on it at high speed. Birds are elevated by their mere ability to fly. From high in the sky, they select their prey and end its life.

This breath-taking spectacle must have impressed human beings independently of their cultures. It is hardly surprising that we find mythological and symbolical meanings attributed to birds of prey in different and disconnected regional, cultural, and historical contexts.[7] There is no need to assume that the fascination with birds of prey stems from one culture which has influenced many others.

The same applies if we go a step further and consider not only the birds themselves, but humans hunting with birds of prey. The earliest evidence for the practice of falconry has recently been traced back to the third millennium BC on the basis of the depiction of specific instruments used for falconry in Hittite representations in Anatolia.[8] Other evidence hints to much later periods, such as the Han Dynasty in China (206 BC – 20 CE).[9] Whether the first falconers threw their birds in Hittite Anatolia, Han China or the lands of Central Asia does not concern us here. Suffice it to say that long before the appearance of an Arabo-Islamic tradition of falconry, this practice was known in several parts of the world some of which contributed substantially to the formation of cultures in Islamic times.

Yet, the very ancient roots of falconry did not guarantee its continuous practice. Even if there had been a tradition of hunting with birds of prey in the Middle East in the third or second millennium BC, it was interrupted for many centuries, and it was only in the second and third centuries CE that the Sassanids and, at about the same time, at a considerable remove, the ancient Germans reassumed this tradition.[10] The tradition of hunting with birds of prey was virtually unknown to the ancient peoples of Egypt, Greece and Italy.[11] In Egypt, the divine character attributed to birds of prey might even have discouraged people from hunting with them.

It is therefore rather surprising to find the oldest illustration of falconry in Southern Europe in Argos in the northern Peloponnesus where falconry was not practised.[12] This mosaic of the fifth century CE consisted originally of seven illustrations which show typical scenes of a hunt with birds of prey including departure, hunting ducks and hares and the return of the hunting party. It probably follows a model from Northern Africa where falconry might have been introduced by the Vandals.

The lack of sources makes it hardly possible to reconstruct the origin of falconry on the Arabian Peninsula. The earliest textual evidence is recorded in pre-Islamic poetry, but it does not reveal whether the Arab Bedouins developed the techniques of falconry themselves or whether they had been inspired by others: Persians, Byzantines, or even Central Asians. Compared with the ʿAbbāsid period which witnessed cross-cultural exchanges on a large scale and the formation of falconry as a ritual of noblemen, the Bedouin origins of this practice were quite humble. For the pre-Islamic Arabs hunting was above all a means of sustenance and a way of honing their military skills.

Even though two of the elements I have mentioned thus far, the majestic character of birds of prey and the practice of hunting with them, have been present in different regions of the greater Middle East, It was above all at the Sassanid courts where hunting with the king of birds became an occupation proper for the kings of human beings.[13] The earliest Middle Eastern texts on falconry were produced in this context.[14] These texts are not preserved in their original form, but they became an important source, possibly even a model, for the Arabic treatises of the ʿAbbāsid period.

Falconry as a ritual at the Sassanid court may have had an impact on the Umayyad Caliphs who were the first Arab rulers known to have hunted with birds of prey. Various historiographical texts record that Umayyad Caliphs enjoyed not only hunting on a large scale but also participated in the care of the animals.[15] Moreover, there is evidence that texts on falconry of Byzantine and Persian origin were collected at the Umayyad courts. This suggests that falconry was one of the rare cases of translations of foreign scientific texts into Arabic before the ʿAbbāsid period.[16] Yet, the traces of practical and theoretical falconry at the Umayyad court are rather fragmentary. The large-scale transmission of foreign knowledge into Arabic under the ʿAbbāsids was yet to come, and this was also the formative period and first bloom of Arabic literature on falconry.[17]

This early interest in scientific aspects of falconry notwithstanding, to say nothing of the immense costs of hunting and the large number of staff employed for the activity itself as well as for the care of the beasts, nothing suggests that ʿAbbāsid courts had an independent institution for hunting. At later Islamic courts there are several instances of such institutions, for example at the courts of the Seljuks, the Mamluks, the Ottomans and the Moguls. The falconer developed into a fixed position in the hierarchy of Islamic courts[18] – a phenomenon which can also be observed at the court of Frederick II. An experienced hunter himself, the emperor knew the requirements of the falconer's profession and their advantages at court, such as the selfless dedication to a task or a living creature, beast or man.[19]

In addition to the flourishing practices of hunting among Muslim elites, the Bedouin traditions were preserved in Arabia throughout the Middle Ages. In Christian Europe on the other hand, the emergence of falconry as an elite pastime accompanied its restriction to noblemen and the prohibition of hunting for common people. In modern times the Bedouin tradition and the noble character of falconry are combined once again in the Arabian Peninsula in the hands of the Sheikhs who owe their economic prosperity to oil.[20]

Sources

A great variety of medieval Oriental sources bears witness to the different contexts, origins and traditions of falconry.

Poems are the most important source for the pre-Islamic and early Islamic traditions of falconry among Bedouins on the Arabian Peninsula. 'Bedouins' should not be understood in a strict sense here. Pre- and early Islamic poetry was also composed by people who lived in cities and occasionally spent time in the desert. Hunting with birds of prey appears in the genres of *fakhr* ('boasting') and *waṣf* ('descriptions').[21] The development of the hunting theme in poetry confirms what other sources suggest, namely that hunting changed from a means of subsistence to a pastime of urban elites. Another important aspect for the development of poetical descriptions of hunting scenes from pre-Islamic to Umayyad and ʿAbbāsid times is the geographical shift from the deserts of the Arabian Peninsula to the fertile regions of Syria and Iraq. This move implied different landscapes and a new variety of game, both of them reflected in the poems.[22]

With the great poet of the ninth century, Abū Nuwās,[23] the *ṭardiyya* ('hunting poem') received a fixed form as an independent poetical genre. In following centuries hunting poems were included by many poets into their *dīwāns*. The following verses by Abū Nuwās reveal the great popularity the saker (in the quotation female) enjoyed among falconers in the medieval Middle East, as it also did in medieval Western Europe, and still does among contemporary falconers:

> There can be no hunting without sharp-sighted sakers, each one greedy for meat, far-sighted
> Displaying the bone of the eye which has no injury; she had not been fed on milk mixed with water
> By her mother, nor was she born on the flat plain, rather in the lofty mountains.
> She takes the jinking desert jacks, attacking them with head raised high,
> With a long [talon] like a short poisoned spear and a beak hooked like a spoon.[24]

Even if they did not have any practical experience in falconry and hunting, these themes must have strongly appealed to the Arab poets with their love for detailed descriptions and unusual words.[25] In this respect, Kushājim, an author of the tenth century, is an exceptional case among medieval Arab poets. In the book he compiled on hunting, *Kitāb al-maṣāyid wa'l-maṭārid* ('Book of Snares and Spikes'), he combined poetical descriptions of animals and the hunt with practical information.[26]

Another writer of Arabic prose who betrays an intimate knowledge of falconry is ʿUsāma ibn Munqidh (1095–1188), a Syrian nobleman and eyewitness of the Crusades. A substantial part of his "autobiography" *Kitāb al-iʿtibār* ('Book of Learning from Example') is dedicated to hunting. It gives an original and almost unique impression of how falconry was practised among Arabs in the medieval Levant. The author presents himself in several instances as an expert in the art of hunting with birds of prey. This is illustrated by the following passage which occurs in ʿUsāma's account of a hunting party with al-Ḥāfiẓ li-dīn Allāh ʿAbd al-Majīd Abū Maymūn in Egypt:

> We went off one day, and one of the austringers was carrying an intermewed goshawk with red irises. We saw some cranes and the master falconer said to the austringer, "Go on ahead and cast off the gos with the reddish irises on them." He did so and the cranes took to flight. The gos bound to one of them some distance away from us and brought it down. I said to one of my attendants on a thoroughbred horse, "Push your horse on up to the goshawk, dismount and thrust the bill of the crane into the ground. Hold it and keep its legs under yours until we reach you." The servant went off and did what I told him. The austringer turned up and despatched the crane. He then gorged the gos.
>
> When the austringer returned, he reported to al-Ḥāfiẓ what had happened and what I had said to my attendant, adding, "O my lord, he talks the way a true sportsman would talk". Al-Ḥāfiẓ replied, "And what other business has this man but to fight and to hunt."[27]

A source of a quite different kind is legal texts which reflect social realities as well as the theoretical debates of the juridical schools of Islam. For the jurists hunting involved several problems. As far as the entertainment at courts is concerned, one might assume that as any element of pre-Islamic or non-Islamic ritual it was regarded with suspicion by "conservative" or "orthodox" jurists. Whether hunting for pleasure was a waste of useful goods was indeed the subject of legal debates. Yet, since there was not a sufficient basis for forbidding this kind of hunting, many scholars (among them Mālik ibn Anas) declared it *makrūh* ('reprehensible').[28] Others considered it permissible and referred to the general declaration in the Qurʾān: "Hunt for yourselves" (5:2).[29]

One of the more crucial problems for the jurists was the question of under which circumstances it was allowed to eat the meat of an animal killed by another beast. Among the food which is explicitly prohibited in the Qurʾān is meat which has been partly devoured by beasts of prey (5:3). On the other hand, the use of animals of prey is explicitly allowed (5:4). An additional problem was involved in the use of hunting dogs since these animals are considered impure in Islam, and particular rituals of purification are required if a dog comes into contact with an instrument used for eating. In his *Bidāyat al-mujtahid* ('Preliminaries for the one who Formulates an Independent Juridical Decision') the Andalusian Qadi Ibn Rushd (d. 1198) described the divisions among the jurists around the question of exactly which animals of prey should be allowed and adds his own explanation which refers to the use of dogs as the key problem:

> The reason for disagreement in this topic is based upon two factors. The first is the analogy for all the predatory animals and birds of prey from the case of the dog, because it is believed that the text has permitted it for dogs, that is, in the words of the Exalted, "And those *jawāriḥ* (beasts and birds of prey) which ye have trained as hounds are trained, teaching them what Allāh taught you" (5:4), unless it is interpreted to mean that the word *mukallibīn* (in the verse) is derived from the pouncing of the predatory animals, and not from the meaning of the word dog.[30]

One might assume that this question of the permissiveness of consuming a certain kind of meat might have affected only the common people who hunted to provide themselves with much-needed food, but the meat of a hunted animal was highly prized and regarded as superior because of the stress the animal suffered when being killed. Caliphs are reported to have joined their companions after the hunt for feasts during which the meat of the game was eaten. Finally, the presence of *fuqahāʾ* ('legal scholars') at hunting parties suggests that these juridical problems were not simply theoretical or casuistic debates and that they were of practical relevance in different strata of society.[31]

A literary category which underlines the significance of hunting in the milieu of courts and vice versa are mirrors of princes. The *Qābūsnāmeh* for instance, a Persian Fürstenspiegel composed in the eleventh century, includes directions about how to carry a falcon.[32] The author recommends:

> If you are fond of hunting, engage in it with falcon, white hawk, royal falcon, leopard (cheetah) or hound, in order not merely to have your hunting without hazard but to ensure that what you take may be of service. (...) If you should choose hawking princes use two methods. Those of Khurasan never fly the hawk from their own hand, while the practice of those of Iraq is to do so. Both are permissible and, if you are not a prince, you do as you please.[33]

Other sources which were produced at courts are letters and financial documents which do not deal primarily with falconry but complete our idea of the significance and context of falconry at courts. Falconry was an expensive pleasure, and falcons a popular gift among noblemen which is confirmed by historiographical accounts.[34] These sources have not yet been systematically explored, but so far coincidental findings have revealed further important aspects of falconry at courts.

A source of an entirely different kind not usually taken into consideration by philologists is art. Here we must largely limit our considerations to the traditions of the Islamic East where humans and beasts have been impressively depicted.[35] In many cases the falconer prince appears as a popular motif. This confirms once again that falconry was not a mere pastime but revealed other, political, qualities.

Scientific texts

The most important source for cross-cultural influences in the field of falconry is another typical product of courts, even though the texts might be identified with another sphere, science. Science as well as falconry was an expensive enterprise, and the production and transmission of certain genres of scientific texts can be traced back, if not always to the courts themselves, at least to their peripheries where local rulers, "noblemen", military and political leaders, and other privileged people served as patrons of translators, philosophers, and other scholars.[36] Islamic courts played a key role in the conservation, transformation, and transmission of the Aristotelian tradition and of Greek philosophy and science in general.

The same applies to various texts which are related with birds of prey. Zoological texts of Greek origin which include ornithological chapters, such as the highly influential books on animals by Aristotle, have been transmitted at courts. Other books on animals were originally composed at Islamic courts with the support of patrons. Al-Jāḥiẓ, author of a famous *Kitāb al-ḥayawān*, is one of the scholars who enjoyed the sponsorship of a court.

Most important among the scientific texts connected with falconry are not zoological, but medical texts.[37] Falcons are delicate animals. They do not reproduce in captivity, but have to be caught as very young animals and trained by humans. They are easily affected by digestive and respiratory diseases. The treatises on falconry reflect these practical needs.[38]

According to what we can reconstruct today on the basis of the few preserved sources the first treatise on falconry written in Arabic was a compilation known among modern scholars as the "work of Adham and Ghiṭrīf", quoted at the beginning of this article (cf. also the stemma at the end of this article).[39] The origin of this text is connected with the courts of the Umayyads Hishām ibn ʿAbd al-Malik (724–743) and al-Walīd II (743–744). The first person after whom the text is named, Adham, has been identified as Adham ibn Muḥriz al-Bāhilī, a military leader who collected texts on falconry, especially of medical contents. These texts were compiled by al-Ghiṭrīf ibn Qudāma al-Ghassānī who was later put in charge of the animals of prey at the ʿAbbāsid court, and whose uncommon name seems to be due to his Christian Syrian descent. Like many of his "compatriots", he played an important role in the transmission of ancient scientific texts.[40] In this case, however, nothing suggests that this text on falconry was translated from Greek into Syriac first and then into Arabic. According to the prologue of one of the versions of the "work of Adham and Ghiṭrīf", the composition of the book was completed at the court of the ʿAbbāsid Caliph al-Mahdī, a key figure in the Graeco-Arabic translation movement.[41] A complete version of the "work of Adham and Ghiṭrīf" has not been preserved, but there are two short versions which are preserved in several manuscripts each. According to their prologues these versions are referred to as the al-Ḥajjāj- and the Iskandar-version.[42]

In terms of the entire medieval Arabic tradition of literature on falconry, the "work of Adham and Ghiṭrīf" is an exemplary case in many respects. It became the most important source for subsequent works with many of the Arabic texts written in later centuries containing quotations or references to this work. Examples are the *Kitāb al-kāfī fī 'l-bayzara* ('Complete Book on Falconry'),[43] probably written in thirteenth-century Northern Africa and relatively independent of other texts, and – as a more general text – the historico-geographical *Murūj al-dhahab* ('Meadows of Gold') by the tenth-century author al-Masʿūdī. Apart from these contributions to Arabic literature on falconry, the structure of the "work of Adham and Ghiṭrīf" served as a role model for most of the Arabic treatises on falconry written in the following centuries.

In one of the two short versions which are preserved, the text begins with a historical and anecdotal introduction to falconry concerning the question who had been the first to hunt with birds of prey. These anecdotes illustrate the symbolical significance of falconry as a ritual of kings. They also underline that the authors of the first Arabic treatises on falconry were well aware of the various dimensions of the ritual. The following quotation from the "work of Adham and Ghiṭrīf" will demonstrate this:

> Al-Ghiṭrīf said: The first who hunted with birds of prey was the Byzantine king (*malik al-Rūm*). He said: We found in the *Book of Khāqān*[44] that a Byzantine king once watched a falcon hunting. (...) He looked at him and was amazed by the clarity and smallness of his eyes and the beauty of his plumage. The king said: "This bird has a weapon, and kings have to adorn their courts with him." So he ordered a number of them to be collected as an ornament for the court. Then a snake appeared to one of the falcons, and the falcon hopped on it and killed it. The King said: "This is a king who becomes angry about what kings become angry about." After a few days he sent a tamed fox to the falcon. The falcon jumped on it and let it escape with severe injuries. The king said: "This is a giant king who does not endure injustice." Then another bird passed the falcon, and the falcon jumped on it and ate it. The king said: "This is a king who defends his territory and does not lose his food." So Khāqān hunted with falcons as did the kings who came after him.[45]

In addition, the second version of the "work of Adham and Ghiṭrīf" contains a fictitious dialogue with Alexander the Great which gave it its name, the Iskandar-version. This is another testimony of the role Alexander played as an outstanding model for the ʿAbbāsid Caliphs. The Arabic tradition of the pseudo-Aristotelian *Sirr al-asrār* (*Secret of Secrets*) bears impressively witness to this image of Alexander.[46]

The second chapter of the "work of Adham and Ghiṭrīf" contains an ornithological description of the birds of prey. The animals are divided up according to their species and classes, characterised, and rated with regard to their qualities for hunting. This part is followed by a chapter on care and training in which general questions of diagnostics are also discussed. The main part of the text consists of the medical treatise proper. The diseases are described one by one according to the corresponding symptoms from head to toe, and subsequently a number of recipes are described for their treatment.

The "work of Adham and Ghiṭrīf" is based on explicit quotations from various foreign sources, such as the book of the Turkish Khāqān, the Persians or the Indians. This tendency is even more evident in other Arabic books on falconry. The *Kitāb al-ṣayd* ('Book of Hunt'), which will be discussed below, contains quotations from a *Kitāb al-Furs* ('Book of the Persians'), a *Kitāb al-Rūm* ('Book of the Byzantines'), a *Kitāb al-Turk* ('Book of the Turks') and a *Kitāb al-Hind* ('Book of the Indians'), as well as a *Kitāb al-buṣarā'* ('Book of the Experts') and a *Kitāb al-Wāthiqī* dedicated to the Caliph al-Wāthiq bi'llāh (reg. 842–847). Even though birds of prey played a major role in the cultures of the peoples these sources are ascribed to (as I have sketched in the first part of my article), the possibilities of identifying these sources are very limited. Some information is available on the origins of the Greek and Persian texts, but the same does not apply to the Indian and Turkish sources. The Arabic texts which claim to have used these two texts do not contain any "Indian" or "Turkish" words whatsoever.[47] These books might have also been written in Greek or Persian (like most other foreign sources of Arabic treatises on falconry), but might have been attributed to two other great peoples of that time who were also known for practising falconry. Aspects of falconry which are discussed in other texts but do not appear in the "work of Adham and Ghiṭrīf" are juridical problems and poetry. Some of the medieval Arabic treatises on falconry do not deal exclusively with falcons but contain similar chapters on other hunting animals, such as dogs or cheetahs.[48]

The key role of the "work of Adham and Ghiṭrīf" in medieval falconry literature is evident not only from its far-reaching influence in the Islamic world, but also from its transmission to the Latin West, where it was translated at the court of Frederick II. Before dealing with this translation I will make some remarks on falconry in Europe before the twelfth and thirteenth centuries.

Falconry in Europe before the twelfth and thirteenth centuries

Falconry itself was not an Islamic import to Europe. Long before the age of translations and cross-cultural contacts ancient Germans and Byzantines hunted with birds of prey. Hunting as a royal activity in Central Europe was well-known from the time of Charlemagne.[49] But at that time and until the twelfth century birds usually did not range among animals used for hunting. Hunting was much closer to fighting and war. Large animals were hunted, and several noblemen are reported to have been seriously injured or even killed during a hunt. This situation changed considerably during the twelfth century with a decrease of danger and the growing popularity of falconry. These developments reflect general tendencies of courtly manners as can also be seen in poetry. Here too, falcons and falconry play an important role and the falcon is used as a symbol for the beloved. The illustrations of the famous Manesse manuscript give an impression of this symbolism in medieval German literature which does not have any equivalent in Arabic poetry.[50]

In addition to these developments within Christian European culture itself, Byzantine and Islamic traditions of falconry as a royal pastime had a great impact on the West. This influence resulted on the one hand from the adoption of certain sophisticated aspects of Islamic culture in the aftermath of the early Crusades,[51] but the importance of the Arabic-Islamic influence on the European tradition of hunting and falconry lies specifically in the scientific approach to this field.[52] The most intriguing example of this development is Frederick II, a passionate hunter and author of a treatise on falconry himself, *De arte venandi cum avibus.*[53] Yet, Frederick, who was well-known in his own time for his fascination with the Islamic world, did not rely on Arabic sources for his treatise. The influence of Arabic science was of a more complex kind and is traceable in the methods the emperor used in *De arte venandi cum avibus* as I will describe below. However, in 1240/41 Frederick commissioned also a Latin translation of an Arabic treatise on falconry. The Latin translation is known under the title *Moamin*. The title is probably a corruption of the Arabic title of the Caliph, *amīr al-muʾminīn* ('Commander of the believers') and suggests that the Arabic Vorlage of the *Moamin* had been dedicated to a Caliph.

This translation is only one out of several which can be traced back or associated with the court of the emperor. In the period of translations of Arabic texts in the Christian world, courts provided an ideal atmosphere. They had all the technical requirements which were necessary for the first step of the adoption of a foreign text, the translation. Frederick's court combined in an almost unique manner the presence of translators for the purpose of diplomatic correspondence and the personal interest of the emperor in scientific problems which created perfect conditions for the adoption and further diffusion of Arabic scientific texts.

As Dimitri Gutas has suggested, this patronage of translation might very well be interpreted as an imitation of Oriental courts in general or the ʿAbbāsid court in particular. The presence of two men in Frederick's entourage corroborates this interpretation. These men served as personal philosophers and translators to Frederick: Michael Scot and Theodore of Antioch, the latter the translator of the treatise on falconry, *Moamin*. Their function might indeed have been inspired by an Arab *ḥakīm*, as suggested by Charles Burnett.[54]

Apart from this general influence of Arabic scientific culture, Frederick's *De arte venandi cum avibus* proves that the presence of philosophers and the translations had not merely a decorative function at the emperor's court, a justification or representation of power on the grounds of knowledge. Frederick himself adopted the principles of Aristotelian science, transmitted by the Arabs, in the composition of his own treatise on falconry. Compared with the Arabic treatises, it has a distinctive structure and applies new principles of observation to natural science.[55] Instead of copying information from other texts the author presented his own descriptions of birds of prey which, because of their meticulousness, stand out among medieval ornithological texts. Even though Aristotle appears as a serious authority, the emperor corrected his explanations on birds and based them on his own observations and his own experience as a hunter. The extraordinary character of *De arte venandi cum avibus* is evident in a manuscript which preserves the copy produced for Frederick's son Manfred.[56] This manuscript is famous for its illustrations which accompany the text and provide details of description of birds, training and care.

Frederick's *De arte venandi cum avibus* remained unfinished: it does not contain any chapter of medical contents even though the author announces it. Still, the emperor clearly went beyond the Arabic treatises on falconry. He set a new standard in the Western world not to be reached for centuries. It could be the extraordinary style of the text which explains why it did not spread, whereas the treatise which was translated from Arabic into Latin, the *Moamin*, spread quickly all over Italy.[57]

Though there is no connection between the original work, *De arte venandi cum avibus*, and the translation, *Moamin*, a comparative analysis of the Arabic Vorlage of the *Moamin* and its Latin translation is revealing for techniques of translation as well as the concept of science in general at Frederick's court.[58]

The Arabic original of the *Moamin* itself is not preserved, but either its Arabic original or the Latin translation is a combination of two Arabic texts which have been identified: one of them is the "work of Adham and Ghiṭrīf", the other one is a *Kitāb al-Mutawakkilī*, dedicated to the ʿAbbāsid Caliph al-Mutawakkil (reg. 847–861). This treatise has not been transmitted separately in Arabic, but it was almost completely translated into Castilian at the court of Alfonso the Wise in 1250,[59] i.e. only ten years after the translation of the *Moamin* at Frederick's court. Furthermore, extensive quotations of the text have been preserved in Arabic in a compilation with the title *Kitāb al-ṣayd* ('Book of Hunt'),[60] which was dedicated to the Ḥafṣid ruler in Tunis, al-Mustanṣir bi'llāh (reg. 1249–1277), and which was probably composed in the middle of the 1250s.

This suggests a possible origin of the *Moamin*. The ties between Sicily and Tunis were close, and Frederick was known even in his own time for sending questions of a scientific nature to the Arab world. The prologue to the encyclopaedia *Livre de Sidrac* sketches a scenario which might have formed the background of the transmission of the Arabic text on falconry which became the *Moamin* at Frederick's court: even though the sources of the *Livre de Sidrac* have been identified as entirely Western, the prologue recounts a different story. It states that the immense wisdom of the ruler of Tunis attracted the attention of Frederick's envoys. When the emperor asked for the source of this wisdom, he heard about the *Livre de Sidrac* whereupon the emperor obtained the Ḥafṣid's permission to have the book translated by Theodore.[61] This story cannot have been entirely concocted, if it was supposed to convey a certain degree of authenticity.

The parallel translations of the *Kitāb al-Mutawakkilī* in the West – in a compilation with the "work of Adham and Ghiṭrīf" at the court of Frederick into Latin, and separately into Castilian at the court of Alfonso – offer extraordinary possibilities for comparing the different techniques of translation at the two courts, and into two different languages. Generally speaking, a comparison of the three versions of the *Kitāb al-Mutawakkilī* reveals that the Castilian translation is much more faithful to the Arabic original than the Latin translation, as Stefan Georges demonstrates in his meticulous study of the *Moamin*.[62] The translator at Alfonso's court explains, for example, that he left out a particular passage of the Arabic text since it concerned only Muslims. This passage dealt probably with the legal problems described above, e.g. the question whether the meat of the game was *ḥarām* or *ḥalāl*. Also on the level of sentences and words the Castilian translation is far more literal than the Latin translation. An interesting phenomenon is that the Arabic text contains words scarcely comprehensible to an Arab reader. These are Persian names of minerals or plants which were definitely unfamiliar to at least one of the scribes (as the corruption of the term reveals) and which are often introduced by "yuqālu lahu" (= "which is called"). If such a word appears in an Arabic recipe, the Castilian translator usually renders the entire passage in his version including the distorted name, whereas the Latin translator leaves it out completely.

Conclusion

Falcons and falconry appear in various contexts and in different cultures and social spheres throughout many centuries and in a geographical region which covers Europe, the Mediterranean, the Middle East and the lands of Central Asia. In cross-cultural relations and when considering the influence of the Islamic traditions of hunting on European culture, it is above all the category of scientific texts which is relevant. Yet, this particular case of transmission needs to be regarded within its broader context. This enables us to understand the character of the impact and to explain why these very specific Arabic texts – medical texts for the treatment of falcons – have been translated at Western courts. The transmission involves at least two larger contexts: on the one hand falconry as a noble pastime, a sport of the kings, a representation of power, a ritual at courts, on the other hand an object of science which in turn is an occupation proper for kings or which at least deserves their support. Falconry can serve as an example of many fundamental changes in the various historical societies involved as well as of developments in the history of science, be it the hunting privilege of the European nobility with all its consequences for common people, be it the imitation of the Sassanid court by the ʿAbbāsids and the rise of the translation movement.

The contexts of the composition of both the "work of Adham and Ghiṭrīf" and the *Moamin* show a characteristic pattern of scientific culture at medieval courts, Islamic and Christian. The ʿAbbāsid court in Baghdad and Frederick's court in Sicily met all the essential conditions present in other courts which were important stages in the transmission of this and other texts on falconry. The scientific activities at the courts of the early ʿAbbāsids and of Frederick II are characterised by the adoption of foreign knowledge and an imitation of another court: the ʿAbbāsids were inspired by the Sassanids, and Frederick by the Arabs. In both situations translators, astrologers, physicians, and philosophers enjoyed the ruler's explicit support. As with astrology, hunting with birds of prey demanded economic affluence and was part of courtly rituals. Even if falconry itself was not an import from a foreign culture (since there had been Bedouin traditions in Arabia and German and Byzantine traditions in Europe), the imitation of another court changed the features of falconry in both cases fundamentally. In both cases its character as a royal pastime became more prominent, and in both cases a corpus of scientific texts developed around this pastime. Falconry became a courtly institution, combining several aspects of cultural activities and representation of power.

I will conclude my text with a quotation which might reveal more than anything else the attitude of medieval Arab (and probably also Western European) noblemen to their falcons. It is again ʿUsāma ibn Munqidh, the Syrian knight, who reveals genuine concern about the animals, but possibly also a certain degree of self-mockery:

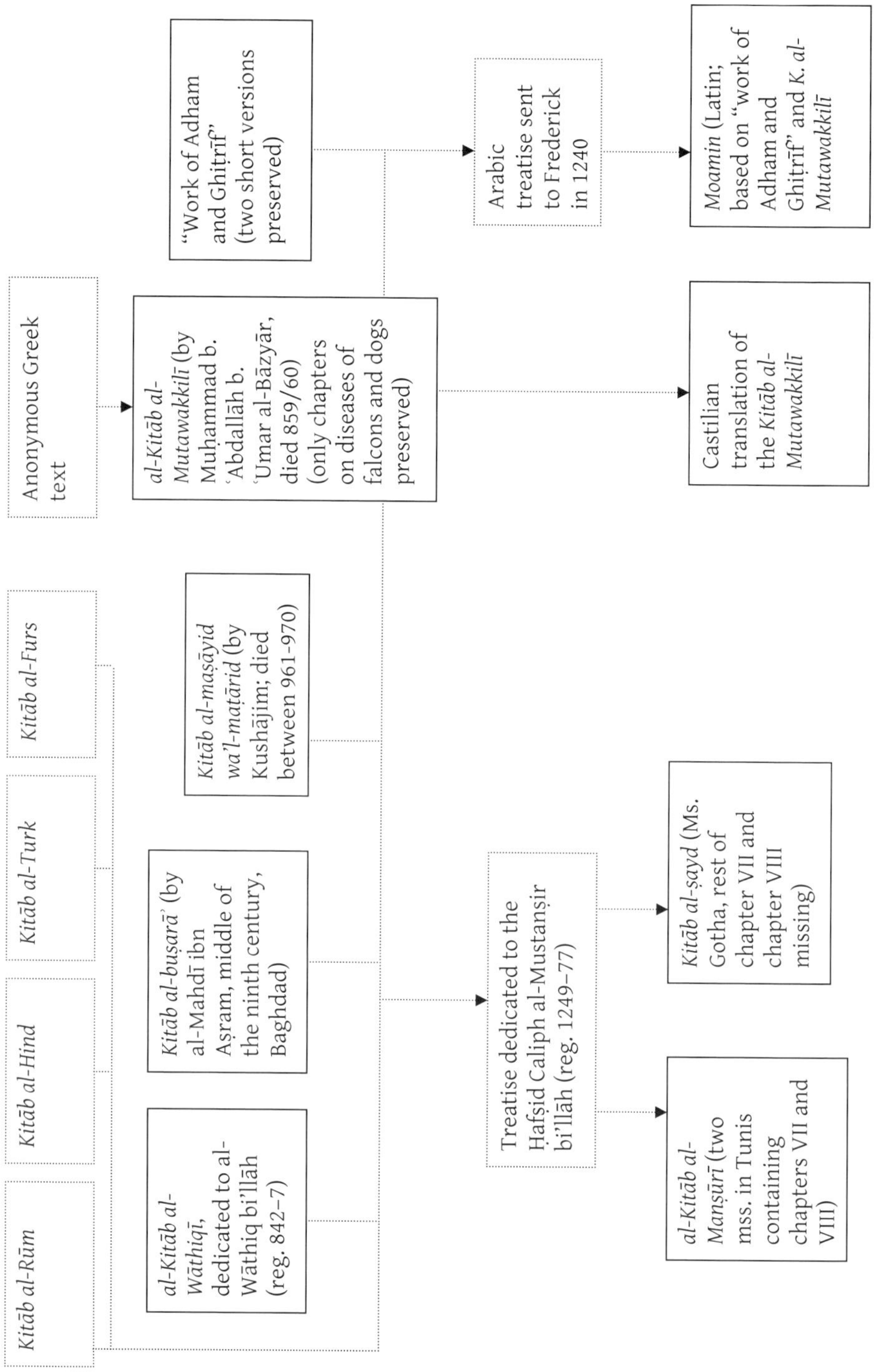

Anonymous Greek text
al-Kitāb al-Mutawakkilī (by Muḥammad b. ʿAbdallāh b. ʿUmar al-Bāzyār, died 859/60) (only chapters on diseases of falcons and dogs preserved)
"Work of Adham and Ghiṭrīf" (two short versions preserved)
Arabic treatise sent to Frederick in 1240
Moamin (Latin; based on "work of Adham and Ghiṭrīf" and *K. al-Mutawakkilī*
Castilian translation of the *Kitāb al-Mutawakkilī*
Kitāb al-Furs
Kitāb al-Turk
Kitāb al-Hind
Kitāb al-Rūm
Kitāb al-maṣāyid wa'l-maṭārid (by Kushājim; died between 961-970)
Kitāb al-buṣarāʾ (by al-Mahdī ibn Aṣram, middle of the ninth century, Baghdad)
al-Kitāb al-Wāthiqī, dedicated to al-Wāthiq bi'llāh (reg. 842–7)
Treatise dedicated to the Ḥafṣid Caliph al-Mustanṣir bi'llāh (reg. 1249–77)
Kitāb al-ṣayd (Ms. Gotha, rest of chapter VII and chapter VIII missing)
al-Kitāb al-Manṣūrī (two mss. in Tunis containing chapters VII and VIII)

It happened that as I was paying a visit to Shihāb al-Dīn in Ḥamā, I arose one morning to find the Qur'ān readers, the *Allāhu Akbar* chanters, and a large crowd of the inhabitants of the town assembled. On asking, "Who is dead?" I was told that it was a daughter of Shihāb al-Dīn. So I desired to walk in the funeral procession, but Shihāb al-Dīn began to argue with me and prevented me. The dead body was carried and interred in Tell-Ṣaqrūn. On their return, Shihāb al-Dīn said to me, "Knowest thou who was the dead one?" I replied, "I was told that it was a child of thine." He said, "No, by Allāh. It was rather the falcon, al-Yaḥshūr. Hearing that it died, I sent and had it brought hither. Then I made for it a shroud and funeral trappings and interred it. For it surely deserved as much."[63]

Notes

1 Ms. Istanbul, Topkapı Sarayı Kütüphanesi, Ahmet III, 2099. Facsimile edition: *The Book on Birds of Prey / Kitāb ḍawārī aṭ-ṭayr* (Publications of the Institute for the History of Arabic-Islamic Science, Series C: Facsimile Editions, 25; Frankfurt, 1986), 2.

2 Cf. the articles on Horus by E.S. Meltzer in *The Oxford Encyclopaedia of Ancient Egypt*, 3 vols. (Oxford, 2001) and by W. Helck in H.W. Haussig (ed.), *Götter und Mythen im Vorderen Orient* (Wörterbuch der Mythologie, 1. Abteilung: Die alten Kulturvölker, 1; Stuttgart, 1965), 360–64.

3 For their mythological traditions cf. E. Schmalzriedt and H.W. Haussig (eds.), *Götter und Mythen in Zentralasien und Nordeurasien* (Wörterbuch der Mythologie, 1. Abteilung: Die alten Kulturvölker, 7; Stuttgart, 1999); J. Baldick, *Animal and Shaman: Ancient Religions of Central Asia* (London, 2000).

4 Cf. *Die Mythologie der Mandschu-Tungusischen Völker* by K. Uray-Kőhalmi in E. Schmalzriedt and H.W. Haussig (eds.), *Götter und Mythen in Zentralasien und Nordeurasien* (as in n. 3), 30 and 146–7 (articles 'Adler' and 'Vogelgeister').

5 Cf. *Die alttürkische Mythologie* by J.-P. Roux in E. Schmalzriedt and H.W. Haussig (eds.), *Götter und Mythen in Zentralasien und Nordeurasien* (as in n. 3), 242–3 (article 'Raubvögel').

6 Cf. *Die türkische Mythologie: Die Mythologie der Ogusen und der Türken Anatoliens, Aserbaidschans, Turkmenistans* by P.N. Boratav in E. Schmalzriedt and H.W. Haussig (eds.), *Götter und Mythen in Zentralasien und Nordeurasien* (as in n. 3), 315–16 (article 'Dumrul').

7 The position of birds of prey in pre-Columbian cultures (for example the eagle in Mexico) is yet another example of the universality of this fascination.

8 J.V. Canby, 'Falconry (Hawking) in Hittite Lands', *JNES*, 61/3 (2002), 161–201.

9 H.J. Epstein, 'The Origin and Earliest History of Falconry', *Isis (International Review of the History of Science)*, 34/6 (1943), 497–509.

10 For a summary of some of the recent research on the early history of falconry cf. M.-D. Gleßgen, *Die Falkenheilkunde des <Moamin> im Spiegel ihrer volgarizzamenti: Studien zur Romania Arabica*, 2 vols. (Beihefte zur Zeitschrift für Romanische Philologie, 269–270; Tübingen, 1996).

11 K. Lindner, *Beiträge zu Vogelfang und Falknerei im Altertum* (Berlin, 1973), 111–19.

12 For a detailed description of this mosaic cf. Lindner, *Beiträge zu Vogelfang und Falknerei* (as in previous note), 136–48.

13 Apparently there is a certain connection between high rank and falconry implied in some of the Hittite representations, but it is hardly possible to specify this connection, cf. Canby, 'Falconry (Hawking) in Hittite Lands' (as in n. 8). Clauson quotes a verse by the poet Kutadgu-bilig at the Karakhanid court which was under the influence of Iranian models. This verse might be a rare indicator of falconry as a royal ritual among Turks: 'Your birds do not let anything that flies fly, and your hunting leipards (!) and dogs do not let anything that goes on its feet escape.' Cf. G. Clauson, 'Some Old Turkish Words Connected with Hunting', in *Die Jagd*

bei den altaischen Völkern, Vorträge der VIII. Permanent International Altaistic Conference vom 30.8. bis 4.9.1965 im Schloß Auel (Wiesbaden, 1968), 9–17, here 12.

14 D. Möller, *Studien zur mittelalterlichen arabischen Falknereiliteratur* (Berlin, 1965), 103–6; the articles 'Bāz' by H. Aʿlam and 'Bāz-Nāma' by M.T. Dānešpažūh in the *Encyclopaedia Iranica*. Cf. also the article on the eagle in Carsten Colpe's discussion of Iranian and Zoroastrian mythology in H.W. Haussig (ed.), *Götter und Mythen der kaukasischen und iranischen Völker* (Wörterbuch der Mythologie, 1. Abteilung: Die alten Kulturvölker, 4; Stuttgart, 1986), 230–32.

15 The first to be described with a passion for hunting is Yazīd I, cf. the article 'Bayzarah' by F. Viré in the *EI*[2].

16 D. Gutas, *Greek Thought, Arabic Culture: the Graeco-Arabic Translation Movement in Baghdad and Early ʿAbbāsid Society (2nd–4th/8th–10th centuries)* (London, 1998). Gutas mentions the treatise composed by al-Ghassānī for al-Mahdī (74). Cf. n. 41.

17 Möller, *Studien zur mittelalterlichen arabischen Falknereiliteratur* (as in n. 14), 107–11.

18 For the Seljuks, H.F. Hofmann mentions the *mīr shikār* in 'A Short Notice on Some MSS. of a Few Books on Falconry, Interesting the Altaist', in *Die Jagd bei den altaischen Völkern* (as in n. 13), 77–89, here 77; cf. also H. Eisenstein, 'Chronologie der Jagd-Emire unter den Mamluken-Sultanen', *Wiener Zeitschrift für die Kunde des Morgenlandes*, 82 (1992), 121–8; id., 'Der *amīr šikār* unter den Mamluken-Sultanen', in C. Wunsch (ed.), *XXV. Deutscher Orientalistentag vom 8. bis 13.4.1991 in München: Vorträge* (Zeitschrift der Deutschen Morgenländischen Gesellschaft, Supplement 10; Stuttgart, 1994), 129–35. E. Lévi-Provençal mentions the position of a *ṣāḥib al-bayāzira* for the court of the Caliph in Cordoba. (*L'Espagne Musulmane au x*[ème] *siècle : Institutions et vie sociale* [Paris, 1932], 55.) For the position of the falconer at the Ottoman court, cf. the articles 'Doğancı' and 'Çakırcı-başı' in *EI*[2].

19 J. Fried, 'Kaiser Friedrich II. als Jäger oder Ein zweites Falkenbuch Kaiser Friedrichs?', in *Nachrichten der Akademie der Wissenschaften in Göttingen*, I. Philologisch-historische Klasse, Jahrgang 1996, 4 (= pp. 115–56); id, „'...correptus est per ipsum imperatorem.' Das zweite Falkenbuch Friedrichs II.", in R. Schieffer (ed.), *Mittelalterliche Texte, Überlieferung - Befunde - Deutungen*, Kolloquium der Zentraldirektion der Monumenta Germaniae Historica am 28./29. Juni 1996 (Monumenta Germaniae Historica, Schriften, 42; Hannover, 1996), 93–124; W. Stürner, *Friedrich II*, ii (Darmstadt, 2000), 429–57; D. Abulafia, *Frederick II: a Medieval Emperor* (London, 2002), 267–70.

20 M. Allen, *Falconry in Arabia* (London, 1980); A. Ali, 'Arab Legacy to Falconry', *IC*, 70/3 (1996), 55–63; F. al-Tamīmī, *al-Ṣuqūr wa'l-ṣayd ʿind al-ʿarab* (Qatar, 1992).

21 E. Wagner, *Grundzüge der klassischen arabischen Dichtung*, 2 vols. (Darmstadt, 1988), i (*Die altarabische Dichtung*), 106–10 and ii (*Die arabische Dichtung in islamischer Zeit*), 46–58; M.J. Rubiera Mata, 'La poesía cinegética árabe', in J.M. Barral (ed.), *Orientalia Hispanica sive studia F.M. Pareva octogenario dicata*, i (*Arabica-Islamica*), Pars Prior (Leiden, 1974), 566–73.

22 G. Rex Smith, 'Hunting Poetry (*ṭardiyyāt*)', in Julia Ashtiani et al. (eds.), *ʿAbbasid Belles-Lettres* (The Cambridge History of Arabic Literature, 2; Cambridge, 1990), 167–84, here 167. In pre-Islamic poetry there are only a few references to falconry which became popular under the Umayyads and ʿAbbāsids (170–71). I am grateful to James Montgomery for drawing my attention to the following studies: J.E. Montgomery, 'Ṭardiyya', in J.S. Meisami and P. Starkey (eds.), *Encyclopedia of Arabic Literature*, 2 vols. (London, 1998), ii, 759–60; id., 'Abū Firās' Veneric *Urjūza Muzdawija*', *Arabic and Middle Eastern Literatures*, 2 (1999), 61–74; P.F. Kennedy, *Abu Nuwas: a Genius of Poetry* (Oxford, 2005), 109–120; J. Stetkevych, 'The Hunt in the Arabic *Qaṣīdah*. The Antecedents of the *Ṭardiyyah*', in J.R. Smart (ed.), Tradition and Modernity in Arabic Language and Literature (Richmond, 1996), 102–18 and id., 'The Hunt in Classical Arabic Poetry: from Mukhaḍram *Qaṣīdah* to Umayyad *Ṭardiyya*', *JAL*, 30 (1999), 107–27.

23 E. Wagner, *Abū Nuwās: Eine Studie zur arabischen Literatur der frühen ʿAbbāsidenzeit* (Wiesbaden, 1965), 265–89.

24 Translation by G. Rex Smith in 'Hunting Poetry (*ṭardiyyat*)' (as in n. 22), 182.

25 Sometimes it seems hardly possible to judge from the poems alone whether falconry was practised in the region where the poem was composed, cf. the different opinions of Rubiera Mata, 'Poesía cinegética' (as in n. 21) and H. Pérès (*La Poésie andalouse en arabe classique au XIe siècle: ses Aspects généraux, ses principaux themes et sa valeur documentaire* [Paris, ²1953], 346–9) on falconry in al-Andalus.

26 An edition of the text has been published by M.A. Ṭalas (Baghdad, 1954).

27 Translation in G. Rex Smith, 'A New Translation of Certain Passages of the Hunting Section of ʿUsāma ibn Munqidh's *Iʿtibār*', *JSS*, 26 (1981), 235–55, here 243–4. Last paragraph taken (with minor changes) from: ʿUsāma ibn Munqidh, *An Arab-Syrian Gentleman and Warrior in the Period of the Crusades*, trans. P.K. Hitti (New York, 1929), 225. Arabic text: *Kitāb al-iʿtibār*, ed. P. Hitti (Princeton, 1930), 194–5. See also the latest publication on this author by Paul M. Cobb, *Usama ibn Munqidh: Warrior-Poet of the Age of Crusades* (Oxford, 2005).

28 E. Gräf, *Jagdbeute und Schlachttier im islamischen Recht: Eine Untersuchung zur Entwicklung der islamischen Jurisprudenz* (Bonn, 1959).

29 Translation Richard Bell: 'But when ye are free (from your state of sanctity) hunt for yourselves.' (*The Qur'an, Translated, with a Critical Re-arrangement of the Surahs*, 2 vols. [Edinburgh, 1937–39].) Slightly different the translation by Arthur Arberry: "But when you have quit your pilgrim sanctity, then hunt for game." (*The Koran Interpreted*, trans. A.J. Arberry [London, 1955].)

30 Quoted from Ibn Rushd, *The Distinguished Jurist's Primer: a Translation of* Bidāyat al-Mujtahid, trans. I.A. Nyazee, 2 vols. (Reading, 1999), i, 552. Chapter XV is entirely dedicated to the problems of hunting.

31 M.M. Ahsan, *Social Life under the Abbasids, 170–289 AH, 786–902 AD* (London, 1979), chapter on hunting.

32 ʿUnsur al-Maʿālī Kaykāvus ibn Iskandar, *Qābūsnāmeh*, ed. Gh.H. Yūsufī (Tehran, 1378 AH), 94–5.

33 Kai Kāʾūs Ibn Iskandar, *A Mirror for Princes: the Qābūs Nāma*, trans. R. Levy (London, 1951), 84–5.

34 Some evidence has been collected by Ahsan (as in n. 31).

35 E. Esin ('The Hunter Prince in Turkish Iconography', in *Die Jagd bei den altaischen Völkern* [as in n. 13], 18–76, especially 32–4 about possible depictions of falconer princes in early illustrations) deals with the ritual and mythological backgrounds of this iconography, typical elements in style and composition and adds brief descriptions of the illustrations of some of the most impressive Ottoman manuscripts, pointing out the connections between shamanistic legacy, heraldic manifestation, ritual and depiction at the court. Cf. also D.L. Shepherd, 'Banquet and Hunt in Medieval Islamic Iconography', in U.E. McCracken (ed.), *Gatherings in Honor of D.E. Miner* (Baltimore, 1974), 79–92. Shepherd observes a transformation "from the Sasanian type attacking wild beasts into a more peaceful version as falconer" (84). Cf. as well E. Koch: 'The Just Hunter: Renaissance Calendar Illustrations and the Representation of the Mughal Hunt', in C. Burnett and A. Contadini (eds.), *Islam and the Italian Renaissance* (Warburg Institute Colloquia, 5; London, 1999), 167–83.

36 Cf. Gutas, *Greek Thought, Arabic Culture* (as in n. 16); J.L. Kraemer, *Humanism in the Renaissance of Islam: the Cultural Revival During the Buyid Age* (Leiden, ²1992).

37 The corpus of medieval Arabic literature on falconry, especially the medical dimension, has been explored by Detlef Möller and François Viré (see the literature cited in this article). Some otherwise hardly accessible articles have been reprinted in two volumes: F. Sezgin (ed.), *Falconry, Texts and Studies Collected and Reprinted* (Frankfurt, 2001). For an introduction to Arabic literature on animals cf. H. Eisenstein, *Einführung in die arabische Zoographie: Das tierkundliche Wissen in der arabisch-islamischen Literatur* (Berlin, 1991).

38 It remains unclear whether these texts were merely theoretical or used in practice. None of

the manuscripts I have studied so far contains marginal notes commenting on a recipe from a practical perspective. Cf. for this questions H. Eisenstein, 'Las obras árabes de medicina veterinaria: tratados médicos o literatura edificante?', in C. Vázquez de Benito and M.A. Manzano Rodríguez (eds.), *Actas, XVI Congreso UEAI* (Salamanca, 1995), 157–63.

39 A German translation has been published by Detlef Möller and François Viré, Al Ġiṭrīf ibn Qudāma al-Ġassānī, *Die Beizvögel (Kitāb ḍawārī aṭ-ṭayr): Ein arabisches Falknereibuch des 8. Jahrhunderts* (Hildesheim, 1988) and without major changes a French translation by the same two scholars, *Traité des oiseaux de vol (Kitāb ḍawārī aṭ-ṭayr)* (Nogent-le-Roi, 2002). No critical edition of the Arabic text has been published, but Möller and Viré based their translations on all available manuscripts and recorded the significant differences. In addition, a facsimile of the manuscript Istanbul, Topkapı Sarayı Kütüphanesi, Ahmet III, 2099 has been published (as in n. 1.) as well as a transcript of this manuscript (N.Ḥ. al-Qaisī and M.N. al-Dalīmī [eds.], *Kitāb ḍawārī aṭ-ṭayr* [Baghdad, 1990].). The "work of Adham and Ghiṭrīf" is part of the Vorlage of a Latin treatise on falconry with the title *Moamin* (cf. below). An edition of the Latin text is currently prepared for publication by Stefan Georges, who summarises in his introduction recent research concerning the Arabic sources.

40 Cf. the article by Peter E. Pormann in this volume.

41 Gutas, *Greek Thought, Arabic Culture* (as in n. 16), 61–74.

42 The first version is named after the scribe at the court of that Caliph, al-Ḥajjāj ibn Khaythama (cf. the passage quoted in the introduction). The second version includes at the beginning a fictitious didactic dialogue with Alexander the Great.

43 An edition, based on the single manuscript preserved in Tunis, has been published by I. ʿAbbās and ʿA. Manṣūr (Beirut, 1983). Aside from the quotation of the "work of Adham and Ghiṭrīf" and possibly of the *Kitāb al-Mutawakkilī* (see below) the sources of this treatise have not been identified and its place within the corpus of Arabic falconry literature has not been studied.

44 According to the Arabic sources, this Khāqān is the king of the Turks. Cf. the introduction to Al Ġiṭrīf ibn Qudāma al-Ġassānī, *Die Beizvögel (Kitāb ḍawārī aṭ-ṭayr)* (as in n. 38), 36–7.

45 Ms. Istanbul, Topkapı Sarayı Kütüphanesi, Ahmet III, 2099 (as in n. 1), 11–12.

46 The literature on the impact of this text is abundant. Cf. Steven J. Williams, *The Secret of Secrets: the Scholarly Career of a Pseudo-Aristotelian Text in the Latin Middle Ages* (Ann Arbor, 2003) and Regula Forster, *Das Geheimnis der Geheimnisse: Die arabischen und deutschen Fassungen des pseudo-aristotelischen* Sirr al-asrār, Secretum Secretorum (Wiesbaden, 2006).

47 Most of the evidence of old Turkish words connected with hunting collected by Gerald Clauson ('Some Old Turkish Words Connected with Hunting,' as in n. 13) stems from a work written in the eleventh century, Kāshgarī's *Dīwān Lughāti 'l-Turk*, and contains no reference to falconry at all (16). Moreover, in this article and all of the research I have been able to consult so far, the medical aspects of falconry among Central Asian peoples are never mentioned. There is a clear focus on training and hunting methods. Cf. as well the scarce evidence of Turkish words in Arabic, Persian and Indian treatises on falconry mentioned in Hofmann, 'A Short Notice on Some MSS. of a Few Books on Falconry, Interesting the Altaist' (as in n. 18).

48 Cf. the articles by François Viré on *Fahd* or *Ibn ʿIrs* in *EI*[2] and the English translation of the chapters on dogs and cheetahs from the *Kitāb al-ṣayd* (see below): T. Clark and M. Derhalli, *Al-Mansur's Book on Hunting: an Introduction, Translation and Notes* (Warminster, 2001). In the entire category of Arabic texts on veterinary medicine, birds of prey have clearly received more attention from modern scholars than other animals. Whereas the sections dedicated to dogs and cheetahs are comparatively short, there is a substantial corpus of horse medicine (*bayṭara*) which parallels the treatises on falconry in its literary history, inner structure, and institutional context of production. Except for a few editions which have been published in the last years, this corpus remains virtually unexplored. Cf. R.G. Hoyland, 'Theomnestus of Nicopolis, Ḥunayn ibn Isḥāq and the Beginnings of Islamic Veterinary Science', in id. and Ph.F. Kennedy (eds.),

Islamic Reflections, Arabic Musings: Studies in Honour of Professor Alan Jones (Oxford, 2004), 150–69 and M. Heide, 'Beschreibung und Behandlung einiger Erkrankungen, die die Extremitäten der Pferde betreffen aus dem Kitāb al-furūsīya wa-l-bayṭara des Muḥammad ibn Yaʿqūb ibn aḫī Ḥizām al-Ḫuttulī', *Die Welt des Orients* 34 (2004), 105–52. One of the future perspectives of such a research should include possible Arabic sources of a treatise on horse medicine composed at the court of Frederick II by Jordanus Ruffus. Cf. J.-L. Gaulin, 'Giordano Ruffo et l'art vétérinaire', *Micrologus*, 2 (1994), 185–98.

49 See the articles by Fried mentioned above (as in n. 19) and W. Rösener (ed.), *Jagd und höfische Kultur im Mittelalter* (Göttingen, 1997).

50 I. Reiser, *Falkenmotive in der deutschen Lyrik und verwandten Gattungen vom 12. bis zum 16. Jahrhundert*, PhD thesis (University of Würzburg, 1963); A.G. Ermes-Körber, *Zwei Künste, beflügelt von einem Ideal: Eine Untersuchung des Falkenmotivs in der Lyrik, Epik und Minneallegorie des 12.–14. Jahrhunderts*, PhD thesis (Amsterdam, 1995). For English literature cf. C.E. Brown, 'Juliet's Taming of Romeo', *Studies in English Literature, 1500–1900*, 36/2 (1996), 333–55.

51 Some of the Arabic sources (such as ʿUsāma ibn Munqidh and the *Kitāb al-kāfī*) mention Frankish falconers, cf. for example *Kitāb al-iʿtibār*, 196 (Arabic text) and G.R. Smith, 'A New Translation of Certain Passages', 244–5 (as in n. 27).

52 For a recent interpretation of the role of falconry (without consideration of the recent debates among Western scholars and the Arabic tradition) cf. D. Boccassini, *Il volo della mente: Falconeria e sofia nel mondo mediterraneo, Islam, Federico II, Dante* (Ravenna, 2003). For Western European medieval literature on falconry cf. the numerous publications by B. van den Abeele, e.g. *La Fauconnerie au Moyen Âge: Connaissance, affaitage et médecine des oiseaux de chasse d'après les traités latins* (Paris, 1994).

53 Edition by C.A. Willemsen (2 vols., Leipzig, 1942).

54 C. Burnett, 'Master Theodore, Frederick II's Philosopher', in *Federico II e le nuove culture*, Atti del XXXI Convegno storico internazionale, Todi, 9–12 ottobre 1994 (Spoleto, 1995), 225–85. Cf. also B. Kedar and E. Kohlberg, 'The Intercultural Career of Theodore of Antioch', *Mediterranean Historical Review*, 10 (1995), 165–76.

55 Apart from the publications by Fried and Stürner (as in n. 19) cf. D. Walz, 'Das Falkenbuch Friedrichs II', *Micrologus*, 2 (1994), 161–84. One should note however that there have been some recent debates about the interpretation of Bottatius' letter which do not yet appear in this article.

56 The manuscript which is preserved in the Vatican library has been reprinted several times in facsimile editions, e.g. *Das Falkenbuch Kaiser Friedrichs II.*, Nach der Prachthandschrift in der Vatikanischen Bibliothek, Einführung und Erläuterungen von Carl Arnold Willemsen (Dortmund, ^{4}1986).

57 In his PhD thesis *Der falken- und hundeheilkundliche Traktat des Moamin: Studien zu Quellen, Entstehung, Überlieferung und Rezeption* (University of Frankfurt, 2004) Stefan Georges presents a critical edition of the Latin text with an extensive introduction which analyses this rapid dissemination. The thesis is currently being prepared for publication.

58 For the relations between the Arabic and Latin texts mentioned in this article see the stemma.

59 Muhammad Ibn ʿAbd Allāh Ibn ʿUmar al-Bazyār, *Libro de los Animales que cazan (Kitāb al-Ŷawāriḥ)*, ed. J.M. Fradejas Rueda (Madrid, 1987).

60 This compilation has not been preserved completely. A single manuscript located in Gotha (Germany) seems to include nearly the entire text consisting of eight chapters, but the rest of book VII and book VIII are missing. Two fragments preserved in Tunis comprise book VII on dogs and cheetahs and book VIII, a glossary of animals. An edition of the Tunis fragments has been published by ʿAbd al-Ḥafīẓ Manṣūr (*al-Manṣūrī fī 'l-bayzara* [Tunis, 1989]) and an English translation of the chapter on dogs by Clark and Derhalli (as in n. 46). An edition of the quotations

from the *Kitāb al-Mutawakkilī* as preserved in the Gotha manuscript in the chapter on diseases of birds of prey has been published by Stefan Georges and myself, cf. Muḥammad ibn ʿAbdallāh al-Bāzyār, *Das Falken- und Hundebuch des Kalifen al-Mutawakkil: Ein arabischer Traktat aus dem 9. Jahrhundert*, ed. and trans. A. Akasoy und S. Georges (Berlin, 2005).

61 E. Ruhe (ed.), *Sydrac le philosophe: Le Livre de la fontaine de toutes sciences*, Edition des enzyklopädischen Lehrdialogs aus dem XIII. Jahrhundert (Wiesbaden, 2000), 2. For a summary of recent research cf. B. Wins, '*Le Livre de Sidrac* – Stand der Forschung und neue Ergebnisse', in W. Brunner (ed.), *Wissensliteratur im Mittelalter und in der frühen Neuzeit* (Wiesbaden, 1993), 36–51.

62 Cf. Georges' thesis mentioned in n. 57 and the articles dealing with the *Moamin*, its sources and the parallel Castilian transmission in the forthcoming J. Fried (ed.), *Wissen an Höfen und Universitäten: Rezeption, Transformation, Innovation*, Akten der Tagung in Frankfurt am Main, 5.–6. Oktober 2001. Cf. also our *Das Falken- und Hundebuch des Kalifen al-Mutawakkil* mentioned in n. 60.

63 Quoted with minor changes from Hitti's translation (*An Arab-Syrian Gentleman and Warrior in the Period of the Crusades*, 235–6), Arabic text: *Kitāb al-iʿtibār*, 206 (both as in n. 27).

4

The Presocratics in Arabic Philosophical Pseudepigrapha[1]

Ulrich Rudolph

I.

If one surveys the history of philosophy, one will without a doubt find thinkers who have influenced intellectual development more than those whom we today call the Presocratics. Nevertheless, whilst examining this same history, one can scarcely find another group of thinkers who have in a comparable manner stimulated the imagination of posterity.

This renowned and exceptional role is explained by their unique historical status, for actually, the Presocratics constitute the very beginning of Western philosophy. They represent the birth of philosophy itself, and that endows them with unsurpassable charm. However, the Presocratics are perhaps the philosophers whose doctrines are the least known of all philosophical teachings. Their works are lost; their fragments are dispersed, thereby permitting of a variety of interpretations. To the charm of the beginning is thus joined the obscurity of their origins, which inexorably leads exegetes to construct multiple interpretations of these ancient philosophical heroes.

Almost all of these speculative interpretations are grounded in references in ancient doxographies. As is well known, the latter fall under two distinct categories: some are complete texts, such as Aetius' *Placita philosophorum*; and some are part of larger texts, such as the famous doxographies of Aristotle or Simplicius, but also those of the Church Fathers.[2] These writers do not introduce their work with the intention of giving a neutral *conspectus* of the history of philosophy, but rather always combine their account with an ulterior but specific end; either they wish to demonstrate that their own ideas were anticipated in the thought of the ancient masters, or they would like to show that their own doctrines are free of the errors committed by the ancient masters.[3] At the same time, however, it is indisputable that these texts also contain information about their objects, even though this information was selectively chosen, subjectively interpreted and occasionally altered in content. One could thus conclude that the doxographic reports of Presocratic philosophy remained, throughout the course of antiquity, circumscribed within a delimited scope. These limitations did indeed make room for a variety of interpretations, original approaches, misunderstandings, mistakes and a certain number of errors and confusions. Yet these accounts, though confused, continued to transmit a traditional understanding of Presocratic doctrines, whether we are dealing with early authorities such as Plato and Aristotle, or later authors such as Simplicius and his contemporaries in Alexandria and Athens.

II.

This picture changes when, beyond the reach of the period, we turn towards the medieval world of the East. For the transmission of Greek philosophy to the Islamic world[4] was not a uniform process limited to the translation of ancient works into Arabic. It also involved other ways of assimilating Greek culture such as paraphrases, commentaries, and even new works of Hellenistic leanings, produced from ancient sources then available.

This observation is particularly evident in the case of the Presocratics. They played a special role in the transmission of Greek philosophy to the Islamic world because, in the course of this development, their reputation as ancient masters, even as mythic philosophical heroes, persistently stimulated the creative imagination of their commentators. Thus from the ninth century onward a series of doxographies concerning the Presocratics appeared in Arabic.

There were, on the one hand, translations from Greek texts. The Arabs translated, for example, Aetius' *Placita philosophorum*[5] as well as Aristotle's *Physics*[6] and *Metaphysics*,[7] which had instilled in them a certain awareness of the Greek sources and had in this way given them an impression of the ideas associated with the names of the Presocratics during antiquity. On the other hand, a new series of doxographies appeared in the East during the ninth century, treatises that certainly seemed to have been written directly in Arabic without being based upon a Greek model or text.

These texts in particular deserve our attention because they alter the literary style of the doxographies with which we were previously familiar. They were not actually intended to enlighten their readers on the thought of the philosophers they cited by name. More often, their authors only touched on the names of the ancient philosophers in order to attribute their own opinions to them. We are dealing therefore with a very unique form of literature. This literature passes on certain ideas and philosophers' names from the Greek into the Islamic world, but in so doing alters the content by depriving them of their original meanings. Even now it is impossible for us to determine how this literature developed in its totality, and the preponderance of this material has yet to be studied or even published. The most that we can provide at present is to offer a provisional outline of this literature, which forms the substance of this article.

The sketch that I wish to provide is based on three different texts. The first deals with philosophical questions; the second takes place on the level of cosmology. The last text is an encyclopedia in which all questions concerning the universe and its creator are discussed. These texts, however, have three common characteristics. They are all pseudepigraphic treatises which seem to have been compiled in Arabic in the ninth century. They are all doxographic commentaries, whether they incorporate a complete text in this form or whether they contain a fragmentary reference from it. And they all pass on a fictitious or, at least, an unconventional account of the Presocratics, which will lead us to conclude with reflections on the role played by these authors at the dawn of Arab scientific writing as well as the differences between this role and the renown of the Presocratics in antiquity.

III.

Our first text, found in a sole surviving Arabic manuscript in the library of the Aya Sofya, is entitled *The Book of Ammonius on the Opinions of the Philosophers.*[8] It is composed throughout as a doxography and it discusses, on first reading, the topics which ancient philosophers would have taught concerning the Creator, the principles of the universe and other metaphysical themes. Among the philosophers cited, we find almost all the Presocratics, but also other celebrated thinkers such as Plato, Aristotle, the Stoics, Epicurus, Plutarch, Proclus, and even Zoroaster and the Indian Brahmans.

However, this 'Ammonius' only rarely transmits the actual teachings of the philosophers referred to by name. For the most part, he simply attributes his own ideas to them. These cases are evident, because the philosophical background of the text is sufficiently clear: he positions his thought, as we shall see, in a Neoplatonist context or, more precisely, in a metaphysical system that combines Neoplatonism with monotheism. However, the method our author uses is decidedly strange and remarkable; for this reason it deserves to be described in some detail.

The text begins with a discussion of the problem of the divine creation of the world. According to Ammonius, all ancient philosophers unanimously agree that God created all things *ex nihilo*. However, despite this general unanimity, there remains in particular one question to explicate: were there eternal ideas in the mind of God before creation or did God create the world with no foreknowledge of any model? This is the *casus belli.*[9]

Thales, the first philosopher in our text, defends the second thesis. According to him, God is the origin of everything, without exception. It then necessarily follows that he created the ideas too.[10] In our text, the position is disputed by Plutarch who promotes a divergent view. According to him we must choose between two possibilities: either we assume that God does not have the model within himself, implying that God himself did not know what he wanted to create – a hypothesis evidently absurd; or, one agrees that God knew his own intentions, in which case it is necessary to conclude that He had this idea within himself. Therefore, one must concede that these ideas have always existed in the mind of God.[11]

Initially, this argument appears to be convincing, but Ammonius hastens to contradict Plutarch.[12] In his view, it is Thales who is correct. Therefore, he must summon a third philosopher, Xenophanes, with the sole purpose of confirming Thales' reasoning by means of other arguments. According to Xenophanes, God is beyond our comprehension, to the extent that all speculation concerning his nature is ultimately futile. It is necessary by definition to admit the omnipotence and superiority of God over all other things; and, accordingly, so too with ideas, which can only be created by God himself.[13]

These preliminary chapters disclose the general character of the text. They reveal that the work is not a doxography *per se*, appearances notwithstanding, but rather a treatise of philosophical and religious persuasion, concealed behind the façade of a doxography.

However, in spite of the general impression conveyed by these chapters, we must attend to detail. For amongst the multitude of speculations intended to express the personal opinion of Ammonius, we also find short remarks which consistently demonstrate that our author did indeed have a genuine knowledge of ancient philosophy. In the chapters just discussed, as we have seen, 'Plutarch' proposed that the Ideas have always existed in the mind of God. This thesis was originally expounded by Middle Platonism[14]: Plutarch of Chaeroneia was indeed a representative of this philosophical movement. Thus, Ammonius integrated a historical element into his account, but not for the purpose of informing his readers, we hasten to add. Rather, he used this doxographical detail to embellish his account and to demonstrate that, in his view, Plutarch was a poor philosopher.

The same method is found in the rest of this text. In order to illustrate this key point, let us give another example. In chapter 13, Thales appears again, and this time explains:

> The first thing that God created...was water. It is the first material that takes on all forms. From this was created all substances, such as the heavens and everything beneath them... This matter which is the origin and end (of our world) is however only the material of corporeal substances... Above the heavens there are other worlds... They are so bright, so beautiful, and so splendid that our minds cannot conceive them. They are created from a spiritual matter the light of which is not conceivable by our intellect... Minds and souls desire it.... (But) they are dependent upon a Creator whose qualities are not known. Intellect can only know this Creator through his works; his essential being is, on the contrary, absolutely unknowable...[15]

Here too, one can see immediately the basic principle of our text. Ammonius uses Thales' name to express his own ideas, at the same time adorning his account with allusions to well-known doctrines propagated under the name of Thales.

The same thing occurs in subsequent chapters which contain the same elements – some traces of ancient doxography, but above all the author's expression of his own philosophical viewpoint. His conviction is confirmed by a multitude of Greek authorities, amongst whom are Anaximenes, Heraclitus, Democritus and especially Empedocles and Pythagoras. However, there are also certain thinkers who are not part of this universal harmony: Epicurus,[16] Plutarch,[17] Zeno the Stoic,[18] Pyrrho the Sceptic[19] and Zoroaster[20] – that is, the authors who were neither Neoplatonics nor Presocratics.

At this point, it only remains to ask which ideas inspired our Ammonius whilst he wrote this astonishing treatise? What exactly was his philosophical and religious background? And what were the sources he used in order to embellish his text with a doxographical underpinning?

Let us begin with the second question: without exception, the doxographical foundation of the text is derived from ancient sources. In most cases, Ammonius cites a work of the Church Fathers entitled *Refutatio omnium haeresium*, a work attributed in various editions to Hippolytus of Rome.[21] In addition to Hippolytus, he has also used other ancient authorities, such as Porphyry and Proclus. We can thus conclude that, as far as doxographical sources are concerned, our author depended exclusively on these ancient predecessors.

The same thing cannot be said of Ammonius' philosophical vision. When his metaphysical doctrines are analysed, we find an accumulation of different ideas of which two stand out clearly: on the one hand there is Neoplatonism, of a type which is very close to extant texts such as *The Theology of Aristotle*[22]; on the other hand, there is the feature we have already pointed out, our author's monotheistic tendencies. These tendencies constitute perhaps the most delicate element in the entire text to evaluate. But this monotheism is also in the end conducive to a detailed analysis which reveals that it is not monotheism *tout court*, but a specific doctrine which finds its origins in Muslim religion.

This origin reveals itself at both the level of vocabulary and doctrine. To take but one example, the discussion between Thales, Plutarch and Xenophanes about the place of Ideas within God's mind remains altogether inexplicable if one does not place it within the context of Islamic doctrine. No Christian would have bothered to refute the fact that God already had conceptions before proceeding to Creation. On the contrary, Christian theologians, influenced by Platonism, entertained precisely this concept. Only Muslim thinkers rejected it. And it is, to be more precise, the Muʿtazilite theologians of the ninth century and the philosopher al-Kindī who unanimously claimed that God did not possess the model by which he could realise his Creation.[23]

We can therefore conclude that our text was written in the ninth century. The author was an expert in Neoplatonic philosophy, but he interpreted this philosophy within the context of Muslim theology. However, the characteristic feature of this text is not its synthesis of philosophy and religion. Its distinctive characteristic comes rather from the fact that its author presents this synthesis as a conviction common to all the Presocratics. This cannot but shock someone who is familiar with ancient doxography, but in the ninth century this was not an isolated case, as we shall see presently.

IV.

Let us now proceed to the analysis of our second text that seems to date from the same period. I am speaking of the *Turba philosophorum*,[24] a text which is much better known than that of Ammonius, but which is, in a certain sense, quite similar.

Firstly, in both cases we are dealing with pseudepigraphic texts. The *Turba*, moreover, does not reveal the name of its author, but it pretends to be the record of the proceedings of a debate between a large gathering of philosophers supposedly presided over by Pythagoras.[25] Secondly, both texts are written with similar motives: each author wishes to express his own philosophical and religious convictions, and these respective convictions resemble each other in that they both combine certain elements of ancient philosophy with theological notions which find their origin in Islam.[26]

The feature which reveals most clearly the parallel between the two works is, however, their literary form. The *Turba philosophorum*, like Ammonius' treatise, has the appearance of a doxographic text, although it is a fictional recreation of a grand assembly of philosophers debating diverse matters – the majority of the participants in this extra-ordinary spectacle are, once again, Presocratics.

The first part of the *Turba philosophorum*, which is what interests us here, is divided into nine chapters. These are without exception characterised by the fact that it is a Presocratic who delivers his speech before an assembly of colleagues and who answers the questions which follow.

The first to speak is Anaximander. He explains that in the beginning God created a certain substance which served as a first principle for the other elements (amongst which the air is, according to Anaximander, the most noble and prominent).[27] This opinion is confirmed by the second philosopher to speak. He reiterates the primacy of air as an element that conserves and organises life in the world – a celebration which is hardly surprising since this philosopher is Anaximenes.[28] The third thinker, Anaxagoras, introduces new ideas into the debate. He supports the idea according to which God created, before everything else, intellect and piety, after which was created the sensible world in which intellect and piety are manifested. This very world consists of four elements of which the most noble, according to Anaxagoras, is not air, but fire.[29]

We have thus arrived at the famous theory of the four elements. There can be no question that this theory represents one of the most important doctrines held by the unknown author of the *Turba philosophorum*, since from that point on he refers to it repeatedly. The fourth, fifth and sixth philosophers (Empedocles, Archelaus and Leucippus) hasten to confirm this theory, while the seventh, Ecphantus, modifies the theory by claiming that a world exists above the heavens, inaccessible to us, and another world beneath the heavens which consists of four elements.[30] Pythagoras, the eighth philosopher to speak, adds some subtle speculations to these considerations. He confirms yet again that God created everything from the four basic elements. But the main point of his speech is the assertion that God, and God alone, existed before creation. God is therefore the absolute principle of all things. He is the infinite ruler since nothing outside him existed before he created it.[31] And this is the second key point of our text, an idea also corroborated by the last philosopher, Xenophanes,[32] who justifies it with some clear references to the Qurʾān.[33]

In this way, the *Turba philosophorum* is a unified whole. Just as Ammonius had done, its author wrote different chapters in order to promulgate a single and unique conviction. This is certainly not as elaborate as Ammonius' doctrine; here we search in vain for the subtle Neoplatonic speculations that characterise Ammonius' treatise. But the principal pathways are almost identical: these are, I repeat, an ancient philosophical and cosmological background, a religious conviction which derives from Islam, and the surprising observation that it could be thought most opportune to present this new philosophico-religious synthesis in the mouths of the Presocratics.

V.

Having reached this point, we could be excused for supposing that the role of the Presocratics in the beginnings of Islamic science was uniform. Hitherto our observations have tended to indicate that the reputation of the Presocratics was incontestable given that they were considered to be the greatest scientific and philosophical teachers of all time. However, this greatly simplifies the complexity of the situation, for there are other ways of construing the role of the Presocratics, as we shall see in the third text.

The third text, called *The Book of the Secret of Creation* (*Kitāb sirr al-khalīqa*), seems to be yet another Arabic treatise written in the ninth century.[34] We are again dealing with a pseudepigraphon, this time attributed to Apollonius of Tyana, a mysterious and late representative of the Pythagorean School.[35] However, *The Book of the Secret of Creation* is not similar in all respects to the two other works that we have examined, but does contain some significant differences.

First and foremost, it is not a doxography. *The Book of the Secret of Creation* is a massive encyclopaedia which describes in six books the Creator, celestial phenomena, minerals, plants, animals and man, that is, all realms of creation. Yet, if we include this work within the context of our discussion, it is because its first book contains some doxographical accounts, albeit very short. It will suffice therefore briefly to summarise their content. Nonetheless, these passages are able to complement the picture we have drawn so far, and so merit mention.

The first part of the *Sirr al-khalīqa* is devoted to a description of God.[36] Its author approaches this subject in two stages, one intended to describe the divine qualities, the other to deal with the different acts of God. The presentation is sufficiently clear and coherent. The author approaches the explanation of this delicate subject in the manner of a theologian, although he occasionally interrupts the course of his argumentation with digressions in response to the objections of his adversaries. It is precisely at this point that we find the passages which interest us because they are presented as doxographical.

In brief, there are three small chapters. The first is attributed to a philosopher whose name in Arabic appears as Munīs. This philosopher upholds the idea that no change occurs within the world here on earth. All perception of change, according to this theory, would be an illusion of the senses. In effect, God created nothing ambiguous or ambivalent. Consequently, all remains in its original state. There is no movement or real change.[37] This opinion is modified in the second chapter. This view is attributed to Plato, a name referring not to the Plato we know but to a certain Coptic Plato. He explains that while it is true that neither movement nor change exist, there are things which move and change.[38] The third philosopher to speak is Calanus, the celebrated Indian who is alleged to have corresponded with Alexander the Great.[39] In our text, he is actually presented as Indian. But this Calanus is not conversing with Alexander. He distinguishes himself by asking absurd theological questions, such as whether God is able to create another God that is similar to Himself, or whether God is able to contain an entire world within a mustard seed.[40]

It is immediately noticeable from an analysis of these three chapters that their content derives from two distinct traditions. Like Ammonius and the author of the *Turba philosophorum*, the author of *The Book of the Secret of Creation* combines allusions to ancient philosophy with an Islamic theological position.[41] The absurd questions, here attributed to Calanus, were known within the discussions that took place in Muslim theological circles of the ninth century. Numerous Arab authors speak about them, occasionally with some variation, throughout the Middle Ages.[42]

The discussion of the reality of change seems, on the other hand, to be rooted in Greek tradition. It forcefully reminds us of the ideas taught by Parmenides and the Eleatic School,[43] and it does not seem out of the question that the 'Munīs' of our text is actually a Greek name distorted in Arabic. It is even possible that we are dealing there with Parmenides himself. But it is equally possible that it is Melissus, a student of Parmenides, who held the same doctrines.[44]

We thus arrive at a conclusion comparable with those drawn from the two previous texts. Once again, an unknown author has revealed to us his Graeco-Muslim convictions. Once again, he does not put forth his point of view as personal, but as a shared perspective that would be generally recognised. At the same time, we must nonetheless concede that there are clear differences between these three texts. For instance, within *The Book of the Secret of Creation* the philosophers mentioned are not seen as ancient heroes and wise masters. Moreover, these thinkers erred in not accepting the absolute truth this text proclaims. On the contrary, they pronounce embarrassing objections that the author of the *Sirr al-khalīqa* is obliged carefully to refute.

VI.

It is evident that this research must be pursued further. As I have stated, there is a whole series of Arabic texts which are, in one form or another, comparable with the three works that we have just considered.[45] These works do, however, permit us to draw some conclusions, for our analysis has shown that they have certain traits in common and exhibit a number of parallel phenomena.

Three observations can, in sum, be made concerning the role of the Presocratics at the dawn of Islamic philosophy:

1) Within the Arabic doxographic texts of the ninth century, the genuine identities and doctrines of the Greek philosophers so named are not the most central issues. It seems rather that the philosophers are given a new role and a new function which is explained by the context of the work in which they are quoted. This function is not always positive. This is what *The Book of the Secret of Creation* shows us, where the philosophers are limited to presenting absurd and embarrassing objections. But in most cases, the image of the Greek thinkers is at least positive. The Presocratics in particular enjoy an enormous prestige. They are venerated as supremely wise men and for this reason often fulfil the function of expressing the author's personal opinion.
2) Consequently, in these works presented to us as doxographies, one can find very few doxographic details that are actually trustworthy. On the contrary, many doctrines are erroneously attributed. One could thus form the impression that these texts give free rein to all sorts of abuses, because on a first reading it seems that their authors made so bold as to assign any doctrine to any thinker.
3) However, this impression turns out to be misleading. For in the final analysis these authors, despite everything, respected certain limits, even if they were not immediately apparent. In this way, there are ancient thinkers to whom they never attribute their own doctrines, such as for example Plutarch and Epicurus, who often play the role of heretics and who merely assert scandalous opinions. On the other

hand, there are philosophers who are always elevated above the others, and here, one must refer to several Presocratics, especially Empedocles and Pythagoras.

Having made these observations, there remains but one question to ask. Do all the results that we have established truly represent later developments that can only be found in Arabic works of the Middle Ages? Or, did comparable phenomena already exist or was there even a precursory movement in doxographic literature in Greek Antiquity?

The reply can only be equivocal because much depends upon the particular aspect we choose to consider. There are certainly some observations that we could apply equally to the texts of Antiquity. For instance, the critique of Epicurus and Plutarch is an element that clearly comes from the Greek tradition. The same can be said of the praise for Empedocles and for Pythagoras, which was widespread in the Neoplatonism of late antiquity. Even the tendency of certain authors to use the Presocratics for their own ends was not unknown in Greek texts. It is perhaps enough here to allude to the works of the Church Fathers and, *a fortiori*, to treatises belonging to the science of Alchemy.

Nevertheless, I remain convinced that the texts that we have analysed could not have been written by an ancient author. For they also represent some aspects that seem to me incompatible with a cultural climate permeated with ancient philosophy and one that makes use of the Greek language. We must call to mind here the boldness with which these authors combined certain thinkers' names with certain doctrines. But we must also stress the incredible prestige that the Presocratics enjoy in some of these texts. One can therefore maintain, as a final conclusion, the idea that the Presocratics play a double role in these ninth century works: from the point of view of historical information and authenticity, they suffer badly; but from the perspective of prestige and authority, at no other time have they been so highly exalted.

Notes

1 A longer version of this article has been published in French in S. Matton and C. Viano (eds.), *L'alchimie et ses racines philosophiques: La tradition grecque et la tradition arabe* (Paris, 2004), 155–70. I want to express my gratitude to John Beach (Université de Montréal) who translated the French version into English.

2 For general information see both B. Wyss, 'Doxographie', in *Reallexikon für Antike und Christentum*, iv (Stuttgart, 1959), col. 197–210, and *Revue de Métaphysique et de Morale*, 3 (1992), special edition: *Doxographie antique*.

3 See for example J. Mansfield, 'Doxography and Dialectic: The *Sitz im Leben* of the Placita', *Aufstieg und Niedergang der Römischen Welt*, II, XXXVI (Berlin, 1990), 3056–3229.

4 G. Endress, 'Die Übersetzungen wissenschaftlicher und philosophischer Literatur ins Arabische', in H. Gätje (ed.), *Grundriss der Arabischen Philologie*, ii (*Literaturwissenschaft*) (Wiesbaden, 1987), 416–506; D. Gutas, *Greek Thought, Arabic Culture: The Graeco-Arabic Translation Movement in Baghdad and Early ʿAbbāsid Society (2nd-4th/8th-10th Centuries)* (London, 1998).

5 The Arabic text has been edited by H. Daiber, *Aetius Arabus: Die Vorsokratiker in arabischer Überlieferung* (Wiesbaden, 1980).

6 See P. Lettinck, *Aristotle's Physics and its Reception in the Arabic World, With an Edition of the Unpublished Parts of Ibn Bājja's Commentary on the Physics* (Leiden, 1994).

7 The Arabic text of the *Metaphysics* has been included in the edition of M. Bouyges: Averroès

(Ibn Rušd), *Tafsīr Mā baʿd al-ṭabīʿa* (*Grand Commentaire de la Métaphysique d'Aristote*), 3 vols. (Beirut 1938–52); cf. M. Bouyges, 'La critique textuelle de la *Métaphysique* d'Aristote et les anciennes versions arabes', *Mélanges de l'Université Saint-Joseph*, 27 (1947–48), 145–52; Ibn Rushd, *Grand Commentaire de la Métaphysique d'Aristote* (*Tafsīr Mā baʿd al-ṭabīʿa*). *Livre Lām-Lambda*, transl. A. Martin (Paris, 1984); Ch. Genequand, *Ibn Rushd's Metaphysics: a Translation with Introduction of Ibn Rushd's Commentary on Aristotle's Metaphysics, Book Lām* (Leiden, 1986).

8 See Ulrich Rudolph, *Die Doxographie des Pseudo-Ammonios: Ein Beitrag zur neuplatonischen Überlieferung im Islam* (Stuttgart, 1989) [henceforward *Doxographie*]. This work comprises an edition of the Arabic text [henceforward *Ammonius*], a translation into German and a commentary.

9 *Ammonius* I.1–3.

10 Id., II.1–12.

11 Id., III.1–11.

12 Id., III.12.

13 Id., IV.1–13.

14 See e.g. Albinus, *Didaskalikos*, in *Platonis dialogi*, vi, ed. C.F. Hermann (Leipzig, 1892), 163, 1. 27-8.

15 *Ammonius* XIII.1–22.

16 Id., XVIII.1–2

17 Id., III.12 and IX.2–7.

18 Id., VI.12; cf. *Doxographie*, 142-7.

19 *Ammonius*, XIX.1–7.

20 Id., XV.1–5; 19; 25–38.

21 See the Greek text that has been reproduced as part of the German translation (*Doxographie*, 82-106.)

22 See *Doxographie*, 121-2, 125-7, 150, 155-8 etc.

23 Ibid., 128-30; cf. 199-204.

24 See J. Ruska, *Turba Philosophorum: Ein Beitrag zur Geschichte der Alchemie* (Berlin, 1931).

25 Ibid., 109.

26 On the *Weltanschauung* of the author of the *Turba* see M. Plessner, *Vorsokratische Philosophie und griechische Alchemie: Studien zu Text und Inhalt der* Turba Philosophorum, *Nach dem Manuskript ediert von Felix Klein-Franke* (Wiesbaden, 1975), 124–34.; see Ulrich Rudolph, 'Christliche Theologie und vorsokratische Lehren in der *Turba Philosophorum*', *Oriens*, 32 (1990), 97–123, especially 121-2.

27 Plessner, 38-40 (*Sermo* 1).

28 Ibid., 45-6 (*Sermo* 2).

29 Ibid., 49-50 (*Sermo* 3).

30 Ibid., 66-7 (*Sermo* 7).

31 Ibid., 72-5 (*Sermo* 8).

32 Ibid., 82-3 (*Sermo* 9).

33 Xenophanes mentions in particular the idea that God has created the world by means of the word "become" (*kun*); the idea is to be found in the Qurʾān in different forms (2:117, 3:48. 3:59 etc.). Compare also *Sermo* 5 (Plessner, 58) wherein Archelaus quotes 112:1–3.

34 The Arabic text has been edited by U. Weisser, *Buch über das Geheimnis der Schöpfung und die Darstellung der Natur (Buch der Ursachen) von Pseudo-Apollonios von Tyana* (Aleppo, 1979) [henceforward *Sirr*]. See as well U. Weisser, *Das „Buch über das Geheimnis der Schöpfung" von Pseudo-Apollonios von Tyana* (Berlin, 1980) [henceforward Weisser]. This book contains an introduction into the work, a German summary of the Arabic text and a commentary.

35 Weisser, 10-28; cf. P. Robiano, 'Apollonios de Tyane', in R. Goulet (ed.), *Dictionnaire des Philosophes Antiques*, i (Paris, 1989), 289–94.

36 *Sirr* I, 1–99; Weisser, 74–88.

37 *Sirr* I, 2.2.10, 26,1–27, 2; Weisser, 77.

38 *Sirr* I, 2.2.11, 28,7-9; Weisser, 77.

39 See C. Muckensturm, 'Cal(l)anus', in *Dictionnaire des Philosophes Antiques*, ii, 157–160.

40 *Sirr* I 3.6.1–3, 67,11–69,5; Weisser, 83.

41 See Ulrich Rudolph, 'Kalām im antiken Gewand: Das theologische Konzept des *Kitāb Sirr al-ḫalīqa*', in A. Fodor (ed.), *Proceedings of the 14th Congress of the Union Européenne des Arabisants et Islamisants* (The Arabist, Budapest Studies in Arabic, 13–14; Budapest, 1995), i, 123–136.

42 J. van Ess, 'Göttliche Allmacht im Zerrbild menschlicher Sprache', *Mélanges de l'Université Saint-Joseph*, 49 (1975), 651–88.

43 See W.K.C. Guthrie, *A History of Greek Philosophy*, ii (Cambridge, 1965), 39-43.

44 Idem, ii, 103-6.

45 For the most part these texts remain in manuscript form. For example, the manuscript Aya Sofya 2450, wherein the doxography of Pseudo-Ammonius is preserved contains another doxographic text which describes the opinions of the Greek philosophers on nature.

5

Islamic Medicine Crosspollinated: A Multilingual and Multiconfessional Maze

Peter E. Pormann

In his *Book of Misers*, the famous littérateur al-Jāḥiẓ (d. 868/9) portrays the Arab physician Asad ibn Jānī as lamenting the fact that he has no patients (and hence no income) because people only trust Christian and Jewish doctors.[1] When some fifty years later the caliph al-Muqtadir ordered that Jews and Christians not be admitted to public office, he excluded two areas: tax administration and medicine.[2] And the celebrated Islamic polymath of Iranian stock al-Bīrūnī, who was born in 973 on the Southern shores of the Aral sea and died shortly after 1050 in Ghazna (Eastern Afganistan), wrote an Arabic pharmacological treatise in which he had the following to say about his Greek predecessor Dioscorides:[3]

> Among the Greeks before the advent of Christianity there were men who distinguished themselves through their great zeal for research and their efforts to advance things to the highest degree and to bring them to perfection. If Dioscorides had lived in our region and had directed his efforts at knowing the things in our hills and valleys, the plants would have all become remedies, and their fruits would have been turned through his expertise into medicaments. Yet the land of the West (Maghrib) won through him and his likes, and, in its victory, let us have a share of the great and laudable scientific and practical benefits.

Al-Jāḥiẓ's anecdote, al-Muqtadir's order and al-Bīrūnī's praise in his preface all illustrate that the Arabic and Islamic medical tradition was heavily influenced by non-Arabic and non-Muslim elements. By the end of the eleventh century, this medical tradition had acquired so much fame and favour that it dominated the medical discourse not only in the Islamic lands, but also in the Christian West, where writings such as Ibn Sīnā's *Qānūn* were eagerly studied in Latin translation and even became university textbooks.

In the present contribution, I propose to investigate how Islamic medicine was shaped through intense crosspollination with ambient cultures and traditions, and how it, in its turn, fertilised the burgeoning university medicine of the Latin Middle Ages. The focus will not only be on medical theory, but also on practical and social aspects of Islamic health care. Institutions such as the newly founded hospitals in the ʿAbbāsid capital stand out as centres of multi-cultural mixing. To plot a course through the maze of different cultures and confessions, it is necessary to approach the subject from different angles. First, we shall look at the pre-Islamic and early Islamic ideas about health and disease, and contrast them with Greek concepts of the body and illness. It is against this background that the most important ambient cultures contributing to the formation of Islamic medicine will be discussed, namely the Syriac and Persian ones. In order to understand how the sophisticated health care provisions in Baghdad emerged from this melting-pot of cultures, it is useful to look at the role of imperial patronage and the contribution of court culture to the development of the arts and sciences. Moreover, to illustrate how crosspollination works in a concrete example, we shall, so to speak, enter the hospitals of Baghdad and see how different factors such as Greek theory and folk knowledge are combined, for instance, in the treatment of rabies. Finally, the impact of the Islamic medical tradition on the Latin West will be explored.

The single most important source for the manners and customs of pre-Islamic Arabs is their poetry. This poetry of the so-called *Jāhiliyya*, the 'time of ignorance' before the advent of Islam, became a model of style and a subject of study from the eighth century onwards, and the earliest extant collections date from this time. It is a subject of scholarly contention whether poems compiled in these collections reflect the linguistic forms used by their authors or whether they were later harmonised from a stylistic and dialectical point of view; regardless, it is safe to say that they illustrate the life of the desert-dwelling Bedouins with all their woes and worries, their wonders and wanderings.[4] Medical care was part of this life, and, by looking more closely at this literature, it is possible to gauge concepts of health and disease in pre-Islamic Arabia.[5]

One striking characteristic of these odes is the recurrence of many terms for a variety of maladies. Some common Arabic words such as *zukām* (cold), *suʿāl* (cough), *khunāq* (angina) and *kalab* (rabies) later become technical terms, employed in the medical literature.[6] Others such *qudād* (grumbling stomach) and *ʿaraj* (lameness) are vague and imprecise. Ophthalmological disorders seem to have been particularly common, and a number of names can be found in the early Arabic poetry. For instance, the word *ramad* (inflammation of the eye), already used in pre-Islamic times, later becomes a technical medical term for ophthalmia.[7] Another Arabic word for a medical condition is fever (*ḥummā*); it occurs, for instance, in a verse by al-Akhnas ibn Shihāb al-Taghlibī, a famous poet who lived in the second half of the sixth century.[8] He compares the heat of his passion for his absent lover to the delirium of feverish individuals in Khaybar, saying:[9]

> Daylong I stood there, while a tremor and burning heat swept over me, as a vehement hot fit comes on a sick man in Khaybar.

The scholion to this verse highlights a crucial aspect of concepts about health and disease in pre-Islamic Arabia, namely magic. The scholiast remarks that the oasis Khaybar was plagued by a chronic violent fever;[10] to protect themselves from it, people coming there would bray ten times like donkeys, because they believed that the fever could be tricked: it would not befall them, if it thought them to be animals.[11] Such apotropaic measures as well as magic in general were thought to be able to ward off disease; this can further be illustrated by the following verse:[12]

> I bestow upon him who is my adversary words which could even finish off the disease pleurisy (*kashaḥ*).[13]

Words used against the poet's foe are deemed to be particularly powerful if they can dispel disease. Priestesses (*kawāhin*), too, appear to have treated people by using both magic and medicinal herbs (*busūm*).[14] And magical spells (*ruqā*) and 'physicians (*ṭabāʾib*)' are two things able to avert death according to another pre-Islamic poet.[15] However, one should not imagine that these 'physicians' were sophisticated medical practitioners; rather, the word *ṭabīb* is etymologically linked to *maṭbūb*, meaning 'enchanted', so that medicine and magic seem to have been closely connected.[16]

However, magic was not the only method used to treat patients. Cupping and cautery as well as some simple remedies, such as camel urine reduced through boiling, are mentioned. The following verses by the famous poet al-Burayq ibn ʿIyād (fl. *c.*600–630)[17] are interesting for a number of reasons:

> Many a wailing woman have I sent away, when the Mirzam[18] rose,/ who wailed, whilst probing the wound so that her palm and wrist disappeared [in the wound],/ [the wound] of a man, whose head is bent and whose wounds exhaled blood,/ [a woman] who separated his joints with a probe (*mīl*) as the comb separates the hair hanging down.[19]

In this passage, the poet boasts of the many women who wail because their male relatives or friends have been wounded by him, proudly claiming to have forced his adversaries to flee while being treated by their womenfolk. In tending to the injuries sustained during battle, the women apparently resort to a primitive form of surgery, since they use a probe to set the joints right. This probe is called *mīl* in Arabic, which is a Greek loan (from *mēlē*, 'probe'),[20] and later becomes a technical term for probe in the medical literature.[21] We therefore see that, at least at some level, even bedouin medical practice, simple and rudimentary as it might have been, employed certain instruments which had Greek names.

Women are specifically singled out as those treating patients, whether by using magic as priestesses or by performing first aid and employing simple surgery as a member of the wounded warrior's family. They are also called by the feminine form of an term for physician (*āsin*), derived from Aramaic *asyā*[22] as in the following verse by Qays ibn al-Khatīm (fl. *c.*600):[23]

> It is of no importance to me that his (i.e. of the son of ʿAbd al-Qays, the poet's adversary) wounds make the eyes of the female physicians (*awāsin*, sg. *āsiya*) turn away, for I praise the affliction they bring.

This verse reminds us, of course, of those by al-Burayq ibn ʿIyād quoted above: in both cases, women are portrayed as treating wounds. However, men are also called *āsin*, as a verse by the poet Muzarrid, a contemporary of Qays ibn al-Khatīm, demonstrates:[24]

> I should have delivered a smashing blow on the Son of Thawb that would have knocked him senseless, at the sight of which every physician (*āsin*) and sick-nurse (*ʿāʾid*, lit. 'someone who visits a patient') would have wailed in [despair].

The picture which emerges from this short survey is that of medical practice in pre-Islamic times being quite rudimentary and often associated with magic. It was typical for women to treat their male relations, and they were called *āsiya* (physician) and *kāhina* (priestess). The first is an Aramaic term, and points to the vocabulary of medicine containing even at this early time non-Arabic elements. Another case in point is the *mīl*, the Greek-derived word for probe, which a woman uses to perform minor surgery. Here, too, the foreign influence seems visible. In the concepts of fever, however, superstition was prevalent.

In stark contrast to these rather basic ideas and methods, the Greek tradition had developed a sophisticated medical system. In the Hippocratic treatise *On the Nature of Man*, written in the fourth century BCE, the author proposes a conception of health and disease which was to dominate medical theory not only for centuries but for millennia to come.[25] It is that of humoral pathology, or the notion that health consists in the balance of the four humours (blood, phlegm, yellow bile and black bile), and that their imbalance results in disease.[26] As this theory expanded, each of these humours was in turn linked to two of the four cardinal qualities, wet or dry, and hot or cold; to one of the four elements; to one of the four seasons; to one of the four ages of man; to one of the four cardinal organs (heart, brain, spleen and liver); and to one of the four natural types of character (melancholic, choleric, sanguine, and phlegmatic). Diseases would be cured and health recovered when the humoral imbalance was restored by removing excessive humours and replenishing deficient ones. This was said to be achieved through a variety of means such as diet, exercise, cupping, venesection, vomiting and so on. The underlying principle of treatment was that of *contraria contrariis curantur* (opposites are cured by opposites). Simple drugs, for instance, were arranged by Galen into different classes according to their drying and moistening, their cooling and warming qualities. If the patient was too hot and dry, a cooling and moistening drug is prescribed and vice versa. This theory, as mentioned, first appeared in the treatise *On the Nature of Man*, part of the Hippocratic Corpus, a collection of writings by different authors mostly composed between 420 and 350 BCE. But it was Galen (129–*c*.216 CE) who really put humoral pathology on the map and made it into the dominant, if not the sole explanation of health and disease. Most subsequent Greek medical authors followed his lead and adopted his theoretical approach.

Another important characteristic of the Greek medical tradition is the search for causal explanations of health and illness. The Hippocratic treatise *On the Sacred Disease* had already rejected the notion that epilepsy is brought about by the Gods, and offered an interpretation in terms of humours.[27] This insistence on knowing the hidden causes of diseases is particularly prevalent in Galen. In his *On the Sects for Beginners*, he argues ferociously against the empiricist, that is to say physicians who rely solely on experience in order to treat patients without trying to explain how and why the malady has come about. Galen was consequently of the opinion *That the Best Physician Is Also a Philosopher*, as he himself explains in a treatise thus entitled.[28] The link between philosophy and medicine grew stronger in Late Antiquity. Neoplatonism with its tendency to combine and harmonise the views of Plato and Aristotle was the dominant philosophy, and in many medical texts of the time reflections of this philosophy are visible. For instance, the four Aristotelian causes (formal, material, final, effective) are used to explain disease patterns. Division into an ever increasing number of parts, a method known as *diæresis*, emerges as an important analytical as well as didactic tool.[29] Such divisions are often represented in form of branch diagrams, presumably as a mnemonic device.[30]

These aspects of the medical ideology of Late Antiquity, which O. Temkin had aptly called Galenism,[31] virtually dominated medical discourse at least in the Greek speaking world. They were, however, particularly salient in late antique Alexandria, which, by the middle of the sixth century, had become the major centre for the study of medicine. It was here that this approach to medicine was perpetuated in many commentaries, abridgments and encyclopaedias, which, in turn, were to have a lasting influence on the Islamic tradition. These commentaries and abridgments often originated from the medical teaching which took place in the many so-called *akadēmiai* (academies) and *mouseia* (museums, i.e. philosophical schools-cum-libraries); the famous Alexandrian library had long been destroyed.[32] The teaching concentrated on a canon of *Sixteen Books of Galen*, deemed to be particularly appropriate for students; this canon included many of the writings which Galen himself had singled out for teaching purposes. Everyone had to study Galen's *On the Sects for Beginners* first, followed by the *Art of Medicine* (*Small Art*), *On the Pulse for Beginners* and *Therapeutics to Glauco*.[33] However, since these Galenic textbooks were thought to be too difficult, or to require additional explanation, they were abridged and commented upon; a product of this activity are the famous *Alexandrian Summaries*.[34] Apart from these commentaries and abridgments, closely linked to medical instruction, another genre became increasingly popular in late antique Alexandria: the medical encyclopaedia. One author who wrote such a work was the seventh century Alexandrian physician Paul of Aegina; his *pragmateia* (handbook) had a significant impact on Syriac and Arabic authors, and helped shape the Islamic medical literature to no small degree.[35]

This was possible because Hellenism in general and Greek medicine in particular were not limited to those reading Greek. Greek thought transcended the boundaries of languages through translation. This happened, for instance, when Greek philosophy was translated into Latin, but also when Greek medical writings were adapted and adopted by a host of different cultures on the Eastern shores of the Mediterranean. Syriac and Persian cultures are two such examples which are of particular interest to us here, since they formed the background against which the Islamic empire was to appear.

It is apparent that the Syriac tradition helped shape the Arabic one to a large extent, for later Arabic sources contain a significant amount of information on Syriac medicine, which, in its turn, is largely based on Galenic medical theory. Despite its great importance for the development of Islamic medicine, there are very few extant original texts which would allow us to assess the exact content of Syriac medical theory. Moreover, Syriac historical sources mostly talk about physicians in an ecclesiastic or monastic context; there are no secular contemporaneous writings about medical history. This makes the interpretation of the evidence quite difficult.[36]

These caveats aside, it is possible to trace a preliminary picture of Syriac medical theory, and, to a lesser extent, practice. Syriac is an Aramaic dialect which became the language of a number of Christian communities in the Levant, Mesopotamia and Persia. The two main rival confessions using Syriac as their liturgical language are the so-called Jacobites and Nestorians, living mostly under Byzantine and Persian rule respectively until the advent of Islam. As early as the second century, translations from Greek, which constituted an important part of Syriac literary activity, were producded; one of the first such translations was the Syriac version of the Bible, the Peshitta (literally 'vulgate'), which is at the core of Syriac literature in general. Soon afterwards, a significant number of theological treatises were rendered into Syriac.[37] It is therefore not surprising that the Syriac tradition, steeped in Christian Hellenism, also turned its interest to Greek philosophical and medical texts.[38] As mentioned above, Alexandria was a centre of learning for both these subjects. Since Jacobite and Nestorian strongholds such as Edessa and Nisibis were well connected through trade roads to Alexandria, Syriac intellectuals often travelled there to study, and brought sophisticated Greek culture back to their own home towns. As a result, many philosophical texts, especially Aristotle's logical works (the *Organon*), and a significant amount of Greek medical writers were translated into Syriac. The most important translator of Hippocrates and Galen was Sergius of Rēsh ʿAynā (a city situated approximately half way between Edessa and Nisibis, and called Raʾs al-ʿAyn in Arabic). A Jacobite priest living in the sixth century, he exemplifies the link between the Syriac medical tradition and Alexandria: having studied medicine and philosophy there, he returned home to translate as many as thirty-two Galenic treatises.[39] Among the translations of Galenic writings which he prepared, we find all the so-called *Sixteen Books of Galen* already mentioned. His choice is, therefore, determined quite significantly by the Alexandrian medical curriculum.[40] But also in his choice of philosophical texts to be translated, he was influenced by this city: he rendered the *Categories* of Aristotle and the *Isagoge* (*Introduction*) of Porphyry into Syriac, which were philosophical core textbooks. His interests demonstrate again the close link between medicine and philosophy developed in Late Antiquity. Sergius' Syriac translations were in wide circulation among the Syriac-reading intellectual elite, at least until the ninth century. Yet, for all their popularity, they are now largely lost, partly because they were superseded by Ḥunayn ibn Isḥāq's renderings.[41]

For a direct impression of Syriac medical writing it is therefore necessary to turn to the so-called *Syriac Book of Medicines*, an anonymous medical treatise in three books first edited by E. A. W. Budge,[42] for it represents the most important extant Syriac medical work. There is a certain amount of debate as to when and where it was written; but even if it was compiled as late as the thirteenth century, it certainly includes much older material, some probably dating back to the sixth century.[43] In its present form, it is, to a large extent, a pastiche of Greek medical theory. There are notably many episodes related in the first person, which are unacknowledged quotations rather than the author's own remarks; this has caused some scholars to arrive at incorrect conclusions, thinking that the 'I' in the text referred to the author rather than his source.[44] As for the content, the *Syriac Book of Medicines* is divided into three parts, the first dealing with diseases from tip to toe and the second with medical astrology, and the third being a collection of recipes, many containing dubious folk remedies quite different from the more scientific outlook present in the other parts of the work. For instance, the ophthalmology set out in part one is based on Greek humoral pathology, physiology and therapeutics. In its approach, however, it is more influenced by late Alexandrian models, rather than Galen himself, as Barbara Zipser and Klaus-Dietrich Fischer have shown in a recent article.[45]

We therefore see that Syriac medical theory, as it appears to us in our limited sources, is truly Galenic, even if it does not always follow Galen to the letter; it reflects the prevalent interpretation of Galen in late antique Alexandria. In the organisation of health care, however, the Eastern Christian tradition in general, and the Jacobite and Nestorian denominations in particular display some innovation when compared to the late antique Greek models they inherited. Timothy Miller has argued that quite sophisticated hospitals, some incorporating medical centres of learning, were invented in the Byzantine Empire, but he has rightly been taken to task for this assessment.[46] The Christian charitable tradition clearly introduced something novel into the medical equation: the Christian hospice. This institution was a place where the poor and the needy, travellers and pilgrims could find rest and shelter for the night or for longer spells of time. They were often linked to monasteries, and were always religious in character. In some, the emphasis was not only on caring, but also curing. On the evidence of monastic rules, preserved not in the original, but in later, amended, versions, scholars have assumed that a medical school, at least partly separate from the monastery, developed in Nisibis, and have interpreted this as the beginning of a secular medical education within the Christian context.[47] But, owing to the brevity and vagueness of these texts, our knowledge of how medicine was taught there remains elusive; moreover, in these institutions, the medical sciences and their teaching were deemed to be inferior to the religious ones.

In Islamic times, many Nestorian Christians were associated with the city of Jundaysābūr. There are legends that this city had a medical academy-cum-hospital as early as the fourth century, but these myths have been dispelled by recent scholarship.[48] This said, there is no doubt that by the end of the eighth century, this city, which was founded by the Sasanian emperor Shāpūr I, had attained high fame for its medical learning. Given its Persian background, it invites us to look at the medical tradition in Sasanian Persia, the other ambient culture in which Islam was to emerge.

Like Syriac culture, Persian culture in general, and the Sasanian medical tradition in particular, was profoundly influenced by Greek ideas, which were to filter into the Islamic tradition.[49] Paul Kunitzsch has argued that Pahlavi translations from Greek were both numerous and important for the transmission of Greek thought into the Arabic world.[50] Pahlavi medicine bears substantial marks of Greek influence, although many indigenous elements are also prevalent. There are two important texts containing sections on Persian medicine, namely the *Dēnkard* and the *Wizīdagīhā ī Zādsparam*. The former is a tenth century Pahlavi compilation on Mazdaean (i.e. Zoroastrian) religion and culture in nine books; book three is of particular interest to us, since it contains chapters on science and medicine.[51] The latter is an anthology, also written in Pahlavi and probably dating from the ninth century; it, too, has important sections dealing with medicine.[52] Both these texts were written during the ʿAbbāsid period, but clearly contain earlier Pahlavi material; they therefore illustrate Persian ideas about health and disease in pre-Islamic times. Without going into any great detail, the picture which emerges from these two sources is a mixed one, thereby reflecting the crosspollination of ideas. On the one hand, Mazdaean concepts of body and soul are clearly visible. On the other hand, Greek ideas of humoral pathology and other fundamental concepts such as the four cardinal qualities (warm – cold; dry – moist) are part of the theoretical framework. J. Hampel has characterised this fusion of traditions in the following way, quoting a difficult passage from the *Dēnkard*: '... the roots of medicine are found in Greek learning, while the doctrine and synopsis (*zayč*) are derived from Iranian wisdom.'[53] Greek influence in Pahlavi therefore manifests itself on two levels: first, there are Pahlavi translations of Greek texts which were later rendered into Arabic; and second, Pahlavi medical thought itself displays strong traces of Greek concepts.

It is therefore evident that Greek thought influenced the ambient cultures in the context of which Islam was to emerge, especially with regards to medicine: pre-Islamic poetry contains Greek and Aramaic loan words, and both the Syriac and Pahlavi medical traditions are profoundly influenced by Greek ideas. To put it differently, the dominant medical ideology not only in Byzantium and Alexandria, but also in the Syriac and Persian traditions was Galenism. And Galenism was only one aspect of more general Hellenistic trends present not only in philosophy and the sciences, but also in literature and popular culture.[54] It is therefore not surprising that many of the conquering Arabs took Greek models as paradigms in many different areas, such as art and architecture.[55]

The field of medicine stands out as an area in which the Arabs espoused Greek theory nearly completely. This wholesale absorption was possible only through a vast translation movement, although the general climate of Hellenistic influence in the Syriac and Persian cultures also played a role. The first Arabic renderings of Greek works appeared in the late eighth century, some of them produced or at least supervised by the Nestorian patriarch Timothy I (728–823).[56] Many of the most important medical texts were translated by Ḥunayn ibn Isḥāq (808–873 or 877), a pupil of Yūḥannā ibn Māsawayh; Ḥunayn ibn Isḥāq surpassed his master and created a circle around himself which included his son Isḥāq ibn Ḥunayn and his nephew Ḥubaysh ibn al-Ḥasan al-Aʿsam. They were all Nestorian Christians, that is to say, people well versed in Syriac language and literature. In that sense, they continue a tradition of Syriac Hellenism discussed above. Yet, as Dimitri Gutas plainly shows, it is a misconception to imagine that the translation movement, culminating in the work of Ḥunayn ibn Isḥāq's circle, was merely a prolongation of previous Syriac translation activity.[57] Ḥunayn ibn Isḥāq's own account of how he rendered the works of Galen, known simply as his *risāla* (epistle), explicitly sets out why and for whom he translated them.[58] Two important trends emerge: 1) The ʿAbbāsid elite commissioned most of these translations; 2) Ḥunayn ibn Isḥāq and his circle produced the vast majority of Syriac renderings of Galenic works. But his *risāla* also illustrates that he and his contemporaries drew extensively on the Alexandrian tradition of Late Antiquity when formulating ideas about teaching and studying medicine. In the entry on Galen's *De methodo medendi* (On the Method of Healing), Ḥunayn ibn Isḥāq remarks:[59]

> These are the books which were read exclusively at the place of medical instruction in Alexandria. They (sc. the Alexandrians) used to read them in the order just mentioned, and gathered each day to read and interpret one of the main works, just as our contemporary Christians gather at the places of learning known as *uskūl* ('school', from Greek *scholē*) each day in order to study one main book, be it by the Ancients or be it a different book. They (the Alexandrians) used to read [the other books by Galen] individually, each on its own, after they had been instructed in these books which we have just mentioned, just like our contemporaries read the commentaries of the ancients.

Galenism was therefore taught and studied through the prism of late antique Alexandria. Yet, the influence of the Alexandrian tradition is not limited to medical instruction. It also made great strides in describing diseases and prescribing medication, as can be seen in the work of the Alexandrian physician and encyclopaedist Paul of Aegina whose work constitutes an important milestone in the development of the genre of the medical encyclopaedia.[60] Like most Galenic works, Paul of Aegina became available in Arabic through the good efforts of Ḥunayn ibn Isḥāq himself, or someone with a similar translation style, most likely a member of his circle.

It is therefore evident that the Arabic translations of Greek medical texts, prepared by Nestorian Christians for their patrons who were, for the most part, members of the ʿAbbāsid elite, constitute a cornerstone of Islamic medicine as it developed in the ninth century. A similar crosspollination of cultures and traditions is evident when looking at another major factor in the provision of health care in the ʿAbbāsid empire, namely the Islamic hospital.[61] Both the Byzantine and Syriac traditions shared charitable concepts of caring for the poor and the needy. On the basis of these ideas, they set up hospices called *xenodocheia* (*ξενοδοχεῖα*, Greek, literally: 'places where one receives strangers') and later *bīmāristānāt* (Persian, literally: 'place of the sick'). The idea of charity also constituted a strong motivation for establishing Islamic hospitals, which were often endowed by means of a *waqf*, a pious trust defined in Islamic law. However, while the Christian hospices never played a major role in health care for the high society or in elite medical learning, research and teaching, Islamic hospitals, founded and funded mostly by members of the ʿAbbāsid courts, moved to centre stage. Unlike their earlier Christian counterparts, these hospitals were secular in orientation: members of various religious backgrounds were admitted both as patients and practitioners, and some high-ranking individuals of non-Arab and non-Islamic backgrounds helped run a number of the most famous early Islamic hospitals. For instance, ʿAlī ibn ʿĪsā, the vizier of al-Muqtadir (reg. 908–932), who oversaw the good governance and construction of various hospitals, was a pious Muslim of Nestorian and Persian stock. Shaghab, who was originally a Greek slave girl but later gained great renown and influence because she gave birth to the future caliph al-Muqtadir, endowed a hospital known as that 'of the Lady (*al-Sayyida*)'. Sinān ibn Thābit ibn Qurra, a Ṣābiʾan of Ḥarrān (Carrhae), administered hospitals and was commissioned by ʿAlī ibn ʿĪsā to help oversee other areas of public health; and al-Rāzī, of Persian origin and born in Rayy, directed hospitals both in his native town and in the capital Baghdad. The cosmopolitan melting pot of Baghdad thus provided a fertile ground for crosspollination by people of many creeds and cultures. This can be seen not only from the external history of the Islamic hospital – in the sense that patrons and practitioners from all sorts of backgrounds were involved in the foundation and management of these institutions –, but also from the medical practices within these hospitals, which will reveal an interesting fusion of diverse concepts.

Sources for our knowledge of Islamic medical theory are extremely plentiful.[62] We have numerous treatises, monographs and encyclopaedias in which the authors set out proper medical practice. These, however, are mainly theoretical and prescriptive works; Arabic medical manuals describing actual practice are much rarer.[63] This said, there are a number of sources for the Islamic medieval period which are particularly rich in information about how physicians really carried out their duties. For instance, al-Rāzī's *Kitāb al-ḥāwī* (*Encompassing Book*, known in Latin as *Liber Continens*) includes a number of case-notes, already edited by Max Meyerhof in the 1930s.[64] Cristina Álvarez-Millán has illustrated that

Rāzī's *Kitāb al-tajārib* (*Book of Experiences*) is a rich mine of information on the author's performance as a practitioner. Unfortunately, neither set of these case-notes contains direct references to hospital practice. By contrast, however, the *Kunnāsh* (*Handbook*) by al-Kaskarī combines Greek medical theory, in both acknowledged and unacknowledged quotes, with practical experience, which the author gained in a variety of hospitals around the 920s and 930s.[65] To give just one example: when discussing rabies, he draws on Greek authors such as Galen, Paul of Aegina, and Rufus of Ephesus. He employed the first two to give a concise account of Greek medical theory on the subject. Rufus, however, fulfils an additional purpose, as can be seen from the following anecdote which al-Kaskarī reproduces from the treatise *On Buying Slaves* (*Peri andrapodismou*). A man sold a slave girl who had been bitten by a rabid dog without realising that the disease was incubating; when it finally broke out, the buyer had to return her for a refund. This story is told to illustrate the point, made by Galen and Paul of Aegina, that one should not allow a wound inflicted by an animal to heal, but rather keep it open and clean it. An additional reason for citing it here, however, is the importance of slave-trade as an economic activity in tenth century Baghdad.[66] In this case, the choice of quoting Rufus is determined not only by the desire to set out the content of Greek medical theory, but also to make it relevant to the readers of the time.

As far as treatment is concerned, al-Kaskarī sometimes departs from his Greek models. For example, he takes the recipe for Archigenes' *hiera* (*ἱερὰ Ἀρχιγένους*)[67] at the end of the chapter from the *Small Dispensatory* (*al-Aqrābādhīn al-ṣaghīr*) by Sābūr ibn Sahl, a Christian physician and pharmacologist (d. 869) from Jundaysābūr.[68] Al-Kaskarī himself stated at the beginning of his work that he would draw on this *Small Dispensatory*, and we know from a different, late tenth century source that Sābūr ibn Sahl's work was popular in hospitals.[69] No less interesting than the written sources are the oral accounts about rabid camels which al-Kaskarī reports:[70]

> 6 (1) I was also told that camels are sometimes stricken by rabies during the violent heat, so that they become rabid, and bite [other] camels. (2) Then the bitten camels are afraid of water and do not drink any so that they die. (3) If a camel which previously had rabies is killed, or dies, and [other] camels eat its meat, they become rabid.

Since camels were not too common on the Greek mainland, they do not figure prominently in the Greek medical literature. The situation is, of course, quite different in Arabia. Therefore, as this quotation shows, al-Kaskarī goes beyond his sources and endeavours to incorporate into his *Handbook* information that is potentially of great relevance for his audience. In summary, one can say that al-Kaskarī's chapter 'On Rabies' combines information from different sources. He chooses Greek medical theory according to his own and his audience's interests, as is evident in the case of the quotation from *On Buying Slaves*. He also uses contemporary information, be it written, like the standard pharmacological text by a Nestorian Christian of Persian descent, be it oral, as in the tales about possible means of transmission in camels, the beasts of burden par excellence in the Arab heartland. This mixture of Greek theory, Persian pharmacology and Arab folk experiences exemplifies the mingling of different traditions in the medical practice of a tenth century physician in Baghdad.

Let us consider two more interesting instances where al-Kaskarī relates his own personal experience. In the first case, al-Kaskarī confirms Greek theoretical learning by his own observation, saying in the chapter 'On Cramps and Trembling':[71]

> A spasm which occurs because of injury is a sign for [imminent] death, as Hippocrates said in his *Book of Aphorisms*.[72] I once saw a group of thieves whose hands and feet were cut off in the hospital.[73] Their limbs became spasmodic because of the amputation. Not a single one of them was saved from death.

Hippocrates, perceived as the legendary father of medicine and the greatest authority on the subject, is not merely accepted as such at face value; rather, al-Kaskarī observes for himself and confirms (as in this case) or rejects Greek medical theory. One might say that his practice was the touchstone for the theory on which he based his medical ideas, as he himself states:[74]

> I for my part only consider valid those things which I have used and proved by experience (*jarrabtuhū*) ...

The second example is that of al-Kaskarī's tending to slave women; he reports:[75]

> In the palace of al-ʿAlawī there was a slave girl who had pimples on her face. Therefore, I wanted to make her gain weight in order to cleanse her face of the pimples. I gave her grain seeds to drink according to the following recipe:
>
> Grains, half a *riṭl* (as dry measure, 'half' becomes 'quarter'). I mixed it with sesame flour, one *riṭl*; I did not crush the grain. I mixed with it half a *riṭl* white sugar. She [sc. the patient] was eating five dirham of it every day for a fortnight, while her meals consisted of *isfīdabāj* meat. On this diet she put on weight. Sometimes it [sc. the meat] was baked together with bread, after *karmān* cumin[76] has been added. From it one can make buns [*gharīf*] and dry them in an oven. Crush it and drink it together with the crumbs.

This remark illustrates a number of points, also apparent from other passages in the *Kunnāsh*. Firstly, it presents further evidence for the importance of slavery at the court of the caliphs. In this example, al-Kaskarī paid special attention to the well-being of slaves, whilst, when discussing rabies, he specifically quoted from Rufus' manual *On Buying Slaves*. Secondly, it demonstrates that al-Kaskarī frequented the palaces of the powerful; the circles in which he moved seem to be those of high society.[77] More important for our discussion is another aspect. Al-Kaskarī gives a recipe and then says that, when taking it, one should eat *isfīdabāj*. This term is a combination of two Persian words, *isfīd* (white) and *bāj* (something to eat), thereby denoting a sort of *blancmange*, a whitish stew of meat and other ingredients.[78] *Isfīdabāj* was a humble dish, and it is revealing that popular food here supplements a treatment based on Greek humoral pathology.

The ninth and tenth centuries were the most formative period for the Islamic medical tradition. It was then that virtually all medical literature available in Greek was translated into Arabic, in some cases with a Syriac intermediary translation also being prepared. It was also a time when the medical works of Syriac authors such as Ibn Sarābiyūn (second half of the ninth century) were translated into Arabic,[79] and when Nestorian Christians writing pharmacological treatises in Arabic, like Sābūr ibn Sahl, contributed to the formation of a medical canon on which subsequent traditions would draw for centuries to come. We also know of Indian medical works rendered into Arabic, often via Persian, but their influence, like that of Persian medicine itself, was mostly felt in the area of *materia medica*.[80] Plants and herbs unknown in the lands of the Greeks were imported into the Islamic world from the four quarters of the globe, and especially the Far East; they were then incorporated into the Arabic pharmacopœias.

Our picture of the genesis of Islamic medicine would be incomplete, however, were we to ignore the medical folklore in the Arab lands. Even in pre-Islamic times, there never was a pure Arabic medical tradition, since the ambient cultures contributed to the rudimentary medical techniques. Likewise, the idea that the 'Medicine of the Prophet (*Ṭibb al-nabī*)' was composed solely of Islamic concepts, pious, pure and unpolluted by foreign elements is unfounded.[81] On the contrary, Galenic ideas such as humoral pathology trickled down into the popular imagination and are found even in cooking recipes.[82] Conversely, popular dishes such as the *isfīdabāj* (blancmange) were used in medical contexts where Greek theory generally dominated. On an institutional level, we saw that the Islamic hospital was a product of intense crosspollination. Set up, funded and directed by people of various backgrounds, it was influenced by earlier Christian charitable ideas, but was also radically transformed and made into something new, even revolutionary, in the provision of health care. This fusion of the manifold cultures present in the melting pot of Baghdad in the ninth and tenth centuries could not have occurred without this congenial and tolerant environment, in which people of diverse creeds and cultures lived and worked side by side, even if some tensions between the communities did exist.[83]

This is not the place to discuss the development of medieval Islamic medicine in all its ramifications.[84] Yet, it is useful briefly to evoke some trends in the evolution of Islamic medicine in order to show how this tradition, itself the result of intense crosspollination, fertilised and shaped medieval European medicine. Three Arabic medical works became especially important for the evolution of medical ideas in the Latin tradition: the *Royal Book* (al-*kitāb al-malakī*) by al-Majūsī (known in Latin as Haly Abbas, d. before 995), hailing from a Persian family of Zoroastrian persuasion as his name ('al-Majūsī', the Mazdaean) suggests;[85] the *Canon of Medicine* (*Qānūn fī 'l-ṭibb*) by Ibn Sīnā (Avicenna, 980–1037), a famous Persian physician and philosopher;[86] and the *Taṣrīf* by al-Zahrāwī (Albucasis, d. 1009 [?]), an Andalusian practitioner.[87] All three works have certain features in common: they are medical encyclopaedias, and thus continued a medical genre popularised through the writings of such luminaries as Paul of Aegina and Ibn Sarābiyūn. In some ways, they constitute summaries and systemisations of the medical theory of their time, often drawing on the previous Greek, Syriac and Arabic medical traditions. As mainly theoretical works, they neglect the practical aspects of health care, which fall by the wayside. The divergent background of these encyclopaedias further illustrates the cosmopolitan nature of the medical and scientific community in the medieval Islamic world. Through Latin translations made in Toledo (Spain), Salerno (Italy), and Antioch (Syria), these encyclopedias became available in Christian lands. They were eagerly read, debated, abbreviated and commented upon. Moreover their inclusion into the medical curriculum of the nascent European universities such as Montpellier, Oxford and Paris ensured their lasting impact on the development of medicine in the West.[88] One of the Latin authors who relied heavily on these translations was the renowned thirteenth century French surgeon Guy de Chauliac, who used the thirtieth book of al-Zahrāwī's *Taṣrīf* (which is in itself a large compendium on surgery) extensively in his *Chirurgia Magna*.[89] Apart from this transmission of ideas through texts and translations, there was also oral exchange in places of contact between Muslims and Christians, such as the Crusader States.[90] Even in the sixteenth century, when the Renaissance and the return to the 'pure sources' of Greek learning was in full swing, Avicenna's *Canon of Medicine* enjoyed immense popularity, and continued to serve as the most important textbook of all university medical students.[91] Arabic medical teaching in its Latin garb did, however, come under increasing attack, and demands to purge the European medical tradition of all things Arabic constantly grew. This development resulted in a conscious rejection of the Islamic elements in the Western medical heritage, and few physicians today realise to what extent the Islamic tradition is part of 'our' legacy.[92]

In the present political and ideological climate, we hear much about the clash of civilisations, and more specifically the antagonism between the Judaeo-Christian and the Islamic civilisations.[93] This question, to be sure, was already broached and eagerly debated nearly a century ago. The German Orientalist C. H. Becker took the philosopher E. Troeltsch to task for thinking that Islam and the West belong to two different cultural zones (or '*Kulturkreise*'); rather, Becker argued, because of their constant mutual intercourse on a variety of levels, they belong together, and therefore, their histories cannot be investigated separately.[94] In the late fifties of the last century, J. Kraemer made a case similar to Becker's, highlighting more specifically the Graeco-Arabic translation movement, which was so important in shaping the Islamic intellectual tradition.[95] In this contribution, we have seen that the Arabo-Islamic world was constantly influenced by surrounding cultures. From pre-Islamic times when women healers went by the Aramaic term for 'physician', *āsiya*, and used Greek loan words, to the heyday of cosmopolitan culture in the ʿAbbāsid capital where people from a great array of backgrounds came together to forge an exciting metropolitan medical tradition; from the shore of the Aral Sea and the lands of the Persian East, whence many of the most famous physicians of Islam hail, to the Christian courts where Arabic medical lore was translated into Latin, we see a constant interchange of culture between East and West, without which medicine, whether in Cordova or Cologne, Cairo or Calcutta, would never have been the same. The essentialist position that Islam and the West are by nature opposed to, and in conflict with, each other flies in the face of the evidence reviewed here of profound crosspollination in the area of medicine.

Notes

1 Al-Jāḥiẓ, *Kitāb al-bukhalāʾ*, ed. G. van Vloten (Leiden, 1900), 109–10, ed. Ṭ. al-Ḥājirī (Dhakhīrat al-ʿArab, 23; Cairo, 1958), 103; *The Book of Misers*, trans. R.B. Serjeant, reviewed by E. Ibrahim (Reading, 1997), 86; quoted below, 149.

2 Ibn Taghrībirdī, *Al-Nujūm al-zāhira fī mulūk Miṣr wa'l-Qāhira (The Stars Shining on the Kings of Egypt and Cairo)*, ed. M.Ḥ. Shams al-Dīn, 16 vols. (Beirut, 1992), iii, 183, ult.–184, 2; cf. M. van Berkel, *Accountants and Men of Letters: Status and Position of Civil Servants in the Early Tenth Century Baghdad*, Academisch Proefschrift (Amsterdam, 2003), 84.

3 Al-Bīrūnī, *Kitāb al-ṣaydana fī 'l-ṭibb (On Materia Medica)*, ed. ʿA. Zaryāb (Tehran, 1991), 12, 10–15; previously edited by M. Meyerhof, 'Das Vorwort zur Drogenkunde des Bērūnī', *Quellen und Studien zur Geschichte der Naturwissenschaften und der Medizin*, 3 (1933), 157–205 and 18 pages of Arabic text, 12, 5–10 of the Arabic text.

4 The question of the authenticity of pre-Islamic poetry has been heavily debated ever since

Ṭaha Ḥusayn published his influential work *Fī 'l shi'r al-jāhilī* (*On Poetry during the Jāhiliyya*) (Cairo, 1926); cf. A. Jones, *Early Arabic Poetry*, 2 vols. (Reading, 1992–96), i, 17–25.

5 A short, but interesting and influential account can be found in the section entitled 'Krankheiten und Heilmethoden (Diseases and Therapies)' of G. Jacob, *Altarabisches Beduinenleben nach den Quellen geschildert* (Berlin, ²1897), 154–8; see also M. Ullmann, *Die Medizin im Islam* (HdO 1. Abt., Erg. 6.1; Leiden, 1970), ch. 1 ('Die altarabische Heilkunde [Ancient Arabic Medicine]'), 15–24, on which many of the following remarks are based.

6 For the use of *kalab* both in Arabic poetry and later in technical medical texts, see M. Ullmann (ed.), *Wörterbuch der Klassischen Arabischen Sprache* (henceforth: *WKAS*) (Wiesbaden, 1955–), i, 310a 28–311a 11 and 573a 14–21.

7 Cf. O. Kahl, 'Ramad', *EI*².

8 *GAS*, ii, 149–50.

9 C.J. Lyall (ed.), *The Mufaḍḍalīyāt: an Anthology of Ancient Arabian Odes*, 3 vols. (Oxford, 1918–24), nº 41, 2.

10 Ibid., i, 411, 10: '*wa-innamā khaṣṣa Khaybara li'anna ḥummāhā ashaddu 'l-ḥummā* (he specifically talks about Khaybar since the fever there is the most violent)'.

11 See al-Qazwīnī, *'Ajā'ib al-makhlūqāt wa-gharā'ib al-mawjūdāt*, ed. F. Wüstenfeld: *Zakarija Ben Muhammed Ben Mahmud el-Cazwini's Kosmographie*, 2 vols. (Göttingen, 1848–9), ii, 60, 5–7.

12 R. Geyer, *Gedichte von 'Abû Baṣîr Maimûn ibn Qais al-'Aš'â, nebst Sammlungen von Stücken anderer Dichter des gleichen Beinamens und von al-Musayyab ibn Àlas* (London, 1928), nº 36, 55; quoted and translated in Ullmann, *Medizin* (as in n. 5), 17.

13 Cf. *WKAS* (as in n. 6), s.v., i, 207a 36–40 and 268b 5–6.

14 This can be inferred from the poet Aktham ibn Ṣayfī saying: 'Our people were informed that we are indeed doomed, and that the priestresses (*kawāhin*) and the medicinal herbs (*busūm*, from syr. *besmā*; cf. S. Fraenkel, *Die aramäischen Fremdwörter im Arabischen* [Leiden, 1886], 261), are powerless', edited by I. Goldziher, *Abhandlungen zur arabischen Philologie*, 2 vols. (Leiden, 1896–99), ii, 16, l. 9; see also ibid., ii, xv, n. 1.

15 J.G.L. Kosegarten (ed.), *The Poems of the Huzailis (Collected by Assukkari)* (London, 1854), n. 2, 3.

16 Cf. Fraenkel, *Aramäischen Fremdwörter* (as in n. 14), 260 and Ibn al-'Anbārī, *Kitāb al-aḍdād*, ed. E. Houtsma: *Kitābo'l-Adhdād sive Liber de vocabulis arabicis quae plures habent significationes inter se oppositas* ... (Leiden, 1881), 150–51; see also M.W. Dols, *Majnūn: the Madman in Medieval Islamic Society* (Oxford, 1992), 262.

17 *GAS*, ii, 130–2.

18 Mirzam is a common name for three stars, β Canis Maioris, β Canis Minoris, and γ Orionis; cf. P. Kunitzsch, *Untersuchungen zur Sternnomenklatur der Araber* (Wiesbaden, 1961), 78–80.

19 This passage is quoted in *WKAS* (as in n. 6), ii, 1313b 12–21 (with many variations).

20 Cf. Fraenkel, *Aramäischen Fremdwörter* (as in n. 14), 261.

21 Cf. P.E. Pormann, *The Oriental Tradition of Paul of Aegina's* Pragmateia (Leiden, 2004), 143–4.

22 In Christian Syriac literature, Christ is often designated as the great *asyā* (physician); cf. N. Allan, 'Hospice to Hospital in the Near East: an Instance of Continuity and Change in Late Antiquity', *Bulletin of the History of Medicine*, 64 (1990), 446–62, 452.

23 Thaddäus Kowalski, *Der Dīwān des Ḳais ibn al Ḫaṭīm* (Leipzig, 1914), nº 1, 9.

24 Lyall, *Mufaḍḍalīyāt* (as in n. 9), nº 15, 15.

25 Hippocrates, *Volume IV: Nature of Man. Regimen in Health. Humours. Aphorisms. Regimen 1-3. Dreams. Heracleitus. On the Universe*, trans. W.H.S. Jones (Loeb Classical Library, 150; Cambridge, Mass., 1931).

26 There are numerous good introductions to the topic of ancient medicine; two recent ones, the first very short and readable, the second authorative with excellent notes and further literature, are the following: H. King, *Greek and Roman Medicine* (Bristol, 2001) and reprints; and V. Nutton, *Ancient Medicine* (London, 2004).

27 Cf. O. Temkin, *The Falling Sickness: a History of Epilepsy from the Greeks to the Beginnings of Modern Neurology* (Baltimore, [2]1971).

28 *Ὅτι ὁ ἄριστος ἰατρὸς καὶ φιλόσοφος*, ed. K.G. Kühn, *Claudii Galeni Opera Omnia*, 20 vols. (Leipzig, 1821–33), i, 53–63; I. von Müller, *Claudii Galeni Pergameni Scripta minora*, 3 vols. (Leipzig, 1884–93), ii, 1–8; the Arabic translation has been edited by Peter Bachmann, *Galens Abhandlung darüber, dass der vorzügliche Arzt Philosoph sein muss* (Nachrichten der Akademie der Wissenschaften in Göttingen, Phil.-Hist. Klasse; Göttingen, 1965).

29 Cf. P.E. Pormann, 'The *Alexandrian Summary* (*Jawāmiʿ*) of Galen's *On the Sects for Beginners*: Commentary or Abridgment?', in P. Adamson et al. (eds.), *Philosophy, Science and Exegesis in Greek, Arabic and Latin Commentaries*, 2 vols. (London, 2004), ii, 11–33.

30 Cf. B. Gundert, 'Die *Tabulae Vindobonenses* als Zeugnis alexandrinischer Lehrtätigkeit um 600 n. Chr.', in K.-D. Fischer et al. (eds.), *Text and Tradition: Studies in Ancient Medicine and its Transmission Presented to Jutta Kollesch* (Leiden, 1998), 91–144 and *Abbildungen* 1–3; E. Savage-Smith, 'Galen's Lost Ophthalmology and the *Summaria Alexandrinorum*', in V. Nutton (ed.), *The Unknown Galen* (London, 2002), 121–38.

31 O. Temkin, *Galenism: Rise and Decline of a Medical Philosophy* (Ithaca, 1973).

32 Cf. M. El-Abadi, *The Life and Fate of the Ancient Library of Alexandria* (Paris, [2]1992); M. Meyerhof, 'Von Alexandrien nach Bagdad', *Sitzungsberichte der preussischen Akademie der Wissenschaften, Phil.-Hist. Kl.*, 23 (1930), 387–429; A Polish archaeological mission led by Grzegory Majderek seems to have uncovered one of these schools; cf. *Neue Zürcher Zeitung*, 27 May 2004, 19.

33 Cf. A.Z. Iskandar, 'An Attempted Reconstruction of the Late Alexandrian Medical Curriculum', *Medical History*, 20 (1976), 235–58.

34 Cf. Pormann, 'The *Alexandrian Summary* (*Jawāmiʿ*) (as in n. 29); id. 'Jean le grammarien et le *De sectis* dans la littérature médicale d'Alexandrie', in I. Garofalo and A. Roselli (eds.), *Galenismo e medicina tardoantica: fonti greche, latine e arabe* (Naples, 2003), 233–63.

35 Cf. Pormann, *Oriental Tradition* (as in n. 21).

36 Cf. L.I. Conrad, 'Varietas Syriaca: Secular and Scientific Culture in the Christian Communities of Syria after the Arab Conquest', in G.J. Reinink and A.C. Klugkist (eds.), *After Bardaisan: Studies on Continuity and Change in Syriac Chritianity in Honour of Professor Han J. W. Drijvers* (Leuven, 1999), 85–105.

37 Cf. S. Brock, 'Greek into Syriac and Syriac into Greek', *Journal of the Syriac Academy*, 3 (1977), 406–22, repr. in id., *Syriac Perspectives on Late Antiquity* (London, 1984), no. II; id., 'Aspects of Translation Technique in Antiquity', *Greek, Roman and Byzantine Studies*, 20 (1979), 69–87, repr. in *Syriac Perspectives*, no. III; 'The Syriac Background to Ḥunayn's Translation Techniques', *ARAM*, 3 (1991), 139–62, repr. in id., *From Ephrem to Romanos* (London, 1999), no. XIV.

38 Cf. M.W. Dols, 'Syriac into Arabic: The Transmission of Greek Medicine', *ARAM*, 1 (1989), 45–52.

39 Cf. H. Hugonnard-Roche, 'Note sur Sergius de Reš ʿAinā (d. 536), médecin et philosphe', in G. Endress and R. Kruk (eds.), *The Ancient Tradition in Christian and Islamic Hellenism* (Festschrift Drossaart Lulofs) (Leiden, 1997), 121–49.

40 Cf. R. Le Coz, *Les médecins nestoriens au Moyen Âge: Les maîtres des Arabes* (Paris, 2004), 39.

41 A perusal of R. Degen, 'Galen im Syrischen: Eine Übersicht über die syrische Überlieferung der Werke Galens', in V. Nutton (ed.), *Galen: Problems and Prospects* (London, 1981), 131–66, shows both the huge amount of Syriac translations prepared by different individuals, and the extent of the loss. See also H. Hugonnard-Roche, *La logique d'Aristote du grec au syriaque: Études sur la transmission des textes de l'Organon et leur interpretation philosophique* (Paris, 2004).

42 *Syrian Anatomy, Pathology and Therapeutics: or The Book of Medicines: the Syriac Text*, Edited from a Rare Manuscript, with an English Translation ..., 2 vols. (London, 1913); the second volume, containing the translation, has recently been reprinted as E.A.W. Budge, *The Book of Medicines: Ancient Syrian Anatomy, Pathology and Therapeutics* (London, 2002).

43 Cf. M. Meyerhof, 'Die Augenheilkunde in der von Budge herausgegebenen syrischen ärztlichen Handschrift', *Der Islam*, 6 (1917), 257–68; cf. Ullmann, *Medizin* (as in n. 5), 100, n. 2 for further literature on the topic.

44 Cf. e.g. M. Ullmann, 'Yūḥannā ibn Sarābiyūn: Untersuchungen zur Überlieferungsgeschichte seiner Werke', *Medizinhistorisches Journal*, 6/4 (1971), 278–96, 291.

45 B. Zipser and K.-D. Fischer, 'Neue Quellen zur antiken Augenheilkunde: der lateinische *Aphorismenkommentar* Lat-A, *The Syriac Book of Medicines* und Theophilos Protospatharios', in I. Andorlini (ed.), *Testi medici su papiro: Atti del Seminario di studio (Firenze, 3-4 giugno 2002)* (Florence, 2004), 3–28.

46 T.S. Miller, *The Birth of the Hospital in the Byzantine Empire* (Baltimore, 1985; repr. with new preface, ibid., 1997); in the new preface (xix–xxvi), Miller discusses some of his critics, trying to refute their arguments; however, his attempts are hardly convincing. For a recent critical assessment of Miller's theses, see P. Horden, 'How Medicalised Were Byzantine Hospitals', *Journal of Interdisciplinary History*, 35/3 (Winter, 2005), 361–89. Incidentally, Le Coz, *Médecins nestoriens* (as in n. 40) follows Miller blindly.

47 Cf. e.g. Coz, *Médecins nestorien* (as in n. 40), 41–3.

48 See, for instance, L.I. Conrad 'Arab-Islamic Medicine', in W.F. Bynam and R. Porter (eds.), *Companion Encyclopedia of the History of Medicine*, 3 vols. (London, 1993), i, 676–727, 688, following M.W. Dols, 'The Origins of the Islamic Hospital: Myth and Reality', *Bulletin of the History of Medicine*, 61 (1987), 367–90, 367–70.

49 A recent survey of this influence can be found in the article 'Greece', *Encyclopaedia Iranica*, 2nd ed., xi, 292–361, especially section x entitled 'Greek medicine in Persia' by G. Russell.

50 P. Kunitzsch, 'Über das Frühstadium der arabischen Aneignung antiken Gutes', *Saeculum*, 26 (1975), 268–82; see also A. Nallino, 'Tracce de opere greche giunte agli Arabi per trafila pehlavica', in T.W. Arnold and R.A. Nicholson (eds.), *A Volume of Oriental Studies Presented to Edward G. Browne ... on his 60th Birthday (7 February 1922)* (Cambridge, 1922), 345–63.

51 Cf. Ph. Gignoux, 'Dēnkard', *Encyclopaedia Iranica*, vii, 284–9. Especially revealing is the chapter entitled 'Exposition regarding Physical and Spiritual Medicine', *The Dinkard*, ed. D.P. Sanjana, Peshotanji Behramji Samjana, 19 vols. (Bombay, 1874–1928), iv, 220–42 (English translation); cf. L.-C. Casartelli, 'Un traité pehlevi sur la médecine', *Le Muséon*, 5 (1886), 531–58.

52 Cf. P. Sohn, *Die Medizin des Zādsparam: Anatomie, Physiologie und Psychologie in den* Wizīdagīhā ī Zādsparam, *einer zoroastrisch-mittelpersischen Anthologie aus dem frühislamischen Iran des neunten Jahrhunderts* (Wiesbaden, 1996).

53 J. Hampel, *Medizin der Zoroastrier im vorislamischen Iran* (Husum, 1982): '[...] daß „Wurzeln der Medizin im griechischen Wissen liegen, aber die Doktrin und die ‚Gesamtschau' (*zayč*) aus iranischer Weisheit (stammen)'.

54 An example of popular fiction is the *Alexander Romance*, which spread through many culture in different recensions and versions; see C. Jouanno, *Naissance et métamorphoses du* Roman d'Alexandre*: domaine grec* (Paris, 2002); F. Doufikar-Aerts, *Alexander Magnus Arabicus: Zeven eeuwen Arabische Alexandertraditie: van Pseudo-Callisthenes tot Ṣūrī*, Proefschrift (University of Leiden, 2003).

55 Quṣayr ʿAmrā, the hunting lodge of the Ummayad princes in the Jordanian desert, illustrates the strong Greek influence on early Islamic art and architecture; cf. the article by Garth Fowden in this volume and his *Quṣayr ʿAmrā: Art and the Umayyad Elite in Late Antique Syria* (Berkley, 2004).

56 Cf. D. Gutas, *Greek Thought, Arabic Culture* (London, 1998), 61; cf. H. Putman, *L'église et l'Islam sous Timothée I (780-823)* (Beirut, 1975).

57 Gutas, *Greek Thought, Arabic Culture* (as in previous note), e.g. 3.

58 G. Bergsträsser, *Ḥunain ibn Isḥāq Über die syrischen und arabischen Galenübersetzungen* (Leipzig, 1925); id., *Neue Materialien zu Ḥunain ibn Isḥāq's Galenbibliographie* (Leipzig, 1932).

59 Ibid., n. 20, 18, 19–19, 1.

60 Pormann, *Oriental Tradition* (as in n. 21), especially 293–9.

61 The following is a short paraphrase of ideas which I have more fully developed elsewhere (cf. P.E. Pormann, 'Islamic Hospitals in the time of al-Muqtadir', in J. Nawas et al. [eds.], *ʿAbbasid Studies: Occasional Papers of the School of ʿAbbasid Studies, Leuven, 27 June - 1 July 2004* [Leuven, 2008] [forthcoming]).

62 Cf. Ullmann, *Medizin* (as in n. 5) and *GAS*, iii.

63 The subject of theory versus practice has recently been broached by P. Horden and E. Savage-Smith (eds.), *The Year 1000: Medical Practice at the End of the First Millennium* (Social History of Medicine, 13/2; August 2000).

64 M. Meyerhof, 'Thirty-Three Clinical Observations by Rhazes (Circa 900 A.D.)', *Isis*, 23/2 (1935), 321–72; repr. in id., *Studies in Medieval Arabic Medicine: Theory and Practice*, ed. P. Johnstone (London, 1984), item V.

65 Cf. P.E. Pormann, 'Theory and Practice in the Early Hospitals in Baghdad – Al-Kaškarī On Rabies and Melancholy', *ZGAIW*, 15 (2003), 197–248.

66 Illustrated by the fact that the future caliph al-Muʿtaṣim once bought 3000 slaves at once; cf. 'Ghulām', *EI*[2].

67 Greek *hiera* < Pahlavi (Middle-Persian) *iyārag* < Arabic *iyāraj*, literally meaning 'holy remedy', denote a special group of compound drugs.

68 Cf. O. Kahl, 'Sābūr ibn Sahl', *EI*[2].

69 Cf. Pormann, 'Theory and Practice' (as in n. 65), 208–9; Ibn al-Nadīm, *Kitāb al-fihrist*, ed. G. Flügel (Leipzig, 1871–72), 297, 9–11, states: 'Sābūr ibn Sahl, the director of the hospital in Jundaysābūr. He was excellent, knowledgeable, and advanced. He wrote the following books: A *Dispensatory*, used in the hospitals (*bīmāristānāt*) and apothecary shops (*dakākīn al-ṣayādila*), 22 chapters. [...]'.

70 Istanbul, Sülemaniye Kütüphanesi, MS Aya Sofya 3716, f. 231b; a facsimile of this manuscript has been produced by F. Sezgin: Yaʿqūb al-Kaškarī, *Kunnāsh fī 'l-ṭibb/Book On Medicine* (Publications of the Institute for the History of Arabic-Islamic Science, Series C, 17; Frankfurt am Main, 1985); the chapter on rabies has previously been edited and translated in Pormann, 'Theory and Practice' (as in n. 65), 228–32, where the present quotation is § 6 on 229 (text), 231 (trans.).

71 Istanbul, Sülemaniye Kütüphanesi, MS Aya Sofya 3716, f. 142a 1

72 Hipp. *Aph.* 5.2: "*Ἐπὶ τρώματι σπασμὸς ἐπιγενόμενος θανάσιμον* (When a spasm occurs as a result of a wound, it is lethal)".

73 In the original: *fa-qad raʾaytu jamāʿatan mimman quṭiʿat aydīhim wa-ʾarjuluhum mina 'l-luṣūṣi fī 'l-bīmāristāni*; from the Arabic it is not entirely clear whether the punishment is actually carried out 'in the hospital', or whether al-Kaskarī just saw the criminals there after they had suffered the amputation elsewhere.

74 Istanbul, Sülemaniye Kütüphanesi, MS Aya Sofya 3716, f. 142; Cf. Pormann, 'Theory and Practice' (as in n. 65), 204–5.

75 Istanbul, Sülemaniye Kütüphanesi, MS Aya Sofya 3716, f. 66b 11-ult.

76 Identity not entirely clear; cf. *WKAS* i. 365b 20–25 and W. Schmucker, *Die pflanzliche und mineralische Materia Medica im* Firdaus al-ḥikma *des Ṭabarī* (Bonn, 1969), no. 649.

77 Cf. Pormann, 'Islamic Hospitals' (as in n. 61).

78 Cf. I.A. Vullers, *Lexicon Persico-Latinum*, 2 vols. (Bonn, 1855–64), s.v.

79 Cf. P.E. Pormann, 'Yūḥannā ibn Sarābiyūn: Further Studies into the Transmission of his Works', *ArScPhil*, 14/2 (2004), 233–62.

80 Cf. Ullmann, *Medizin* (as in n. 5), 103–7; A. Siggel, *Die indischen Bücher aus dem* Paradies der Weisheit über die Medizin *des ʿAlī ibn Sahl Rabban aṭ-Ṭabarī, übersetzt und erläutert* (Wiesbaden, 1951).

81 P. Johnstone, 'Tradition in Arabic Medicine', *Palestine Exploration Quarterly*, 107 (1975), 23–37.

82 Cf. G. Endress, 'Die Wissenschaftliche Literatur', in H. Gätje and W.-D. Fischer (eds.), *Grundriß der arabischen Philologie*, 3 vols. (Wiesbaden, 1982–92), iii, 117 (8.8.3 'Medizin');. M. Marín and D. Waines, 'The Balanced Way: Food for Pleasure and Health in Medieval Islam', *Manuscripts of the Middle East*, 4 (1989), 123–32, 124b: 'Many of the culinary manuals, however, have a purpose beyond the mere transformation of raw ingredients into cooked dishes for the table. The opening chapters of al-Warrāq's *Kitāb al-ṭabīkh* are devoted to the 'natures' of various foodstuffs, and their suitability for different temperaments, and seasons as well as for specific bodily functions or disorders. The Hellenistic background of food lore is everywhere apparent: [...]'

83 For evidence of tension, see P.E. Pormann, 'The Physician and the Other: Images of the Charlatan in Medieval Islam', *Bulletin of the History of Medicine*, 79/2 (2005), 189–227.

84 For an overview and further literature on this topic, see M. Ullmann, *Islamic Medicine* (Edinburgh, 1978); and P.E. Pormann and E. Savage-Smith, *Medieval Islamic Medicine* (Edinburgh, 2007).

85 Al-Majūsī, *Kāmil al-ṣināʿa al-ṭibbiyya*, facs. edn. F. Sezgin (Publications of the Institute for the History of Arabic-Islamic Science, Series C, 16; Frankfurt am Main, 1985); cf. Ullmann, *Medizin* (as in n. 5), 140–6.

86 Ibn Sīnā, *Qānūn fī 'l-ṭibb*, 2 vols. (Būlāq, 1294/1877); 5 vols. (Beirut, 1408/1987); cf. G. Strohmaier, *Avicenna* (Munich, 1999).

87 Al-Zahrāwī, *Kitāb al-taṣnīf li-man ʿajiza ʿan al-taʾlīf* (*Arrangement [of Medical Knowledge] for One Who is Unable to Compile [a Manual for Himself]*); facs. edn. F. Sezgin, *A Presentation to Would-Be Authors On Medicine* (Publications of the Institute for the History of Arabic-Islamic Science, Series C, 31/1-2; Frankfurt am Main, 1986); cf. E. Savage-Smith, 'al-Zahrāwī', *EI*^{2}.

88 Cf. D. Jacquart, *La science médicale occidentale entre deux renaissances* (Ashgate, Variorum: Aldershot, 1997); C. Burnett, *Arabic into Latin in the Middle Ages: The Translators and their Audience* (Ashgate, Variorum: Aldershot), in preparation.

89 M.R. McVaugh (ed.), *Inventarium sive Chirurgia Magna Guigonis de Caulhiaco* (Guy de Chaliac), 2 vols. (Leiden, 1997), i, xiii; Ullmann, *Medizin* (as in n. 5), 151, and W. von Brunn, 'Die Stellung des Guy de Chauliac in der Chirurgie des Mittelalters', *Sudhoffs Archiv*, 12 (1920), 85–100; 13 (1921), 65–106.

90 J. Pahlitzsch, 'Ärzte ohne Grenzen. Melkitisch, jüdische und samaritanische Ärzte in Ägypten und Syrien zur Zeit der Kreuzzüge', in K. Steger and K.P. Jankrift (eds.), *Gesundheit - Krankheit: Kulturtransfer medizinischen Wissens von der Spätantike bis in die Frühe Neuzeit* (Cologne, 2004), 101–20. The question of whether Islamic hospitals influenced the development of Christian ones, especially since crusaders were familiar with them, cannot be discussed here; for further information, see, e.g., M. Amouroux, 'Colonization and the Creation of Hospitals; The Eastern Extension of Western Hospitality in the Eleventh and Twelfth Centuries', *Mediterranean Historical Review*, 14 (1999), 31–43 and L.I. Conrad, 'Usāma ibn Munqidh and Other Witnesses to Frankish and Islamic Medicine in the Era of the Crusades', in Z. Amar, E. Lev and J. Swartz (eds.), *Medicine in Jerusalem Throughout the Ages* (Tel Aviv, 1999), xxvii–lii.

91 Cf. N.G. Siraisi, *Avicenna in Renaissance Italy: the Canon and Medical Teaching in Italian Universities after 1500* (Princeton, 1987).

92 For a detailed discussion of this development, see P.E. Pormann, 'La querelle des médecins arabistes et hellénistes et l'héritage oublié', in V. Boudon-Millot and G. Cobolet (eds.), *Lire les médecins grecs à la Renaissance: Aux origines de l'édition médicale*, Actes du colloque international de Paris (19–20 septembre 2003), coll. Médic (Paris, 2004), 113–41.

93 Cf. S.P. Huntington, *Clash of Civilization and the Remaking of World Order* (New York, 1996).

94 Cf. E. Troeltsch, *Schmollers Jahrbuch für Gesetzgebung, Verwaltung und Volkswirtschaft im Deutschen Reiche*, 44 (1920), 633–80; C.H. Becker, 'Der Islam im Rahmen einer allgemeinen Kulturgeschichte', *ZDMG*, 76 (1922), 18–35, repr. in id., *Islamstudien*, i (Leipzig, 1924), 24–39, 24.

95 Cf. J. Kraemer, *Das Problem der Islamischen Kulturgeschichte* (Tübingen, 1959).

6

Byzantine, Western European, Islamic and Central Asian Influence in the Field of Arms and Armour from the Seventh to Fourteenth Century AD

David Nicolle

This is a vast and varied field, so it is perhaps best to focus on a few very different examples of military technology in order to illustrate significant aspects of the subject. Nevertheless, a general introductory overview might be useful. Since the period under consideration covers eight centuries, there were inevitably huge changes within the technological and military capabilities of the four civilisations under consideration. In the seventh century AD Western Europe was a technological, economic and military backwater. In most such respects it was also the heir of Rome. The only significant new influences had stemmed from the Eurasian steppe cultures, beyond whom lay Iran and ultimately China. These new influences were introduced by migrating or conquering Germanic peoples, some of whom had themselves been significantly influenced, militarily and technologically, by steppe cultures.

Nevertheless, some scholars have made a great deal of the quality of early medieval European sword-blades. Yet these blades, though exported to both the Byzantine and Islamic worlds, were not as highly regarded outside Western Europe as they were within it. Furthermore "Frankish" blades, as they were widely known outside Western Europe, were themselves an exception where the general standard, sophistication and volume production of early medieval Western European armaments were concerned. On the other hand, by the eleventh and twelfth centuries things were already changing and by the fourteenth century Western Europe had become an economic, technological and military powerhouse.

Like Western Europe, the early medieval Byzantine World was militarily and technologically the heir of Rome, but whereas Western European arms and armour remained largely rooted in Late Roman traditions, Byzantium continued to learn from its militarily highly effective foes. Before the twelfth century Byzantium had little to learn, and learned little, from Western Europe. Its teachers lay to the east and north; namely Sassanian Iran and its Islamic successors, and, to an even greater extent, the largely Turkic peoples of the Eurasian steppes. In fact military and technological adaptability was a major factor in the Byzantine Empire's prolonged and remarkable survival within a broadly hostile world.[1] It was also an adaptability which stood in stark contrast to the deep seated conservatism of so many other aspects of Byzantine civilisation.

The military backwardness and isolation of the Arabian Peninsula during the immediate pre-Islamic period has been greatly overstated. This is not only the case amongst non-Islamic historians, whose focus has been on the Graeco-Roman and early Byzantine Mediterranean worlds or on the magnificent civilisations of the Iranian world. It is also seen amongst traditional Islamic historians who emphasised Arabia's supposedly primitive military heritage, and thereby highlighted the almost miraculous character of the early Islamic conquests. Here is perhaps not the place to argue this point in detail, except to suggest that the first two generations of Arab-Islamic armies were not that different from their immediate neighbours, nor was their military technology particularly backward. Indeed, in terms of infantry archery these armies probably enjoyed an advantage over the Byzantines and almost certainly did so over the Sassanians. The military preoccupations of both these longer-established Middle Eastern empires had previously been northwards, where they faced the highly developed and highly effective horse-archery traditions of steppe peoples – that was, of course, when they were not fighting each other. The story of the original Arab bow has yet to be properly told.[1a] Suffice to say that it was a large weapon which seems to have existed in a variety of construction techniques which included what was virtually a simple "longbow" – to use anachronistic English terminology – and which shot heavy arrows which could penetrate most armour of that period.

If the Byzantines were enthusiastic learners in matters military, then the Islamic Arabs and those who subsequently became the military-political elites of Islam's Middle Eastern heartlands, were even more eager to take the best from whatever military technology was available. As a result the armies of what has been called the Classical or Golden Age of Islamic civilisation (eighth to tenth centuries AD) absorbed the military technologies and tactical traditions of the Byzantine Middle East, of Sassanian Iran and of Turco-Iranian Central Asia. In fact, the latter proved to be the fountainhead of the most significant military-technological developments in the medieval Islamic world and, to a lesser extent, of many other cultures as well. Meanwhile India, on the easternmost frontiers of medieval Islam, and Western Europe on the other most distant frontier, were both sources of sword-blades, but of little else. I would suggest that in both cases the blades in question were more significant in literary terms, and perhaps as stylistic influences, than they were in strictly practical military terms.

The fourth major culture which cannot be ignored in this context is Central Asia. As already stated, this served as a fountainhead of military, technological, tactical, and even fashionable influences. For the Islamic, and to a lesser extent the Byzantine worlds, the Turco-Mongol steppes were also a significant source of military recruitment; not just for soldiers but for commanders and eventually ruling elites as well. Behind Central Asia lay China, which some historians have seen as the fountainhead of practically everything, especially in the technological and military fields. However, the evidence suggests that the more advanced steppe cultures were at least equal partners with China in many such matters. Certainly it would be a gross oversimplification to regard the Iranian, Turkish and Mongol nomadic peoples of the Eurasian steppes merely as transmitters who channelled the technological brilliance of China to Western Asia and Europe.

The five aspects of medieval arms and armour to be considered below are potentially important where the question of inter-cultural influence is concerned. The first is an example of the problems of textual and pictorial interpretation, and concerns the earliest illustration and description of a counterweight *manjanīq* or mangonel which is in a famous manuscript written by Murḍā ibn ʿAlī ibn Murḍā al-Ṭarsūsī for Saladin. The second is an example of how archaeology can help with a question which has been discussed for almost two centuries; namely medieval Western Islamic and Western European swords. The third illustrates how archaeology can pose entirely new questions; namely the importance of hardened leather "hoop" armour in the Islamic Middle East, its origins and its possible link with the sudden reappearance of semi-rigid body armour in thirteenth and fourteenth century Western Europe. The fourth will look at some pieces of medieval armour which have been known for decades but have not, as far as I am aware, been studied as a group, probably because they are geographically and culturally very dispersed; namely anthropomorphic iron visors. The fifth looks once again at a question which has been discussed for well over a century; namely whether scale armour existed in early or high medieval Western Europe. Here recent discoveries made by French archaeologists in the Provençal Alps have undermined the argument of several generations of armour specialists, myself included, that there was no scale armour in Western Europe during this period.

I.

The counterweight mangonel or trebuchet is generally believed to have have been invented in the eastern Mediterranean region during the twelfth century. That is when the first confirmed evidence of its existence emerged in the remarkable treatise written for Saladin by Murḍā al-Ṭarsūsī.[2] The latter was, as far as we can tell, a military scholar or senior technician working in Egypt who may have been of Cilician-Armenian origin. However, a careful reading of the relevant section in al-Ṭarsūsī's book, *Tabṣirat arbāb al-albāb*, suggests that, for the author, the counterweight *manjanīq* was not a new weapon. Like virtually everything else in al-Ṭarsūsī's book, it was apparently rooted in the military technology of the preceding Fāṭimid Caliphate which Saladin overthrew when he seized control of Egypt in the second half of the twelfth century. Furthermore Fāṭimid military technology was itself rooted in the military technology of the earlier ʿAbbāsid Caliphate and much of what appears in al-Ṭarsūsī's book is actually of tenth or even ninth century ʿAbbāsid origin.

Although there is no evidence that the counterweight *manjanīq* was of ninth century ʿAbbāsid origin, there is evidence that rudimentary forms of counterweight *manjanīq* existed in the tenth century. In other words some stone-throwing weapons based upon the traction or beamsling principle already relied on the downward motion of a counterweight rather than on a team of men or women pulling ropes. So far the earliest tentative evidence for the counterweight *manjanīq* which I have been able to find dates from the mid-tenth century, and is in a description of the fortified city of Tarsus in Cilicia shortly before it fell to the Byzantines in 965 AD.[3] At that point the walls of Tarsus supposedly had one hundred towers, and of these twenty supported or were armed with an *ʿarrāda*, which I believe to have been the most common form of relatively small man-powered beamsling mangonel.[4] Another twenty each had a "large" *manjanīq* or mangonel. Only three towers were described as being armed with a *manjanīq* of a type called *ḥ-r-r-ī*. Unfortunately the short vowels were not shown so the precise meaning of this Arabic word in this context remains unclear. It could, however, be rooted in the meaning of "free" or "independent",[5] but independent of what? Perhaps the name indicated that this particular form of *manjanīq* was free or independent of a team of rope pullers, in which case three of the towers of Tarsus might have had early forms of counterweight *manjanīq*. Another less likely meaning could be rooted in the concept of "stoney",[6] and it is worth noting that the counterweight in al-Ṭarsūsī's counterweight *manjanīq* consisted of a net full of large stones.

The remaining towers of mid-tenth century Tarsus were defended by *qisiyy al-rijl* or "foot bows", in other words early forms of hand-held crossbow, which opens up the fascinating question of the use and spread of the crossbow during the early medieval period.

Meanwhile there is little evidence for a Byzantine origin for the counterweight mangonel, despite a widespread assumption that the Byzantine Greeks, with their remarkably literate tradition of military training manuals, were more likely to have invented such a significant siege weapon than were the Arabs. Of course the Muslim Arabs' own tradition of technical military and other manuals remains virtually unknown outside a handful of specialists. Subsequent evidence from the Islamic Middle East, some of it relating to Byzantine siege weapons, is circumstantial, though interesting and relatively abundant. In fact the first specific reference to a Byzantine counterweight mangonel was in 1165 AD during the siege of Zevgminon – now Zemunik in Croatia.[7]

Al-Ṭarsūsī's own description of a counterweight *manjanīq* has been widely misunderstood. It is also worth pointing out that the well-known copy of the *Tabṣirat arbāb al-albāb* now in the Bodleian Library is the original, signed by al-Ṭarsūsī himself.[8] This manuscript could, indeed, have been written as early as 1169 when Saladin became *wazīr* or "Prime Minister" of what was then still officially the Fāṭimid Caliphate in Egypt.

After describing the forms of manpowered *manjanīq* currently in general use, al-Ṭarsūsī went on to describe and illustrate what he called the *Farsi* or Persian *manjanīq*[9] (Fig. 1). This had a supporting frame and a beamsling essentially the same as those of al-Ṭarsūsī's Turkish *manjanīq* which was, according to the author, the easiest to erect. He provided a great deal of detailed information about things such as the best wood, the necessary metallic elements, and the proportions of the beamsling which should be on each side of the axle. The counterweight was to consist of a large net or bag made of hemp rope containing rocks. It was certainly not the wooden container attached to a smaller axle and containing various sorts of heavy materials used in almost all later counterweight mangonels or trebuchets. The net was itself attached by three hemp ropes to a large iron ring in the shorter end of the beamsling.

This brings us to a very significant point. The supporting frame of the stone-throwing weapon was no taller than that of the simpler man-powered Turkish, Arab and "Frankish"

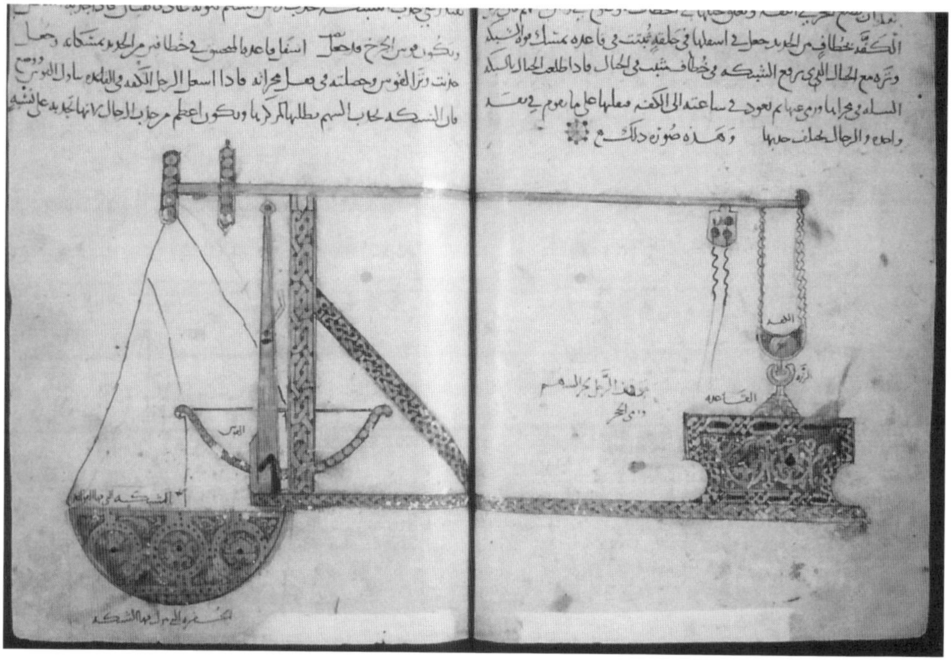

Fig. 1a: The manjanīq fārisī, illustrated in al-Ṭarsūsī's manuscript (Oxford, Bodleian Library, MS Hunt. 264, ff. 134v–135r, Oxford).

or European *manjanīqs*. So the bag of rocks would have hit the earth as it dropped unless, as al-Ṭarsūsī explained, an elongated hole or trench was excavated between the base-frame timbers of the machine (Fig. 1b). This enabled the bag of rocks to complete its arc or drop when the weapon was released. Why had this problem not yet been solved by simply increasing the height of the frame? Perhaps al-Ṭarsūsī's Persian *manjanīq* was still a rare and primitive machine, or perhaps it had originally been developed for use in a position where there was already space for the counterweight to swing free. Perhaps such an earlier version had been mounted on a wooden platform on a fortified tower. Certainly early beamsling mangonels were used as much, if not more, in defence of fortifications than in attacking such places. Similar problems might have been faced when the earliest counterweight mangonels were mounted on European castle towers in the late twelfth century, where such machines were still a considerable novelty. So it was very interesting to learn that a hole or trench was apparently found in the upper platform of what was originally the main tower in the early thirteenth century Plantagenet castle at Bressuire, in the Poitou region of western France. The tower in question is a solid half-round "great tower" in the middle of the castle's northern wall.[10] Its location overlooking a vulnerable side of the castle, as well as its solid construction and its considerable size when compared to other towers on the northern wall, strongly suggest that it was used as an artillery emplacement for stone-throwing mangonels. Perhaps the latter included one of the first counterweight types which would soon revolutionise fortress design in the Islamic World, the Byzantine Empire, and Western Europe.

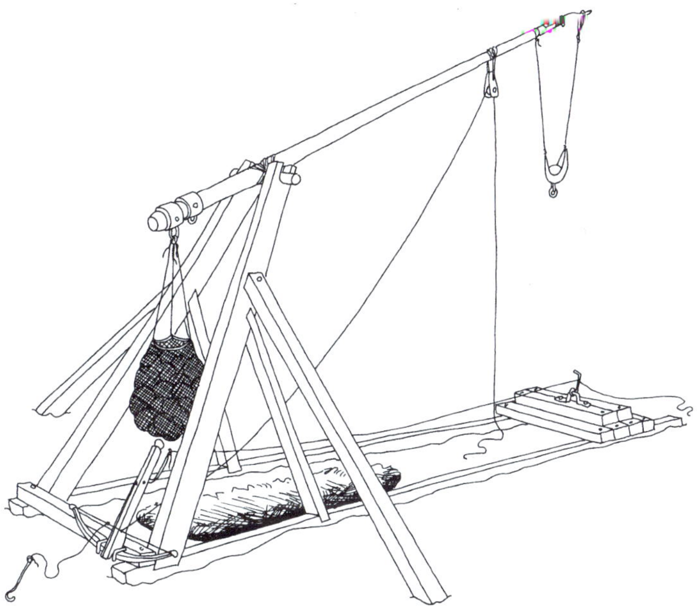

Fig. 1b: Author's reconstruction of al-Ṭarsūsī's counterweight manjanīq.[10a]

II.

The second topic concerns early and high medieval swords in the Iberian Peninsula and North Africa. Until recently archaeology has played a very small role in the study of medieval Iberian and North African arms and armour, both Christian and Islamic. On the other hand there has been considerable study of texts and of such subjects as mining, metallurgy and sword-making in the wider context of medieval Christian and Islamic cultures. Thus we know that the majority of sword blades were manufactured in relatively few production centres but were exported across a huge area. Meanwhile the making of sword-hilts tended to be more localised, and consequently hilts varied considerably in their design. Hilts, or rather the various parts of a hilt, were also subject to changes in fashion and the spread of such fashions from one culture to another.

The basic character of Medieval European swords is known from abundant surviving examples.[11] These can shed light on the meaning of contemporary Islamic weapons terminology where, for example, al-Bīrūnī describes eleventh century imported European swords as being of the *qalʿa* type with a fuller or groove down the blade.[12] He also stated that they were made of *shaburqan* or *shabraqan* "female" or "soft" iron rather than the early forms of steel seen in Indian blades. Evidence from the Muslim "customers" shows that the Maghrib was importing European swords in the ninth century[13] and that this continued to be the case throughout most of the medieval period. It is also likely that some, perhaps even a majority, of the blades exported from al-Andalus to North Africa and other Muslim countries were of northern origin, with Andalusian merchants merely acting as middle-men.

Meanwhile a number of misleading myths persist where medieval Islamic swords are concerned. At its most extreme this represents all such weapons as being curved sabres of the post-medieval Turco-Persian type. Even when the predominance of straight-bladed weapons in most parts of the Islamic world up to the thirteenth century has been accepted, the character of the earliest forms is rarely understood. In the central Arab lands swords seem at first to have been relatively short stabbing, rather than slashing, weapons and were designed for infantry rather than cavalry warfare. As such they had several features in common with the Roman *gladius*. Hilts also reflected a Roman, early Byzantine and Sassanian-Persian heritage, and for several centuries Turkish traditions from Central Asia had only a localised impact. Meanwhile the remarkable collection of old swords preserved in the Topkapı Museum and Islamic Treasury in Istanbul almost certainly includes weapons from very early Islamic times, perhaps even from the seventh century as pious Muslims believe. Furthermore, several of these weapons have features in common with a broken tenth or eleventh century straight sword from Nishapur; all of them represent a separate tradition from that seen in early medieval Western Europe.

Written information from northern Africa during these centuries tends to be patchy and not particularly specific, while pictorial evidence is rare and difficult to interpret. Yet by the thirteenth century Ibn Saʿīd al-Maghribī stated that the Berbers of North Africa had lighter swords than the Andalusians[14] who were, by that time, under strong Christian Spanish military influence.

Documentary, pictorial, and archaeological evidence all point to the existence of a separate Iberian military tradition evolving between the eighth to eleventh centuries. Such a tradition obviously owed much to previous or neighbouring traditions, yet it also became increasingly different from the rest of the Islamic world, as well as from the rest of Western Europe. This was largely because of the survival of early Islamic military-technological traditions here in the Far West. There are many aspects to this question, but this article will focus on just two, both of which concern the hilt. The first is the presence or absence of an integral pommel-shaped enlargement at the end of the tang of surviving sword blades, while the second is the phenomenon of a tubular metallic sheath around the grip.

It is clear that several different types of sword were being used by the army of the Caliphate of Cordova during the tenth century.[15] Namely the *afranjī* "Frankish" or Western European, the *ʿarabī* or "Arab", and the *ʿidwī* which is normally translated as "Berber from the other side of the Strait of Gibraltar".[16] This name might, however, be a sexual pun comparable to the names give to various medieval Islamic siege engines; a slightly differently spelled the word would mean "penis like".[17]

Two swords found in Martin's Cave on the near vertical eastern flank of the Rock of Gibraltar are relevant in this context (Figs 2a–b). Though known for almost a century and a half,[18] they have only recently been studied and published in detail,[19] having been hidden away in store either in the British Museum or in the Royal Armouries.

The two swords from Gibraltar confirm these trends while also showing how structural and technological differences remained. A lot could be made of various aspects of their hilts, especially the decorated one. However, it is their spherical pommels which are relevant here. A small quotation in an Arabic source from al-Andalus cannot be said to prove the

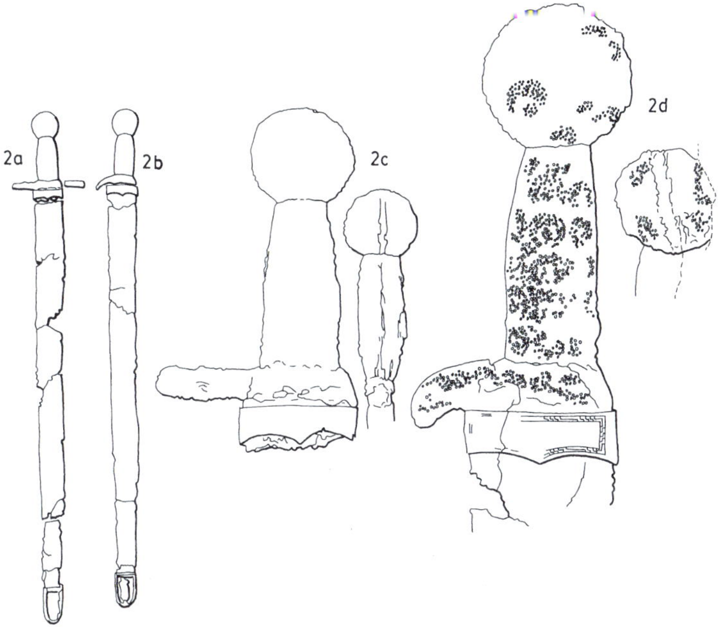

Figs 2a-d: Two swords from Martin's Cave, Gibraltar, Andalusian or Moroccan, mid-twelfth century

a: Undecorated sword with straight quillons (British Museum, inv. no, 67.12.23.2, London). b: Sword with decorated hilt and curved quillons (British Museum, inv. no, 67.12.23.1, London). c: Detail and side-view of the hilt of the undecorated sword with straight quillons, minus the broken piece of quillon (British Museum, inv. no, 67.12.23.2, London). d: Detail and side-view of the hilt of the decorated sword with curved quillons (British Museum, inv. no, 67.12.23.1, London).

identity of the first and most decorated sword from Martin's Cave but it certainly fits that weapon. This sentence stated that "some of the Andalusian swords had the tops of their hilts (pommels) inscribed in the manner of the scales of a pine-cone, except that this (the real pine-cone) is in relief and that (the decorated sword pommel) is inscribed."[20]

The spherical pommels (Figs 2c–d) on the Gibraltar swords are associated with relatively short grips and are examples of those short-hilts which were designed to fit snugly into the base of the palm of the hand rather than to extend beyond the hand.[21] Whereas the length of the grip reflected variations in fencing technique, differences in the design of the pommel tended to be a matter of fashion rather than function.[22] Though not unknown in medieval Christian Western Europe, the spherical pommel was very rare. It was found in several areas but seems most strongly associated with the Iberian peninsula or with swords of possible Iberian origin during the twelfth and thirteenth centuries; one possible example being a weapon said to have come from Palermo Cathedral, via Saragossa Cathedral, to the Musée de l'Armée in Paris.[23]

Another of the relatively few surviving examples in medieval Christian Western Europe

Fig. 3a: Bronze cylinder, perhaps part of a sword-hilt, from Qaryat al-Faw, capital of the Kinda tribal confederation, first–fifth century AD, Arabia (King Saud University Museum, Riyadh).

was found on what the late Ewart Oakeshott described as a small Castilian "riding sword", which is now thought to be in the Royal Armouries.[24] Not until much later did the spherical pommel become more widespread. Almost by definition, the spherical pommel is not a feature which will be very clear in art, particularly two dimensional art, as it can so easily be confused with the disc-shaped pommel. Nevertheless where it can be identified, or presumed with some confidence, the artistic evidence supports the idea that the spherical pommel was primarily a Middle Eastern and Mediterranean fashion.

Next comes the question of the Metal-Covered Grip. The all-metal or metal-covered grip had not, as far as I am aware, been a feature of Western European swords since the late Roman and very early medieval periods. The gold-covered grip and guard was then typical of what are considered "princely" weapons in the Hun period, this fashion being continued for a while by Franks and Goths.[25] Metal-covered grips were also seen on early Scandinavian weapons, but these were entirely different in design and purpose from the Gibraltar swords and other Islamic swords.

In contrast, the integral metal grip was typical of many Islamic weapons, particularly those of early or specifically Arab origin. Here a distinction must be drawn between Islamic weapons where the grip is structurally metallic and other swords where the grip is covered with a thin sheet of precious or polished metal for decorative or anti-corrosive reasons. The origins of the former type of hilt remain unknown, as do so several aspects of early Arab-Islamic military technology. The earliest known example may be a bronze cylinder with one remaining rivet through it, found during excavations at Qaryat al-Faw in Saudi Arabia (Fig. 3a). This site was probably the capital of the pre-Islamic Kinda tribal confederation and dated from the first to fifth centuries AD.[26] The bronze cylinder has not been identified as part of a sword hilt, but it is remarkably similar to the very few surviving examples of such sword hilts of early Arab-Islamic provenance.

The most similar object forms part of the grip of an all-bronze hilt on an extraordinary sword found in the wreck of the late tenth or early eleventh merchant ship off the island of Serçe Liman in south-western Turkey (Fig. 3b). Here the lower sections of the grip consist of such a cylinder attached to the tang by a single rivet.[27] The ship itself is now believed to be of eastern Mediterranean Arab-Islamic origin. In stylistic terms this weapon,[28] with its double-edged and almost certainly straight blade and its cast-bronze sword-hilt, could be interpreted as being within a "sub-Roman" tradition. Metallurgical analysis of

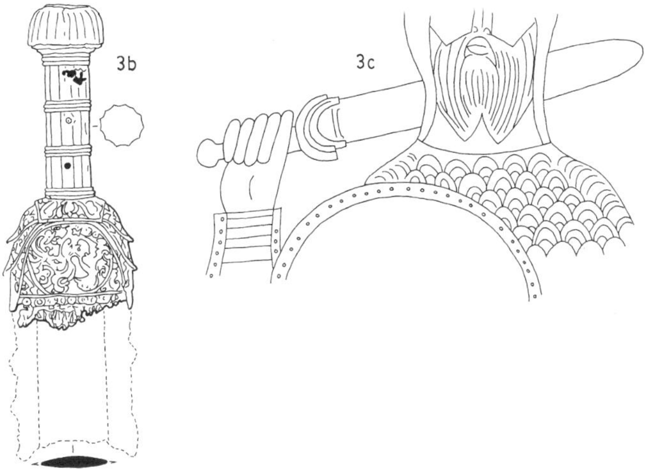

Figs 3b–c

b: Bronze hilt of a sword found in the wreck of a late tenth or early eleventh century Islamic shipwreck off the island of Serçe Liman (Castle Museum, inv. GW 56, Bodrum). c: Sword of Goliath, relief carving, early tenth century Armenian (in situ Church of Gagik, Agtamar, Lake Van).

the hilt proves that, despite its decoration of Hindu Indian or Zoroastrian Persian origin, the hilt includes ores mined close to Tehran or the Caspian coast of Iran. The sword might well have been made in Armenia, on the borderlands of the Islamic and Byzantine worlds. In overall appearance it is virtually identical with a weapon wielded by the Philistine giant Goliath in a tenth century Armenian carving on the church of Agtamar, on a small island in Lake Van (Fig. 3c). Here Goliath is armoured in the manner of those Turco-Iranian elite cavalrymen who served in the Caliphal army. Other evidence indicates that the metallic grip had a long history in Arab and Berber areas, clearly surviving beyond the Middle Ages, especially in those regions which escaped strong Turkish military influence.

The overall shape of the bronze Serçe Liman sword-hilt is different to that of both the iron-hilted Gibraltar swords, and an unprovenanced sword in the Museo Arqueológico in Seville (Fig. 3d) and a similar weapon in the Alava Museum in Vitoria. Yet structurally they are all similar and must surely be members of the same technological family. The grip of the Seville sword is said to be of bronze or brass and is decoratively divided lengthways into four panels. One of these panels contains a worn Arabic inscription which seems to include the word *al-baraka*.[29] The others contain stylised plant motifs, only one of which seems to be within the normal Islamic decorative tradition.[30] The sword in the Alava Museum in Vitoria (Figs 3e–f) is very similar but apparently undecorated. To some extent the decorated metal grip might subsequently be reflected in later Andalusian sword-grips made from other decorated materials such as ivory.

Another interesting sword was found with the bones of its presumed owner and the remains of a sheath in the wreck of a small boat alongside the wreck of a larger vessel off the French Mediterranean coast near Agay (Fig. 3g). The main ship has been identified as

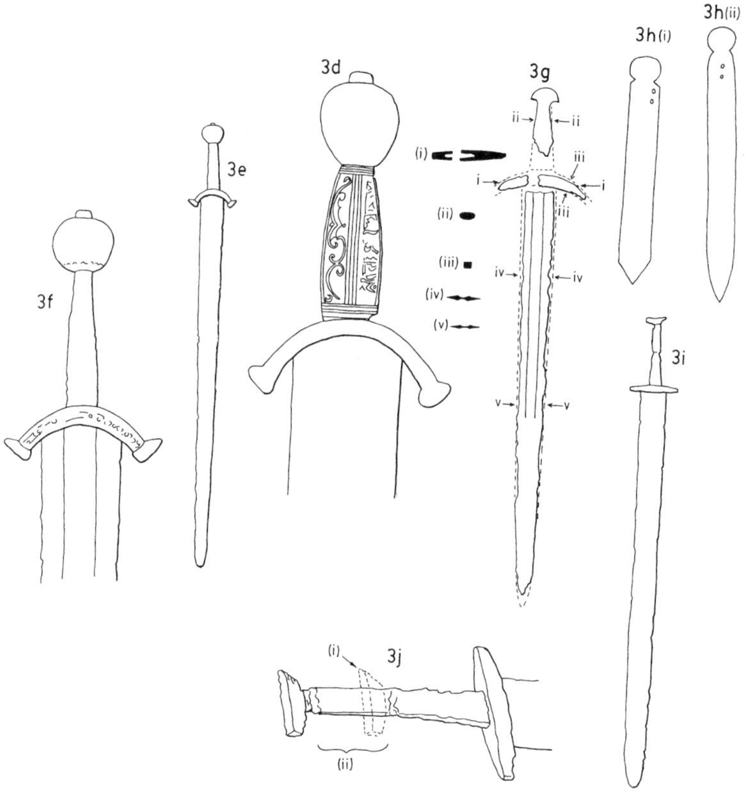

Figs 3d–3j

d: Hilt of a sword, fourteenth–fifteenth century, Andalusian (Archaeological Museum Seville). e: Sword from Tarragona, possibly eleventh–thirteenth century, Andalusian or Spanish (Archaeological Museum of the Province of Alava, Vitoria). f: Hilt of the sword from Tarragona (Archaeological Museum of the Province of Alava, Vitoria). g: Sword from the wreck of an Islamic ship, off Agay, North African Islamic, eleventh or early twelfth century (Museum of Underwater Archaeology, St. Raphael). h: Illustrations of a Yemeni samsam sword-blade in later copies of Al-suyūf wa-ajnāsuhā by al-Kindī (i: after A.R. Zaki; ii: after Hammer Purgstall). i: Andalusian sword found with a cache of Islamic coins, c.880 AD, in its present condition (private collection). j: Detail of the hilt of the sword found with a cache of Islamic coins, c.880 AD, showing the presumed original position of the cross-bar pommel (i), and the piece of modern iron welded to the existing hilt (ii) (private collection).

tenth century and probably of North African origin. However, the Museum of Underwater Archaeology at St. Raphael has now proposed a rather later, eleventh or even twelfth century, date for this weapon. Though incomplete, the hilt of the Agay sword has several features in common with those from Martin's Cave in Gibraltar. Most obvious are the curved quillons, but more significant is the way in which the end of the tang broadens into the shape of the now lost pommel. Although the pommel of the Agay sword was not spherical, the way in which its two halves were presumably sandwiched around this broadened tang is identical to the Gibraltar swords and some other medieval Arab rather than Turco-Persian swords. It is certainly unlike the system of construction seen in medieval

Western European swords.[31] Furthermore such a pommel shaped broadening of the end of a sword-tang appears in stylised but still recognizable drawings in later copies of al-Kindī's text on swords (Fig. 3h). More tentative evidence for a pommel-shaped extension might be seen on a recently published Andalusian sword, dated to the late ninth century because it was found with Islamic coins of that date (Figs 3i–j). This appears to have a horizontal bar-shaped extension at the end of its tang. Unfortunately the tang was broken and has had a new piece of iron welded between the original tang and the pommel extension, making the whole thing rather peculiar.

III.

The third topic under consideration is hardened leather "hoop armour" which, until quite recently, seems to have existed only in what might be called textual interpretation. Now we have an abundance of such armour, some of which has been published[32] and some of which is currently in an archaeological store in Damascus and is as yet unpublished. In fact it is now thought likely that all this material may originally have come from Damascus. Suffice to say that, until these items came to light, the best known evidence for medieval armours made from hoops of hardened leather was in Carpini's description of the Mongol armour he had seen in Central Asia. Over a century earlier al-Ṭarsūsī also described the making of hardened leather in considerable detail. However, these sources had almost invariably been interpreted in terms of the hardened leather lamellar armour with which we were already familiar. Where these sources did not quite fit this interpretation, armour historians – myself included – tended to assume that Carpini did not fully understand the technology of what he observed, or, in the case of al-Ṭarsūsī, any confusion came from our inability to understand the author's original text.

Now we have almost complete cuirasses made of hoops of hardened leather. Each of these hoops is made of several layers of leather, sewn and perhaps also glued together (Fig. 4a–b). Several have a decorative outer layer which gives an almost fish-scale or feather effect which seems to have no practical function. Some incorporate small iron hinges and all seem to have been kept together by vertical leather straps, usually on the inside, though on at least one armour these straps were on the outside. The most complete of these hardened leather armours has been subjected to radio-carbon dating tests (Fig. 4c), producing the astonishing optimum date of 1220 AD.

Some pieces made in the same manner, which came from a clearly dateable archaeological context, are now being studied in Damascus.[33] This context, being the very late fifteenth or very sixteenth century may be outside the period under consideration, but the armour fragments are potentially even more significant because they may be elements from a horse-armour rather than armour for a man (Figs 5a–b). As such they are probably unique.

Within Western European pictorial or art-sources, the presence of a more rigid form of armour over a mail hauberk but beneath a fabric surcoat can be indicated by a guard-chain emerging from a slit or hole in the surcoat and then being joined to the hilt of a sword or dagger (Figs 6a–b). These guard-chains became more common in the fourteenth

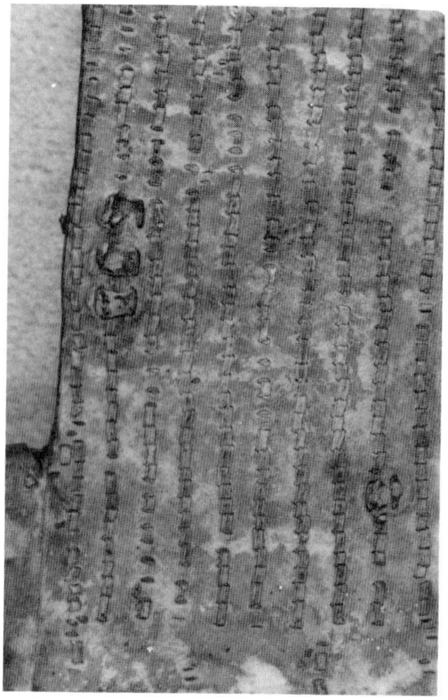

Figs 4a–c

a (top): Exterior detail of the stitching of a laminated hardened leather cuirass, probably from the Citadel in Damascus, Mamluk Islamic twelfth or thirteenth century (private collection). b (top right): Interior detail of the stitching of a laminated hardened leather cuirass, probably from the Citadel in Damascus, Mamluk Islamic twelfth or thirteenth century (private collection). c (right): Yellow-stained laminated hardened leather cuirass, probably from the Citadel in Damascus, Mamluk Islamic, radio-carbon optimum date of 1220 AD (private collection).

century and were designed to stop a man losing his weapon during the tumult of combat. Nevertheless their presence provides no information about the structure of the unseen rigid or semi-rigid armour beneath the surcoat. It is only when something more specific is illustrated that we can say anything further. However, most of the earliest illustrations normally have one feature in common, and that is their apparently "hooped" structure (Fig. 6c). Occasionally vertical rather than horizontal divisions dominate and the latter style is assumed to illustrate an early form of the coat-of-plates or pair-of-plates which incorporated substantial iron scales or small plates. Most of the illustrations of the "hooped" form also illustrate what are taken to be the heads of rivets securing presumed iron

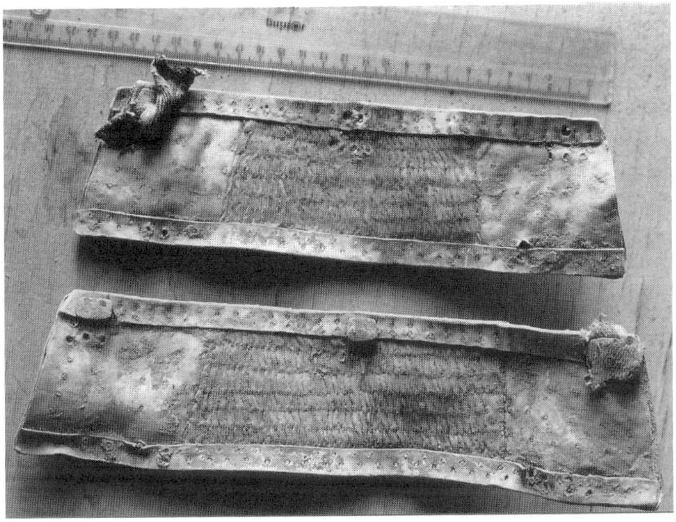

Fig. 5a: Exterior of pieces of hardened leather armour excavated in the Citadel of Damascus, perhaps a fragment of horse-armour, Mamluk late fifteenth or very early sixteenth century (author's photograph).

Fig. 5b: Interior of pieces of hardened leather armour excavated in the Citadel of Damascus, perhaps a fragment of horse-armour, Mamluk late fifteenth or very early sixteenth century (author's photograph).

elements inside the apparent hoops, though they might also show how the hoops were fastened to a fabric exterior (Figs 6d–f). As such these riveted and "hooped" body armours might be called coats-of-plates, though they might equally be reinforced versions of an earlier armour or *cuirie* simply consisting of hardened leather "hoops".

It is misleading to try to put the "hooped" style and the style in which presumed iron elements consisted of vertical rather than horizontal plates, in chronological order. Indeed the evidence indicates that both were used around the same time. One form might have been more popular in one or other part of Europe, and the overall picture does seem to suggest that the "hooped" structure was initially more popular in the south while the

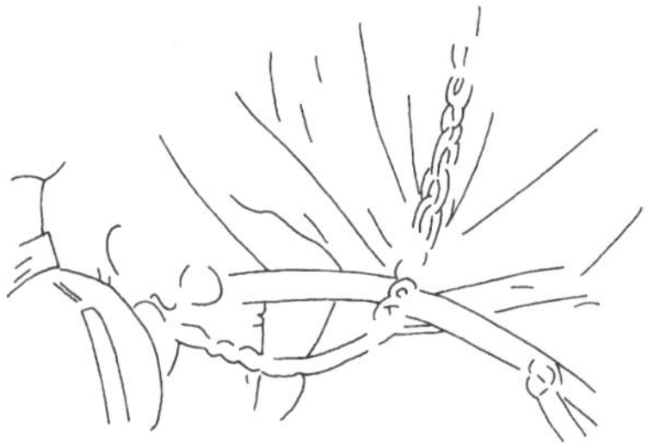

Fig. 6a (left) Effigy of an unnamed knight wearing a brimmed helmet, mail hauberk, perhaps hardened leather gauntlets and leg armour, with a single guard-chain from a presumed coat-of-plated beneath his surcoat, English, second half of the thirteenth or early fourteenth century (in situ Church of St. John the Baptist, Mamble, Worcestershire).

Fig. 6b (top) Detail of the worn effigy in Mamble church, showing a single guard-chain emerging from the centre of the wearer's surcoat.

Fig. 6c (bottom) Effigy of an unnamed knight, showing the side buckles and straps of a coat of plates worn beneath the surcoat (in situ Abbey, Pershore, Worcestershire).

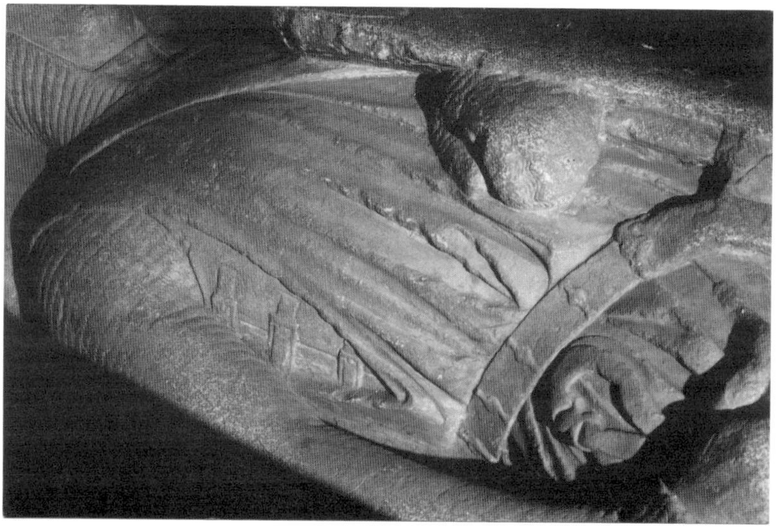

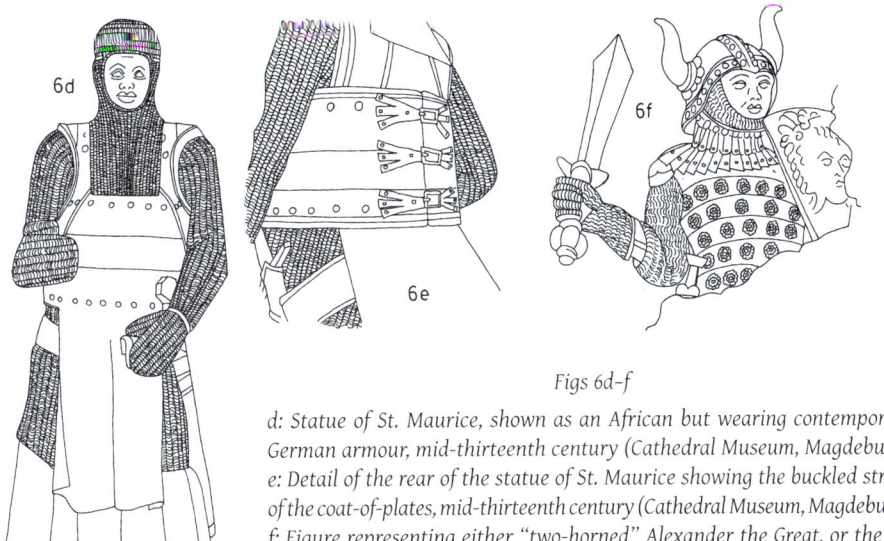

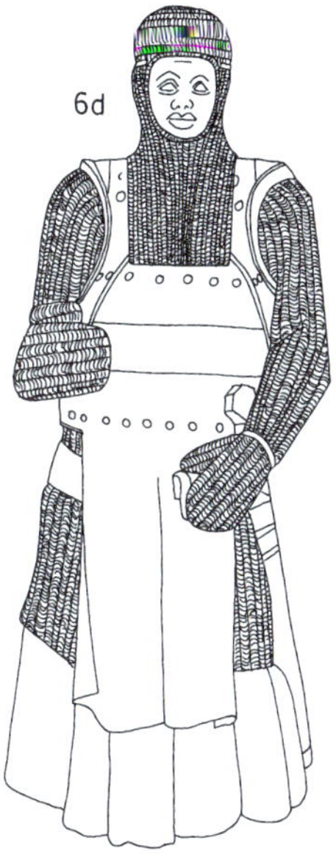

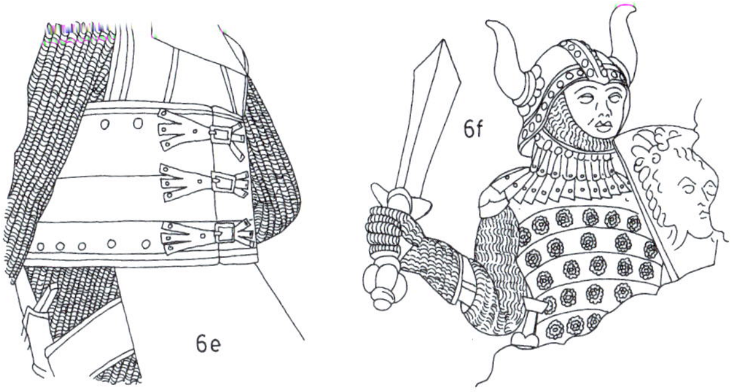

Figs 6d–f

d: Statue of St. Maurice, shown as an African but wearing contemporary German armour, mid-thirteenth century (Cathedral Museum, Magdeburg). e: Detail of the rear of the statue of St. Maurice showing the buckled straps of the coat-of-plates, mid-thirteenth century (Cathedral Museum, Magdeburg). f: Figure representing either "two-horned" Alexander the Great, or the Sin of Pride, carved capital, mid-fourteenth century Venetian (in situ, Doge's Palace, Venice).

"vertical" style was more popular in the north. Eventually, however, the "hooped" style was adopted everywhere, probably because it was more efficient.

Armour of "hooped" construction had, of course, been known long before the medieval period. It protected the limbs of Seleucid Greek cavalry in what is now Afghanistan[34] and probably elsewhere in the Hellenistic world, as well as forming the basis of the Roman legionary's famous cuirass. Subsequently, the idea of fusing ordinary laced lamellar armour into rigid or semi-rigid strips by coating them with numerous layers of lacquer was developed in Japan. It is also possible that both the hardened leather *cuirie* and the "hooped", splinted or simply scale-lined *coats-of-plates* used in medieval Western Europe were indigenous developments which owed little or nothing to outside influences, either from the Byzantine World, the Islamic World or the Mongols.[35] Clearly these armours were adopted at a time when the military superiority supposedly enjoyed by mail-armoured knightly cavalry was under threat from crossbows and latterly also from longbows.[36] Here it is only fair to point out that the very idea of a knightly domination of medieval warfare has itself been convincingly challenged in recent years.[37]

Nevertheless the interesting possibility, or indeed probability, remains that the sudden adoption of early forms of rigid or semi-rigid body armours in Western Europe from the mid-twelfth to early fourteenth centuries was influenced by the more sophisticated armament technologies of neighbouring civilisations. This is not to suggest that such technology was transferred directly. Indeed it seems more likely that Western European armourers adopted a concept rather than directly copying an armour, and that the Islamic concept of the "hooped" hardened leather cuirass first influenced armourers and their customers in northern Italy; perhaps specifically in maritime republics such as Venice (Fig. 6f).

Fig. 7a: Iron visors from the Byzantine Imperial Great Palace in Istanbul, probably mid-twelfth century (present location unknown; St. Andrews University Library Photographic Collection).

If this is correct, then it seems likely that iron-rich Europe replaced the hardened leather hoops of the Islamic *jawshan* with iron hoops. Given the vulnerability of hardened leather to damp, especially when it was of reconstituted or layered construction, one might guess that the seagoing Venetians would have been keen to change from leather to iron.

The fourth topic is that of anthropomorphic face-masks or visors. Most surviving early examples come from Russia and the Ukraine, though some were also found in the ruins of the Byzantine Great Palace in Istanbul (Fig. 7a). Here they appear to have been in the same or a similar archaeological context as some interesting fragments of iron lamellar armour. The latter were fused together by fire and were stuck to a coin of the Emperor Manuel I (1143–1180 AD). The first published report on these finds suggested that, because these nine iron masks were found all together in one spot, they might have had something to do with military "games" or ceremonies such as those described during the tenth century in the *The Book of Ceremonies*.[38] This was a fair assumption at the time when it was written, since nothing comparable was known from such a period. Furthermore these masks have strong similarities with the far more realistic face-mask visors worn by some Hellenistic and Late Roman cavalry. So there was little reason for the British archaeologists, with their all too typical Eurocentric and classicist mindset, to look further afield for alternative parallels.

However, we now have plenty of alternative sources of inspiration and perhaps even origin for the iron masks from the Byzantine imperial capital. One decorated example was found in what was, before the Mongol conquests, the Turkic Khanate of Bulgar on the upper Volga river (Figs 7b–c).[39] Others have been excavated in southern Russia and the Ukraine, where some are associated with a people known in Russian history as the "Black Hats". This people were semi-settled ex-nomads of Turkic origin and speech who, having been forced out of the western extremity of the vast Eurasian steppes by other nomadic peoples

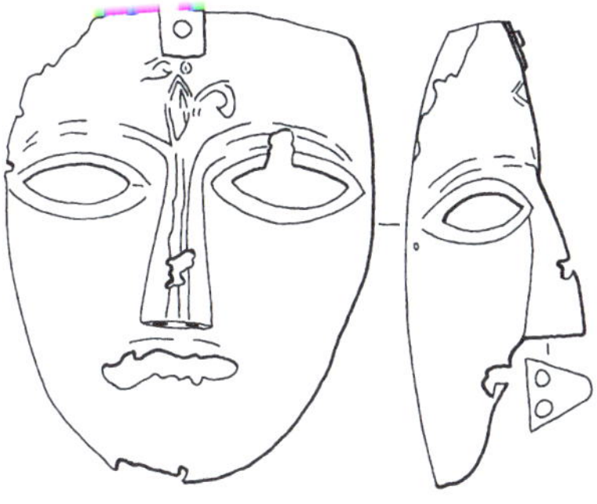

Figs 7b (top) and 7c (right): Iron "face-mask" visors found in the territory of the Khanate of the Volga Bulgars, probably early thirteenth century (current location unknown; drawing after I.L. Ismailov & V.N. Markov, in Khalikov [et. al. (eds.)], Volgskaya Bulgariya i Mongolskoe Nashestvie [as in n. 39]).

pushing westward, became frontier allies or vassals of Kievan Russia. Others are roughly associated with the Kipchaq Turks – known to the Russians as the Polovtsy and to most other Europeans as the Cumans (Fig. 7d). Pictorial and somewhat later archaeological sources then indicate that comparable metallic face-masks were occasionally used in Iran from the fourteenth century onwards. Taken altogether, the evidence supports the thesis that the face-mask visors from Constantinople are likely to have been worn by heavily armoured cavalry of Turkic origin in Byzantine service. Certainly the Byzantine Empire recruited horsemen from the steppes, or from ex-nomadic peoples who, like the "Black Hats" of Russia, had been forced out of the steppes by powerful new arrivals.

Might such iron masks have had some influence upon the early development of rigid visors in early fourteenth century Europe? The timing is about right. During the second half of the twelfth century fixed face-protecting visors came into use, almost

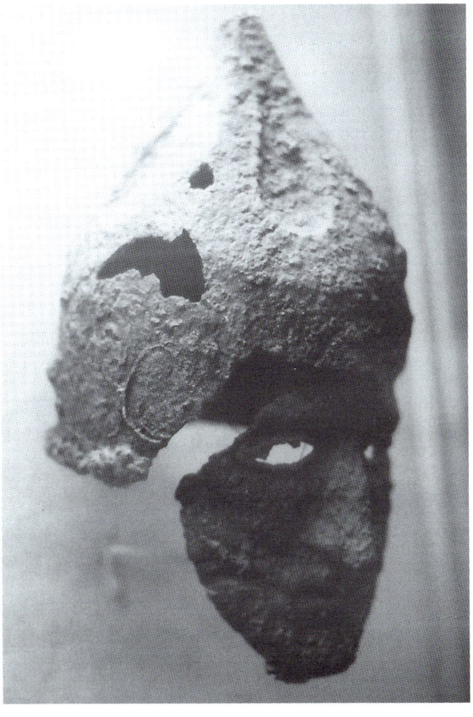

Fig 7d: Helmet and visor from gravesite near Kovali, south-east of Kiev, Kipchaq early thirteenth century or Mongol Golden Horde late thirteenth early fourteenth centuries (Hermitage Museum, St. Petersburg).

Fig. 7e: Bascinet with so-called "dog-faced" visor, German mid- or late fourteenth century from Hungary (Hungarian National Museum, Budapest).

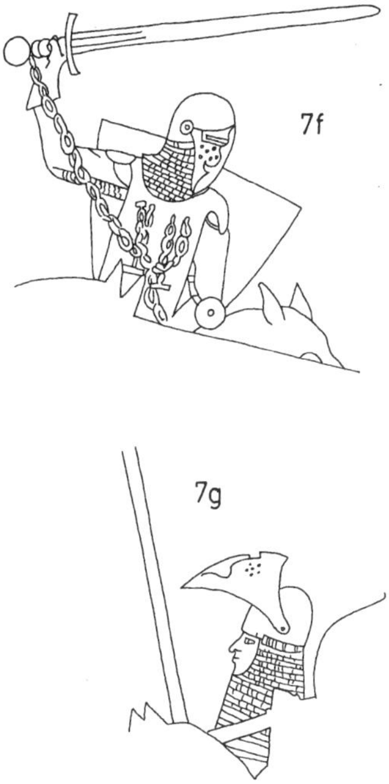

Fig. 7f–g: Details from a wall-painting of mounted Ghibeline (f) and Guelph (g) knights in combat, c.1340 AD, Italian (in situ Castle of Sabbionara, Avio).

certainly in response to the rising threat from infantry archery; at this date primarily from crossbows. This style then developed into the so-called *great helm* of the late twelfth to early fourteenth century. Such a form of helmet provided splendid protection but greatly restricted visibility. It was also extremely heavy and made breathing difficult. So it is no surprise that, with the development of the lighter *bascinet* helmet which protected most of the head but not the face, moveable and indeed removeable visors also appeared. Some were attached by a hinge on the brow of the helmet (Fig 7e), like those from Eastern Europe and probably the examples from Constantinople, but more commonly they were attached to a pair of swivels on the sides of the helmet (Figs 7f–g). In both cases the visors could be raised to permit easy breathing and unimpaired visibility. Furthermore the earliest such moveable visors were almost flat or only slightly domed in profile, much like the Turkic and Byzantine examples. Only later did distinctive so called "dog-faced" and "pig-faced" visored *bascinets* appear. The former were pointed and the latter very prominently domed.

IV.

The final topic concerns scale armour in medieval Western Europe. Here archaeology, instead of offering an entirely new form of armour, has provided evidence which apparently overthrows a long-held argument that a particular form of military technology simply did not exist. Most armour historians, myself included, had argued that what might at first glance look like scale armour – as illustrated in manuscripts from, for example, the Carolingian period – actually showed ordinary mail armour. The apparent similarity with downwards overlapping fish-like scales was merely an artistic convention at a time when detailed technological accuracy was not uppermost in the minds of the monkish illuminators (Fig. 8a).

Fig. 8a: "The Psalmist pursuing his enemies", Psalm 17 v. 38–39 (Stuttgart Psalter, Würtembergische Landesbib. Biblia Folia 23, f. 21v, Stuttgart).

This interpretation is probably still true of virtually all early medieval pictorial sources, since there is a total lack of archaeological evidence for such scale armour as opposed to the real though rare evidence for lamellar armour. Furthermore, it has been extremely rare for those scale armours which did exist at various times and in various cultures, to include anything like sleeves; at least sleeves in the normally accepted meaning of the word, going right around the arms and covering the wearer's armpits. It is, in fact, effectively impossible to make a scale armour with complete shoulder, upper-arm and armpit protection. On the other hand illustrations of sleeveless scale armour do exist. One such armour of highly debateable date but obvious scale construction exists in the Alava Museum in Vitoria (Figs 8b–c). It might date from the later medieval period, though an early modern Chinese origin has also been suggested.

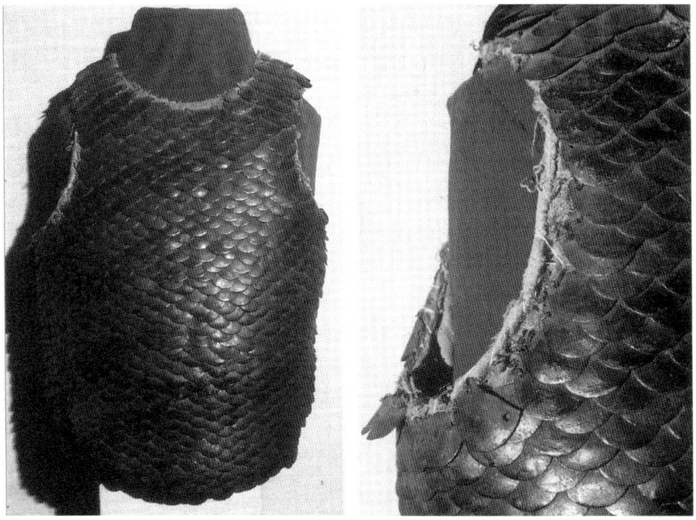

Figs 8b (left) and 8c (right): Scale armour, said to be Spanish thirteenth or fourteenth century (Archaeological Museum of the Province of Alava, Vitoria).

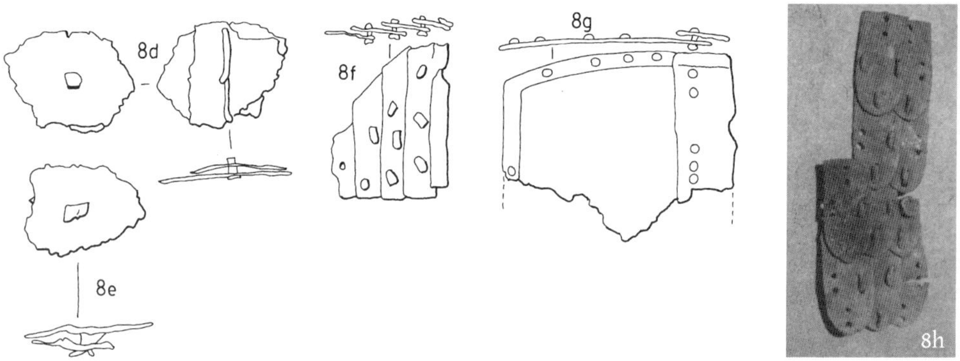

Figs 8d–h
d–e: Scale armour from Charavines, Provençal French, start of eleventh century (Colardelle [et. al.], 'L'armement des chevaliers-paysans de Charavines au XIe siècle', [as in n. 40]). f–g: Fragments of loose-rivetted lamellar from the gravesite at Verhniy Chiryurt, tumulus 5, Khazar, seventh–eighth century (after Gorelik, 'Arms and Armour in South-Eastern Europe in the Second Half of the First Millenium AD' [as in n. 41]). h: Fragment of rivetted bronze lamellar armour, from Dura Europos, Syro-Roman, third century (Yale University Art Gallery, New Haven).

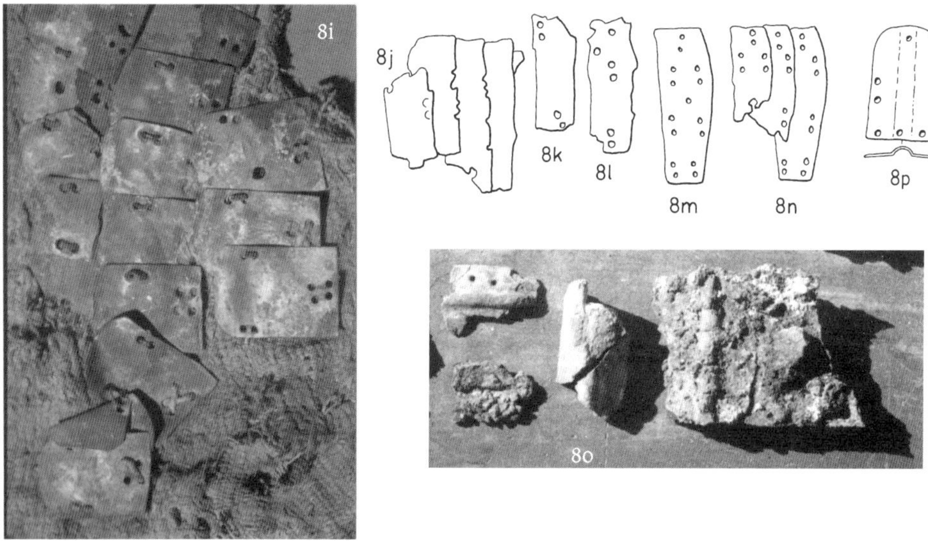

Figs 8i–p
i: Fragment of rivetted bronze scale armour with fabric backing, from Dura Europos, Syro-Roman, third century (Yale University Art Gallery, New Haven). j–n: Magyar lamellar from gravesites at Lagerevo in Bashkiria, seventh–eighth century and Manvelovka, Dnipropetrovs'k region, ninth century (after Gorelik, 'Arms and Armour in South-Eastern Europe in the Second Half of the First Millenium AD' [as in n. 41]). o: Fragments of corroded iron lamellar armour from the Byzantine Imperial Great Palace in Istanbul, probably mid-twelfth century (present location unknown; St. Andrews University Library Photographic Collection). p: Author's reconstruction of a single lamel from the Byzantine Great Palace, Istanbul.

The above-mentioned archaeological evidence for scale armour in eleventh century south-eastern France has only recently been published (Figs 8d–e). According to one article about the military finds at Colletière, near Charavines in the Departement of Isère, many polygonal iron plates or scales were found. These were identified as elements from a *brunia* cuirass.[40] Though severely corroded, each iron scale originally had a large split-pin in the centre, secured by a large roughly cut washer. The space between the washer and the back of the scale certainly suggests that some relatively thick material such as a leather backing for the whole armour was originally present.

An alternative though less likely explanation for the space between the washer and the scale is that these were examples of the "loose rivetting" system used in Khazar armour from the steppes of southern Russia in the seventh or eighth centuries (Figs 8f–g).[41] Loose rivetting was a sophisticated system which permitted increased flexibility and increased strength when compared to ordinary lamellar armour, though it also demanded greater metalworking skills. The "loose rivetting" system had apparently disappeared with the fall of the Roman Empire and would not reappear in Western European armour until the end of the fifteenth century. Perhaps the most abundant Roman examples are amongst the third century AD finds from Dura Europos in Syria (Figs 8h–i). Here most of the scales or lamellae were of bronze, while their split-pins or rivets were copper. But before disregarding the Khazars and their loose rivetted cuirasses, it might be worth noting that the Magyars had been culturally as well as politically very closely associated with the Turkic Khazars before their migration into, and conquest of, what is now Hungary (Figs 8j–n).[42] Furthermore, the Magyars campaigned deep into Italy and Germany in the tenth century. So the possibility of some Hungarian Magyar influence upon the unexpected iron scale armour from Colletière should not be disregarded.

More significantly, perhaps, a case has recently been made for the use of a slightly different form of partially laced and partially rivetted lamellar armour in the Byzantine Empire (Fig. 9), at least from the eleventh century onwards.[43] This would seem a more likely source of direct inspiration for the scales from Colletière. A written description of the very oxidised scales from the Byzantine Great Palace[44] also seems to indicate the presence of a single hole for a lost rivet, as well as the paired holes used in lacing (Fig. 8p). Many years ago I argued that much early Arab-Islamic armour was of scale rather than mail construction, though relying on textual rather than archaeological or pictorial sources.[45] Subsequently I largely withdrew from this position, though I still believe that Arab-Islamic armourers may have exchanged technological and stylistic influences with their early and high medieval southern European counterparts.

Fig. 9: Reconstruction of Byzantine riveted and laced lamellar armour (after Dawson, 'Suntagma Hoplon' [as in n. 43]).

However, a magnificent scale-lined rather than scale covered armour has recently been found by a French and Syrian archaeological team in the Citadel of Damascus (Fig. 10a). It is around five

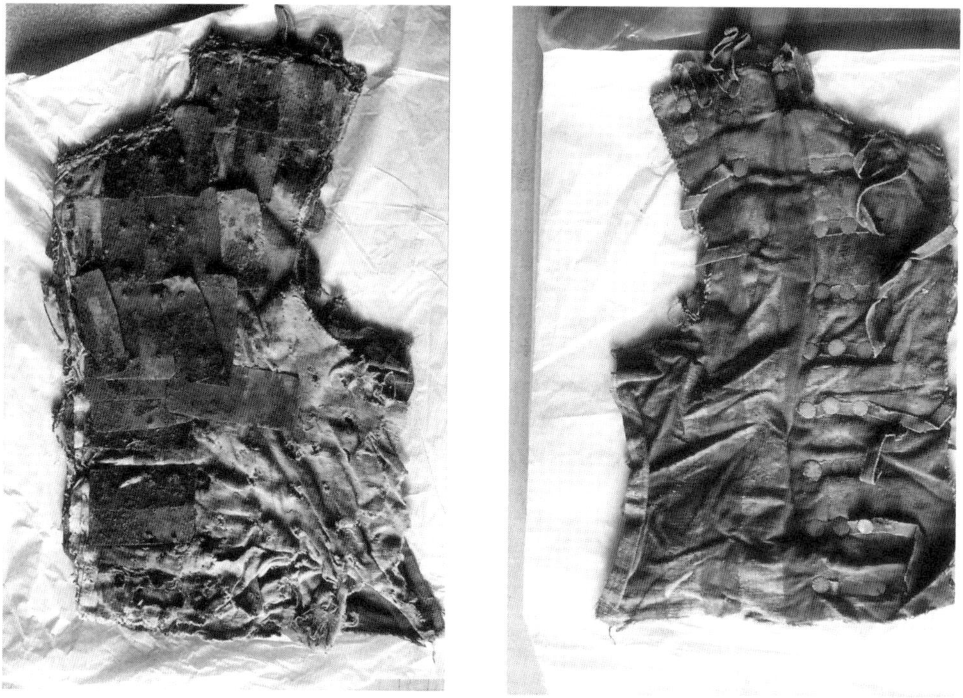

Fig 10: a (left) Interior of a scale-lined qarqal excavated in the Citadel of Damascus showing some iron scales still attached, Mamluk late fifteenth or very early sixteenth century (author's photograph). b (right) Exterior of a scale-lined qarqal excavated in the Citadel of Damascus showing the fine velvet outer layer of fabric, Mamluk late fifteenth or very early sixteenth century (author's photograph).

centuries later than the Colletière finds but seems to be a late example of a form of armour known as a *qarqal* which had been known for at least two hundred years. This magnificent garment will feature prominently in the forthcoming publication of the late medieval archaeological finds from the Damascus Citadel (Fig. 10b).[46]

Notes

1 D.C. Nicolle, 'Byzantine and Islamic Arms and Armour: Evidence for Mutual Influence', *Graeco-Arabica*, 4 (1991), 299–325; D.C. Nicolle, 'No Way Overland? Evidence for Byzantine Arms and Armour on the 10th–11th Century Taurus Frontier', *Graeco-Arabica*, 6 (1995), 226–45.

1a D.C. Nicolle, 'Archery', in *Encyclopaedia of Islam* 3rd edition (Leiden, 207), 155–60.

2 C. Cahen, 'Un traité d'armurerie composé pour Saladin', *BEO*, 12 (1947–48), 103–60; a more complete and correct edition has recently been made by Dr. Shihab al-Sarraf, *Tabṣirat arbāb al-albāb* (awaiting publication).

3 C.E. Bosworth, 'Abū ʿAmr ʿUthmān al-Ṭarsūsī's Siyar al-Thughūr and the Last Years of Arab Rule in Tarsus (Fourth/Tenth Century)', *Graeco-Arabica*, 5 (1993), 183–95.

4 C. Cahen, article *ʿArrāda*, in *EI*[2]; Cahen believed that the *ʿarrāda* was a single-armed torsion powered stone-throwing machine like the Roman *onager* from which he believed it had developed. However, by the later medieval period the *manjaniq ʿarrāda* was clearly a small man-

powered *manjanīq* or beamsling mangonel, as seen in ibn Aranbughā al-Zaradhkāsh, *Al-Anīq fī 'l-manajanīq*, ed. I. Hindī (Aleppo, 1985), figs. 23 and 26 on pages 109 and 118. I believe the evidence indicates that it was always a weapon of a similar kind. Furthermore the similarity between the name *ʿarrāda* and the word *ʿarida* meaning a crossbeam resting on a fulcrum used to raise heavy weights (E. Wiedemann, *Aufsätze zur Arabischen Wissenschafts-Geschichte*, i [Hildesheim, 1970], 192) cannot be ignored. Perhaps early Muslim soldiers, like soldiers everywhere, used puns and visual imagery when giving names to their weapons, and a beamsling stone-thrower with an axle as its fulcrum did indeed look like a kicking ass or donkey when it was shot. Finally it is worth drawing attention to a siege weapon used in thirteenth century Islamic northern India. It was known in Persian as a *khark*, again meaning "little ass", but a description of its use strongly suggests that it was a form of ram or bore having nothing in common either with a late Roman *onager* or an Arab-Islamic *ʿarrāda* (Muḥammad ibn Manṣūr Fakhr al-Dīn Mubarakshāh, *Adab al-ḥarb wa'l-shujāʿa*, ed. A.S. Khwansari [Tehran, 1969], 424).

5 *Ḥurr* = free, unrestrained, unadulterated, noble, and various other related meanings.

6 *Ḥarra* (pl. *ḥarr*, or *ḥarrāt*) = stoney area, volcanic lava field.

7 P.E. Chevedden, 'The Artillery Revolution of the Middle Ages: the Impact of the Trebuchet on the Development of Fortifications' (unpublished paper, 1990), 28–31, quoted in K. DeVries, *Medieval Military Technology* (Peterborough, Ontario, 1992), 138, n. 34.

8 Ms. Hunt 2640.

9 In twelfth century Egypt the term *Farsī* was often used to indicate a somewhat unspecific "eastern" part of the Islamic world beyond Syria and the Jazirah (upper Mesopotamia) but not as far as Khurasan; in other words the heartland of the Great Saljuq Turkish Sultanate around south-western or western Iran (the region of Fars itself) plus much of what is now southern and central Iraq.

10 This hole or trench was noted when the castle of Bressuire was first studied archaeologically in the nineteenth century. I am indebted to Marie-Pierre Baudry for bringing this fact to my attention.

10a I now consider the crossbow shown in al-Ṭarsūsī's illustration of a counterweight *manjanīq* (Fig. 1a) to be evidence that al-Ṭarsūsī himself, or more likely the person who made the illustrations, did not understand the text upon which this particular illustration was based. The work *jarkh* could mean either "crossbow", which seems largely pointless in this context, or a "winch", which would not only make much more sense but which would very soon become a normal featuer of such weapons, as it may in reality always have been.

11 I. Peirce, *Swords of the Viking Age* (Woodbridge, 2002); E. Oakeshott, *Records of the Medieval Sword* (Woodbridge, 1991).

12 Muḥammad ibn Aḥmad al-Bīrūnī, *Kitāb al-Jamāhīr*, ed. F. Krenkow (Hyderabad, 1936), 248–9; J.W. Allan, *Persian Metal Technology, 700–1300 AD* (Oxford, 1979), 72.

13 Ibn Khurradādhbih, in C. Courtois, 'Les rapports entre l'Afrique et la Gaule au début du Moyen Âge', *Cahiers de Tunisie*, 2 (1954), 136.

14 E. Lévi-Provençal, *L'Espagne musulmane au Xème siècle* (Paris, 1932), 144–6.

15 E. García Gómez, 'Armas, Banderas, Tiendas de Campaña, Monturas y Correos en los 'Anales de Al-Hakam II' por 'Isà Razi', *al-Andalus*, 32 (1967), 163–4.

16 From *ʿudwa* = side, slope, shore, etc.

17 Using the letter *ḍād* rather than *dāl*.

18 G. Busk, 'On the caves of Gibraltar in which human remains and works of art have been found,"' in *Congrès international d'anthropologie et d'archéologie* (Norwich, 1868), 134–6.

19 D. Nicolle, 'Two Swords from the Foundation of Gibraltar', *Gladius*, 22 (2002), 147–200.

20 Al-Maqqarī in R. Dozy, G. Dugat, L. Krehl and W. Wright, *Analectes sur l'histoire et la littérature des arabes d'Espagne*, ii (Leiden, 1858–61), 397, ll. 14–15, trans. D. Nicolle; H. Pérès, *La poésie andalouse en arabe classique au XIe siècle* (Paris, 1953), 352.

21 R.E. Oakeshott, 'Some Medieval Sword-Pommels', *Journal of the British Archaeological Association*, 3 ser. 14 (1951), 55.
22 Ibid. 49.
23 Ibid. 68–9.
24 R.E. Oakeshott (in correspondence with the author, 9-1-1989).
25 J. Werner, *Beiträge zur Archäologie des Attila-Reiches* (Munich, 1956), 43.
26 A.R. al-Ansary, *Qaryat al-Fau: A Portrait of Pre-Islamic Civilization in Saudi Arabia* (London, 1982).
27 J. Schwarzer and E.C. Deal, 'A Sword Hilt from the Serçe Liman Shipwreck', *MASCA Journal*, 4/2 (1986), 52.
28 Castle Museum, inv. GW56, Bodrum, Turkey.
29 Fermando Fernández Gómez, of the Museo Arqueológico de Sevilla (in correspondence with the author, December 1989).
30 Prof. E. Baer (in correspondence with the author, 20-1-1990).
31 A.G. Visquis, 'Présence Sarrazine en rade d'Agay au Xme Siècle', in *Rencontre d'Archéologie Sous-Marine de Fréjus. Saint-Raphael* (St. Raphael, 1975), no page numbers.
32 D.C. Nicolle, 'Jawshan, Cuirie and Coat-of-Plates: An Alternative Line of Development for Hardened Leather Armour', in D.C. Nicolle (ed.), *Companion to Medieval Arms and Armour* (Woodbridge, 2002), 179–221, plates XIII-1 to XIII-45.
33 "Mission franco-syrienne de la citadelle de Damas" (IFEAD-DGAMS), headed by S. Berthier and S. Khalifeh with financial support from the General Directory for Antiquities and Museums of Syria, the French Ministry of Foreign Affairs, Total E et P Syria, and Nestlé Syria.
34 The mid-second century BC Seleucid corslet body armour found at Ai Khanoum in Afghanistan was of iron scales, but there was also "hooped" iron armour for the legs; both of these items of armour being used by heavy cavalry; F. Grenet, J.-C. Liger and R. de Valence, 'L'Arsenal', in 'Campagne de Fouille 1978 à Ai Khanoum (Afghanistan)', *Bulletin de l'École Français d'Extrème Orient*, 68 (1980), 60.
35 M.S. Lacy, *Coat of Plates to Brigandine: the Evolution of Cloth Covered Armour 1250–1500*, MA thesis (Reading University, 1992), 7.
36 A.P. Jones, 'The Attack of Plate Armour by Longbow Arrows', *Château-Gaillard*, 11 (1983), 167–8.
37 M. Bennett, 'The Myth of Supremacy of Knightly Cavalry', in M. Strickland (ed.), *Armies, Chivalry and Warfare in Medieval Britain and France* (London, 1998), 304–16.
38 G. Brett, 'Small Finds', in G. Brett (ed.), *The Great Palace of the Byzantine Emperors (First Report)* (London, 1947), 99.
39 I.L. Izmailov and V.N. Markov, 'Zheleznaya Maska - Zabrolo s Territorii Volgskoya Bulgarii', in I.L. Izmailov et al. (eds.), *Volgskaya Bulgariya i Mongolskoe Nashestvie* (Kazan, 1988), 120–25.
40 M. Colardelle, J-P. Moyne and E. Verdel, 'L'armement des chevaliers-paysans de Charavines au XIe siècle', in M. Heyer-Boscardin (ed.), *Wider das „Finstere Mittelalter": Festschrift für Werner Meyer zum 65. Geburtstag* (Schweizer Beiträge zur Kulturgeschichte und Archäologie des Mittelalters, 29; Basel *c.*2002), 107–9.
41 M. Gorelik, 'Arms and Armour in South-Eastern Europe in the Second Half of the First Millenium AD', in D.C. Nicolle (ed.), *A Companion to Medieval Arms and Armour* (Woodbridge, 2002), 134–5 and fig. XI-5.
42 Ibid., fig. XI-12.
43 T. Dawson, 'Suntagma Hoplon: The Equipment of Regular Byzantine Troops, *c.*950 to *c.*1204', in Nicolle (ed.), *A Companion to Medieval Arms and Armour* (as in n. 41), 89 and figs. VII-2 & VII-12.
44 Brett (as in n. 38), 99.
45 D. Nicolle, 'Arms Manufacture and the Arms Trade in South-Eastern Arabia in the Early Muslim Period', *The Journal of Oman Studies*, 6 (1983), 231–8.
46 To be published in the collections of the Institut Français d'Études Arabes de Damas.

7

Memories of Egypt in Medieval Venice

Deborah Howard

Apostles and epistles

In a letter to Doge Andrea Dandolo written in 1352, Petrarch justified his own passion for travel with an analogy that he knew would ring true in the Venetian mind: "The Apostles travelled far, and barefoot journeyed to the most distant lands. One or another was sent to Ephesus, to Syria, Greece, Rome, India, Egypt. Their bodies wandered in the most rugged regions; they suffered all the misadventures of land and the wide waters; but their hearts were fixed upon heaven. Today, indeed, the bodies of our 'apostles' rest on golden beds, while they send their thoughts afar over land and sea."[1]

In death as in life, the bodies of the Apostles had experienced the adventures of travel. Robbed from its burial place in Alexandria by two Venetian merchants in AD 829, St Mark's body now lay on its 'golden bed' in the ducal chapel of Venice. Here, in the mosaics, the Doge could see an encomium of the experience of travel: an anthology of gilded memories of foreign lands.

The celebrated *translatio* of the relics of St Mark had achieved a compression of both time and space, by situating the physical 'body' of the Evangelist in present and future time, in the very heart of Venice. But if his martyred remains were to be truly naturalised in Venice, this process had to involve the deliberate importation of aspects of the identity of ancient Alexandria.

The Venetian experience of travel

Just as Venice derived its wealth and power from transporting goods from the east to sell to the markets of Western Europe, so, too, the city could gain religious and intellectual stature by the importation of memories and ideas to feed the imagination of the western mind. Travel reminiscences involved all five senses – heat and cold, hunger and thirst, noise and silence, fear and amusement, bustle and solitude. Sensory perceptions infused the Venetian collective memory. In his account of the *translatio*, the thirteenth century chronicler Martino da Canal remarked that, when St Mark's tomb was opened, it seemed as if all the spices of the world had been brought to Alexandria – an analogy implying immeasurable value as well as sensual pleasure.[2] Like the Apostles, to quote Petrarch's letter again, Venetian merchants "wandered in the most rugged regions; they suffered all the misadventures of land and the wide waters." Their misfortunes ranged from interception by pirates or hostile warships to those irritations that we all remember, such as the Venetian merchant who forgot his purse containing 15 gold ducats under his pillow in an overnight lodging in Corfù.[3]

The limitations of verbal language as a vehicle for transmitting such complex patterns were recognised by the Council of Ten when they issued instructions to their ambassadors in the sixteenth century. Reports were to follow a set progression in both time and space, starting with the site of the foreign place and its name in antiquity, moving through climate and nature (including both 'bontà' and 'tristizia' – good and sad aspects), to the inhabitants and finally to the elite.[4] Letters from merchants tended to be more limited in scope, relaying the prices and availability of merchandise, and offering only scanty personal impressions. "I am healthy and safe, as are the goods I brought with me. And yes, I have sold and bought almost everything I had to do," wrote the merchant Vanino from Alexandria to his colleague in Venice in 1347.[5] Some travellers recorded their travel reminiscences in writing on their return, as much for their own pleasure as for posterity, Marco Polo being the most celebrated example. After a series of voyages between 1557 and 1562, the Venetian merchant Alessandro Magno copied out his journals in a vellum-bound volume, now in the Folger library: "There being nothing more enjoyable, for those seeking the world, than the memories of past events, I have decided for this reason and as a relaxation ['per passar l'otio' – the very opposite of 'negotio' = trade] to write up the details of my journey."[6]

The oral narratives of returning travellers and merchants constructed a more flexible mental picture of the eastern Mediterranean than written accounts, because their transmission involved dialogue and spontaneous questions from the listeners. Thus the communal culture of the city could be enriched and shared by wives and children, by confessors and doctors, by local merchants and tradesmen, and by artists and craftsmen.[7] But Martino da Canal asserted that it was the limited time-frame of oral memory that justified his own literary effort: "One person has already died, another is dying and a third is being born, and therefore one cannot record what happens except through writing and pictures."[8]

It was through the mediation of text and images that architectural identities had to be transported across the seas, for we have no record of Venetian masons or architects travelling between Venice and the Islamic world before the Fall of Constantinople in 1453. This article investigates the motivations and mechanisms underlying such cultural diffusion in the twelfth and thirteenth centuries.

Venice and Alexandria

In a literate society, travellers' tales were integrated into a verbal discourse that already existed in the heritage of classical and Christian writings. It was this dialogue with older written traditions that allowed new experiences to be authenticated, as they were absorbed into the city's cultural memory, and to be given heightened local significance by a process of analogy and mimesis. The effectiveness of Venice's acquisition of aspects of the identity of Alexandria was to depend on this dialectic process.

Like that of Venice, the foundation of Alexandria was shrouded in myth. Just as several Venetian chronicles claimed a Trojan pedigree, Alexandria's beginnings were rooted in Homeric lore. According to Plutarch, Homer himself – "a man with very hoary locks and of venerable aspect" – appeared to Alexander in a dream, quoting two lines from the Odyssey:

> An Ile there is by surging seas embrac't
> Which men call Pharos, before Ægypt plac't.[9]

On waking, Plutarch relates, Alexander "saw now that Homer was not only admirable in other ways, but also a very wise architect, and ordered the plan of the city to be drawn in conformity with this account." Like that of Venice in AD 421, Alexandria's foundation in 332 BC was associated with a specific date, both being supposedly founded on the twenty-fifth of the month.[10] Such chance conjunctions provided the context for the interlocking structure that underpinned the process of civic *emulatio.*

The Venetians were not the first to compare their homeland with Alexandria. Already in antiquity, the Greek geographer Strabo likened the site and climate of Alexandria to that of Padua, Ravenna and Altinum (the nearest Roman town to the site of Venice itself).[11] All of these were marshy cities, he explained, but they remained healthy because of the purifying effect of the winds and tides, a passage echoed by both Vitruvius and Alberti. Like Plutarch, Diodorus Siculus described the site of Alexandria in terms evoking that of Venice, lying between a great marshy lake and the sea.[12] Between 1306 and 1321 the Venetian traveller Marin Sanudo Torsello expounded his case that the next Crusade should strike at Muslim power in Egypt because the Venetians were so familiar with such terrain from their own experience at home.[13]

The physical resemblances between the two sites extended to the wider context, both geographically and commercially. Both were situated near the mouths of great rivers, the Nile and the Po, their navigable channels needing regular dredging to prevent them from silting up. Like Alexandria in ancient times, the Venetians constructed a canal link – the Brenta – to ease the transport of goods between the hinterland and the port. In Hellenistic and Roman times Alexandria was normally described as lying *by* Egypt ('ad Aegyptum'), rather than *in* Egypt, for its cultural and commercial orientation, like that of Venice, looked outwards towards the Mediterranean.[14] According to Diodorus, Alexandria was widely considered "to be the first city of the civilised world, and it is certainly far ahead of all the rest in elegance and extent of riches and luxury."[15] Writing in about AD 80, Josephus was among those who praised the trading success of the city: "To this port are carried all the commodities which the country lacks for its welfare, and from it the surplus local products are distributed to every quarter of the world."[16] Like medieval Venice, the ancient city had been equipped with shipyards, granaries and warehouses, and had minted its own coins; and among the local industries, Alexandria's renown as a centre for glass manufacture anticipated Venice's success in the same craft. Even in the fifteenth century, the Egyptian port was still regarded as a marketplace linking two different worlds[17] – precisely the same strategic commercial role that defined Venice's trading success.

The Alexandria of antiquity was certainly a metropolis worthy of emulation. Ancient sources remarked on its beauty, prosperity and size: Ammianus Marcellinus was one author who called the city 'vertex omnium civitatum'.[18] According to Diodorus the census returns at the time of his visit recorded a population of 300,000, greater than the largest population ever to be recorded in Venice in the second half of the sixteenth century.[19] During the Middle Ages, however, under the Islamic caliphates, the centre of gravity within Egypt itself shifted inland to Cairo, leaving Alexandria as a rundown maritime outpost. In 1326 the Muslim traveller Ibn Baṭṭūṭah described Cairo, rather than Alexandria, as "mother of all cities... boundless in multitude of buildings, peerless in beauty and splendour".[20] Despite his standpoint as a Christian pilgrim, the German priest Felix Faber, too, was impressed by his visit to Cairo in 1483, writing of "this enormous city, the most formidable in the world", whereas he had found Alexandria "a desolate town".[21] Like Rome at the start of the fifteenth century much of the ancient city of Alexandria was *disabitato.* Faber painted a poignant picture of its faded glory: "Every day houses collapse one after another, and there are only miserable ruins, inside imposing fortifications. The population is small. Apart from the mosques, the houses of the Mamluks and officials, and the *fondaci* [trading posts], the town is almost deserted, and the houses still standing are uninhabited."[22]

Like a martyred saint, the spirit had gone out of Alexandria, ready to be resurrected on foreign soil.

Egypt in the San Marco mosaics

It was in the apostle's 'golden bed', San Marco itself, that the most explicit recollections of Alexandria and Egypt were to be translated into visual imagery in Venice, not only in the narratives of the Marcian legend, but also in the Old Testament cycle in the atrium. Evocations of Egypt could endow the narratives with biblical authenticity, making them believable in the literal sense, yet transporting the worshipper effortlessly into the realm of the supernatural by alluding to the exoticism of far-away lands. As Serlio wondered in his *Dell'antichità* published in Venice in 1540, "What should we ourselves say of the absolutely extraordinary remains of Egypt, which seem more like dreams and visions than real objects?"[23]

In the *Stories of St Mark* in the Chapels of St Clement and St Peter on either side of the choir of San Marco, datable to the first half of the twelfth century, Alexandrian settings play an intrinsic part in the narrative. In the *Baptism of Anianus* in the chapel of St Peter (Fig. 1), Alexandria is given a simple lobed roofline like that of San Marco itself at that time, but firmly labelled 'ALESANDRIA', as if to make explicit the congruence between the two cities. In the late fifteenth century Gentile Bellini was to use the same device in his *St Mark preaching at Alexandria,* now in the Brera, though by then the reference was understood and the 'luggage label' no longer needed.

The scene of *The Martyrdom of St Mark* in the Cappella di San Pietro (Fig. 2) shows the saint suspended by a rope around his neck from the towers of Alexandria with that city's most celebrated monument, the Pharos, directly above his head. In antiquity, the great lighthouse had been distinguished by its three tiers – square at the base, octagonal in the middle and cylindrical at the summit. When this mosaic was executed, it was still standing,

Fig. 1: Baptism of Anianus, *mosaic, early twelfth century. Venice, San Marco, Cappella di San Pietro. Courtesy of the photographic archives, National Gallery of Art, Washington DC.*

Fig. 2: Martyrdom of St Mark, *mosaic, early twelfth century. Venice, San Marco, Cappella di San Pietro. Courtesy of the photographic archives, National Gallery of Art, Washington DC.*

though sadly mutilated. Its condition had dramatically deteriorated since the Arab conquest in AD 641: badly damaged under Caliph al-Walīd in the early eighth century in a mistaken search for treasure inside, the upper parts had been restored in brick and stucco rather than the original gleaming white ashlar, their height now much reduced.[24] The descriptions (and one schematic sketch) by Arab travellers in the twelfth and early thirteenth centuries suggest that the form depicted in the Cappella San Pietro was based on first-hand knowledge of its actual state at the time. The glow inside the cupola, however, must have been superimposed on the information in traveller's reports, through recourse to ancient texts. When Ibn Ṭūlūn had a wooden-domed mosque erected on top in about 875, the blazing fire and complex mirror system of the ancient lighthouse were no longer to be seen.[25]

Not only does the recognisable inclusion of the Pharos signify a particular geographical identity, but also, as one of the Seven Wonders of the Ancient World lit by the perpetual fire burning at its summit, the Pharos adds stature to the apostle's role as a powerful source of spiritual light, its lantern open to reveal the golden light emanating from within. It appears again with its lantern alight, once more placed directly above the saint's head in *The Burial of St Mark* in the same chapel, though in a more schematic form.

The atrium mosaics

It was in the atrium during the thirteenth century that the opportunity to evoke Egyptian settings offered its widest scope. Here the impact of travel and trade on the visual imagination may be observed in the Old Testament scenes from the *Book of Genesis* that decorate the chain of domes. Even the idea of surrounding the nave of the church on its two free sides with a succession of low cupolas may have been intended as an allusion to eastern models, for repeated domes were beginning to appear in mosque and madrasa architecture from Aleppo to Isfahan.

As Demus stressed, the atrium mosaics show an insistent desire to focus on stories with Egyptian settings, whereas events that largely preclude this, such as the stories of Isaac and Jacob, are omitted.[26] As if to underscore this particular choice of programme, the exterior of the north wing of the atrium displays a relief of *The Flight of Alexander the Great* (Fig. 3). Founder of Alexandria and the ruler over an enormous empire, Alexander seems to be intended as an image of temporal power, with specific reference to Alexandria, rather than an anti-Christ figure or an image of pride, as has been suggested.[27] The king rides in triumph in his chariot, drawn by mythical griffins, holding aloft the sticks with joints of meat that tempted the beasts to take to the skies. He is portrayed in the guise of a Byzantine emperor, probably taken from coin images (which would explain his lack of a lower body). The life of Alexander was familiar not only from ancient writings, but more particularly from the hugely popular *Alexander Romance* of Pseudo-Callisthenes, mentioned for instance by Marco Polo.[28] At the end of the *Alexander Romance*, Zeus through an oracle instructs Ptolemy to carry the body of the dead conqueror to its final resting place in Alexandria, enacting the divine prophecy revealed to Alexander at the opening of the *Life:*

Fig. 3: Flight of Alexander the Great, *stone relief, c. twelfth century. Venice, San Marco, north side (exterior). Osvaldo Böhm, Venice.*

Here in this city always you shall dwell
In life and death. The city which you built
Shall be your tomb. This I, your sire, swear,
Oh Alexander.[29]

Thus the *translatio* and burial of Alexander offered the perfect classical analogy for the fate of St Mark's relics, as well as a potent image of state.

It has been realised for over a century that the manuscript known as the *Cotton Genesis* was used as the basic source for the figure compositions of the atrium mosaics (apart from the final Moses cupola which is not found in the *Book of Genesis*).[30] Badly burned in a fire in 1731, this famous Greek manuscript is now in the British library. It consists only of a series of fragments, known either as charred scraps of parchment or from the water colours made by George Vertue soon after the fire. Most scholars accept the tradition that the *Cotton Genesis* was made in Egypt – possibly in Alexandria itself – at about the end of the fifth or the beginning of the sixth century.[31] The Alexandrian provenance, whether true or mythical, gave this source a poignant relevance.

It was above all in the architectural backgrounds of the atrium mosaics that the imagination of the local designer(s) transcended the prototypes in the *Cotton Genesis*. This important modification, observed repeatedly by Weitzmann, led Demus to search almost in vain for similar treatments of architecture within the traditions of Byzantine art. To Demus, the settings showed "a somewhat barbaric love of showiness, of material splendour", for he recognised (but did not entirely sympathise with) the desire to evoke one of the great trading emporia of the east.[32] Finding only isolated reminiscences from sites as far apart as Serbia and Kiev, he tentatively suggested illuminated manuscripts as the means of transmission. Before returning to this important question we must address the mosaics themselves.

The entire north side of the atrium is dominated by Egyptian settings: the *Story of Joseph* occupies three domes, and the *Life of Moses* the fourth. The prominence given to Joseph inside the atrium further emphasises a Christian justification of temporal power. In Egypt, according to the *Book of Genesis*, Joseph was placed second in command to the king himself:

> And Pharaoh said unto Joseph, See I have set thee over all the land of Egypt.
>
> And Pharaoh took off his ring from his hand, and put it upon Joseph's hand, and arrayed him in vestures of fine linen, and put a gold chain about his neck;
>
> And he made him to ride in the second chariot which he had; and they cried before him, Bow the knee: and he made him ruler over all the land of Egypt. (*Genesis*, 41, 41–43)

Joseph's namesake, Josephus, in his *Jewish Antiquities*, records how Jacob could scarcely believe the news of his son's destiny: "living in splendid fortune, sharing with the king the government of Egypt and having well-nigh the whole charge of it in his hands."[33]

Thus Joseph becomes a prototype for St Mark himself, described as the founder of the church in Alexandria by Eusebius, and depicted as Bishop of Alexandria in one of the spandrels of the north atrium. The association between Joseph, Mark the Evangelist and the image of Alexander in triumph on the north façade as three figures of authority in Egypt would not have gone unnoticed. Material success, temporal power and the ability to manage scarce resources of food – all these aspects of the Joseph story offered themes of particular relevance to the fortunes of the Venetian state. Dale has even suggested that Joseph served as a pre-figuration of the office of Doge.[34] It is not inconceivable that the prominent position of the great state granaries, erected on the waterfront opposite Piazza San Marco in the 1340s (on the site now occupied by gardens), may have evoked Joseph's prudent storage of reserves of grain.

The Egyptian settings had to evoke a set of memories, personal or retold, of a distant land. Potiphar's wife, an image of temptation, is richly dressed and framed by colourful, airy pavilions. Pharaoh is seen enthroned beneath a cusped arch topped by an exotic, eclectic skyline; in another scene he banquets in front of a similar archway draped with luxurious curtains (Fig. 4); and in a lunette he dreams on a cushioned divan. In his position of authority, Joseph occupies dignified buildings almost as rich as those of Pharaoh himself. Following the identification relayed by medieval travellers such as John Mandeville, Joseph's granaries are given the form of the great pyramids of the Nile (Fig. 5), although one of the scenes in the Cotton Bible had given them the more correct beehive shape. Of course, as the German pilgrim Felix Faber prosaically remarked of this tradition, there isn't even enough space inside the pyramids for a man to stand upright – a problem energetically represented in a sketch in Alessandro Magno's diary.[35]

The fact that a manuscript source of Egyptian derivation for the Old Testament figure compositions has been identified, namely the *Cotton Bible,* leads us to investigate whether

Fig. 4 (left): Butler serving Pharaoh, *mosaic, thirteenth century. Venice, San Marco, north atrium, second Joseph cupola, pendentive. Courtesy of the photographic archives, National Gallery of Art, Washington DC.*

Fig. 5 (below): Joseph's barns, *mosaic, thirteenth century. Venice, San Marco, north atrium, third Joseph cupola, detail. Courtesy of the photographic archives, National Gallery of Art, Washington DC.*

Fig. 6: Banquet scene, *from the* Maqāmāt *of al-Ḥarīrī, 1237. Paris, Bibliothèque Nationale, ms Arabe 5847 ('Schefer* Maqāmāt*'), f. 47v. Bibliothèque Nationale de France, Paris.*

other collections of miniatures may have been at hand to inspire the designers of the atrium mosaics. Many of the characteristics of the anecdotal detail in the mosaics can also be found in illustrated manuscripts of the Muslim world, such as versions of the *Maqāmāt* (Assemblies) of al-Ḥarīrī, a series of stories focusing on two main characters: a verbally acrobatic picaresque hero and the narrator, a bourgeois travelling merchant. In his compilation of all thirteen surviving illuminated versions of the *Maqāmāt,* Oleg Grabar remarked on the paradoxical role of these entertaining, visually self-sufficient illustrations as an accompaniment to intricate written texts characterised not by visual imagery but by verbal subtlety and complexity.[36] All but two of the known illustrated *Maqāmāt* manuscripts date from the thirteenth and early fourteenth century – for instance, the celebrated Schefer *Maqāmāt* in the Bibliothèque Nationale in Paris (ms. arabe 5847) is dated AD 1237 (Fig. 6). Such a book could therefore have been imported well before the atrium mosaics reached completion in about the mid-thirteenth century. Another popular illustrated narrative in the Islamic world was the *Ḥadīth Bayāḍ wa-Riyāḍ* (Story of Bayāḍ and Riyāḍ).[37] It is the capacity to delight and entertain *without the support of their own texts,* that made such images so easily adapted to another text within a totally different culture.

This was an unusual period in the history of Islamic art when representational images proliferated, in both book illustration and the applied arts.[38] Intriguing parallels suggest that thirteenth century illustrated Arabic books may have been available in Venice to enliven the eastern atmosphere, especially in the Egyptian scenes. These include details such as banquet scenes, trees silhouetted in bold abstract patterns against a bright sky, tents and open pavilions, figures of power seated on cushioned thrones, ships floating on schematically rippled water, figures reclining on divans, and laden camels. Most of all, the mosaics share with Arabic book illustrations the use of pose and gesture to express human emotions – the very emotions of trade and travel: anger, submission, gratitude, tiredness, friendship.

The process of assimilation reveals how such an extraneous visual culture had to be transformed. The vocabulary and emotion may be Islamic, but the pictorial language of the Venetian mosaic masters is distinctively Byzantine. At the same time, the roomy architectural spaces are far removed from the flatness of Islamic illustrators; and indeed, they are unusually deep even within the Byzantine tradition. As Demus observed, they are closer to the spatial systems then evolving in mainland Italian art.[39] Jean-Philippe Antoine argued the efficacy of such enhanced volumes in Italy at this period for locating ideas in the memory.[40] As classical memory systems such as the *Ad Herennium* stressed, backgrounds arranged in series – particularly unfamiliar and noticeable backgrounds – offered the ideal compartments for committing ideas to memory.[41] In the cupolas of San Marco's north atrium, the spectator's mind could perambulate round and round the rhythmic spatial sequences, exploring spaces deep enough to locate a thought, but not separate enough to interrupt the flow of the narrative.

The Zen chapel

From the south, the visitor arriving by sea originally entered the atrium of San Marco through a barrel-vaulted vestibule, now known as the Cappella Zen. The vault of the vestibule was decorated, probably in the third quarter of the thirteenth century, with the first full visual cycle narrating the *praedestinatio* of St Mark.[42] According to the text from which the cycle derives, the hymn transcribed by Martino da Canal in 1274, St Mark's visit to Venice – and the angel's prophecy that the lagoon should be his final resting place – took place *before* his mission to Alexandria.[43] Thus the story justified the (re-) capture of the saint's body and the reclaiming of Alexandria's identity and success.

Most striking of all is the vivid and memorable depiction of the Pharos of Alexandria (Fig. 7). Unlike the earlier representations of the Pharos in the Cappella di San Pietro (Fig. 2) it is not hoisted to the rooftops, as a symbolic beacon over the head of the saint, but planted firmly on the seashore. The domed lantern is not lit, but instead the whole tower

Fig. 7: Saint Mark's Voyage to Alexandria, *showing the Pharos, mosaic, c. 1270s. Venice, San Marco, Cappella Zen. Courtesy of the photographic archives, National Gallery of Art, Washington DC.*

glows with the luminous whiteness of its stone walls. The three storeys are clearly differentiated, decreasing telescopically upwards, each with a balustraded terrace. The close-range details – the stepped shoreline and the huge, arched watergate – give a deceptive immediacy. What has been lost in the process of revision is the three-dimensional solidity of the tower that the earlier mosaicists seemed to understand. Here, the image stands as insubstantial as a stage-flat. This Pharos is a vivid representation, not of its state in the thirteenth century, but of the lighthouse as it stood in Hellenistic times. Instead of the memory of a returning traveller, we see evidence of true humanistic research, based on classical texts and/or coins or reliefs.[44]

The façade mosaics

However schematic, the new *all'antica* imagery of the Pharos proved compelling. As the most memorable detail in the Zen Chapel vault, it appears in almost identical guise in the continuation of the same cycle across the lunettes of the façade, depicting the *Translatio of St. Mark's relics,* probably carried out in the 1260s. Only the last of these scenes, the *Carrying of St. Mark's body into the church of San Marco,* over the Porta Sant'Alippio on the northernmost portal of the façade still survives today, but the other lunettes are known from their detailed reproduction in Gentile Bellini's *Procession in Piazza San Marco,* signed and dated 1496, now in the Accademia in Venice.

Book illustrations from the Arab world seem to have been used once again to inspire the two scenes of the theft of the body from Alexandria in the right-hand façade lunette, now destroyed, but also recorded by Gentile Bellini. The two-dimensional silhouette of an open pavilion, with a glowing lamp suspended from the roof, forms the setting for the two robbery scenes (Fig. 8), borrowing the conventional portrayal of mosque interiors from

Fig. 8: Theft of St Mark's Body from Alexandria, *mosaic of the thirteenth century, formerly on the right hand lunette of the façade of San Marco. Detail from Gentile Bellini,* Procession in Piazza San Marco, *signed and dated 1496, Venice, Galleries dell'Accademia. Osvaldo Böhm, Venice.*

Arabic painting, such as the *Maqāmāt* Illustrations already mentioned (Fig. 9). Any viewer familiar with the art of Islamic books at this time would have recognised this stylised representation, its simplified *mode* of depiction directly appropriated from Muslim visual tradition as an allusion to the daring theft of the apostle's body.

Fig. 9: Mosque scene, *from the* Maqāmāt *of al-Ḥarīrī, 1237. Paris, Bibliothèque Nationale, ms Arabe 5847 ('Schefer* Maqāmāt*'), f. 143. Bibliothèque Nationale de France, Paris.*

The last Venetian Pharos

When he painted his *Procession* in 1496, Bellini could now see a three-dimensional, large-scale reproduction of the Pharos, newly erected on Venetian soil. This was Mauro Codussi's *campanile* (bell-tower) for the cathedral church of San Pietro di Castello (Fig. 10), for which the architect received the commission in 1482. With its three superimposed tiers – quadrangular at the bottom, octagonal in the central zone and circular at the top – and its gleaming white ashlar masonry, Codussi's *campanile* was an explicit reference to the ancient Pharos of Alexandria, now given its true three-dimensional geometry. (Sadly, the domed top storey of the *campanile* of San Pietro was removed in 1670 because the structure became unsafe.) The crucial point at issue is that the commission did not, as has usually been assumed, involve the total reconstruction of the campanile, for the tower had been newly rebuilt in 1463–74.[45] Minor lightning damage may have been the catalyst for Codussi's project, but the commission involved, not the reconstruction, but the cladding of the new brick tower in white limestone from Istria. In other words, a new identity was consciously sought for the existing *campanile.* As the first bell-tower in Venice to be completely faced in Istrian stone, it stands

Fig. 10: Mauro Codussi, campanile of San Pietro di Castello (formerly the cathedral of Venice), refaced 1482–8. The crowning dome was removed in 1670. Deborah Howard.

at the eastern end of the city, as a beacon for the sea-borne traveller approaching (or returning) from the east. Indeed, like the original Pharos of Alexandria, it was cited in shipping guides as a point of reference for navigation when entering the port of Venice.

The Pharos of Alexandria itself had now totally disappeared. In 1480, just two years before the start of the new campanile of San Pietro di Castello, the Sultan Qā'it Bey had destroyed the last remains of the great lighthouse in order to erect his hefty fort on the promontory at the mouth of Alexandria's double harbour. The sight of the Pharos rising anew on Venetian soil gained added potency through its recent final obliteration in the hands of the Mamluk sultan. The appropriation of Alexandrian identity in Venice was still a potent intention.

Conclusion

Spaces are recalled by the traveller through a Proustian array of sensations, sound and movement, as well as sight – memories that may be brought home in the form of material objects, visual depictions or verbal accounts. In the composite self-image that the city compiled from this rich array of experiences, spectators could recognise the city's cultural fertility through recourse to their own individual visual repertoire, ranging from exotic travellers' tales to first-hand recollections of travel. We may recall the comment in Magno's diary, "There being nothing more enjoyable, for those seeking the world, than the memories of past events..."[46] 'Memories of past events' encoded in the architecture and decoration of St Mark's brought the eastern world of biblical times into the city's cultural traditions. As a cradle of Christianity, where the Bible had been translated into Greek, Alexandria was not only a symbol of temporal power but also an eloquent devotional allusion. Like the display of spoils pillaged from a foreign city, the visual representation of the remembered appearance of another place could be revealed through a process of distillation, recombining elements to imbue these 'stolen' memories with their new Venetian meaning.

Notes

Note: This article is based on material contained in my book *Venice & the East: the Impact of the Islamic World on Venetian Architecture 1100–1500* (New Haven, 2000), from which it draws extended passages, mainly from Chapter 3, here reproduced by kind permission of Yale University Press.

1 Petrarch, *Letters from Petrarch*, ed. and trans. M. Bishop (Bloomington, 1966), 133, letter from Vaucluse, France, 26 February 1352.

2 Martino da Canal, *Les estoires de Venise: Cronaca veneziana in lingua francese dalle origini al 1275*, trans. A. Limentani (Florence, 1972), 18–20.

3 Folger Library, Washington DC, ms. V.A. 259 (= De' Ricci 1317/1): Alessandro Magno, *Account of his Journeys to Cyprus, Egypt, Spain, England, Flanders and Germany, and of Brescia, 1557–1565*, f. 73v.

4 Pietro Donazzolo, *I viaggiatori veneti minori: Studio bio-bibliografico* (Rome, 1927), 6–7.

5 Raimondo Morozzo della Rocca, *Lettere di mercanti a Pignol Zucchello (1336–1350)* (Venice, 1957), 88.

6 Magno, *Account of his Journeys* (as in n. 3): "Non essendo cosa più dilettevole, che vada cercando il mondo quanto lo aricordo all'huomo delle cose passate, ho deliberato per questo et per passer l'otio tenir conto particular del presente viaggio."

7 D. Howard, *Venice & the East: the Impact of the Islamic World on Venetian Architecture 1100-1500* (New Haven, 2000), 62–4.

8 Da Canal (as in n. 2), 154: "car li un sont mort et li autre meurent at li autre naissent, si ne pevent pas conter a toz ce que a lor tens estoit fait, se il ne nos fait a savoir par escrit ou par peintures."

9 Plutarch, *Lives*, VII, trans. B. Perrin (Cambridge, Mass.: Loeb Classics, 1919), xxxvi, 1–6. Translation of Homer, *Odyssey*, iv, 345–6 from George Sandys, *A Relation of a Journey begun An. Dom. 1610* (London, 1615), 111.

10 For details of these legendary dates, see Howard (as in n. 7), 232, n. 15.

11 Strabo, *The Geography*, trans. H.L. Jones (Cambridge, Mass.: Loeb Classics, 1917–32), v, 5, I, 7. Strabo visited the city in 25–24 BC. See also L. Bosio, 'Note per una propedeutica allo studio storico della laguna veneta in età romana,' *Atti dell'Istituto Veneto di Scienze, Lettere ed Arti*, CXLII (1983–4), 95–126, on 104–6.

12 Plutarch, VII (as in n. 9), xxvi, 4; Diodorus of Sicily, *Works*, (Cambridge, Mass.: Loeb Classics, 1963), viii, trans. C. Bradford Welles, xvii, 53, 3.

13 Marin Sanuto ditto Torsello (Marinus Sanutus dictus Torsellus), *Liber secretorum fidelium crucis super terrae sanctae recuperatione et conservatione* (Hanover, 1611), book 1.

14 P.M. Fraser, *Ptolemaic Alexandria* (Oxford, 1972), i, 107; ii, 196–7; P. Green, 'Alexander's Alexandria', in B. Gilman (ed.), *Alexandria and Alexandrism* (Malibu, Calif., 1993), 3.

15 Diodorus VII (as in n.12), xvii, 52, 5.

16 Josephus, *The Jewish War* (Books IV-VII), trans. H.St.J. Thackeray (Cambridge, Mass.: Loeb Classics, 1928), iv, 615.

17 Felix Fabri (= Faber), *Le voyage en Egypte 1483*, trans. J. Masson (Paris, 1975), 722.

18 Ammianus Marcellinus, *Res gestae*, trans. J.C. Rolfe (Cambridge, Mass.: Loeb Classics, 1935), 22, 16, 7.

19 Diorodus (as in n. 12), xvii, 52, 6,

20 Ibn Baṭṭūṭah, *The Travels of Ibn Battuta, AD 1325-1354*, ed. H.A.R. Gibb, trans. C.F. Beckingham, i (Hakluyt Society, 110, 1958), 41.

21 Fabri (as in n. 17), 400 (on Cairo) and 725 (on Alexandria).

22 Fabri (as in n. 17), 725.

23 Sebastiano Serlio, *Sebastiano Serlio on Architecture, Books I-V*, trans. V. Hart and P. Hicks (New Haven, 1996), 244.

24 H. Thiersch, *Pharos: Antike, Islam und Occident: Ein Beitrag zur Architekturgeschichte* (Leipzig, 1909), 41–4.

25 Al-Maqrīzī, *Déscription topographique et historique de l'Égypte*, trans. U. Bouriant, i (Paris, 1895), 7.

26 O. Demus, *The Mosaics of San Marco in Venice* (Chicago, 1984), ii, 67–76.

27 V.M. Schmidt, *A Legend and its Image: the Aerial Flight of Alexander the Great in Medieval Art* (Groeningen, 1995), 7, 18–19, 68.

28 Schmidt (as in n. 28), 41–2; Marco Polo, *The Travels*, trans. R. Latham (Harmondsworth: Penguin Classics, 1958), 49. On the medieval versions of the *Alexander Romance*, see especially G. Cary, *The Medieval Alexander*, ed. D.J.A. Ross (Cambridge, 1956).

29 Pseudo-Callisthenes, *The Life of Alexander of Macedon*, trans. E. Hazelton Haight (New York, 1955), 40–41.

30 K. Weitzmann and H.L. Kessler, *The Cotton Genesis: British Library Codex Cotton Otho BVI* (Princeton, 1986), 3–6, 18–20.

31 H. Buchtal, *Historia Troiana: Studies in the History of Medieval Secular Illustration* (London, 1971), 53; Demus (as in n. 26), ii, 95; Weitzmann and Kessler (as in n. 30), 6, 30–34.

32 Demus (as in n. 26), i, 81.

33 Josephus, *Jewish Antiquities* (Books I-1V), (Cambridge, Mass.: Loeb Classics, 1930), ii, 168–9.

34 T. Dale, 'Inventing a Sacred Past: Pictorial Narratives of Saint Mark the Evangelist at Aquileia and Venice *c.* 1000–1300', *DOP*, 48 (1994), 53–104, on 97.

35 Fabri (as in n. 17), 449; A. Magno, *Account of his Journeys* (as in n. 2), f. 132; sketch reproduced in Howard (as in n. 7), fig. 80.

36 O. Grabar, *The Illustrations of the Maqâmât* (Chicago, 1984), 3–4.

37 Cf. C. Robinson, *Medieval Andalusian Courtly Culture in the Mediterranean:* Hadîth Bayâd wa Riyâd (London, forthcoming).

38 D. James, *Arab Painting* (Edinburgh, 1978), 15–38; Grabar (as in n. 36), 4.

39 Demus (as in n. 26), 1984, ii, 165–6.

40 J.-P. Antoine, 'L'arte della memoria e la trasformazione dello spazio pittorico in Italia nel Ducento e Trecento,' in L. Bolzoni and P. Corsi (eds.), *La cultura della memoria* (Bologna, 1992), 96–116.

41 *Ad Herennium*, trans. H. Caplan (Cambridge, Mass., 1954), 209. See also F.A. Yates, *The Art of Memory* (London, 1966); M. Carruthers, *The Book of Memory: a Study of Memory in Medieval Culture* (Cambridge, 1990).

42 Demus (as in n. 26), ii, 73. On the conversion of the space to the Zen Chapel in 1503–15, see B. Jestaz, *La Chapelle Zen à St. Marc de Venise* (Stuttgart, 1986).

43 Da Canal (as in n. 2), 340–43.

44 For examples see Howard (as in n. 7), 91

45 ASV, Mensa Patriarcale, busta 60, Registro di Cassa, I (formerly busta no. 69) 1483–1485, published in Pietro Paoletti, *L'architettura e la scultura del Rinascimento in Venezia* (Venice, 1893), i/2, 101, docs. 67–9. For further discussion see Howard (as in n. 7), 94–99. For the alternative interpretation that the *campanile* was completely rebuilt from 1482, see L. Puppi and L. Olivato Puppi, *Mauro Codussi* (Milan, 1977), 45–50, 187–90; J. McAndrew, *Venetian Architecture of the Early Renaissance* (Cambridge, Mass., 1980), 262–7.

46 See above, n. 6.

8

Latin Averroism

John Marenbon

This is a polemical paper.[1] Even the title is polemical, hard though you might find that to believe. For about a century from 1852, when Ernest Renan's *Averroès et l'averroïsme* was first published, Latin Averroism was one of the labels – like 'twelfth-century Platonism' or 'fourteenth-century nominalism' – which was happily used by historians of medieval philosophy to order and shape their subject. The first Latin Averroists, we were told, were the Arts Masters at Paris in the 1260s and 1270s, notably Siger of Brabant and Boethius of Dacia, who were the objects of Bishop Tempier's censures in 1270 and (among others) in 1277, and who were attacked by Aquinas in his treatise on the *Unity of the Intellect*. Despite these onslaughts, Averroism flourished in early fourteenth-century Paris, where John of Jandun was its most extreme proponent and Ramon Llull its fiercest critic; it informed Marsilius of Padua's influential *Defensor Pacis*, and went on to become one of the main schools of thought in Bologna in the fourteenth, and Padua in the fifteenth and sixteenth centuries. Or so the old story went, because we are now told that 'Latin Averroism' is not a term that should be used about thirteenth century thought at all: it is a misnomer for 'Radical Aristotelianism'.

I shall be arguing, by contrast, that there is an understanding of Latin Averroism by which it did indeed begin with Siger and Boethius and continued through to the sixteenth century, and which is close to what medieval scholars themselves had in mind when they talked of *averroistae* or, in certain contexts, appealed to (or distanced themselves from) the Commentator (as Averroes was called).

***

Although his view of Latin Averroism remained dominant for a century, beneath Renan's impressive construction there was from the beginning an unresolved tension which would eventually destroy it. Renan was, by training and inclination, a philologist and historian, determined to use the new, scientific historical methods to reach an accurate view of the past, untainted by religious or other prejudice. In *Averroès et l'averroïsme*, he set out to extend scientific, historical knowledge into an area which predecessors, such as Victor

Cousin, had neglected. He wanted to map out, first the work and thought of Averroes himself, and then its influence in medieval Europe which, from a glance at library catalogues he could have told was vast. His account of Latin Averroism is, therefore, set out as a survey of where and how the Latin translations of Averroes were used, from the mid-twelfth to the sixteenth century. But Renan's very concern to take account of all the evidence led to there being another strand, perhaps the dominant one, in his account. He looks at the doctrines which were explicitly identified as 'Averroist' by medieval writers (usually hostile ones), and he finds a set of views which, he recognises, have little to do with anything Averroes himself thought. Averroism, by this account, is – as Renan summarises it – 'denial of the supernatural, of miracles, angels and devils and divine intervention; and the explanation of religious and moral beliefs as the result of imposture' (behind this final comment is the fact that Averroes was often held, in the medieval West, to have originated the blasphemy that the religions of the world had been founded by three imposters: Moses, Christ and Muhammad). The concluding paragraph of *Averroès et l'averroïsme*, goes on to give a remarkable account of how an imaginative historian can respond to such pseudo-history:

> Aristotle and Averroes could scarcely have expected that this is what their thought would be reduced to. But, for those figures who are raised up as symbols, we must always distinguish their lives as people from their lives beyond the grave, what they were in reality and what opinion has made of them.

The history of Averroism is, Renan says, 'properly speaking nothing but the history of an enormous misunderstanding', but then 'we do not *create* with a text that we understand too accurately'.[2]

Renan's successors took little notice of this sophisticated understanding of the history of misconceptions. In one sense, Pierre Mandonnet's monograph on Siger of Brabant and Latin Averroism, published in 1899, filled in the gaps of the structure Renan had erected and so stengthened it. From the texts of those who had attacked it – Aquinas, Giles of Rome – and the condemnations of Étienne Tempier, Bishop of Paris, Renan had asserted the presence in the Paris Arts Faculty in the 1260s and 1270s of a Latin Averroism which involved doubting the truths of Christianity. In Siger of Brabant, hardly more than a name for Renan, Mandonnet provided this movement with a spokesman and a leader. Whereas Renan had been almost entirely vague about the doctrinal content of Latin Averroism, apart from its associations with disbelief, Mandonnet – who edited a number of Siger's writings – felt able to associate with it the four fundamental doctrines: denial of divine providence over contingent things; eternity of the world; the fact that there is only one intelligence for all humans; the denial of free will.[3]

Mandonnet also added a wealth of detail about the translations of Aristotle, and the controversies and condemnations in the university. But all this had the effect of obscuring – what Mandonnet himself indeed seems hardly to have understood – that the central strand in Renan's work was a history of misunderstanding; that, if Latin Averroism was to be a useful notion historiographically, it could not be understood in terms of the real use of Averroes.

It only needed another historian to approach the subject in the same spirit, rigorous, bold but narrow-minded, and exercise the same intellectual vigour in criticism as Mandonnet had done in constructing his case, for the edifice of Latin Averroism to crumble. Fernand van Steenberghen fulfilled this role. He argued that the one point in common between Averroes' own particular doctrines and the thinkers called or identified as Averroists was just the third of Mandonnet's four fundamental doctrines, best put as the claim (explained below) that there is only one 'potential intellect' for all humankind. But how could anyone be described as an Averroist on such slender grounds? Siger and the others were rather radical, heterodox Aristotelians, who wished to accept all of Aristotle's teaching even when it conflicted with Christian doctrine; not until John of Jandun, who worked in Paris in the early fourteenth-century, is Van Steenberghen willing to admit that there was a genuine Latin Averroist.[4]

Other, more recent sallies have tried to level what still remained of Renan's edifice, especially the arguments made by the distinguished Dominican scholar, R.-A. Gauthier,[5] that Siger was an unimportant, timid figure, who, at the time he was most outspoken knew his Averroes mainly at second-hand, through Aquinas and Albert the Great. As a result, historians of philosophy today, even those most inclined to value the work of men such as Siger, are reluctant to use the phrase 'Latin Averroism'.

And, of course, they are right, if we are supposed to take the term 'Latin Averroism' as making a scientific claim about the influence of Averroes – as Renan half-supposed and Mandonnet took for granted. Suppose, though, that we follow the other half of Renan's account, and recognise that the Averroes who stands behind Latin Averroism is a figure who has been 'raised up as a symbol' and that we are dealing with the history not of influence but of creative misreading or partial reading; but that, instead of the vague and philosophically vacuous disbelief, free-thinking and libertinism that Renan linked to Averroism, we discover an interesting and unexpected philosophical position ...

***

Let us take a step back. From the most basic fact about the translation and knowledge of Averroes' works in the Latin Middle Ages, it should be obvious that Latin Averroism could never be a story about the real views Averroes himself had. Averroes was a highly prolific commentator of Aristotle, but he was also the author of two important works on the nature of philosophy and its relation to religious teaching: one – a detailed refutation of al-Ghazālī's *Incoherence of the Philosophers* – called *The Incoherence of the Incoherence*, and the other his *Decisive Treatise on the Relation between Religion and Philosophy*, as well as a treatise on theology (*The Explanation of the Sorts of Proofs in the Doctrines of Religion*). The commentaries contain many interpretations of Aristotle that are peculiar to Averroes, but they are a work of exegesis, an attempt to explain what Aristotle – whom Averroes held in almost exaggerated regard – had written. In one sense, they are indeed the most serious expression of Averroes's views, since he regarded the arguments expounded in them as demonstrative. In his other writings, he was often writing for a wider audience or for a particular purpose, and he may have been willing to include in them views that he did not really hold, or positions that were persuasive but he did not think could be demonstrated. None the less, a good deal of his most characteristic, individual thinking is found when he is not simply expounding Aristotle. Moreover, an understanding of the real Averroes would need to take account of his position as a close follower of the Almohad ruler of Muslim Spain and North Africa, Abū Yaʿqūb Yūsuf and a practising *qāḍī* and expert on religious law.

In the Latin West, only a part of Averroes became known. Many of his commentaries were translated into Latin and they became part of the required reading for anyone taking a university course, since they were indispensable as aids to understanding Aristotle. The *Incoherence of the Incoherence,* however, was not put into Latin until 1328 and was not widely circulated, whilst the *Decisive Treatise* was not translated in the Middle Ages. And the neglect of these polemical works of Averroes is not at all surprising. The relation between philosophy and religion is, no doubt, a subject of equal interest for Christians and for Muslims, but the Islamic context in which Averroes formulated his views made them untranslatable into terms that Christians could understand and assimilate, even if – through the intermediary of a Jew – the Arabic words could be put into Latin. And so, if 'Latin Averroism' is to refer to anything beyond the widespread, though selective use of Averroes's commentaries – in which case the philosophical culture of the medieval universities will be without exception Averroistic, it must be to a body of thought that does not depend on Averroes' most characteristic ideas but stands, rather, in a complex, oblique relation to him.

I suggest that a useful way to use the label 'Latin Averroist' – one which has the virtue of by and large picking out the writers who in the Middle Ages were called *averroistae* or described as Averroes's followers (usually by their critics) – is to apply it to those writers who

(a) accepted Averroes' view that there is only a single potential intellect;
(b) concentrated their efforts on reaching and examining an accurate account of Aristotle's ideas – usually based on that presented by Averroes – even where these positions are incompatible with Christian teaching (in particular, the position that the world has no beginning); and,
(c) adopted some sort of strategy to explain why they, though Christians, did (a) and (b)

(a) and (c) call for further comment, and (a) requires a detour into Aristotle's theory of cognition, as expounded in his *De anima.*

For Aristotle, thinking about something – grasping it with the intellect – requires the form, which makes the thing the sort of thing it is – to inform the intellect.[6] When I grasp intellectually what-it-is-to-be-a-man, then the form of man, that which makes a man into a man, informs my intellect. Just as matter, which is pure potency, becomes something in actuality through a form, the intellect is potentiality, waiting to be informed and made actual by what it cognises. Aristotle thus envisages the capacity for thinking as a potential intellect (*intellectus possibilis*). But he did not consider that the process of intellectual cognition could be explained just by reference to the forms in individual things, and the potential intellect. He also posited another intellect, an active one, which was able to take the enmattered forms from individual things so as to inform the potential intellect. Is Aristotle talking here about individual human cognisers saying that every person has both an active and a potential intellect? Yes, said some interpreters, including Aquinas. But many readers, from antiquity onwards, thought Aristotle meant that there is just one active (or 'agent') intellect, identified either with God or with the lowest of a series of emanated celestial Intelligences, which serves all human beings. It was this interpretation that became standard within the cosmological system elaborated by al-Fārābī and adopted by Avicenna. Most Latin theologians of the mid-thirteenth century also adopted a version of it in which the active intellect was identified with God.[7] This view still left people with their own individual potential intellects, and so it presented no threat to Christian doctrines. Averroes's innovation – or depravation, as Aquinas called it – was to argue that, like the active intellect, the potential intellect is one for all people.[8] Averroes is still able to individuate thoughts, linking them to particular human beings, by reference to the sense-images which, according to Aristotle, must accompany all thinking.

Averroes's interpretation is, therefore, less far-fetched than it may sound at first, and it was intellectually attractive to scholars wanting to be faithful to Aristotle and yet make sense of his text. But it was clearly unacceptable to Christians, because it denied humans any individual immortality and so made reward and punishment in the after-life impossible. For this reason, Latin Averroism has feature (c): those Christian thinkers who adopted Averroes's reading needed to offer some explanation for how *they* could hold it. One possibility was to say that they were engaged in a purely exegetical task, and that Averroes's had indeed interpreted Aristotle correctly but Aristotle was wrong. But, for most of them, their view of how the world can be understood by reason was so bound up with Aristotle's conception of it, that they could not claim just to be exegetes. Usually they deny that they are actually asserting the truth of the views they have taken from Aristotle when they contradict Christian faith. This type of reflection is missing in the very earliest of Siger's surviving works, a commentary on Book III of *De anima*, but it was provoked and became common once the first-order interpretations along the lines of (a) and (b) started to be attacked (as Siger's was). Many historians have tended to react to these reflections in one of two antithetical ways: either they have seen them as insincere, mere fig-leaves to allow them to continue to propound heretical views without being called to account for them, or else they have used them as evidence that the Latin Averroists were really Christian fideists. I suggest that, rather, we should see them as putting forward a serious philosophical position, one of the very few examples of a medieval relativism.[9]

Relativist theories rightly have a bad name in philosophical quarters, especially when, as in the present case, they concern truth. Their proponents are likely to be caught in blatant self-contradiction, or else to be pushed towards a scepticism they may not want to embrace. The opponents of the Latin Averroists were quick to exploit this weakness, formulating the claims they wished to attack in a manner that allowed no escape. So, in the preface to the 219 propositions he condemned in 1277, Bishop Tempier writes:

> They say that these things are true according to philosophy, but not according to the Catholic Faith, as if there were two contrary truths, and as if, over against the truth of Holy Scripture, there were truth in the sayings of gentiles who are damned ...[10]

On this account, it is as if they simply said 'It is true that *p*' and 'It is true that not-*p*'. At the end of *De unitate intellectus*, as Alain de Libera has shown,[11] Aquinas sets up a neat logical trap for this type of crude relativism. The Averroist, he tells us, asserts that 'I conclude by reason that necessarily the intellect is one in number, and yet I firmly hold the opposite by faith'.[12] But if it is necessary that the intellect is one in number, then it is impossible that it is not one in number, and so Christian faith, according to the Averroist, requires its adherents to accept the truth of an *impossible* proposition – one that even God could not make true.

The Latin Averroists' own pronouncements, however, tend not to embody this crude and easily rejected relativism, but a type of procedural or practical relativism about truth and the pursuit of knowledge. Such relativism accepts that there can be no contrary truths, but it marks out a space in which practitioners of a given discipline can develop arguments and positions within the terms of that discipline. This procedural relativism allows in some cases for arguments to be developed for a proposition *p*, and for *p* to be entertained and perhaps used as a premise in arguing that *q* and *r*, even where, ultimately, it is accepted that there are reasons for rejecting *p* (and *q* and *r*) as false. Consider the complex relativism developed by Boethius of Dacia, who was clearly linked with Siger by contemporary and later antagonists. Boethius used the eternity of the world (rather than the unity of the potential intellect) as his test case. He regarded each branch of knowledge as self-contained, built – as Aristotle explained in the *Prior Analytics* – on its own, self-evident first principles. It is among the principles of natural science that there can be no change, unless it is preceded by prior change, which is its cause, and so the scientist must deny that the world had a beginning and that there was a first man. But why, Boethius has an imaginary objector ask, when it is 'the truth of the Christian faith and the unqualified truth that the world had a beginning', should the scientist, just because it is the case that 'the principles of his branch of knowledge do not extend to such difficult and hidden works of divine wisdom' *deny* these truths? Boethius replies that it is because the truths destroy the principles of his branch of knowledge that he must deny them; otherwise he could accept them. But, then, is the scientist not asserting falsehoods? No, because when he says, 'The world is eternal' he must be taken as meaning 'According to natural principles, the world is eternal.' Similarly, the truth of the Christian's assertion that the world had a beginning depends on the acknowledgement that this is indeed possible through the power of a principle greater than any natural one.[13]

Logically, then, the solution to the problem raised by Boethius lies in the simple observation that '*p* is true according to X' is perfectly compatible with 'not-*p* is true according to Y' or even simply 'not-*p*'. But is the implication of this solution not the rather unremarkable one, that physical science brings imperfect knowledge, whereas Christian doctrine gives the truth – *simpliciter*, without qualification? In a passage from a different work, *De somniis*, Boethius does indeed write:

> And this is the cause of error to many people who believe that natural scientists want to demonstrate any conclusions without qualification, when they demonstrate them to follow from causes with respect to which or supposing which it is impossible that those conclusions should be otherwise. Given, however, that both those causes and so those conclusions are able to be impeded, the scientists do not therefore intend to demonstrate such conclusions without qualification.[14]

But if Boethius had just wanted to say that physical science is unreliable, why would he have erected such an elaborate and provocative framework in order to protect the truth of the statements made by scientists? That is why I say that he wished to develop a procedural relativism. Boethius's theory allows the scientist to go on doing his science according to the rules of his discipline. Though a Christian, he is entitled – indeed obliged – to deny certain Christian doctrines, and he can do so without speaking against Christianity. Although the truths of Christianity are true without qualification, they cannot replace the branches of knowledge elaborated by the scientist, or the metaphysician, or the mathematician or whatever, because they do not consist of demonstrations founded on self-evident principles.

The leading Averroist of the early fourteenth century, John of Jandun, had a similar position, although it was less elaborately presented. John has recently been the object of an important, revisionary study,[15] which shows that his use of Averroes was far less direct than has been thought, and that he often moulded his reading of Aristotle and his commentator in order to answer problems set by the discussions of his own day. But this discovery does not bear on the stance that John takes where Aristotle, interpreted with the help of Averroes, contradicts Christian doctrine. There are many passages in John's work where he affirms, in the strongest terms, that a Christian position, which goes against the interpretation he has been giving, is to be accepted: as he says on one occasion (Commentary on *De anima* III, quaestio 5), 'it is certain that divine authority should command greater faith than any reasoning devised by men, just as the authority of a single philosopher is stronger than some piece of weak reasoning put forward by a child.' Yet, for about 99 per cent of the time in his commentaries, John is striving to put exactly the sort of philosophical arguments which, here, he says can be so easily dismissed when they happen to conflict with the faith. These hundreds of pages are not wasted, though, because the dismissal of the Aristotelian arguments is itself non-argumentative: indeed, John says that 'a person who tries to refute some of the arguments against this position [that of Christian teaching] in another way will, because of the inadequacy of his arguments, make the position improbable rather than supporting it.'[16] John's professions of faith are not, as was once thought, ironic. But they do sound too profuse and easy, a necessary exaggeration to leave John free to pursue the type of reasoning he enjoyed and preserve its value as an activity of an utterly incomparable kind to proposing truths of the faith.

Were there space, it would be good at this point to look at the development of the Latin Averroist tradition – especially at how it came to flourish not only in Bologna and then Padua but also in Erfurt and Krakow.[17] Most recent historians of philosophy – especially Anglophone ones – have tended to write Latin Averroism out of their accounts; the term is rejected with respect to the thirteenth century, and when it comes to the fourteenth and fifteenth centuries, the historians' focus is firmly North of the Alps and the West of the Rhine. Perhaps if they could be persuaded of the real intellectual interest of the Latin Averroists, they would be less willing to perpetrate so distorted a view. Rather, though, than enter into this little known and difficult area, I would like, as I promised at the beginning, to spend the final part of this paper looking at the most fascinating and distinguished of all the Latin Averroists – one who, unlike most of the others, never formally attended a university and is best known for what he wrote, not in Latin, but the vernacular: Dante Alighieri.

***

I want to insist, against the grain of most recent scholarship, that the mature Dante, the Dante of the *Commedia*, is rightly described as a Latin Averroist. The two pieces of evidence I shall bring are his political treatise, the *Monarchia*, and the famous appearance of Siger of Brabant in Paradise.[18]

The *Monarchia*, scholars now agree, is a work written near the end of Dante's life, when the *Paradiso* was being or had been composed.[19] Dante's aim there is to show that the Roman Emperor should be the supreme ruler of humankind, and not be subject to the Pope in temporal matters. If not, there will be no universal monarchy, and without a universal monarchy, there will be no peace. Without peace humankind will not reach its goal. But what is the goal of humankind? Dante presents it in blatantly Averroistic terms.

Humankind's goal is its peculiar activity, which can be performed only by humankind as a whole. What distinguishes men from other animals, says Dante, is their ability to apprehend through the potential intellect (that is to say, engage in intellectual thought). Such apprehension, he argues, is the peculiar activity, not of individual humans but of the whole of humankind, because only through a great many people can the whole of the intellectual potency be made actual. He writes (I, 4): 'the peculiar work of the human race taken as a whole is to actualize always the whole power of the potential intellect ...' (*proprium opus humani generis totaliter accepti est actuare semper totam potentiam intellectus possibilis*).[20] So, at least, the Latin translates. But readers of the translation by Prue Shaw, the editor of the latest and best edition, are told, rather: 'the activity proper to humankind considered as a whole is constantly to actualize the full intellectual potential of humanity ...' The divergence between her version and the Latin is certainly not due to carelessness or incompetence on her part:[21] rather, Dr Shaw refuses to believe that Dante is committing himself to the Averroist position on a single potential intellect which his phrasing so clearly implies – and in this she is at one with every other commentator I have read.[22] Yet what else is he doing?

Even two scholars so outstanding as Étienne Gilson and Bruno Nardi do not convince on this point. Gilson writes that 'What Averroes wants to actualize the potential intellect entirely is a being; whereas, to reach the same end, what Dante looks to is a society – the universal society of all the individual potential intellects which constitute the human race.'[23] If, explains Gilson, Dante had accepted that there was just one potential intellect, then the goal of humanity would be realised in any case, by the mere existence of such an intellect; there would be no need for a society at peace under a universal emperor. But not only does this explanation leave Dante's reference to 'the potential intellect' in the singular quite unmotivated, it also seems to miss the point: the goal of humanity would not be achieved by the mere existence of a single potential intellect: it demands the actualisation of that intellect to the greatest possible degree – something which requires the work of individual humans living in a peaceful society. Bruno Nardi rightly thought that Gilson underestimated the extent of Dante's Averroism, but his own view comes down to his saying that when in the *Monarchia* Dante refers to *the* potential intellect in the singular, he has in mind the species of which the individual potential intellects are members. But is potential intellect a species? And, even if it were, how can a species be actualised?[24]

Most commentators are willing, like Gilson, to allow that, in the *Monarchia*, Dante did put forward a species of 'political' Averroism, and they accept the links between Averroist thinking and the conclusion of the treatise, where he contrasts two types of happiness, one achievable in an earthly state, ruled by a universal monarch according to philosophical teachings, the other to be enjoyed only in heaven and attained through Christian teaching. I maintain that the *Monarchia* is a genuinely Averroistic work, in which Latin Averroism is not qualified or diluted, but developed into a political theory.

The other striking piece of evidence for Dante's Averroism is provided by this famous passage from the *Paradiso.*

> Questi onde a me ritorna il tuo riguardo,
> è 'l lume d'uno spirto che 'n pensieri
> gravi a morir li parve venir tardo:
> essa è la luce etterna di Sigieri,
> che, leggendo nel Vico delli Strami,
> sillogizzò invidïosi veri.

> This one, from whom your gaze comes back to me, is the light of a spirit for whom, amid his grave thoughts, death seemed slow to come. This is the eternal light of Siger who, teaching in the rue du Fouarre [where the Paris arts masters had their schools], demonstrated by syllogistic arguments unpalatable truths.

By Dante's time, Siger of Brabant was well on his way to becoming a symbolic figure, like Averroes. To put him so unexpectedly into Paradise, along with the great Church Fathers and the leading modern Domincans – Albert and Aquinas – and Franciscan – Bonaventure – seems like an open declaration of Averroism, if of an eclectic variety. Yet historians have offered the most far-fetched reasons for avoiding this obvious inference. Mandonnet suggested that Dante did not know who Siger was. Gilson argued that Siger was included because he stood for philosophy, but not for Siger's particular views about philosophy and religion. Van Steenberghen said, using first one and then another commentary of doubtful authenticity as his evidence, that Siger is in Paradise because, at the end of his days, he had converted to Thomism and Dante must have know this.[25]

I am saying that Dante – although he was influenced by Aquinas, Bonaventure and many others – can and should be labelled as a Latin Averroist. But there are two apparently crushing objections to this view, which may well account for the scholars' failure to draw this, as I contend, obvious conclusion. The first is another passage from the *Purgatorio*:

> ... quest' è tal punto,
> che più savio di te fe' già errante,
> sì che per sua dottrina fe' disgiunto
> da l'anima il possibile intelletto,
> perché da lui non vide organo assunto.
> (XXV, 62-6)

> ... this is such a point that once it led someone wiser than you into error, so that, according to his teaching, the potential intellect is not joined to the soul, because he did not see any organ which was taken up for use by it.

These lines clearly refer to Averroes and they declare that the doctrine of the single potential intellect is an error.

The second reason is simply this: accepting the Averroist view that there is only one potential intellect involves denying that individual human souls are rewarded or punished in the after-life. But if there is anyone in the Middle Ages who we know accepted the doctrine that souls are rewarded or punished, it is Dante, who wrote his great poem precisely on this theme.

These points are objections, however, only if one forgets the character of Latin Averroism as having a second-order doctrine as well as first-order positions. Latin Averroists do not propose that it is the unqualified truth that there is only one potential intellect, merely that this is the conclusion to which natural reasoning leads. By denying the Averroist doctrine of the potential intellect where he does, Dante actually shows himself to be a truer Averroist than if he always followed it. In the passage from the *Purgatorio*, Averroes is treated with great respect, and no philosophical objection is put forward to his view. But it is absolutely appropriate that Statius, the speaker at this point (and a Christian convert, according to Dante) should reject it; so would Dante, when engaged with theology rather than philosophy. And, of course, the *Commedia* is explicitly a theological poem, concerned primarily not with the government of earthly society, but with humanity's supernatural end: Dante should not regard the best philosophical teaching about the soul and the intellect when he is writing it, but look rather to revealed theology.

***

There is one side of Latin Averroism which this paper has left almost unmentioned: the detailed, uncontroversial use of Averroes's commentaries by a whole range of writers, not just in metaphysics and natural science, but also in logic – take, for instance, Robert Kilwardby. I have preferred to put to one side this 'real' Latin Averroism and concentrate on what one might want to call a phantom Averroism – a set of ideas and attitudes which could not have existed unless Averroes had been read, but do not in the main reflect what Averroes wrote or thought. Certainly, there are many tales to be told about the detailed borrowings, but I am not sure whether these tales make up a story. In logic, perhaps, they do, because of the way that logicians working in diverse contexts and cultures face, at least to some extent, the same problems. In most other areas, the difference in the framework of later medieval Latin Christian culture from that of Islam in the twelfth century meant that, whereas at the microscopic level its scholars often followed Averroes with precision and diligence, at the macroscopic level on which the historian needs to make sense of their procedure, they are following a symbol or an image (even in cases and areas less striking than what I have identified in particular as Latin Averroism). A helpful analogy might be that of my looking, through an elaborately and closely-wrought grid at an intricate mosaic immediately behind it. If I come right up to the grid and put my eye to one of the gaps, I can see through to the mosaic without obstruction, but I see only a very small patch of it, not enough to make out the scene which is depicted there. But, as I move away from the grid so as to take in a wider view of the mosaic and understand what it is about, the grid interferes more and more with my vision, so that what I see is not the mosaic itself, but the mosaic as shaped by the grid.

In short, if we want to think about Latin Averroism (and one might say the same for other themes, such as medieval Platonism), it is more profitable to think, not in terms of influence, but – as the theme of this volume instructs us – of crosspollination. It may be a misplaced philologism which assumes that the scholar need only discern and bring together the details, for a meaningful narrative to emerge. As Renan put it: 'For a philologist, a text has a single meaning, but the philologist's scrupulous interpretation does not satisfy the human spirit which has put its life and its predilections into it.' To which we might add that what the historian, as opposed to the philologist, seeks to understand *is* this life and its predilections. And so even the historian of philosophy must often tell a story of phantoms and illusions.

Notes

1 My paper was written to present Latin Averroism and some of the historiographical problems associated with it to the participants in the 'Crosspollinations' conference on which this book is based – specialists in a variety of areas, but not for the most part in medieval philosophy. I have retained its polemical and broad-ranging character for the printed version. It is *not* a presentation of new scholarly research, but an introduction to an area of medieval thought too often passed over hastily in English-language accounts.

2 E. Renan, *Averroès et l'averroïsme* (Paris, 2002), 298–9. This new edition contains a valuable historiographical introduction by Alain de Libera. On the historiography of Latin Averroism, including Renan's part in it, see R. Imbach, 'L'averroïsme latin du XIIIe siècle', in R. Imbach and A. Maierù (eds.) *Gli studi di filosofia medievale fra otto e novecento: Contributo a un bilancio storiografico* (Rome, 1989), 191–208.

3 P. Mandonnet, *Siger de Brabant et l'averroïsme latin au XIIIe siècle, 1ère Partie, Étude critique* (Louvain, 1911), 112.

4 F. van Steenberghen, 'L'Averroïsme latin', in id., *Introduction à l'étude de la philosophie médiévale* (Louvain, 1974), 553–4.

5 R.-A. Gauthier, 'Notes sur Siger de Brabant', *Revue des sciences philosophiques et théologiques*, 67 (1983–84), 201–32 and 68, 3–49.

6 Aristotle puts forward his theory in Book 3 of his *On the Soul*. For a good English translation, with full commentary, see *De Anima, Books II, III*, transl. with introduction and notes D.W. Hamlyn (Oxford, 1968).

7 For a thorough treatment of the history of this doctrine in Arabic philosophy, see H.A. Davidson, *Alfarabi, Avicenna, and Averroes, on Intellect* (New York, 1992); for a succinct account of some of the Latin doctrines, see Z. Kuksewicz, 'The Potential and the Agent Intellect', in A. Kenny, N. Kretzmann and J. Pinborg (eds.), *Cambridge History of Later Medieval Philosophy* (Cambridge, 1982), 593–601.

8 Averroes gave different interpretations of Aristotle's view of the active and potential intellects at different stages in his career. The view that there is one potential intellect alone is the one fully expounded in his long commentary on *On the Soul*, which has survived – apart from some recently discovered fragments – just in Michael Scotus's Latin translation (Averroes, *Commentarium magnum in Aristotelis de anima libros*, ed. F.S. Crawford [Cambridge, MA., 1953]; cf. Averroes, *L'Intelligence et la pensée: Sur le 'De anima'* [Paris, 1998] for a French translation and detailed commentary). This position is usually taken to be Averroes's final one, but even that has been disputed: see Averroes, *Middle Commentary on Aristotle's 'De anima'*, ed. and trans. A.L. Ivry (Provo, 2002). On the evolution of Averroes ideas on the Intellect, see Davidson, *Alfarabi, Avicenna, and Averroes, on Intellect* (as in previous note).

9 On Siger of Brabant, see not merely F. van Steenberghen, *Maître Siger de Brabant* (Louvain, 1977), but the more up-to-date and sympathetic study F.-X. Puttallaz and R. Imbach, *Profession: Philosophe. Siger de Brabant* (Paris, 1997).

10 R. Hissette, *Enquête sur les 219 articles condamnés à Paris le 7 mars 1277* (Louvain, 1977), 13: 'Dicunt enim ea esse vera secundum philosophiam, sed non secundum fidem catholicam, quasi sint due contrarie veritates, et quasi contra veritatem sacre scripture sit veritas in dictis gentilium dampnatorum ...'

11 A. de Libera, *L'Unité de l'intellect de Thomas d'Aquin* (Paris, 2004), 506–11.

12 Aquinas, *Opera omnia iussu Leonis XIII P.M.*, xliii (Rome, 1976), 314:408–21: 'Nec minoris presumptionis est quod postmodum asserere audet Deum non posse facere quod sint multi intellectus, quia implicat contradictionem. Adhuc autem grauius est quod postmodum dicit: 'per rationem concludo de necessitate, quod intellectus est unus numero; firmiter tamen teneo oppositum per fidem.' Ergo sentit quod fides sit de aliquibus quorum contraria de necessitate concludi possunt; cum autem de necessitate concludi non possit nisi uerum necessarium, cuius oppositum est falsum impossibile, sequitur secundum eius dictum quod fides sit de falso impossibili, quod etiam Deus facere non potest: quod fidelium aures ferre non possunt.'

13 Boethius of Dacia, *Opuscula*, ed. N.G. Green-Pedersen (Copenhagen, 1976), 364–6.

14 Boethius of Dacia, *Opuscula* (as in previous note), 387:176 – 388:184: 'Et ista est causa deceptionis multorum qui credunt physicos velle simpliciter demonstrare conclusiones aliquas, cum demonstrant eas per causas respectu quarum sive ex quarum suppositione impossibile est illas conclusiones aliter se habere. Cum tamen et causae illae et per consequens conclusiones illae natae sunt recipere impedimentum, ideo non intendunt physici tales conclusiones simpliciter demonstrare.'

15 J.-B. Brenet, *Transferts du sujet: La noétique d'Averroès selon Jean de Jandun* (Paris, 2003).

16 John of Jandun, *Super librum Aristotelis de anima substilissimae quaestiones* (Venice, 1561), iii, q. 5: 'Et puto, quod qui per alium modum nititur solvere rationes quasdam contra istam postionem ipse ex insufficientia solutionis magis redderet hanc positionem improbabilem quam sustinet eandem .. .'

17 See *L'Averroismo in Italia* (Accademia Nazionale dei Linci, Atti di convegni Lincei, 40; Rome, 1979); Z. Kuksewicz, *Averroisme bolonais au XIVe siècle* (Wroclaw, 1965) and *De Siger de Brabant à Jacques de Plaisance: La théorie de l'intellect chez les averroïstes latins des XIIIe et XIVe siècles* (Wroclaw, 1968) and especially F. Niewöhner and L. Sturlese (eds.), *Averroismus im Mittelalter und in der Renaissance* (Zurich, 1994).

18 This final section of my paper presents more briefly the argument I give in J. Marenbon, 'Dante's Averroism', in id. (ed.), *Poetry and Philosophy in the Middle Ages: a Festschrift for Peter Dronke* (Leiden, 2001), 349–74.

19 Scholars used to suggest an earlier date, but there is now very strong evidence that a cross-reference to the *Paradiso* in I, 12 (*sicut in Paradiso Comedie iam dixi*) is authentic: see Dante, *Monarchy*, trans. P. Shaw (Cambridge, 1996), xxxviii–xxxix; *Dante's 'Monarchia'*, trans. with commentary by R. Kay (Toronto, 1998), xx–xxxi; A. K. Cassell, *The 'Monarchia' Controversy* (Washington, 2004), 203–4.

20 Dante, *Monarchy*, trans. P. Shaw (as in previous note), 8.

21 Indeed, in the translation which Shaw published the year previously (Dante, *Monarchia*, ed. and trans. P. Shaw [Cambridge, 1995], 11), with parallel Latin text, she translates literally and correctly. Other recent translators (e.g. Kay, as in previous note, 25) have also given literal and accurate versions of the passage, but have not wished to interpret the passage in an Averroistic way.

22 For some recent rejections of the idea that Dante is an Averroist in proposing his argument here, see Dante, *Monarchia*, ed. and trans. P. Shaw (1995), 10, n. 7; Dante, *Dante's 'Monarchia'*, trans. with commentary by R. Kay, 20–21 (both as in previous note).

23 E. Gilson, *Dante et la philosophie*[2] (Paris, 1953), 170

24 Critique of Gilson. B. Nardi, 'Dante e la filosofia', *Studi Danteschi*, 25 (1940), 5–42 (rep. in id., *Nel mondo di Dante* [Rome, 1944], 209–45), 29–31. Most revealing of Nardi's own attitude is an early essay ('Il concerto dell'Impero nello svolgimento del pensiero dantesco', *Giornale storico della letteratura italiana*, 78 [1921], 1–52 [rep. in id., *Saggi di filosofia Dantesca* (Florence, 1967), 215–75]); he maintains the basic view here even in his edition of the *Monarchia* (Dante, *Opere Minori*, ed. P. Mengaldo, B. Nardi et al., ii [Milan, 1979]) from the end of his career. For more details on Nardi's complex position, see Marenbon, 'Dante's Averroism' (as in n. 18), 362–5.

25 Mandonnet, *Siger de Brabant* (as in n. 3), 301–7; Van Steenberghen, *Maître Siger de Brabant* (as in n. 9), 165–76. See also, for a much more convincing discussion (though taking a different view from that proposed here) P. Dronke, *Dante and Medieval Latin Traditions* (Cambridge, 1986), 143–4.

9

Islamic Crosspollinations

James E. Montgomery

My interests in, and aspirations for, the notion of 'crosspollination' are broadly captured in two moments in the creative lives of two prodigiously talented individuals of very different backgrounds, both in significant ways 'typical' products of their eras and their metropolises: the composer Leonard Bernstein (d. 1990) and al-Jāḥiẓ (d. 255/868–9).

When Eileen Sherwood is arrested and taken to the Christopher Street station house in the musical *Wonderful Town* (1953–1954), the Irish cops, dancing to the tune of an Irish jig, claim her for their own and boisterously serenade her, declaring the nostalgia which her Irishness ('the fairest colleen that iver I've seen') evokes. Eileen (a girl from Ohio) points out the error of their identification ('Mother's a Swede/Dad's a Scot'), but the cops will have none of this, for they have set their hearts on her Irishness, identifying her remonstrations as playful 'blarney' and situating her ('you come from Killarney, you're Irish, Eileen!').

Betty Comden and Adolf Green's lyrics (to the book by Joseph Fields and Jerome Chodorov) hilariously send up the dictates of identification which one group can impose on another, in a show which wonderfully captures the idea and reality of New York in the 1950s, which (like Baghdad in the third/ninth century) was a cosmopolitan magnet for talented individuals of all backgrounds, creeds, ambitions and abilities.

In a work written during the first half of the third/ninth century and devoted to the linguistic peccadilloes of various craftsmen and professionals (*Risāla fī ṣināʿāt al-quwwād: An Epistle on the Crafts of the Leading Exponents*), ranging from military commanders to street-cleaners, farmers to grooms, the theologian al-Jāḥiẓ has the physician Bukhtīshūʿ declare his love in the following poem:

> Our relationship drank the phial of avoidance and thus the intestines of union were loosened in diarrhoea;
> My love smote me with the palsy of separation, causing me to forget the criticisms of those who upbraid me.
> Thus the heart of the beloved is emaciated by consumption, while my mind (*qalb*) is afflicted with the morbid restlessness of ennui.

> And my heart (*fu'ād*) is pleuritic and sickly – I have lost my ability to treat myself, Ibn Masawayh!
> If Buqrāṭ (Hippocrates) and Jālīnūs (Galen) were in my condition, they would pass their nights in even greater despondency.[1]

As outlandish as this poem may sound to us, it conforms to the established tradition and conventions of Arabic amatory verse composed to bemoan the collapse of a relationship: the figure of the distraught lover, emaciated with loss of appetite, his mental faculties in a state of deranged disorder, is commonplace and is, of course, familiar also in the European tradition. Bukhtīshū' the physician, however, has at his disposal a barrage of medical and scientific terms to diagnose with exactitude the symptoms of love-lorn grief: diarrhoea, palsy, consumption, ennui, pleurisy. He is, however, a physician who cannot heal himself, and takes consolation in the fact that even those legendary medics, Hippocrates and Galen, would have been found wanting in the face of such a disease. Indeed, their despair would have been greater than his.[2]

Bukhtīshū' and the individual whom he addresses in his poem, Ibn Māsawyah, were Nestorian Christians, as were so many doctors in classical Islamic society, and the profession was hereditary in their families, the medical elite of the fabled infirmary of Jundaysābūr (Gondeshapur), a township in Khuzistan east of the Tigris. This Bukhtīshū' was, in all probability, the personal physician of the 'Abbāsid Caliphs, al-Ma'mūn, al-Wāthiq and al-Mutawakkil, the great-grandson of Jurjīs ibn Bukhtīshū' ibn Jibrīl ibn Bukhtīshū' who, in 148/765, came from Jundaysābūr to Baghdad to treat the Caliph al-Manṣūr. Yuḥannā ibn Māsawyh, the addressee of the poem, was also a prominent physician and an important figure in the commissioning of Greek-Arabic translations, with a particular interest in the anatomical works of Galen.[3]

Such was the prominence of Christian (and Jewish) physicians in 'Abbāsid Iraq, that we find the following lament, also in a work by the self-same theologian, al-Jāḥiẓ: his celebrated *Kitāb al-bukhalā'* (*Treatise on the Parsimonious*):

> Asad ibn Jānī ... was a physician. Once he was rather short of business and was asked by someone, 'There is a pestilence raging this year, and diseases are widespread. Now, you are learned, you have patience and have served [your patients well], you can communicate your diagnoses clearly and have insight, so how has your business come to fare so badly?' 'In the first place,' he replied, 'People know that I am a Muslim, and folk decided before I took up medicine, indeed before I was even created, that Muslims do not succeed as physicians. My name is Asad. My name should have been Ṣalīb or Jibrā'īl, Yūḥannā or Bīrā. My patronymic is Abū 'l-Ḥārith, but it should have been Abū 'Īsā, or Abū Zakariyā' or Abū Ibrāhīm. I wear a robe of white cotton, but my robe should be of black silk. My words are those of an Arab, but my pronunciation should be the dialect of the people of Jundaysābūr'.[4]

The point of the anecdote, however, is that Asad ibn Jānī's complaint about the popularity of Christian and Jewish medics (his alleged pauperism) functions as a device for the concealment of his miserliness.

These two passages seem to me to capture at least some of what I understand by the title which I gave to the Colloquium in Trinity Hall, Cambridge, and which gave rise to this collection of articles: *Islamic Crosspollinations*. In al-Jāḥiẓ's passage we have a sophisticated society in which many different religious creeds mingle, with a highly developed literary language and egregious intellectual accomplishments, serving a court in Baghdad which allowed for the flow of ideas and practices. Asad's lament demonstrates that such intermingling was not confined to the elites alone, however. In Bukhtīshūʿ's love poem, the two traditions of Arabic amatory verse and Hippocratic/Galenic medicine are seamlessly woven together. The resultant combination is peculiar, in both Arabic and English, but is certainly not preposterous in Arabic.

The term 'crosspollination' is certainly unusual and perhaps requires an explanation. In order to furnish such an explanation, I would like to pass under review some of the methods and paradigms which have been applied, within the discipline of Islamic Studies, to the complex and nebulous issues surrounding the processes, means and devices which individual Arabophone Muslims, or groups of Muslims, have either had at their disposal or contrived to avail themselves of, when engaging with other, predominantly non-Muslim, individuals, groups of individuals, texts, concepts and practices. This review will include a consideration of methods such as the search for 'influence', the discernment of cultural contacts, the identification of diffusion and/or migration, the argument for appropriation and its implications for transmission and transformation (i.e. *trans-lation* in its widest intellectual sense).[5] Where appropriate, attention will also be paid to emergent paradigms in the study of identities, such as transculturation, transplanting, hybridity, polygenesis and intersection.

Influence

Within a discipline determined by philological perspectives, such as the practice of tracing texts back through various corruptions to an originary moment (establishing the stemma),[6] or the charting of the divagations of meanings accorded to any given word or concept across time, the observation that one people, society or set of practices may have influenced another people, society or set of practices seems quite warranted. And in fact there is a plethora of works which set out to exemplify the influence of one set of ideas or practices (generally essentialised as a religion: 'Islam', or as 'Islamic culture', for example) on another (sometimes exemplified by a geographical area: 'Europe', for example).[7] Perhaps the most fiercely contested (and resented by some) are those studies which apply the standard of 'influence' to the question of Islamic origins. I propose to consider these only in so far as they arise in discussions of the origins of Islamic law.[8] The motivation of the quest for 'influence' is (explicitly or implicitly) the determination of 'originality', a concept which is naturally suggested by an interest in 'origin', though such suggestions are all too defeasible, are never irrefragable, and are woefully prone to prejudice – 'originality' being a Romantic aesthetic and a facile means of misreading.

It is important to bear in mind throughout the long discussion which follows that it is not the 'factuality' (for want of a better word) of two or more peoples using, sharing or developing a practice, idea or custom which is in question, but rather the implications and consequences of the methods which are applied to the re-presenting of that 'factuality'; and that these methods are not tidy or discrete categories, but to a large extent can overlap and intersect with each other with considerable variations and to differing degrees (as happens, for example, when 'influence' becomes 'impact' and is recast as 'migration').

I propose to consider four exercises in 'influence': W. Montgomery Watt, *The Influence of Islam on Medieval Europe*;[9] *The Arab Influence in Medieval Europe*, ed. D. Agius and R. Hitchcock;[10] Patricia Crone, *Roman, Provincial and Islamic Law*;[11] Donald Ostrowski, *Muscovy and the Mongols: Cross-cultural Influences on the Steppe Frontier, 1304-1589*.[12]

The Influence of Islam on Medieval Europe was first delivered during December 1970 as a series of lectures before the Collège de France. It was published in English by Edinburgh University Press as volume 9 in their *Islamic Surveys* series, intended to give 'the educated reader something more than can be found in the usual popular books' in the form of surveys which presented not merely 'an outline of what was known and generally accepted, but also indicating the points at which scholarly debate continued' (v). Thus the book is a product of that edenic moment in Islamic Studies when it was uncustomary to reflect upon, let alone question, the methodological principles informing the approach which one brought to bear on a given issue. Accordingly, Montgomery Watt does not, as far as I can see, discuss what he means by 'influence' or devote any attention to the problems surrounding the kinds of processes which he describes or even explain how an incorporeal entity such as 'Islam' (whatever we may mean thereby)[13] can in fact interact with a geographical region (however fuzzily articulated: even if we were to extend the meaning of the toponym to the very limit, it is still difficult to envisage whether the inhabitants of the Iberian peninsula, or Sicily or Carolingian France would ever have thought of themselves as 'Europeans').[14] So we are led perforce to consider the book as the realisation of the method.[15]

There are six chapters and one appendix: 'Islamic Presence in Europe'; 'Commerce and Technology'; 'Arab Achievements in Science and Philosophy'; 'Reconquista and Crusade'; 'Science and Philosophy in Europe'; 'Islam and European Self-Awareness'. A cornerstone of Watt's approach is discernible in the Appendix, 'List of English Words Derived from Arabic' (85–92).

Words, of course, are the philologist's bread and butter. As concrete entities, their histories can be mapped, and their meanderings plotted, their origins approximated, and their presence verified. The 'list contains English words which have passed through Arabic at some stage in their history' and its 'chief interest is to indicate our debt to medieval Islam' (85). But words are messy and slippery and the weight of their evidence uncertain – thus Watt havers between Arabic as source and Arabic as medium,[16] and in the process presumes that Arabic and Islam are co-extensive, and that all speakers of Arabic are Muslim. The important thing to note, however, about this list is: a) that the phenomenon is observable and capable of being charted through the empirically ascertainable traces which it leaves behind; b) that the consequence of the phenomenon is a response characterised by indebtedness, though whether material (financial), moral, spiritual or religious is unclear; and c) that it is teleological: an improved, and indebted, 'Europe' is the (satisfactory) end of the process.[17] And the first paragraph of the book informs us that any account of the phenomenon, for it to have genuine worth, must consider it 'in its totality' (1).

This totalising empiricism is evident in the first chapter, 'Islamic Presence in Europe', which is essentially an overview of military activity: 'the occupation of Spain and Sicily by Muslims' and 'military impact' (2, 4 etc.); 'Arab expansion'; 'to the inhabitants of Spain the invasion of 711 may have come as a bolt from the blue' (5); 'expansionist pressure' and '"barbarian" invasion' (9). Influence, then, is something which is *exerted*, presumably through an act, or acts, of violence and is beneficial, though the impartation of these benefits may not be intentional, but may 'overflow into a neighbouring territory' (1), and hence Watt can talk of a 'meeting' between Europe and Islam (82).

Watt's analysis of the phenomenon does not end here, however. In Chapter Six, entitled 'Islam and European Self-Awareness', 72–84, he moves to consider what this phenomenon has meant and continues to mean for Europe over the centuries. He notes that the 'image of Islam' is 'distorted' (73) and that it contrasts with the prevalent image of Europe ('Christendom': 80); that this imagistic 'distortion ... among Europeans was necessary to compensate them' for 'the feeling of inferiority with which western Europe confronted Islamic civilization' (82).[18] Yet, as Watt believes he has shown, Europe is indebted to Islam, confrontation with which belittled Europe (in European eyes) and 'provoked Europe into forming a new image of itself' through a reaction against Islam, and this distortion has led to a lack of European self-awareness (which ought rightly to consist of an avowal of indebtedness):

> In this post-Freudian world men realize that the darkness ascribed to one's enemies is a projection of the darkness in oneself that is not fully admitted. In this way the distorted image of Islam is to be regarded as a projection of the shadow-side of European man. The violence and excessive sexuality ascribed to Saracens existed also in Europe, even if contrary to the Christian ideal (85).[19]

This passage comes as quite a surprise in the context of the book, precisely because it seems so out of context. It is worth considering its implications for how Watt seems to envisage the 'influence' of Islam on Europe.

We may begin by noting that, in addition to the imprecise reference to Freud, Alfred Adler's notion of the 'inferiority complex' looms large in Watt's conceptualisation.[20] Yet however much Watt may dilute a Freudian analysis of the phenomenon (*au pied de la lettre*), we may note that, in Freud's words,

> Consciousness of one's own weakness and helplessness – inferiority according to Adler's terminology, – if it can be prolonged from childhood into adult life, is the final basis of neurosis.[21]

So Watt seems here to approach European anxiety with regard to Islam as a neurosis, and this surely requires investigation. As far as I can see, Watt nowhere uses the term 'anxiety' to describe the relationship he establishes, but a brief consideration of the Freudian understanding of neurosis will prove illuminating.

Freud's mature conception of the psyche in its ideal state of tensionless tranquillity (which he labelled the 'Nirvana principle' in his 1920 work, *Beyond the Pleasure Principle*)[22] owes as much to the philosophers of Classical Antiquity as it does to the psychophysics of Gustav Theodor Fechner (1801–1887) and the phylogeneticism of Jean-Baptiste Lamarck (1744–1829), who held that acquired characteristics were inherited.[23]

In the use of Fechner's principle of absolute stability ('in which there exists no energy or movement in a given system [Freud's state of Nirvana]'), it is hard not to detect the spirit of Aristotle's unmoved mover or the absoluteness of Plotinus' 'One', while in the teleology of Freud's psychological economy, predicated upon his kinetic notion of 'cathexes' (bursts or charges of psychical energy),[24] whereby every psyche mechanistically strives for tranquility through the elimination of emotions and the neuroses engendered by traumas, whether acquired or inherited, one can readily hear inflections of the Stoic goal of *apatheia*, the Sceptic aim of *ataraxia*, or even the Muslim practice of *sukūn al-nafs* (psychic quietude) or Qur'ānic *iṭmi'nān* (equanimity, imperturbability).

When Freud boldly and imaginatively declares that 'the aim of all life is death',[25] as well as adapting Fechner's thermodynamics to his mechanistic notion of pleasure,[26] he is doing philosophy in a long tradition which starts with Socrates and has appealed to thinkers as diverse as Michel de Montaigne and Martin Heidegger.[27]

For Freud (and to simplify outrageously), the mind was a battlefield, a struggle between the conscious, the preconscious and the unconscious for mastery of emotional affects. On the occurrence of a trauma, which generates a surplus of psychic energy, the mind tries to dissipate or discharge this kinetic surplus. Failure adequately to do so results in neurosis. The trauma may merely be ostensible and may unlock previous traumas, working in tandem with memories of them, to produce a fixation.[28] Those individuals who are thus fixated seem

> As though they could not manage to free themselves ... and were for that reason alienated from the present and the future.[29]

Fixation need not necessarily lead to or be occasioned by a neurosis but there can be no neurosis without 'fixation to a particular phase in the past', and thus fixation may involve the obsessive repetition or recreation of the traumatic incident often in some form of displacement, generally symbolic, with which the patient may feel unconnected. This process, then, is characterised by an inability to move on, psychically and often physically.

In Watt's account, the Muslim invasion in 711, for example, 'a bolt from the blue' to the inhabitants of Spain (5), is a traumatic event, while Europe's repeated inability to acknowledge fully the extent of the debt to the Muslims is tantamount to a neurotic fixation to the past.[30] Like the woman in love with her son-in-law and described in Freud's 'General Theory of the Neuroses', Europe's debt to Islam, 'a monstrous and impossible thing, could not become conscious; but it remained in existence and, even though it was unconscious, it exercised a severe pressure'. This experience resulted in a displacement in which the woman became convinced that her husband was having an affair with a young girl. Thus

> Her own love had not become conscious to her, but its mirror-reflection, which brought her such an advantage, now became conscious as an obsession and delusion. No arguments against it could, of course, have any effect for they were only directed against the mirror-image and not against the original which gave the other its strength and which lay hidden, inviolable, in the unconscious.[31]

And we may also remind ourselves of Watt's remarks concerning the 'projection of the darkness in oneself that is not fully admitted' (*Influence*, 83) discussed above.

It was Josef Breuer (1842–1925) who discovered a technique for bringing to the consciousness 'the unconscious processes which continued the sense of the symptoms', as a result of which process 'the symptoms disappeared'. This was in the celebrated case of Anna O. (Bertha Pappenheim, treated between 1880 and 1882) which became the 'foundation of psychoanalytic therapy ... the thesis that symptoms disappear when we have made the unconscious predeterminants conscious'.[32]

Psychoanalysis, like the construction of stemmata in textual criticism, is retrogressive, reconstructing past dissimilarities from the ostensible similitudes of present phenomena, and regularly filling in the gaps in transmission, be it of texts or memories.[33]

Through his account of the influence of Islam on Europe over the centuries, then, Watt set out 'to fill up all the gaps in the patient's memory, to remove his amnesias'. His act of historical psychoanalysis (in the spirit of Freud's *Totem and Taboo* [1913])[34] is aimed at countering the thirteen centuries of repression which can now be seen to have occasioned a long 'violent opposition ... against the entry into consciousness of the questionable mental process'.[35] The prize is the religious rapprochement so sorely required by the ecumenism which informed much of Watt's work,[36] and in the end, Watt can be said to be more interested in 'Europe' than in 'Islam'.[37]

At first blush, *The Arab Influence in Medieval Europe* (*Folia Scholastica Mediterranea*) (1994), a collection of papers presented at a conference held in Oxford in April, 1990, reads like a commentary upon Watt's book.[38] In addition to the similarity in the title, the six contributions touch on aspects discussed by Watt. Thus, the topics of Chapters One, 'Islamic Presence in Europe' and Four, 'Reconquista and Crusade' (1–14 and 44–57) feature in Eduardo Manzano Moreno's 'Christian-Muslim Frontier in Al-Andalus: Idea and Reality' (83–99); the contents of Chapter Two, 'Commerce and Technology' (15–29), are the subjects of 'The Role of Trade in Muslim-Christian Contact During the Middle Ages' by David Abulafia (1–24), 'Arabic Fine Technology and Its Influence on European Mechanical Engineering' by Donald Hill (25–43), and 'The Influence of the Metalwork of the Arab Mediterranean on that of Medieval Europe' by James Allan (44–62); in 'An Islamic Divinatory Technique in Medieval Spain' (100–125), Charles Burnett sheds light on one facet of the scientific heritage discussed by Watt in Chapters Three, 'Arab Achievements in Science and Philosophy' (30–43), and Five, 'Science and Philosophy in Europe' (58–71), while David Wulstan ('Boys, Women and Drunkards: Hispano-Mauresque Influences on European Song?', 136–137) and Philip Kennedy ('Muslim Sources of Dante?', 63–82) investigate items touched upon by Watt under the rubrics of 'the spread of Islamic culture into Europe' (27–28) and 'the contrasting image of Europe' (79–80), respectively. The similarities, however, are superficial.

Through the simple substitution of one preposition ('in') for another ('on') in the title of the collection, the editors, Agius and Hitchcock, take the notion of 'influence' as a given rather than a demonstrandum, and while the full import of the term 'Arab' is unclear to me, it is presumably intended to include Arabic-speakers irrespective of religious denomination (for example, Iberian Arabophone Jews and Arabic-speaking Christians).[39] By 'Europe', the editors intend 'not solely ... the Iberian Peninsula ... but also ... the wider arena of the Mediterranean basin' (vii), although the awkwardness of applying the notion 'Europe' to diverse peoples such as Iberians, Italians and Sicilians remains. Within the conceptual domain of 'influence', Agius and Hitchcock incorporate 'contact and interaction', 'transmission', 'literary and cultural impact', encroachment and dissemination, absorption and exploitation, development and embellishment, permeation and experience.

Yet traces of the teleological paradigm of the philologists persist, when they talk of:

> A Europe that had apparently lost contact with its classical heritage. What the Muslims absorbed and exploited from the classical world, the Europeans received, and eventually developed and embellished (vii).

What these 'Europeans' received is not, of course, a hermetically sealed classical heritage kept alive by the Muslims, but bodies of knowledge, techniques, theories, concepts and notions transmogrified, reforged, Arabicised, Islamicised and revivified – in sum an Islamic heritage created by Muslims and acquisitioned by schools of (non-Muslim) translators working to their own ambitions, circles of patronage, religious visions and scientific enthusiasms.[40]

'Influence' is predicated upon contact, and the evidence for Muslim-Christian contact is so apparent as to be indubitable – perhaps even in no need of verification. And yet was exchange (of practices, techniques and craft technologies as opposed to comestibles and merchandise) the result of trade or conquest?

David Abulafia makes a distinction 'between the borrowing of Arabic terms as a result of Christian conquest of Muslim lands, and borrowings actually effected through trade' (2), noting the various ambiences through which a merchant may have moved in the thirteenth century, from reconquered Majorca where Islamic civilisation was vestigial, to a Valencia where Muslims endured as the majority, living under an Aragonese king, to Muslim North Africa, where western merchants were constrained to operate in governmentally sanctioned *funduq*s. The lesson he draws from his detailed survey of mercantile activities from approximately 1000 to 1400 CE is that:

> It was increasingly possible to conduct trade in the produce of the Muslim world without having to set foot in that world. It is true ... that in formal terms the western merchants never managed to adjust in their favour the balance of trade with the Islamic world. However, following on from the defeat of Muslim navies and from the triumph of western textiles in the Mediterranean, the capture of Arab agricultural technology confirmed the massive ascendancy of western merchants in their trade with Islam by the end of the Middle Ages (19–20).

If this is so, then territories in which Muslim and non-Muslim lived cheek by jowl – Sicily, the Iberian Peninsula, the Fertile Crescent – assume greater prominence in attempts to reconstruct the phenomena of 'influence'. Traditionally, of course, these territories have been viewed through the lens of irreconcilable confrontation and hostility, as lands geographically and religiously sundered in which 'Islam' was pitted against 'Christendom'.

Eduardo Manzano Moreno dissects the medieval and modern historiography of this frontier, remarking upon the explanatory appeal of such polarities, the mutual antipathies of which are deemed so natural as to be taken for granted. His analyses are a timely reminder of the fictiveness of notions such as 'frontier',[41] ethnic distinctiveness and 'Europe' ('it is important always to bear in mind that the whole medieval territory was itself a "frontier"' (96), and of the persuasive hegemony of the literate elites who controlled the reins of textual representation, be they historiographical (with polemical and legitimising fantasies of heroic defence of soil and repulsion of intruders) or jurisprudential (in definitions of the obligations of Reconquista and Jihād).

This 'ideological frontier' was a vision of the Iberian Peninsula which both Muslim intellectuals and Christian clerics had in common!, and the applicability of the paradigm of 'influence' as an identifiable occurrence facilitated by contact across a divide is invalidated by what Moreno refers to as 'the real frontier' (the Duero valley), an area of 'political fragmentation' and 'absence of neat religious boundaries' (93) populated by peoples who by the fourth/tenth and early fifth/eleventh centuries, 'at some time and somehow had become at least partially arabised' (95), Christians (some of them priests) with Arabic names, the results of 'a complicated pattern of assimilation' (96).[42] Talk of 'influence' in cases such as this is nugatory and illusory.[43]

The value of 'influence' as a hermeneutic is discredited (despite his protestations to the contrary) by David Wulstan in his musicological survey of 'the possibility of a Hispano-Mauresque influence on European lyric' (139).

The starting-point of his literate and formalistic study is the not unreasonable assumption that 'it does seem inconceivable that when Arab instruments were imported into Europe, the gramophone came without any disks' (139). Yet, even if one allows for the possibility of 'influence' (which some have denied):

> And although several Mauresque elements can be detected in the troubadour and trouvère traditions, the relationship between the cultures was as promiscuous as that imputed to some of the characters in the lyrics themselves: it was at the same time more indirect, and its by-blows were more miscegenated, than proponents of the 'Arabic theory' might have hoped ... the interchange between the cultures was mostly at a level beneath the notice of the literary sources: it was the vulgar *zajal* ... which provided the melting-pot, not the literate *muwashshaḥ*, despite its Romance *kharajāt* and the possible influence of its rhyme-schemes. It was the popular 'songs of the Christians' which influenced, and were influenced by, the *zajal*, not the troubadour lyrics of Guillem IX of Aquitaine and his successors' (158–9).

At this point the idea of 'influence' seems simply bankrupt. And insult is added to injury when Donald Hill, at the end of his survey, abandons (unilinear) 'influence' in favour of the more open, and distinctly multilinear, notion of 'diffusion', which is especially suited to the study of the spread of technologies, achieved via 'contacts among craftsmen, by travellers' reports and by the inspection of earlier constructions' (41).[44] Although he discusses routes of transmission, he does not privilege the Iberian Peninsula over Byzantium or Sicily or the Fertile Crescent during the Crusades, and even talks of the mechanical escapement as 'an invention that was grafted onto an array of ideas that were Arabic in origin' (42).

'Influence' as a hermeneutic produces its most satisfying results when it is applied to material objects (Hill's survey of fine technology is almost exclusively text-based) and James Allan's account of how Islamic metalwork reached Europe and the changes it wrought is a good example, especially as it is combined with a common-sensical assessment of the 'quirks' or 'echoes of survival' (44 and 46), the possible limitations of their appeal (as in his evaluation of the influence of ''Abbāsid Iraqi silver bowls with niello inlay' on the pulpit of Henry II in Aachen [46–8]) and an appreciation for slippage in the applications of techniques, styles and schemes across a variety of media. His investigation of Boris

Marshak's theories concerning the interrelationship of various thirteenth century cups and ciboria of Near Eastern origin discovered in Europe leads him to suggest that:

> Islamic metalworking is providing a source not only for very ordinary, European, secular objects like the base metal ewers, but also for European objects of great splendour with a specific, sacred function (56).

This suggestion (that European high culture, including sacred objects, may have been produced through an engagement with Muslim traditions and practices) finds a curious echo in Philip Kennedy's excellent discussion of the much-contested Muslim sources of Dante (63–82).

In the spirit of Watt's analysis of European anxiety and in the wake of María Rosa Menocal's influential treatment, after Harold Bloom, of 'the anxieties of influence',[45] Kennedy locates Dante in his native Florence and also in a 'Europe which in moulding its intellectual identity was in the shadow of elements of Islamic culture' (64), and sees in *The Divine Comedy* 'the revindication of a European identity in the shadow of the incursions of another culture' (64). This is the influence of antagonism,

> The product of a Europe engaged, anxiously at times, in the absorption, transformation and reappropriation of literary elements preserved in Arab sources (79).[46]

By this stage, we have left the dynamics of 'influence' as (benign, or even, neutral) cultural improvement far behind, and are left pondering whether 'appropriation' is not a more productive designation for the assertive agonistics of the phenomena thus described.

In 1875 Alfred von Kremer considered the theory of the genesis of Islamic law out of Roman law which had enjoyed some favour in European circles for the previous one hundred and fifty years.[47] Parthenogenesis, to use a term introduced into these discussions by D. Santillana, was clearly impossible: the concept of creation *ex nihilo* (or its analogue, divine revelation) sits ill with the philological approach. For von Kremer, Roman influence on Islamic law would have been mediated by borrowings from Jewish law.[48]

It is this question to which Patricia Crone turns in her monograph from 1987, *Roman, Provincial and Islamic Law: the Origins of the Islamic Patronate*, part of her wider programme to investigate the role which greater Syria (the Roman province of Arabia) played in the evolution of the Islamic polity.[49] The crucible in which she chooses to test the metal of the postulate is *walāʾ*, the institution whereby, she argues, the Arab Muslims of the first two centuries 'regulated the status of freedmen and converts' (35) in the Islamic community.[50]

In the first chapter of the work, 'The State of the Field' (1–17), Crone surveys the deficiencies of previous non-Muslim approaches to the question,[51] proposes the tendentious nature of the presentation of the birth and growth of Islamic law encountered in the Islamic tradition ('virtually every legal institution being traced back to pre-Islamic Arabian practice and/or rulings by the Arabian Prophet and his immediate successors', 2), and lambastes a degeneration in the quality of thinking on the issue of institutional or cultural phylogeneticism evinced throughout the twentieth century. She attributes this latter to the demise of philology and its replacement by a wishy-washy sociology of empathy:

> As the old-fashioned Orientalist has given way to the modern historian, Arabist or social scientist with a tender post-colonial conscience and occasionally more substantial interest in maintaining Muslim good-will, both the inclination and the ability to view the *Werden und Wesen* of the Islamic world from the point of view of the Fertile Crescent have been lost, and Islamic Civilisation has come to be taught and studied with almost total disregard for the Near East in which it was born (6–7).

The up-shot of this trend in scholarship seems, according to Crone, to be a sort of collective navel-gazing combined with a gullible willingness on the part of non-Muslims to be duped by the Islamic tradition into considering Islamic law as a product of 'an Arabian void' (3) hermetically sealed from the wider world in which it was born.

Obviously, Crone agrees with the philological abhorrence of parthenogenesis and is a fervent advocate of the hermeneutic of 'influence'. This leads her, with other philologists, to attempt to locate the growth of Islamic law, for 'influence' can only be exerted through channels of borrowing. Of crucial significance for the validity of location are those residues of Roman law found in Islamic law but not encountered in Jewish law (for it has been taken as a given that Islamic law is basically a younger, and impoverished or less sophisticated, derivative of its Judaic precursor). The candidature of the Syro-Roman lawbook of Nestorian Iraq is rejected (12), and Egypt and Syria elected in its place, but they too prove not wholly satisfactory for:

> The extent to which Roman law was actually practised in Syria and Egypt is of course an altogether different question ... the law of the Near Eastern provinces was never wholly Romanised and ... numerous peregrine institutions survived under a more or less Roman veneer.[52]

As an antidote, she proposes 'provincial law': 'the non-Roman law practised in the provinces of the Roman empire, especially the provinces formerly ruled by Greeks' (1), not 'an autonomous system competing with that of Rome ... but seen through alien eyes and supplemented by numerous alien institutions' (15). And 'provincial practice contributed far more to the Sharīʿa than did Roman law' (14; see 91–92).

Provincial law and Roman law were messy mixtures which varied from place to place, their ingredients were nowhere uniform or standard, and their agents were dispersed across time and place.[53] Such messiness is naturally difficult to pinpoint or determine (and it is not always obvious to me that it is appropriate to attempt such a thing) and on page 15 we are presented with the surprising suggestion that, just as Romanised provincial law may have influenced Islamic law, so 'Islamic law may well prove to be the single most important corpus of information on the nature of legal practice in the Near East'. So profound is Crone's conviction in the hermeneutic of 'influence' that such circular reasoning does not strike her as the special pleading it so clearly is.[54]

We may also note, in her presentation, that Roman and provincial law are both chronologically prior to Islamic law and intellectually superior. According to the reasoning underlying the laws of 'influence' as identified by Gibb, one system can only influence another if that system happens, in some sense, to be superior to that which is being influenced. 'Influence' (and borrowing) are predicated upon a hierarchy of accomplishment.[55]

Borrowing requires borrowers, and it is to the Umayyads, who, according to Schacht, created Islamic law, that Crone now turns. On the basis of an earlier book, *God's Caliph: Religious Authority in the First Centuries of Islam*, co-written with Martin Hinds,[56] she identifies 'all legal authority, be it legislative or adjudicative' as 'concentrated in the caliphs' (15), as a consequence of which 'law in the first century of Islam was caliphal law' (16). The caliphs resided in Syria and 'caliphs of God are more likely than scholars to have felt at liberty to borrow foreign law' (16) – though why they should have inclined to such authoritarian liberties is not explained; nor is it at all as clear as Crone's pronouncement would have us believe.[57]

Umayyad law 'cannot be studied directly' but it must be 'reconstructed partly from early *ḥadīth*[58] and partly from a systematic comparison of *sunnī* and heretical law, archaic elements being fairly common in the latter' (16). In this regard, it resembles the Romanised provincial (or provincialised Roman) law to which Islamic law is held to testify.

Crone is all too aware of the deficiencies of her evidence, but the problems lie not with 'primarily the lack of source material ... but rather a lack of imaginative nerve' (16). We may be gulled into accepting 'Islamic civilisation' as 'Ḥijāzī culture writ large' by 'a documentary sleight of hand' (17) but our gullibility can be dispelled by a brief consideration of the non-textual material presented to us by Islamic art, and for her Umayyad art is, simply put, Greek art continued.[59] A lack of decent documentary evidence and recourse to imaginative nerve – we can be forgiven for thinking of Schacht's 'cardboard citadel' (11).

The distortions of 'influence' do not become fully apparent until the 'Conclusion' of Crone's study (89–99), in which she establishes that 'provincial law ... amounted to a legal *koinē* – a way of regulating things, usually of Greek or ancient Near Eastern origin, which was known to and understood throughout the provinces which were to form the heartlands of Islam' (93), a set of practices some of which, it would seem, were shared by 'the pre-Islamic Arabs themselves to some extent' (92), including 'manumission with *paramonē*', 'the paramonar service contract', a type of 'succession pact common in the provinces' and the type known as '*adoptio in fratrem*' (93). 'To some extent', then, 'law in Arabia would thus appear to have been Near Eastern law, or an archaic version thereof, not simply tribal law unique to the peninsula'.

This is a very important observation and its most natural implication is that Arabia formed part of the ancient Near East and shared in many of its legal practices, be they provincial, Roman, their hybrid forms, or Judaic. But this cannot be, because, for Crone, Arabian law is something distinct from Near Eastern law, and though I struggle to find a definition of Arabian law, despite the numerous asseverations of its existence, it seems to be the customary tribal law still in evidence in 'modern Arabia' (see 44–49).[60] And then, in an interpretative move familiar from the first of Gibb's three laws of 'influence',[61] we recognise the importance of demonstrating 'the familiarity of the pre-Islamic Arabs with the Near Eastern *koinē*': it 'may have assisted its victory in Islam' (97).

So strongly attached is Crone to the dynamic of 'influence' and its dictate that borrowing be topographically located that she is unable to pose the questions demanded by the evidence which she presents: how provincial was Arabian law (by which I mean the legal systems of the pre-Islamic Hijaz)? and how Judaised was this law?[62]

Clearly, I concur with a considerable amount of Wael Hallaq's criticisms of Crone's argument (see note 11). What I find quite astonishing, however, is that for all the judiciousness of his observations concerning the ancient Near Eastern and pre-Islamic Arabian character of the institutions referred to by the term *walāʾ*, he, like Crone, is so wedded to the polemic of 'influence' and its requirements of chronological precedence and topographical location, that he resurrects a nineteenth century philological creation, the 'distinctive Semitic character' of the society of the Fertile Crescent, as a 'fundamental fact'.[63] In so doing, he is merely participating in a 'classic Orientalist creed' of the type that he attacks elsewhere.[64]

In order to comply with Crone's exhortations against the intellectual and methodological insularities of scholarship in contemporary Islamic Studies, I wish now to review Donald Ostrowski's examination of the Mongol contributions to Muscovite society and institutions, in *Muscovy and the Mongols: Cross-Cultural Influences on the Steppe Frontier, 1304–1589*.

Ostrowski examines four areas of possible 'influence', be it alleged or denied: 'administration, political institutions, and the military'; the 'seclusion of women'; 'oriental despotism'; and 'economic oppression' (ix and 35). He describes a spectrum of polarised views on the subject, from the indigenes, 'those who believe Muscovite institutions are indigenously "Russian" ... in part ... continuations of Kievan institutions and ... in part ... created to meet uniquely Muscovite needs' (a heroic process of survival and creativity which was achieved despite nefarious and deleterious Mongol overlordship) (2), to the Eurasianists, 'those who believe Muscovite institutions are all imports ... an imitation of other societies, in particular Byzantine, Mongol, or European' (7–8)[65] to the combinationists, those who propose 'a model that combines the Byzantine and Mongol influences' (9).

This presentation offers us a series of debates which bear some interesting similarities to the study of Islamic origins. Those who suggest that the Mongols may have brought some benefit to the Muscovites are designated as anti-Russian, and those who champion the Russian cause of the Muscovites tend to be pronouncedly hostile to the Mongols. According to Ostrowski, one of the reasons for the appeal of this polarity is 'because Muscovy is presented as being totally different from any other society' (5), 'a failure to integrate Muscovite history into world history' which 'risks keeping the Muscovite field arcane and absolute' (7). The first position is representative of those who specialise in Muscovite and Russian studies, the second of those who consider the phenomenon from a specialism outwith Russian studies (12). Muscovy is thus an oxymoron, 'free from outside influence and influenced from the outside'.

However, and like Islam, Muscovy is not *sui generis*,[66] and to demonstrate this Ostrowski distills three categories of 'opposing features' from twelve types of influence identified by Peter K. Christoff in a study of Russia in the early nineteenth century:[67]

> Imposition by the source culture (target culture is passive) vs. borrowing by the target culture (target culture is active); imposition or borrowing along a broad front vs. imposition or borrowing initially as a wedge or along a narrow front, which might then expand to a broader influence; and sudden, immediate change vs. gradual, long-term change (250).

Such categorisation is achieved for each instance via three lines of inquiry:

1. Where does an institution or practice come from? What were its antecedents both internally and externally?

2. How did it function? What was its structure? What purpose did it serve?
3. Why did it end? Was it ended intentionally by human intervention or did it phase itself out through non-use? Did outside influences replace it with a new institution or practice or amalgamate it with the old institutions or practice to form a hybrid? (16).

These lines of inquiry are grounded in three basic principles:

> (1) that the institution or practice existed in the source culture; (2) that its existence in the source culture coincided in real time with its appearance in the target culture; and (3) that a mechanism for its transference from the source culture to the target culture was operative (34–35).[68]

We may have left behind Gibb's ideal of the improvement of one people or culture under the benign influence of another, superior, one. We can note that in order to deflect the relevancies or critiques of chauvanist scholarship Ostrowski has formulated some useful criteria for a mechanistic and formal schematisation of 'influence', and we can approve of his insistence that 'once borrowed, an institution or practice acquires its own integrity and dynamic' (35), but I am struck by how 'imposition' and 'borrowing' pull in opposite directions and by the complete absence of agency in his scheme: who are the imposers and who the borrowers; how do we identify them?; what are their motives, aspirations, lived experiences? Have we really left the hegemonic dimensions of 'influence' behind? And nowhere in the book, as far as I can determine, does he actually question the relevance or appropriateness of 'influence' as a hermeneutic.

Ostrowski's work is an impressive piece of scholarship but at its completion, it is difficult to see what an approach based on 'influence' has left to offer. No matter how delicately refined or carefully formulated, 'influence' places an excessive emphasis on either donor or recipient: a pro-donor stance tends to imply an anti-recipient position; it is relentlessly unilinear (and seems incapable of reversal), and occludes or elides participation by agents in its realisations: there is no way to escape or to alter what the planets determine, for 'influence' persists in preserving its astrological significance.[69]

The only means of salvaging 'influence' as a hermeneutic is to read it against itself, by following Harold Bloom's lead and defining it as a creative act of 'misprision' or 'misreading' borne out of the anxiety of priority and authority.[70] For Bloom 'influence' is metaphoric, its importance lies in its consequences not in its effects. Thus literary history, and its foundational principle – the detection of influences, is saved as a series of idiosyncratic, competitive and ambivalent, creative misreadings of the past:

> Influence-anxieties are embedded in the agonistic basis of all imaginative literature.[71]

Poetic influence thus detected does not diminish originality,[72] for Bloom is at pains to maintain the creative status of the poets he discusses, the life-cycles of the 'poet-as-poet' (7). Misprision, misreading, anxiety and anguish, contamination, priority and authority, contribute to poetry as *poiēsis*, as an act of making, of genuine creativity, and to the agents of this creativity, the maker: the *poiētēs*.

No theory or account of the dynamics and productivities of intellectual engagements and interactions can afford to ostracise either misprision or the creativity it may give rise to. Bloom sounds the death-knell of 'influence' by depriving it of its agency, by demonstrating that its trajectories are unpredictable, tangential and contingent rather than chartable and unidirectional, and are fundamentally predicated upon the misadventurous anxieties generated by miscomprehension.[73] If we are to use 'influence', then, we must view it as a creative process which derives its agency and success from distortion, or reaction against, or even 're-creation' of the source of influence.[74]

Culture

> Men of all quarters of the globe, who have perished over the ages, you have not lived solely to manure the earth with your ashes, so that at the end of time your posterity should be made happy by European culture. The very thought of a blatant European culture is a blatant insult to the majesty of Nature.
> Herder, *Ideas on the Philosophy of the History of Mankind.*[75]

> In the future, it will be a relief to find a place without culture.
> Talking Heads, *Stop Making Sense.*[76]

Most studies of 'influence' with which I am familiar (and their analogues, works which set out to identify 'borrowings') seek to establish a conduit or channel (say, through trade), or a region of contact and contiguity, usually geographical (the Mediterranean as a geocultural entity, Sicily or al-Andalus, or the Frankish kingdom of Outremer, as melting-pot, for example), sometimes a frontier, an arena within which borrowing can take place or through which 'influence' may operate.

The most ready version of such an approach is that of 'cultural contact', and it works best when applied to material culture. One of the best and most persuasive examples with which I am familiar is the exhibition 'Iraq and China: Ceramics, Trade and Innovation', mounted at the Arthur M. Sackler Gallery of The Smithsonian Institution, Washington DC, from 4 December 2004 to 17 July, 2005.[77]

Two phenomena framed the exhibition: the radical transformation, unusually swift and apparently without precedent, in 'the humble character of Near Eastern pottery' produced in Basra during the third/ninth century, and the great 'Majolica' tradition of al-Andalus and Renaissance Europe.[78] Furthermore Chinese experiments with cobalt blue and the emergence in the fourteenth century of Yuan blue-and-white porcelain are viewed from the vantage point of tin glaze and luster ceramic techniques developed in the Islamic world, 'among the greatest contributions made by Islamic artists to the world's history of ceramics'.

The exhibition was able to tie these technological advances in the beginning to ʿAbbāsid trade out of Basra with China and in the fourteenth century to dissemination from Fatimid Egypt to 'Iran, Syria, and across North Africa to the Mediterranean Sea and southern Europe', and ultimately back to China itself. The intricate and breathtaking processes of engagement, experimentation and exchange were beautifully brought out in the displays.

Yet, what happens when we extend our definition of culture beyond the material, to 'cultures' in contact? Let us take as a brief example the work done by George Makdisi on institutions of learning in the Muslim world and the Christian West. His magisterial surveys of scholasticism and humanism are conveniently presented in an envelope article, 'Religion and Culture in Classical Islam and the Christian West'.[79]

My purpose here is not a criticism of Makdisi's bold theories, but simply to consider his use of the term 'culture' in a context of transmission of ideas. What fascinates me is the postulate that a possible borrowing in one society (or set of societies) of a guild structure and attendant educational practices and values (culture?)[80] developed in another society could be understood to operate precisely as the pottery techniques passed back and forth between China, Iraq, and Europe. Both phenomena, after all, 'occurred chiefly through silent penetration' and both preclude the possibility that they were 'the result of a natural and spontaneous development'.[81]

On the basis of this observation, would we, *mutatis mutandis*, be entitled to speculate about the development of a (cognate) aesthetics in those societies for which the potters fired their merchandise?[82] And if this were the case, we would presumably be constrained to adopt a (Geertzian) vision of culture as an ordered symbolic system which itself could be borrowed *at the same time or as part of the same process* as the borrowing of a material technique or artifact. This question arises most pointedly in what we imagine to be happening when Greek scientific and philosophical texts were rendered into Arabic during the Translation Movement.

In brief, according to Makdisi, then:

> Both the Christian university and the Islamic college were scholastic guild institutions, and performed the same essential scholastic functions. The college was the first institution of learning of the Islamic scholastic movement; it was as essential to Islamic scholasticism as the university was to scholasticism in the Christian West ... The college, as a guild school rather than merely a hospice, was an Islamic creation, as the university was a creation of the Christian West. The Christian West preserved and perpetuated the scholastic structure for posterity by adopting the Islamic scholastic guild and the Islamic charitable trust, by incorporating them both, and by fusing the college and the university into one institution, and thus creating the college-university.

In an end-note we also learn that 'what the university does owe to classical Islam is the scholastic structure of higher learning and the license to teach, the doctorate, to which it led'.[83] This doctorate, indeed, was possibly one of the most significant of all cultural calques in modern European history, for it 'was eventually to become one of the factors leading to the Reformation' (10).

When I reviewed this article and the book in which it is contained in 2001, I struggled to understand what Makdisi and the other contributors might mean by 'culture'. As I re-read the work now, I am no better informed and can simply repeat what I said then: 'I suspect that what Makdisi means by "culture" is essentially what Matthew Arnold referred to in *Literature and Dogma* as "the best that has been known and said"'.

There is, though, one sense in which culture might suit Makdisi's analyses perfectly. It is the non-metaphorical meaning still evident in our use of the adjective 'cultivated', and prevalent before the word began its totalitarian career and became invested with overwhelming explanatory power: its 'primary meaning ... in husbandry, the tending of natural growth'.[84] For education is precisely the tending and tilling, in a most real and non-metaphorical sense, of minds and societies. Consider the ambivalence of 'culture' in the following remark (as well as its substantive bedfellows) by John Milton, from his *The Readie and Easie Way to Establish a Free Commonwealth* (1660): 'spread much more Knowledg and Civility, yea, Religion, through all parts of the land, by communicating the natural heat of Government and Culture more distributively to all extreme parts, which now lie num and neglected'.

In general, though, I would argue that the use of a notion such as culture, surely a prime example of what Ian Hacking refers to as an 'elevator word',[85] gains in its descriptive efficacy precisely because of its indeterminacy, through echoing terms such as 'material culture'. In so doing, it facilitates the construction of the genealogy or the identification of the transmitting conduit required by the logic of philology and the hermeneutic of 'influence' in ways which do a disservice to many of the important issues which Makdisi's work raises.

Culture as cultivation obviously plays a significant part in my promotion of cross-pollination, and I would wish to hold on to the contingencies and permutations of invention, of borrowings and lendings and returns (culture as collage and collecting),[86] together with a determination not to shy away from the possibilities of endogenous development, whilst emphasizing the unitary aspects of diversity[87] and the simultaneity of lived narratives of destruction/extinction and creation/transformation.[88]

Cultivation figures in James Clifford's analyses of ethnography and the cultures it purports to describe (an activity of central significance to the so-called *Writing Culture* Group,[89] of whom Clifford was the quasi-official secretary), as in his reading of Aimé Césaire's 'neologistic' cultural politics, for whom 'culture and identity are inventive and mobile. They need not take root in ancestral plots; they live by pollination, by (historical) transplanting', 'as inventive process or creolized "interculture"'.[90]

Consider the following instance of such a transplanting, the presence, in Avicenna's metaphysical thinking on the subject of divine knowledge, of a ninth century Arabic Neoplatonic reading of the demiurgic design argument as expounded in Plato's *Timaeus*.[91] Based on passages contained in the *Theology of Aristotle*, the Arabic version of Plotinus' *Enneads* IV–VI, as edited and presented by Porphyry, and attributed to Aristotle in the most substantial version extant in Arabic,[92] D'Ancona argues for the centrality of an inventive reading, by the circle of al-Kindī, of Plotinus' reading of Plato's *Timaeus*.[93] Manifestly, transplanting and crosspollination are zygotes, if not indeed monozygotic (the gametes being culture and cultivation).

Transculturation, a politicised cognate of transplanting, is a calque of a Spanish term coined by the Cuban sociologist Fernando Ortiz in the 1940s, developed in the 1970s by Angel Rama, an Uruguayan literary critic, and recently popularised by Mary Louise Pratt in her monograph, *Imperial Eyes: Travel Writing and Transculturation*.[94] Pratt explains how it was intended to

> Replace the paired concepts of acculturation and deculturation that described the transference of culture in reductive fashion imagined from within the interests of the metropolis.[95]

Pratt's interests lie exclusively with the imperial and colonial experience, more specifically with the colonised and how they, as marginal or subordinated, 'select and invent from materials transmitted to them by a dominant or metropolitan culture', and to what varying extents colonised peoples can 'control what emanates from the dominant culture'. In the case of the Greek-Arabic Translation Movement in an ʿAbbāsid context, we are presented with a phenomenon in which the metropolis, caliphal Baghdad, controlled and determined, with varying degrees of success, what it absorbed from the Hellenistic heritage. In this context, 'transculturation' would be synonymous with 'appropriation', which I consider presently.

For Pratt, transculturation is a phenomenon of what she calls 'contact zones' – 'social spaces where disparate cultures meet, clash and grapple with each other, often in highly assymetrical relations of domination and subordination' – deriving her notion of 'contact' from linguistics, where it is a descriptor of improvised pidgins which eventually become creolised. In her system, 'contact' aims

> To foreground the interactive, improvisational dimensions of colonial encounters ... A 'contact' perspective emphasizes how subjects are constituted in and by their relations to each other. It treats the relations ... not in terms of separateness or apartheid, but in terms of copresence, interaction, interlocking understandings and practices, often within radically asymmetrical relations of power.[96]

The contact zone[97] is often dominated by linguistic cornucopia, such as Norman Sicily, for example, where shortly after the Norman invasion, Norse, Arabic, French, Spanish, Italian (or other vernacular variants of Romance languages), Greek, Berber, Hebrew and Latin, may all have been in use, though trilingualism (Arabic, Latin and Greek) was probably only to be encountered in the Greek Christian community.[98]

As nexus of copresence and improvised identities, of intercultures, inter-references and interferences,[99] as site of ideational intersections and intertexts,[100] the contact zone[101] provides a fecund model within which to situate, topographically as well as intellectually, the processes of crosspollination in the histories of Classical Islam. It is a supple concept which permits reflections which incorporate, but are not constrained by, geography,[102] upon social or cultural actors (such as Ibn Faḍlān, Usāmah ibn Munqidh, Ibn Jubayr and Ibn Khaldūn),[103] or upon intersecting ideologies, intellectual systems, ideas, and theologies (for example, ninth century Arabic Neoplatonism and the *Kalām* doctrine of divine unicity [*Tawḥīd*], or Epicurean geometry and *Kalām* atomism).[104]

The contact zone, then, is the locus of contiguity. Contiguity permits travel and traversal (*trans-lation*). A special form of travel is 'migration', either as wandering or as displacement. It is thus that I have considered, in 'Al-Sindibād and Polyphemus, Reflections on the Genesis of an Archetype,' the centuries-long Odyssean wanderings of the man-eating giant in Middle Eastern mythical and epic traditions.[105]

Appropriation

> Yet, as the notion of hostile takeover present in a term such as 'appropriation' implies, adaptation can be oppositional, even subversive. There are as many opportunities for divergence as adherence, for assault as well as homage.
> J. Sanders, *Adaptation and Appropriation*.[106]

The obverse of the 'worn coin' of 'influence' is 'appropriation'. The preliminary and defining statement of the 'hard'[107] version of 'appropriation' is A.I. Sabra's 'The Appropriation and Subsequent Naturalization of Greek Science in Medieval Islam: a Preliminary Statement.'[108]

This is a seminal article, which, with majestic clarity, explodes the notion that the Arabic-speaking scientists, philosophers and speculative thinkers of the third/ninth century were passive receptors and preservers, serendipitously fortunate intermediaries in their interactions with the scientific heritage of Late Antiquity. According to Sabra, this attitude is a bicipital interpretation of 'a merely kinematic account of the transmission of scientific knowledge from one culture to another' (223/3). It can take the form of either 'reductionism' ('the achievements of Islamic scientists were merely a reflection, sometimes faded, sometimes bright or more or less altered, of earlier [mostly Greek] examples' [223/4]); or 'precursorism' (which 'reads the future into the past, with a sense of elation' [224/4]).

The situation to which Sabra applies the paradigm of 'appropriation' is this:

> As for cross-cultural transmission, it is clear ... that its presentation in isolation from cultural factors would remain an incomplete description, one which cannot by itself explain large transformations that frequently occur when cultural boundaries are crossed (225/5).

Appropriation, in its demand for explanations which 'reception may not call for' (228/8) and which a 'preoccupation with the question of influence' (227/8) may distort or occlude, enables the presentation of this series of events thus:

> Greek science was not thrust upon Muslim society any more than it was later upon Renaissance Europe. What the Muslims of the eighth and ninth centuries did was to seek out, take hold of and finally make their own a legacy which appeared to them laden with a variety of practical *and* spiritual benefits. And in so doing they succeeded in initiating a new scientific tradition in a new language which was to dominate the intellectual culture of a large part of the world for a long period of time. 'Reception' is, at best, a pale description of that enormously creative act (225–6/6).

This process of appropriation is holistic, for it incorporates not merely scientific and philosophical knowledge, but also a Hellenistic epistemology, i.e. a Hellenised attitude to science and philosophy,[109] what Ragep calls 'the moral economy of science'.[110]

Sabra's thesis, for the Islamic context, is a process of acquisition, assimilation, and naturalisation, leading to 'decline'. Therefore, a contextually rich series of approaches is demanded by Sabra's model of appropriation. In fact, Dimitri Gutas' seminal study of the Greek-Arabic translation movement[111] could have been written in response to the following questions which Sabra poses:

> What, then, were the forces that combined to produce this great cultural movement? What was it that urged the ʿAbbāsid authorities to embark upon this enterprise? Why the emphasis on 'the philosophical sciences', not just useful medicine and astrology and alchemy? What were the relations of this enterprise to other trends – cultural, religious and political – in the Islamic world? ... In short, how do we explain that forceful and, in a sense, unexpected act of appropration? (228/9–10).

Gutas presents 'a study of the major social, political, and ideological factors that occasioned the unprecedented translation movement from Greek into Arabic in Baghdad ... an effort to explain it as a social and historical phenomenon' (xiii). His is not a unilinear explanation of what is 'a very complex social phenomenon', for 'no single circumstance, set of events or personality can be singled out as its cause' (7), though the foundation of Baghdad in 145/762 by Caliph al-Manṣūr (reg. 136–159/754–775) emerges as both creative catalyst and the stage upon which two centuries of dynamic activity were played out (see, e.g., 19, and 189–91). This is because the 'Graeco-Arabic translation movement ... cannot be understood apart from the social, political, and ideological history of the early ʿAbbāsid empire, of which it was an integral element' (189) and it responded to the requirements of a scientific context which sought from it answers to the questions it demanded.[112] In sum, 'the approaches to ninth-century Islamic societies must be as textured as the societies themselves' (160).

One feature of these societies which, however, Gutas neglects to consider is religion, or better: spirituality, which leads him to overlook, for example, the intellectual and spiritual activities of the Arabic-speaking Christians with whom the ninth century Muslims interacted, in polemic, debate and research activities; or leads him to present al-Maʾmūn's *miḥna* (inquisition) in basically a-religious terms.[113]

In what is a very concise monograph, Gutas devotes next to no space to theorizing the phenomenon which he so ably and convincingly roots. In fact, on pages 6–7 he robustly rejects this activity as it tells us 'nothing about the subject under discussion', and 'everything about the background and ideological orientation of the scholar using such theoretical constructs' (6). One approach which is rejected outright, in a footnote on page 187, is 'appropriation':

> I would ... hesitate to call the process of transmission from Greek into Arabic ... an 'appropriation' – a surreptitiously servile term – and prefer to call it what it really was, a creation of early ʿAbbasid society and its incipient Arabic scientific and philosophical tradition'.

Contrast this view of appropriation with the following remark by Julia Sanders:

> Appropriation is frequently involved in a process of reading between the lines, offering analogues or supplements to what is available in a source text, and drawing attention to its gaps and absences.[114]

This is precisely how, in his stimulating article in this volume, Ulrich Rudolph approaches the intriguing role which the Arabicised Presocratics played in Arabic philosophical intellectualism.[115] Such a rejection of 'appropriation' seems to represent a shift in Gutas' thinking away from the receptiveness to it as a notion which he occasionally entertains in other studies.[116]

Now, when he establishes the movement's 'legacy abroad' (175–86), specifically in relation to the 'first "Byzantine humanism" of the ninth century' (175), he argues vigorously for the influence of 'the scientific and translation movement in Baghdad' on a 'ninth-century Byzantine renaissance', on the basis that 'outside influences affect a society only if there are internal and innate factors that make it receptive to such outside influences' (178). And it emerges from this discussion that it is this latter proposition which his work sets out to document. So, despite a hearty rejection of the viability of Gibb's three laws of cultural influences (6), and a sustained critique of essentialised and a-historical reifications of the Graeco-Arabica, with an endorsement of Edward Said's appreciation of the heterogeneities and impurities of imperial cultures, in this instance Gutas continues to operate within the historiographical parameters which Gibb tried to constitutionalise as laws.[117]

Gutas' study is also an exploration, refinement and development of some key concepts in Rosenthal's vision of the Greek-Arabic phenomenon. Rosenthal subscribes to the notions of cultural improvement and of inferior and superior levels of attainment of civilisation typical of his generation of scholars, and outlined above in the discussion of Watt's notion of 'influence':[118]

> The pre-eminence of the achievements of the higher civilization was apparent on every level and inexorably demanded that the new rulers acquire them ... The Arabs were favourably inclined towards the superior culture and used what it had to offer.[119]

The Muslims 'adopted' the classical heritage, a process initiated by geographical and cultural contiguity (1–2 and 12); and in keeping with the kineticism of 'influence', the result of the revivification of 'the heritage of classical antiquity' was a new outlook on life, giving Islam an intellectual direction that, owing to insufficient original preparedness, it would not have taken on its own (12). Yet, for Rosenthal, unlike so many of his contemporaries, this was a 'consciously creative act' out of 'which was born what we call Islamic culture' (12).

One notion developed by Rosenthal to great effect which, as far as I am aware, Gutas has not developed is that the 'practical' and 'theoretical' utilitarianisms subtending the translation movement were necessary but not sufficient conditions for its success. According to Rosenthal, this was due to the centrality of 'the role of knowledge (*ʿilm*) as the driving force in religion and, thereby, in all human life' (5).[120]

I have read Gutas' wonderful monograph on numerous occasions. It is a deeply impressive work for the breadth of its erudition, accuracy of its analysis and the force of its argument. Each time I read it, it is as if I am reading an astonishingly informative, detailed and precise guide to one of the world's great cities. The maps are clear, I can form a good sense of its districts and principal thoroughfares, of its architectural splendours, the ambitions of those who built the city, commissioned its buildings and patronised its architects, but I am left with little idea of what it would be like to live there.[121] That I think that we can never ultimately recover any such realities for even an immediate past does not, I hold, require of us that we avoid the question altogether.

I have decided not to consider theories of 'assimilation' as a category of its own, as they can be accommodated to either influence, migration, diffusion, or appropriation (as in Sabra's 'naturalization', for example). One of the most sustained exercises in understanding the Islamic engagements with late antiquity as assimilation and naturalisation is Joel L. Kraemer, *Humanism in the Renaissance of Islam: the Cultural Revival during the Buyid Age*.[122] So Kraemer speaks of influence, integration, cultural contact and naturalisation, and yet the following statement in the article strikes a discordant note: 'the *falāsifa* avoided arousing the apprehensions of a traditional society, thereby succeeding to preserve and transmit *an alien cultural legacy* within the orbit of Islam' (161/357, emphasis added).[123] Roshdi Rashed, 'Greek into Arabic' (as in note 108), combines appropriation, assimilation and invention, by identifying three laws of assimilation (159), referring to a 'natural path' (162) and introducing a 'dormant library' thesis which is not dissimilar to Aziz al-Azmeh's synchronic 'floating repertoire' of 'institutions, metaphors, iconographies and problems concerning power',[124] an approach very much generated within a 'diffusionist' paradigm.

Diffusion

If 'influence' is one of the scales in which such phenomena are measured, its antonym is 'diffusion' (in its intransitive sense), the paradigm in which 'influence', 'assimilation',[125] 'borrowing,' 'contact' and 'migration' can coalesce. A diffusionist account of these processes of interchange can be predicated upon either agency or passivity, depending on whether the verb is construed as transitive or not.

Any inflection of agency, a characteristic of the diffusionist accounts with which I am familiar, will tend to stress 'influence', or its analogues. An intransitive account is an extremely difficult scholarly accomplishment in that it is by its nature resistant to exposition, and does not too readily present any convenient taxonomic structure. As a result, many diffusionist accounts make the most of the semantic ambiguity inherent in 'diffusion', juxtaposing agency with passivity.

Other accounts capitalise upon the indeterminacy of diffusion, notably through the notion of 'la voie diffuse,' to endow specious or tenuous links with usually unwarranted corroborative force, often at the expense of contextualised readings of the phenomena thus presented. In the end it is often a matter of emphasis which distinguishes diffusionist accounts from those based on cultural contact.

The spread of cultivars and agricultural techniques is the subject of Andrew M. Watson, *Agricultural Innovation in the Early Islamic World: the Diffusion of Crops and Farming Techniques, 700–1100.*[126] Diffusion is a natural paradigm in which to set the spread of such practices and products. After all, such 'connections ... are often complex, unobservable and uncertain' (2).

Watson understands 'diffuse' in its transitive sense, and is positive in his admiration for 'the overall achievement of early Muslims in diffusing a wide range of useful plants over a large area' (2).[127] His vision of diffusion involves the 'initial transfer' of 'novelties', and their 'secondary diffusion' as these 'rarities' are changed into 'commonplaces' (2), in a series of collaborations between Muslims and neighbours, peasants and landowners whether conquered or forced into migration (6). According to Watson,

> Attitudes, social structure, institutions, infrastructure, scientific progress and economic development all played a part in the making of this medium of diffusion (2).

Probably the most resolutely diffusionist study of the pre-modern Muslim past with which I am familiar is the monograph by Aziz al-Azmeh, *Muslim Kingship: Power and the Sacred in Muslim, Christian and Pagan Polities.*[128] In a modern reworking of a pre-modern concept favoured by Muslim geographers, the girdle of the earth (*minṭaqat al-arḍ*),[129] al-Azmeh identifies a topographical contact zone for his study of kingship, 'the Late Antique Mediterranean-West Asian (or Near Eastern) civilisation belt which had a particular coherence in terms of spatial and temporal continuity' (x). While 'Muslim polities were specific inflections of Late Antique discursive and visual forms and modes of enunciating royal and imperial power' (x), al-Azmeh's interest in them is not one informed by 'comparatism' (xiii–xiv) or driven by a search for the taxonomy of genealogy, but rather because they suggest 'interesting levels of generality, and possibly universality, of certain tropes for the representation of imperial power and its relations to divinity' (x), or 'common repertoires of floating symbols and tropes' (xii; 10).

The ubiquity of these repertoires allows him to discern filiations, identify cultural signatures and point to elements of 'concordance and generality', whilst avoiding the restrictions of comparison (xiii), and promoting specificity over individuality (xv). When these repertoires are enunciated, their enunciations emerge as protean variations on a number of awesomely perdurable 'conceptual and visual elements' (5), so that Alexander the Great

> Appears not so much a Greek conquering the Persian empire as the last Achaemenid, succeeding legally to the throne and adding Greece to Iran (8).

The varying inflections of power to which Alexander's life can be made to give voice are representative, for al-Azmeh, of how

> Modalities and modules of culture are diffused, by superimposition, adaptation and renaming (9).

Although al-Azmeh's 'symbolic and discursive currency' is at times reminiscent of Otto Pretzl's 'worn coins' of Hellenism, and his comparisons can at times seem superficial, the appeal of his approach is its openness and readiness to disregard boundaries and compartmentalisation.

A particular aspect of 'diffusion' is the reconstruction of influence and borrowing by means of the 'voie diffuse'.[130] In 1977 C. Versteegh essayed just such an approach for the early history of Arabic grammar in his *Greek Elements in Arabic Linguistic Thinking*.[131]

His account is based on the concept of the *calque* and seeks to establish 'the process of Greek influence on Arabic grammar' (ix). This influence is of two types, via 'a direct and an indirect way of transmission', with the direct ('contact between Arabic grammarians and Hellenistic culture') preceding the indirect ('Arabic translations of the works of Aristotle and his commentators') (1). The locus of direct transmission is 'the living practice of grammar which existed all over the Near East' (7), in the cultural centres of Hellenism, particularly its monasteries.[132] Though erudite and sophisticated, Versteegh's case remains intriguing and promising, but sadly tenuous at best and tendentious at worst.

Ultimately the deficiencies of many diffusionist accounts, as Versteegh himself notes (xi), are their dependence on the hermeneutic circle, in which a presumption of contact predisposes the construal of any evidence of contact as proof of contact, and the circumstantial character of the probabilism of their evidence. Thus he sums up 'the main points of our evidence for the thesis of a direct contact between the first representatives of a new method of describing language and the last representatives of the old' as:

> The Arabian conquest of the culturally superior civilization that was Hellenism, the geographical location of Baṣra and Kūfa near Hellenistic centres of education, the fact that there were many bilingual people, and the presence of some striking similarities between Greek and Arabic grammar (13).

Versteegh himself recognises the probabilism of his case (x–xi) and in subsequent publications he has retracted much of his thesis.[133]

The weaknesses of this method have been dissected with supreme precision by Dimitri Gutas, 'Pre-Plotinian Philosophy in Arabic (other than Platonism and Aristotelianism): A Review of the Sources'.[134] Gutas identifies two lines of textual transmission, direct and indirect.[135] Contrary to the distinction made by Versteegh, both are text-based, and do not carry any temporal connotations. In the case of direct transmission, the translation will be effected directly upon an original (itself at one of the many variant stages of textual degeneration from an author's autograph); in the case of the latter the transmission can be primary, secondary and derivative, depending upon the incorporation of the translated material in the work whence it is derived by its translator.

There is no room in this system for any non-textual transmission. In the first place, the repertoire of material is determined by whatever was 'available, either as an idea or a cited text, or as a discrete written work, in the philosophy of late antiquity' (4941) (effectively the Alexandrian tradition) and by whatever was available, on the same terms, 'to Syriac-speaking Christians' (4943). In the second place, Gutas suspects that 'the expression remains ... a catchall for explaining anything which is felt ... to be allochthonous in the nascent Islamic civilization' (4945). As such it is all too vulnerable to the impressionism and prejudices of a cultural reductionism that discerns in Islamic civilisations of the period a lack of 'originality' (4948–9), denies outright any of the possibilities of polygenesis and neuters the specificities of 'appropriation' (4947–8).

Here is the crux of the problem of the study of this and cognate phenomena; how do we chart the process of textual transmission reliably and at the same time recognise that these texts are but the faintest glimmerings of some two centuries of the most sustained, imaginative and passionate intellection imaginable, and that we must give voice to what are almost mute vestiges of the dreams, aspirations, enthusiasms, and spiritual exercises of all those members of the societies who brought these works into existence?

With Gutas' magisterial work on the study of the Graeco-Arabica we have, in a sense, come full circle to the symbiosis which obtains between 'influence' and philology. Even though Gutas' brand of scholarship is philology at its most subtle, nuanced, imaginative and persuasive, philology is a *Weltanschauung* which, like narrative history, requires of its practitioners that they perform a daring high-wire act if they are not to tumble into the trap of determinism and meliorism.

Crosspollination

Nature, and especially horticulture, has regularly served as a metatextual language for reflecting upon and describing the dynamics of creation and the creative process. Among the most famous, and perhaps scientifically the most sonorous and significant, is Charles Darwin's coinage, 'natural selection,' in his *The Origin of Species by Natural Selection, or the Preservation of Favoured Races in the Struggle for Life* (1859).

In this imaginative act of anthropomorphism, Nature, personified, acts like a husbandman, selecting which stock to graft, which to breed and which to mingle. This bold metaphor proved so epistemically successful that it soon transmogrified into scientific substance, in that process which Harold Bloom has referred to as 'facticity'.[136]

Less famous, perhaps, than 'natural selection', is Darwin's use of the 'tree' to capture 'evolutionary organization':

> Darwin needed a metaphor in which degree gives way to change and potential, and in which form changes through time. He did not simply adopt the image of a tree as a similitude or as a polemical counter to other organisations. He *came upon* it as he cast his argument in the form of diagram. This 'materialisation' of the image is important in understanding its force for him. It was substantial, a condensation of real events, rather than a metaphor. Here we come back to the problems he faced in adapting language available to him (a language so steeped in natural theological suggestions) to a world of material history in which things must find their explanations, their analogies, and their metaphors, within the material order.[137]

This tree is of uncommon resemblance to the *stemma codicum* of Classical philology, and philology and Darwinian evolution are perfect instances of what today we would describe as an 'interdisciplinarity'.[138] In Islamic Studies, it has a modern avatar in (western, non-Muslim) *ḥadīth* scholarship.[139]

The philological dimension points to the conceptual convergences between Darwin and Freud. As Ludmilla Jordanova succinctly expresses it, 'this raises the question of metaphor – was it that society and nature were *like* each other, that is linked through a metaphorical language, or was it rather that they were different aspects of the *same* thing for which only one language was need, social phenomena being merely more complex organic ones?'[140]

Beer suggests that the inspiration for Darwin's recourse to horticulture in his conceptualisation of 'natural selection' may be found in his passion for Shakespeare. She refers specifically to *King Richard III*, Act III, Scene 7, ll. 124–6, Buckingham's attempt to bring Richard, Duke of Gloucester round to his views on the right of succession through the judicious use of the metaphor subtending the notion of 'royal stock':

> This noble isle doth want her proper limbs;
> Her face defaced with scars of infamy,
> Her royal stock graft with ignoble plants.

'Grafting' was a favourite of Shakespeare's. In *The Sonnets* (Sonnet 15.10–14), it is the crowning move in a witty and passionate appeal to the beloved to accede to the poet's importunacies: the poet as Creator promises immortality to the object of his desire through procreation and through poetic immortalisation:

> Where wasteful Time debateth with Decay
> To change your day of youth to sullied night,
> And all in war with Time for love of you,
> As he takes from you, I ingraft you anew.[141]

In *The Winter's Tale*, Act IV, Scene IV, ll. 89–96, it becomes a bold speculation by King Polixenes on the respective merits of the creative capacities of man and nature, concluding that man's abilities to improve nature are in fact nature's as man is, after all, a product of nature:

Yet nature is made better by no mean
But nature makes that mean: so over that art,
Which you say adds to nature, is an art
That nature makes. You see, sweet maid, we marry
A gentler scion to the wildest stock,
And make conceive a bark of baser kind
By bud of nobler race. This is an art
Which does mend nature – change it rather – but
The art itself is nature.[142]

Lastly, and in the spirit of Shakespeare, a very palimpsestuous writer and a genius at 'ingrafting' new plots onto old stories, it is hardly surprising that 'grafting' suggests itself to Gerald Prince as a convenient way of conceptualising the myriad varieties of transtextuality, of the textual interrelations and interactions of hypertext and hypotext as catalogued by Gérard Genette, *Palimpsests: Literature in the Second Degree.*[143] Of course, perhaps the most widely used instance of the environmental turn in late twentieth century cultural theorizing is Homi Bhabha's notion of 'hybridity', a hubristically though enticingly miscegenating paradox of sterility and creativity, itself profoundly though remotely indebted to Darwin's notion of 'hybridism,' what Milne, after Wilson Harris, calls 'a certain void or misgiving which attends every assimilation of contraries'.[144]

In 1999 Lenn E. Goodman published an intriguing monograph entitled *Jewish and Islamic Philosophy: Crosspollinations in the Classic Age*[145] in which he wished to explore the long symbiosis between Jewish and Islamic philosophical ideas, nourished by kindred scriptures and stimulated by a shared intellectual heritage that runs back not only to a cousinage in scriptural texts and ritual practices but also to a shared patrimony in the great philosophical texts and discussions of classical and Hellenistic antiquity (x).

The work contains seven chapters, many of which are devoted to exploratory comparisons of thinkers from radically different epochs, traditions and societies who can be contemplated for their engagement with several notions fundamental to the human condition within the Abrahamic and Classical tradition: thus, the philosophical consequences of the pietism of Baḥyā b. Pāqūdā and Immanuel Kant for their understandings of human choice within a divinely organised and sustained universe (Chapter 3); the hedonistic impulse in the psychology, physiology and ethics of Epicurus and al-Rāzī[146] (Chapter 2); the role of the empiricism of Thucydides and Ibn Khaldūn in their presentation of human agency and the dynamic of historical change (Chapter 7).[147]

In Chapter One ('Crosspollinations'), Goodman outlines the three crosspollinatory concepts which resonate, for him, throughout the traditions which he means to explore: prophetical revelation ('Hearing God's Voice in Words');[148] the Delphic maxim 'know thyself' ('"He who knows himself knows his Lord"') and the Abrahamic valorisation of the Platonic ideal of *homoiōsis theōi*, of godlikeness, as classically formulated in the *Theaetetus*;[149] and thirdly, "the visiting upon human beings of the consequences of their actions, either communally or individually" ('God's Act in History') (24).

These ideas, of course, are in and of themselves philosophically cognate, for they frequently interact and can be mutually dependent. History, for example, can be understood as a human response to the revelation of God's words, what Mircea Eliade described as 'history regarded as theophany.'[150] Or, ethics can be conceived not solely as an abstract codification of the imperatives of divine revelation (with jurisprudence being left with the task of divining the divine intent in cases not covered explicitly in the revelation), but as lived practice, the telos of which is the 'imitation of the divine in so far as is in one's power'. The normative role of the life and practice of the Prophet Muhammad within the daily life of a Muslim, for example, or the dynamics of the 'imitatio Christi' impulse come to mind.[151] Failure to live up to such standards, whether as an individual or as a group of individuals, is an importance constituent of possible responses to catastrophe or success – thus, defeat at the hands of the Meccans for the nascent Islamic community at the Battle of Uḥud in the year 3/625 came to be viewed as a sign of Allah's disapproval of the sincerity and credal comportment of the Believers.

So why choose 'crosspollinations' in particular? In the first instance, I relish its metaphorical appeal, its promise of insight but not at the expense of a specific commitment to consequence (though of course this is not to suggest that it is uniquely without its own epistemic commitments). I also hope that it will include 'more than the maker ... at the time knew', though some may judge that 'crosspollinations' is more parsimonious than my aspirations for it.[152] And then, I prefer the term 'crosspollinations' over its cognate 'crossfertilisations', because I was deterred by the emphasis in the latter on the activity of the fertiliser, of some guiding agency, and attracted by the room which the former seemed to allow for randomness and contingency, like the process of pollination itself, while continuing to suggest agency in that a botanist may pollinate one plant with the pollen of another.

Reasoning analogously, I want to suggest that the interface between one society and another, between one set of practices and another, between one people and another, between one intellectual tradition and another, need not always be accounted for in intentionalist terms (e.g., purpose, agency or utility): al-Jāḥiẓ, in the chirurgical love song translated above on page 148–49, is clearly revelling in the intellectual permutations which the amatory and 'physickal', the Arabic and the Greek, traditions proffered. We eradicate much, I have argued, if we are too restrictive, too linear, too causal in our attitudes and interpretations for thus we often become deaf to the wider resonances of the phenomenon.

By preferring the term 'Islamic' over 'Muslim', my purpose is two-fold: 'Muslim' would have placed the emphasis on agency, on those doing the crosspollination, which would have been completely appropriate if my design were to highlight agency; 'Islamic' highlights the roles of Islam(s) as an ever-shifting series of inclusive and collaborative traditions which have proved, since their inception, remarkably open, fertile and fecund in both their receptiveness to ideas, practices and customs irrespective of their provenance, and in their donation of such phenomena. This use of 'Islamic' also allows us to remember that not all the creators of Islamic artefacts were Muslims.[153]

The critic may, upon considering the somewhat grandiose claims I make for 'cross-pollination' and my severe critique of a limited application of 'influence', echo the assessment pronounced in Disraeli's *Tancred* (1848) of Robert Chambers' ambitious treatise, *Vestiges of the Natural History of Creation* (1844), satirically referred to as *The Revelations of Chaos*, namely that, 'it explains everything, and is written in a very agreeable style'.[154] And the critic may well be correct in her assessment.

For my own part, I should like to mimic how the American composer John Adams describes the tangos of Ástor Piazzolla, that they

> Speak to us with the authority of genuine feeling. Their roots lie in Buenos Aires's jumble of colliding cultures: Spanish, German, Jewish, Native American, Italian. It is a true multi-culture yet not smoothed out and neutered by self-consciousness. It is a discovery like the best of all discoveries: unexpected, multi-faceted, volatile, generous.[155]

Crosspollination is not a theory but an approach, one which provides a vision of Islam considerably at variance to some versions of Islam currently prevalent. It is a vision of a crosspollinatory and crosspollinated Islam, standing between Antiquity and Medieval Europe, an open, dynamic and vibrant system which thrived on, and pulsated with, diversity.

Notes

1 Al-Jāḥiẓ, *Rasāʾil*, ed. ʿA. al-S. Hārūn (Beirut, 1991), i, 383, 6-10; there is a partial translation in *The Life and Works of al-Jāḥiẓ: Translations of Selected Texts*, trans. Ch. Pellat (translated from the French by D.M. Hawke) (London, 1969), 114–16; see also J. Sadan, 'Kings and Craftsmen – A Pattern of Contrasts. On the History of a Medieval Humoristic Form', *SI*, 56 (1982), 5–49, especially 10–21. On al-Jāḥiẓ, see J.E. Montgomery, 'Al-Jahiz (circa 776–868 or 869)', in M. Cooperson and S.M. Toorawa (eds.), *Arabic Literary Culture, 500-925* (Detroit, 2005), 231–42.

2 See the excellent article by Dimitri Gutas and Hans-Hinrich Biesterfeldt, 'The Malady of Love', *JAOS*, (1984), 21 55 (repr. in D. Gutas, *Greek Philosophers in the Arabic Tradition* [Aldershot, 2000]).

3 See Ibn Abī Uṣaybiʿa, *ʿUyūn al-anbāʾ fī ṭabaqāt al-aṭibbāʾ*, ed. A. Müller (Konigsberg, 1882), i, 206, 16–20. On these physicians as patrons of Syriac translations, see G. Bergsträsser, 'Ḥunain ibn Isḥāq über die syrischen und arabischen Galen-Übersetzungen', *Abhandlungen für die Kunde des Morgenlandes*, 17/2 (1925), index; G. Endress, 'Wissenschaftliche Literatur', in H. Gätje (ed.), *Grundriß der arabischen Philologie. Band II: Literaturwissenschaft* (Wiesbaden, 1989), 424. For their scientific connection with al-Jāḥiẓ's sometime patron Muḥammad ibn ʿAbd al-Malik known as Ibn al-Zayyāt, see J.E. Montgomery, 'Al-Ǧāḥiẓ and Hellenizing Philosophy', in C. D'Ancona (ed.), *The Libraries of the Neoplatonists* (Leiden, 2007, 443–56). On Christian physicians, see H. Putman, *L'église et l'islam sous Timothée I (780–823): étude sur l'église nestorienne au temps des premiers ʿAbbāsides: Avec nouvelle édition et traduction du Dialogue entre Timothée et al-Mahdi* (Beirut, 1975), 95–104; M. Dols, 'Syriac into Arabic: the Transmission of Greek Medicine', *ARAM*, 1 (1989), 45–52; E. Key Fowden, 'The Lamp and the Wine Flask: Early Muslim Interest in Christian Monasticism', in this volume (on monasteries as loci of medical knowledge) 1–28; and generally Peter E. Pormann, 'Islamic Medicine Crosspollinated: A Multilingual and Multiconfessional Maze', in this volume 76–93.

4 Al-Jāḥiẓ, *Kitāb al-bukhalāʾ*, ed. M.Ṭ. al-Ḥājirī (Cairo, 1982), 102, 2–16. Compare how, in sixteenth century Aleppo, Leonard Rauwolf (1535–1596) successfully practised medicine among both itinerant European merchants and the Ottoman elite, despite the stricture that 'infidel physicians were not supposed to heal Christians and vice-versa': see S. Brentjes, 'The Interests of the Republic of Letters in the Middle East, 1550-1700', *Science in Context*, 12 (1999), 435–68 (at 445).

5 As Walter Benjamin declares, 'translation passes through *continua* of transformation, not abstract ideas of identity and similarity' (quoted from H. Bhabha, *The Location of Culture* [London, 1994], 212). For Bhabha, 'the performativity of translation' is 'the staging of cultural difference ... in

the act of translation the content or subject matter is made disjunct, overwhelmed and alienated by the form of signification'. The referentiality and communicability of the original is destroyed by 'the "foreign" element that reveals the interstitial' (227): thus, following Paul de Man, the original is sent into permanent exile (228).

6 For some thoughts on the merits and demerits of Classical stemmata scholarship as applied to Arabic texts from the first three Islamic centuries, see J.E. Montgomery, 'Editor's Introduction', in G. Schoeler, *The Oral and the Written in Early Islam*, trans. U. Vagelpohl and ed. J.E. Montgomery (London, 2006), 1–27.

7 H.A.R. Gibb, 'The Influence of Islamic Culture on Medieval Europe', *Bulletin of the John Rylands Library*, 38 (1955), 82–98. The place of this article within Gibb's vision of Islam is discussed briefly by Edward Said, *Orientalism* (London, 1991, first publ. 1978), 280, who notes that, if we follow Gibb's vision, 'the West took from Islam only those nonscientific elements that it had originally derived from the West', thus rendering Muslim scientific and intellectual traditions 'a mere conduit for elements that are not *sui generis* Islamic'.

8 An instructive example which raises many of the issues pertinent to debates surrounding Islamic origins is the disagreement over the late-Umayyad early-ʿAbbāsid origins of the *kalām*, Arabic-Islamic speculative theology predicated upon dialectic as epistemic and ethical methodology. Note that it is often unclear whether what is at stake in such discussions is the origins of theology as an intellectual exercise or the specific dialectical method itself. According to Josef van Ess, 'The Beginnings of Islamic Theology', in J.E. Murdoch and E.D. Sylla (eds.), *The Cultural Context of Medieval Learning* (Dordrecht, 1975), 87–111, the *kalām* 'started as an inner-Islamic discussion' (111) borrowed from eastern Christian theological practice and forged in the conceptual and logical universe of Stoicism: see also J. van Ess, 'Political Ideas in Early Islamic Religious Thought', *BJMES*, 28 (2001), 151–64; while for Michael Cook, 'The Origins of *Kalām*', *BSOAS*, 43 (1980), 32–43, its formal roots lie in Syrian (and Syriac) Christianity. Rosalind Gwynne, *Logic, Rhetoric and Legal Reasoning in the Qurʾān: God's Arguments* (London, 2004), has established the extent and significance of formal structures of rhetorical argumentation in the Qurʾān, arguing for their 'internalisation' by Qurʾānic scholars: see also J.D. McAuliffe, '"Debate with them the Better Way": The Construction of a Qurʾānic Commonplace', in A. Neuwirth, B. Embaló, S. Günther, and M. Jarrar (eds.), *Myths, Historical Archetypes and Symbolic Figures in Arabic Literature: Towards a New Hermeneutic Approach*, Proceedings of the International Symposium in Beirut, June 25th-June 30th, Beirut 1996 (Wiesbaden, 1999), 163–88; whereas one of Richard M. Frank's most enduring and seminal contributions to the understanding of the *kalām* is to insist that we discern therein a series of attempts to establish an intellectually and spiritually credible theology in response to, and consonant with, the divine revelation: for his most explicit and sustained statement of this position, see *Beings and their Attributes: the Teaching of the Basrian School of the Muʿtazila in the Classical Period* (Albany, 1978), especially 8–11; and S.H. Griffith, 'ʿAmmār al-Baṣrī's *Kitāb al-Burhān*: Christian *Kalām* in the First ʿAbbāsid Century', *Le Muséon*, 96 (1983), 145–81 (repr. in Griffith, *The Beginnings of Christian Theology in Arabic: Muslim-Christian Encounters in the Early Islamic Period* [Aldershot, 2002]). In another study I propose to explore the centrality to the Muslim theological and scientific project of appreciation for the argument from design (*tadbīr*), so central a feature of Qurʾānic anthropology, and its role in the Christian cosmos. The porousness of these religious and intellectual traditions, Byzantine, Syriac Christian and Umayyad Islamic, has been discussed by Averil Cameron and Larry Conrad, *The Byzantine and Early Islamic Near East* (Princeton, 1992), 18–19, 19–20; see also A. Cameron, 'New Themes and Styles in Greek Literature: Seventh-Eighth Centuries', in ibid., 81–105; S. Griffith, 'The Prophet Muḥammad: his Scripture and his Message according to the Christian Apologies in Arabic and Syriac from the First ʿAbbasid Century' in U. Rubin (ed.), *The Life of Muḥammad* (Aldershot, 1998), 345–92; L.I. Conrad, 'Theophanes and the Arabic Historical Tradition: Some Indications of Intercultural Transmission', *Byzantinische Forschung*, 15 (1990), 1–44; A. Cheddadi,

Les Arabes et l'appropriation de l'histoire: Émergence et premiers développements de l'historiographie musulmane jusqu'au IIe/VIIIe siècle (Paris, 2004); D. Pingree, 'The Greek Influence on Early Islamic Mathematical Astronomy', *JAOS*, 93 (1973), 32–43; S. Brock, 'Syriac Culture in the Seventh Century', *ARAM*, 1 (1989), 268–80 (on the manifold ambivalences to Hellenism evident in Syriac culture). The contribution on monks and monasticism by Elizabeth Key Fowden in this volume is a marvellous reflection on the dynamic.

9 Edinburgh 1972. These lectures were translated into French by G. Humbert as 'L'influence de l'Islam sur l'Europe médiévale', *REI*, 40 (1972), 7–41 and 297–327; *REI*, 41 (1973), 127–56.

10 Reading 1994.

11 Cambridge 1987. I shall also consider Wael Hallaq's various ripostes to Crone's theories: 'Use and Abuse of Evidence: The Question of Roman and Provincial Influences on Early Islamic Law', *JAOS*, 110 (1989), 79–91 (repr. in his *Law and Legal Theory in Classical and Medieval Islam* [Aldershot, 1994], Article IX, 1–36: I shall refer to this version of the work); 'The Quest for Origins or Doctrine? Islamic Legal Studies as Colonialist Discourse', *UCLA Journal of Islamic and Near Eastern Law*, 2 (2002–3), 1–31; 'Introduction' in W. Hallaq (ed.), *The Formation of Islamic Law* (Aldershot, 2004), xiii–xxxiii; *The Origins and Evolution of Islamic Law* (Cambridge, 2005).

12 Cambridge 1998. This book is not, of course, a product of the discipline of Islamic studies proper but rather medieval and early modern Eurasian history.

13 Said, *Orientalism* (as in n. 7), 303 notes how in *The Cambridge History of Islam* (1970), 'Islam is a geographical designation applied chronologically and selectively as it suits the experts'.

14 By 'Europe' 'Western Christendom' may be intended. See 82, where the sub-title, 'the significance for Europe of the meeting with Islam' finds expression as 'the significance for Western Christendom of its meeting with Islam' in the first paragraph. In general, Watt (*Influence* [as in n. 9], 95, note 6) owes his idea of Europe to Christopher Dawson, *The Making of Europe: an Introduction to the History of European Unity* (London, 1953), which contains two chapters entitled 'the Rise of Islam' and 'the Expansion of Moslem Culture' (107–17 and 118–34) and which sets out to chart 'the rise of the medieval unity'. For Dawson by Europe is meant 'above all ... the formation of that society of peoples ... more than any geographical unit' (225). Watt seems also to owe some of his understanding of contact with 'the higher civilisation of the Islamic and the Byzantine world' as a catalyst of European development to Dawson: see *Making*, 228–9, where he singles out 'aristocratic courtly culture', 'vernacular literature' and 'the assimilation of the Graeco-Arabic scientific tradition and the rise of a new intellectual culture in the West'. This idea, however, is central to another work which influenced Watt in his thinking: G.E. von Grunebaum, *Islam: Essays in the Nature and Growth of a Cultural Tradition* (London, 1955), who argues that 'the backwardness of the Arabian Peninsula in relation to the cultural level of the neighboring countries made the early development of Islam largely a process of adjustment to the traditions of the older Near Eastern civilizations', in a series of 'accidental contacts', over which 'composite culture of medieval (and modern) Islam' 'an Arabic veneer' was spread, since 'not a single borrowing proved effective, let alone lasting, unless Arabized in terminology and cast into a familiar thought-pattern' (13–14, and passim). Consider also the following judgement: 'But for Greek logic and dialectics, Greek metaphysics and psychology, and the Hellenized theology of eastern Christendom, the Muslim could never have stated and upheld his faith in terms of doctrine' (119)! This book also grew out of a seminar on 'Islam and the West' in 1953: see xiii. In his *Modern Islam: the Search for Cultural Identity* (Berkeley, 1962), 40, von Grunebaum characterises Islam by its lack of vital interest 'in the structured study of other cultures, either as an end in itself or as a means toward clearer understanding of its own character and history'. Compare the withering criticisms of von Gruenbaum by Said, *Orientalism* (as in n. 7), 296–9 and 304–5; and A. Laroui, *The Crisis of the Arab Intellectuals: Traditionalism or Historicism?*, trans. D. Cammell (Berkeley, 1976), 44–80 ('The Arabs and Cultural Anthropolgy: Notes on the Method of Gustave von Grunebaum'). A modern solution to the fuzziness of such

geographies is to recognise the fuzziness but proceed, fuzziness notwithstanding. A convenient example is O. Remie Constable, *Trade and Traders in Muslim Spain: the Commercial Realignment of the Iberian Peninsula, 900-1500* (Cambridge, 1996), xxiii.

15 In an earlier work, *Islam and the Integration of Society* (London, 1961), Watt applies to what he terms 'the creation of Islamic mores' Gibb's formulation of three laws of cultural influence (assimilation preceded by the cultivation on the part of the recipient society of an interest in the area to be assimilated; elements thus assimilated can nourish only in so far as they are consonant with these preceding activities; rejection of all aspects of the assimilated elements not consonant with its *Weltanschauung*: see Gibb, 'Influence of Islamic Culture' (as in n. 7), especially 85–7; Watt, *Islam and Integration*, 184-209). In the case of Watt's lecture series (published as 'Influence'), Gibb's system is not applicable because the Muslim invasion of Spain in 711 invalidates Gibb's fundamental rule of assimilation in accordance with an attraction generated by 'an already existing activity' in those elements which are to be classed as 'genuinely assimilated' (184). Hence, the invasion is traumatic, and is strangely reminiscent of how, according to von Grunebaum, 'during the great age of Islam, Greek philosophy and Greek science had battered the walls of orthodoxy' (*Islam: Essays* [as in previous note], 28); i.e., this is acculturation as assault, which the editors of the series in which von Grunebaum's *Islam* appeared (Robert Redfield and Milton Singer) refer to as 'domestication'. Presumably 'foreign elements' are thought of as wild animals (x).

16 See 'Influence' (as in n. 7), 10: 'there is something almost incredible and, because of that, fascinating in the story of how the ancient cultures of the Middle East became transformed into Islamic culture ... Many of the bearers of the previous cultures became Muslims ... In this region of the world mankind had had experience of millennia of urban civilization, going back to Sumer and Akkad and Pharaonic Egypt, and all that had been retained as valuable from these millennia now came to be expressed in Arabic'. So to whom is medieval Europe indebted: the Muslims, or the ancient Mesopotamians and Egyptians? And note that 'cultural levels' are incremental through incorporation and assimilation (of 'alien wisdom and learning' [11]), simultaneously with the natural development of 'a central core for the new culture ... out of the main interests of the Arab Muslims' (11), that core being the Muslim response to the Qurʾān. This approach is further explored by Watt in his *Islam and the Integration of Society* (as in n. 15), Chapters 6, 7, and 8 (see 278 for example) and is pursued in the spirit of von Grunebaum, *Islam: Essays* (as in n. 15).

17 Von Grunebaum explains that his 'profile of Muslim civilization' is 'intended to deepen the self-understanding of Western civilization' for it 'is both close enough to the Western view of the world to be intellectually and emotionally understandable and sufficiently far removed from it to deepen, by contrast, the self-interpretation of the West' (*Islam: Essays* [as in n. 15], 1). Such hybris is possible because of the 'failure on the part of the Muslim world ... to achieve, and largely even to attempt, an analysis of the fundamentals of its civilization' for the benefit of both the Muslim himself and the West (185). See also Laroui, *Crisis* (as in n. 14), 62, 68–9. According to Gibb, writing in 1931, 'oriental literature may once again perform its historic function, and assist us to liberate ourselves from the narrow and oppressive conceptions which would limit all that is significant in literature, thought, and history to our own small segment of the globe': 'Literature' in Th. Arnold and A. Guillaume (eds.), *The Legacy of Islam* (Oxford, 1931), 209. See the discussion of this dimension to Gibb's thought in Said, *Orientalism* (as in n. 7), 256–7, who refers to an inter-war 'dialectic of cultural self-consciousness'. That the 'Orient existed for the West' is an observation fundamental to Said's *Orientalism*: see 204, 271, 279–80 (and passim).

18 It must be noted that Watt's identification of Europe's inferiority to Islam is, despite its limitations, a bold and controversial reversal (pronounced before the Collège de France!) of what Said, following Jean-Jacques Waardenburg, perceives as the 'Orientalist consensus on Islam: latent inferiority' (*Orientalism* [as in n. 7], 209).

19 Watt here builds upon the work done by his doctoral student Norman Daniel, *Islam and the West: the Making of an Image* (Oxford, 1993, first publ. 1960). Daniel's work is especially instructive a), for its ability to bring out contemporary Muslim rejuvenation of Christian hostilities to Islam and their redirection against Christianity and the West; and b) for how it foregrounds the persistence, in modern (non-Muslim) approaches, of medieval concepts and perceptions of Islam; see, for example, his brief critique in *Islam and the West*, 325-6, of Patricia Crone and Michael Cook, *Hagarism: the Making of the Islamic World* (Cambridge, 1977). Note also some other contributions by Daniel: *The Cultural Barrier: Problems in the Exchange of Ideas* (Edinburgh, 1975); *The Arabs and Medieval Europe* (London, 1986). I have not been able to consult his article, 'The Arab World and Europe – Principles and Procedures of Intercultural Relations', *Die Dritte Welt*, 5 (1977). Watt may have found support for the underlying notion of the 'mirror-image' in the influential work by Jean-Jacques Waardenburg, *L'Islam dans le miroir de l'Orient* (Paris, 1962). See the discussion in Said, *Orientalism* (as in n. 7), 209–10.

20 Alfred Adler (1870–1937) developed a psychoanalytical sociobiology out of a postulated link between organ inferiority and overcompensation, since 'if the defective organ happened to be an erotogenic zone, overcompensation might either lead to neurosis or perversion' and thus, given the former, 'there could be no "organ inferiority" without some degree of "sexual inferiority"': see F.J. Sulloway, *Freud: Biologist of the Mind. Beyond the Psychoanalytic Legend* (Cambridge, Mass., 1992), 428–31. Freud referred to Adler's theories as 'paranoivelties': J. Farrell, 'Paranoia Methodized', in F. Crews (ed.), *Unauthorized Freud: Doubters Confront a Legend* (New York, 1998), 239–41.

21 S. Freud, *Introductory Lectures on Psychoanalysis*, trans. J. Strachey (*The Pelican Freud Library*, 1; Harmondsworth, 1976), 455. Freud rejects inferiority as the agent of neurosis in favour of the libido and separation from the mother.

22 'The dominating tendency of mental life, and perhaps of nervous life in general, is the effort to reduce, to keep constant or to remove internal tension due to stimuli (the "Nirvana principle", to borrow a term from Barbara Low...) – a tendency which finds expression in the pleasure principle; and our recognition of that fact is one of our strongest reasons for believing in the existence of death instincts': S. Freud, *Beyond the Pleasure Principle, Group Psychology and Other Works*, trans. J. Strachey (*Standard Edition*, 18; London, 2001), 55–6. This state of Nirvana was accessible to the psychologically healthy through the realisation of regular, satisfying sexual orgasm: see A. Storr, *Freud: a Very Short Introduction* (Oxford, 1989), 25.

23 See Sulloway, *Freud* (as in n. 20), 404–9 (Fechner) and 274–5 (Lamarck).

24 See Freud, *Introductory Lectures* (as in n. 21), 380, editor's note, and 314–15: 'the term "traumatic" has no other sense than an economic one. We apply it to an experience which within a short period of time presents the mind with an increase of stimulus too powerful to be dealt with or worked off in the normal way, and this must result in permanent disturbances in the manner in which the energy operates'. Strachey coined the term 'cathexis' as a 'scientific' way of rendering Freud's *Besetzung*: see N. Luckhurst, 'Translator's Preface', in S. Freud and J. Breuer, *Studies in Hysteria*, trans. N. Luckhurst (London, 2004), xxxvii–xxxix and the works referred to in her note 4.

25 Freud, *Beyond the Pleasure Principle* (as in n. 22), 38.

26 See Sulloway, *Freud* (as in n. 20), 407–8, who sees in Freud's thinking a 'particularly creative transformation of ideas' in which he used Lamarckian biogenetics 'as a key conceptual bridge between two otherwise distinct forms of the Fechnerian principle of stability', the 'absolute' and the 'animate, repetitive and ahistorical notion of approximate stability'.

27 See P. Hadot, *Philosophy as a Way of Life*, trans. Michael Chase (Oxford, 1995), 93–101.

28 Or there may be no actual traumatic occurrence, but, according to the mature version of the theory, instinctual (sexual) impulses manifest as phantasies. Thus 'psychical reality was of more importance than material reality': S. Freud, *An Autobiographical Study, Inhibitions, Symptoms and Anxiety, Lay Analysis and Other Works (1925-1926)* (*Standard Edition*, 20; London, 2001), 34.

29 Freud, *Introductory Lectures* (as in n. 21), 313.

30 Europe is not alone in this inability, however. In his earlier book, Watt had written that contemporary Islam is characterised by a failure to accept its (Judaeo-Christian) past, which 'is as unhealthy for a society as it is for an individual', and is in sore need of avowing its indebtedness to the 'cultural heritage' of the 'conquered peoples' which 'the new Islamic culture ... continued' (*Islam and Integration* [as in n. 15], 275 and 278). Thus 'the Islamic community' claims 'that much of the traditional wisdom of the Middle East came from Muhammad (as was proved by the existence of Traditions!)', which is a 'failure to admit their dependence on their predecessors': 'a community where there has to be systematic pretence of this kind would seem to be far from healthy. For centuries, Islam has managed "to get away with it", but the exposure of the Islamic world to modern Western scholarship has revealed the true state of matters to many thinking Muslims, while at the same time it has placed Muslims in general (because of their natural defensive reaction) at a disadvantage in assimilating some aspects of the learning of the West' (279).

31 Freud, *Introductory Lectures* (as in n. 21), 287–93 (quotations taken from 291). According to Luckhurst, 'Translator's Introduction', (as in n. 24), xl, 'Freud's language mirrors the bodily language of the hysteric: he uses a physical vocabulary to describe the psychical, just as the hysteric's symptoms are a translation of psychical distress into the physical.' See further J. Lacan, 'The Mirror Stage as Formative of the *I* Function as Revealed in Psychoanalytic Experience', in *Écrits: a Selection*, trans. B. Fink (New York, 2002), 3–9.

32 Freud, *Introductory Lectures* (as in n. 21), 320 and 321. For the case of Anna O., see Freud and Breuer, *Studies in Hysteria* (as in n. 24), 25–50; M. Borch-Jacobsen, 'Anna O.: the First Tall Tale', in Crews, *Unauthorized Freud* (as in n. 20), 10–21; J. Forrester, *The Seductions of Psychoanalysis: Freud, Lacan, Derrida* (Cambridge, 1990), 15–29 and 318–23; on Freud's Breuer period, see Sulloway, *Freud* (as in n. 20), 22–100.

33 Freud and Breuer, *Studies in Hysteria* (as in n. 24), 143, 'liked to compare it to the technique of excavating a buried city'. See also 'Introduction' by R. Bowlby, xviii–xx and Forrester, *Seductions* (as in previous note), 4. Despite Harold Bloom's assertion that Freudian synecdoche (as, for example, the representation of health by neurosis) has been misprised as facticity ('Criticism, Canon-Formation, and Prophecy: The Sorrows of Facticity', in J. Hollander [ed.], *Poetics of Influence* [New York, 1988], 406–7), Freudian psychoanalysis is resolutely philological in character, not only in terms of the similarities between its reconstruction of the past and the technique of reconstruction of stemmata in textual criticism (for example, like textual criticism, 'the libido passes through such a long course of development ... one which has many breaks in it': Freud, *Introductory Lectures* [as in n. 21], 371), but also in its reliance upon linguistic usage and erroneous or free linguistic usage as a determinant of unavowed intention or meaning. This is most evident in Freud's theory of the *Fehlleistung*, the slip of the tongue or parapraxis: S. Freud, *The Psychopathology of Everyday Life*, trans. A. Tyson (*The Penguin Freud Library*, 5; London, 1991). For a discussion of the influence of the Classicist Jacob Bernays, Freud's uncle by marriage, on Freud's theory of catharsis, see J.E. Montgomery, 'Convention as Cognition: On the Cultivation of Emotion' in G.J. van Gelder and M. Hammond (eds.), Takhyīl: *The Imaginary in Classical Arabic Poetics. Volume 2: Studies* (Oxford, in press); on the theatricality of psychoanalysis and the role which Sophocles' *Oedipus Rex* played in determining much of its paradigms, see Bowlby, 'Introduction', in Freud and Breuer, *Studies in Hysteria* (as in n. 24), vii–xiv. Another apposite facet of Freud's reasoning was his prodigious capacity for generalisation, which he shares with much philologically informed historiography, and for anthropomorphizing 'wholesale designations ... used as proper nouns', which he shares with Said's Orientalists (*Orientalism* [as in n. 7], 277).

34 'A study of the beginnings of human religion and morality ... mankind as a whole may have acquired its sense of guilt, the ultimate source of religion and morality, at the beginning of its

history, in connection with the Oedipus complex' (Freud, *Introductory Lectures* [as in n. 21], 375). Perhaps a better analogy to Watt's ambition is the fascinating passage at the end of a lecture on 'The Fixation to Traumas – the Unconscious', where Freud places psychoanalysis on a par with the abandonment of the geocentric cosmos and Darwin's theories of human evolution as the three most serious blows to the 'naïve self-love of men' and 'human megalomania' (Freud, *Introductory Lectures*, 326). Talal Asad profitably compares the 'business of identifying unconscious meanings in the task of "cultural translation"' with psychoanalysis, and remarks on the dynamic of authorship/authorization implicit in 'the power to create meanings for a subject through the notion of the "implicit" or the "unconscious", *to authorize them*": T. Asad, 'The Concept of Cultural Translation in British Social Anthropology', in J. Clifford and G.E. Marcus (eds.), *Writing Culture: the Poetics and Politics of Ethnography* (Berkeley, 1986), 161 and 162.

35 This and the previous quotation are taken from Freud, *Introductory Lectures* (as in n. 21), 335 and 323 respectively.

36 A further example of the combination in Watt's thinking of ecumenism and psychoanalytical theory (this time the ideas of C.G. Jung) is his book, *Islam and the Integration of Society* (as in n. 15), which contains a chapter entitled 'The Integration of the Psyche' (252–83), and a regular theme of which is that 'certain ideas or images or symbols ... release the energies of the psyche' (284–5). See the explication of neurosis and world-religions on 252–3. In this case Islam functions as the device whereby the reader can reflect on 'the place of religion in Western society' 'with relative detachment', and secure in the knowledge that this 'lesser emotional involvement' will 'reduce the distortion' caused by an 'initial bias' to religion in general (*Integration*, 1–2). Are we to infer, then, that Watt's earlier Jungian psychoanalysis of Islam was substituted a decade later by his Freudian psychoanalysis of Europe?

37 For Makdisi's series of erudite studies of 'influence' which suggest that Western institutions of higher learning are the product of the importation into medieval France and Italy of the Islamic scholastic system, see *The Rise of the Colleges: Institutions of Learning in Islam and the West* (Edinburgh, 1981). Makdisi's intent is ultimately chauvinistic and it is possible to entertain polygenesis as opposed to causality and borrowing or to point to divergent traditions of professionalisation in both traditions. A paradigm, such as 'influence', which is predicated upon a narrative dynamics of cause and effect, is perpetually liable to counter-narratives. It is interesting to note that a central activity of Said's *Orientalism* is the tracing of 'influence ... among the guild of professional Orientalists' (274): see his discussion of the legacy of Massignon and Gibb's 'formation' under the aegis of Duncan Black McDonald (274–7). Many of Said's analytical methods are intriguingly analogous to those deployed by the Orientalists he describes – not least is the emergence of his 'Orientalist' as an antitype of the Orientalist's 'Arab'.

38 As far as I can determine, Watt's book is not referred to in the volume. See further the reviews by L. Harvey, *JIS*, 6 (1995), 283–6 and M. Shatzmiller, *IJMES*, 29 (1997), 117–19.

39 Though note their comment on viii: 'the impact of the Arabs and Islam on medieval Europe'. It is a measure of the book's success that the contributors forced a more liberal and extensive interpretation on the term 'Arab' than the editors may have intended.

40 Hugo of Santalla may have developed his interest in the Arabo-Islamic technique of 'sand-divination' (*ʿilm al-ramal*) out of a response to a quotation, preserved in a work of Isidore of Seville, in which Varro refers to *geomantia*, in addition to *hydromantia*, *aeromantia* and *pyromantia*: see Burnett, 'Islamic Divinatory Technique' in Watt (ed.), *The Arab Influence*, 109. And the interest of these Arabic geomantic texts is that they did not originate in the central Islamic lands but 'appear to have originated in Spain' (100). See also his 'Divination from Sheep's Shoulder-Blades: A Reflection on Andalusian Society', in D. Hook and B. Taylor (eds.), *Cultures in Contact in Medieval Spain: Historical and Literary Essays Presented to L. Harvey* (London, 1990), 29–45.

41 For a further discussion of the notion of 'frontier', see below note 97. I am not fully convinced that by the Arabic term *thaghr*, the English 'frontier' is meant; 'march' is perhaps more

appropriate. For a philological attempt to determine topographical exactness, and so political reality, for the tenth and eleventh centuries out of terms such as *thaghr* and *kūra* (an administrative district) in Andalusī Arabic texts, see J. Bosch Vilá, 'Considerations with Respect to "*Al-Thaghr* in al-Andalus" and the Political-Administrative Division of Muslim Spain', in M. Marín (ed.), *The Formation of al-Andalus. Part 1: History and Society* (Aldershot, 1998), 377–87.

42 See also the remarks of Wulstan, 'Boys' (in Agius and Hitchcock [ed.], *The Arab Influence*), that 'the children of a mixed household would often follow the religion of the parent of the same sex ... when a daughter of such a household addresses her mother in a *kharja*, is the word *mama* Romance or Arabic?' (164–5; see further 155–6). It seems fatuous even to attempt an answer. D. Wasserstein, 'The Language Situation in al-Andalus', in M. Fierro and J. Samsó (eds.), *The Formation of al-Andalus. Part 2: Language, Religion, Culture and the Sciences* (Aldershot, 1998), 3–17 provides a useful survey of the problems and issues involved. Compare the account of the Guyanese wedding of 'an East Indian Muslim woman and an East Indian man whose parents reared him as a Christian, although they themselves had a Hindu background', provided by L. Drummond, 'The Cultural Continuum: A Theory of Intersystems', *Man*, NS 15 (1980), 360–63.

43 Despite Harvey's insistence in his review on the existence of 'a cultural divide' (284).

44 Hill wishes to demonstrate 'the influence of Arab engineering on the development of European machine technology' by 'examining the antecedents of a single machine', i.e. the mechanical clock, the elements of which, with the exception of the mechanical escapement, 'were present in Arabic horology' before its invention towards the end of the seventh/thirteenth century' (35). It is this last, but vital piece, 'without a doubt the invention of an anonymous European clockmaker', which seems to divert his presentation from the demonstration of 'influence' to the permutations of 'diffusion' and grafting. On 'diffusion', see 169–71.

45 M.R. Menocal, *The Arabic Role in Medieval Literary History* (Philadelphia, 1987), 115–35; H. Bloom, *The Anxiety of Influence: a Theory of Poetry* (Oxford, 1997). In her study of Muslim interest in Christian monasticism in this volume, Elizabeth Key Fowden presents monastic culture as 'spiritual provocation or ... aesthetic source' (18).

46 See further P. O'Brien, 'Islamic Civilisation's Role in the Waning of the European Middle Ages', *The Medieval History Journal*, 2 (1999), 387–404, which pursues the implications of what he identifies as 'Islamic superiority', 390–96.

47 *Culturgeschichte des Orients unter den Chalifen* (Vienna, 1875), 532–47.

48 He is not the only scholar to have sought to emphasise the centrality of Judaic influence on the development of many 'characteristic' features of Islam, from Josef Horowitz to John Wansbrough. A sample: J. Horovitz, 'The Antiquity and Origin of the *Isnād*', and 'Further on the Origin of the *Isnād*', in H. Motzki (ed.), *Ḥadīth: Origins and Development* (Aldershot, 2004), 151–8 and 159–61; see also the discussion by G. Schoeler, 'Oral Torah and *Ḥadīt*: Transmission, Prohibition of Writing, Redaction', in *Oral and Written* (as in n. 6), 111–41, 208–14; H.J. Liebesny, 'Comparative Legal History: Its Role in the Analysis of Islamic and Modern Near Eastern Legal Institutions', *The American Journal of Comparative Law*, 20 (1972), 38–52 ('reception of foreign institutions in early Islamic law was non-systematic and the intent to take over a foreign legal institution was not officially stated' [38]; for all the force of this assertion, his analysis is remarkably circumspect); J. Wansbrough, *The Sectarian Milieu* (Oxford, 1978); J.R. Wegner, 'Islamic and Talmudic Jurisprudence: the Four Roots of Islamic Law and their Talmudic Counterparts', *The American Journal of Legal History*, 26 (1982), 25–71 ('We may never know for sure if Shāfiʿī sat, literally or metaphorically, at the feet of talmudic sages – just as we may never know for sure if the Caliph ʿUmar "had a Jewish lawyer at his elbow"' [71]; despite the circumspection of her conclusion, the burden of her case is precisely that they did do so); Crone, 'Jāhilī and Jewish Law: the *Qasāma*', *JSAI*, 4 (1984), 153–201; M.A. Cook, 'The Opponents of the Writing of Tradition', *Arabica*, 45 (1997), 437–530.

49 In addition to *Hagarism* (as in n. 19), which she wrote with Michael Cook, see also *Slaves on Horses: the Evolution of the Islamic Polity* (Cambridge, 1980).

50 See Hallaq's remarks on the two aspects of *walāʾ* Crone discusses: 'Use and Abuse of Evidence' (as in n. 11), 7–9.

51 Her demolition of the seminal works of Joseph Schacht on the origins of Islamic jurisprudence (7–12) is a tour-de-force: 'his perspective was that of the purebred Arabist to whom the pre-Islamic Near East is *terra incognita*' (7); 'the idea that *Roman* law was transmitted by *Greek* rhetoric in the *Persian* province of Iraq is so patently implausible that it could only have been proposed by a scholar to whom the non-Islamic world was unknown territory about which anything could be said and nothing checked' (10).

52 The notion of 'peregrine institutions' is one which, to my knowledge, Crone unfortunately does not enlarge upon or explore, nor does she explain how they fit in with 'influence', which is unilateral and hegemonic. It is also not quite clear to me how identifying borrowings as 'residues' (e.g., 16) fits in with 'influence'.

53 Hallaq, 'Use and Abuse of Evidence' (as in n. 11), 3–4, notes, 'Crone attempts no investigation of what the sources of provincial law may have been, nor does she explore who the people applying this law were. But it seems that in Crone's mind these people are associated with the lofty Hellenic culture, and not with their uncivilised southern neighbours in the Peninsula'. Thus, according to this train of thought, her notion of 'provincial law' reveals the same degree of essentialisation as Watt's 'Europe' or 'medieval Islam'.

54 She attributes this observation on the relevance of Islamic law to the nature of Late Antique legal practice to Carl Becker, though in the passage she refers to on page 115, note 66, as far as I can make out he makes no mention of law or any other specific but refers vaguely to 'späten Hellenismus'.

55 Typically, borrowing will also be part of a vision of culture as primordial and discrete: see R. Brightman, 'Forget Culture: Replacement, Transcendence, Relexification', *Cultural Anthropology*, 10 (1995), 518–21 and 524.

56 Cambridge, 1986.

57 On the basis of the arguments presented, I struggle to discern how this amounts to an '*a priori* case for a Roman and/or provincial component in Umayyad law' (16).

58 Hardly, according to the epigones of Goldziher, the most reliable of sources! See her discussion on 30–31.

59 That the situation is hardly as simple as Crone would have it, and that the Umayyads were inventive (and discerning) patrons of the art they consumed, are a couple of the conclusions to be made from reading several excellent works on Ḥijāzī architecture (*pace* her note 160 on 121) and Quṣayr ʿAmra: J. Johns, 'The "House of the Prophet" and the Concept of the Mosque', in J. Johns (ed.), *Bayt al-Maqdis: Jerusalem and Early Islam* (Oxford, 1999), 59–112; G. Fowden, *Quṣayr ʿAmra: Art and the Umayyad Elite in Late Antique Syria* (Berkeley, 2004). The main thrust of his contribution to this volume, 'Greek Myth and Arabic Poetry at Quṣayr ʿAmra', 29–45, is that we must try to understand what these processes of interpretation may have been.

60 The notion that pre-Islamic Arabia was an intellectual and cultural vacuum, common to much thinking on the period, is explored in J.E. Montgomery, 'The Empty Ḥijāz' in J.E. Montgomery (ed.), *Arabic Theology, Arabic Philosophy. From the Many to the One: Essays in Celebration of Richard M. Frank* (Leuven, 2006), 32–97. Hallaq, 'Use and Abuse of Evidence' (as in n. 11), is constrained to reconstruct this aspect of Crone's thinking from her other works: 4–5.

61 Gibb, 'Influence' (as in n. 7), 85: 'cultural influences ... are always preceded by an already existing activity in the related fields'.

62 Any approach to the issue of pre-Islamic Arabia and its Near Eastern environs would have to account for the significance of Arabia as a peripheral zone, an area in which the Near Eastern *koinē* may, for example, have been stretched, adapted and explored in a bewildering variety of permutations. I owe this brilliant observation to Dr A. Marsham, previously of Pembroke College, Cambridge.

63 'Use and Abuse of Evidence' (as in n. 11), 6: 'The Arabs of Syria and the Syrian desert preserved their Semitic rites, language, and above all their traditional laws, old tribal structures and ancestral customs'. See also 27–8: 'if the institution of slavery in the pre-Islamic Near East was characteristically Semitic, as von Kremer rightly asserted, then one must be reluctant, when similarities urge the notion of cultural influences, to claim borrowing from non-Semitic sources'. He has pursued this line of argument in his other works *Origin and Evolution* and his 'Introduction' to *The Formation of Islamic Law*, where, on page xxxi, he notes how in its creation of Roman law the imperial state 'appropriated' the 'Semitic cultural forms prevalent in the Fertile Crescent'.

64 *Origin and Evolution* (as in previous note), 3–4.

65 The philological turn is especially apparent in a representative quotation from Dimitri Obolensky, who speaks of 'the local "recensions" which Byzantine civilisation underwent in medieval Russia' (8). See also the discussion of Alexander Yanov's Marxist development of this as 'local corruption' on pages 10–11.

66 See *Muscovy* (as in n. 12), 12–18, for Ostrowski's solution to this stalemate. For a discussion of this tendency in the study of Islamic origins, see Ch.F. Robinson, 'Reconstructing Early Islam: Truth and Consequences', in H. Berg (ed.), *Method and Theory in the Study of Islamic Origins* (Leiden, 2003), 101–34, and Montgomery, 'The Empty Ḥijāz' (as in n. 60). Ostrowski's plea (*Muscovy*, 26–7) that 'future historians of Muscovy' must be trained 'not only in Slavic and western European languages and history ... but also in Byzantine, Central Asian, and Chinese languages and cultures' (26) is strikingly reminiscent of Crone's exposition of what she sees as deficiencies of mid- to late-twentieth century Islamic studies.

67 *The Third Heart: Some Intellectual Ideological Currents and Cross Currents in Russia 1800-1830* (The Hague, 1970), 14–15 (according to *Muscovy* [as in n. 12], 249–50).

68 In Chapter 2, Ostrowski meets all three criteria to demonstrate how Muscovy borrowed 'administrative procedures from the Qipchaq Khanate' (*Muscovy* [as in n. 12], 63). See further *Muscovy*, 131–2.

69 Bloom, *Anxiety* (as in n. 45), 26–7.

70 *Anxiety* (as in n. 45), 30.

71 *Anxiety* (as in n. 45), xxiv.

72 See also John Hollander, 'Introduction' in Bloom, *Poetics of Influence* (as in n. 33), xi–xlvi.

73 However, Bloom wishes to retain for himself the critic's prerogative to judge, to identify a poet as Poet, and to compose a coherent literary-historical narrative by investing 'source-study ... the history of ideas ... the patterning of images' with their customary values, however misprised his work may reveal them to have been.

74 As an example of such a wary application of 'influence', I should refer to Schoeler's explorations of the resemblances between late antique Alexandrian teaching methods and the transmission of learning in early Islam (see *Oral and Written* [as in n. 6], 42–3: he refers to 'structural similarities ... not direct dependences', 48), and his identification of the presence of *ḥadīth* methodologies in Graeco-Arabic *falsafa* (60). It is 'influence' as recreation which informs the excellent contributions to this volume by Anna Akasoy, Peter E. Pormann and John Marenbon ('The Influence of the Arabic Tradition of Falconry and Hunting on Western Europe', 46–64, 'Islamic Medicine Crosspollinated: A Multilingual and Multiconfessional Maze', 79–93, and 'Latin Averroism',135–47 respectively). Through the erudition which they bring to bear on their chosen materials and the control of their sources, they are able to generate a convincing fusion of 'influence' and 'crosspollination'. The traditions of medicine and falconry which they study so effectively intimate possible answers to a disingenuous query posed by Igor Stravinsky, 'The Author Asks for a Moratorium on Value Judgements', in connection with his opera *The Rake's Progress*: 'Can a composer re-use the past and at the same time move in a forward direction?'

75 This quote is taken from R. Williams, *Keywords: a Vocabulary of Culture and Society* (London, 1983), 89.

76 1983.

77 Another marvellous example is the article by David Nicolle included in this collection, 'Byzantine, Western European, Islamic and Central Asian Influence in the Fields of Arms and Armour from the Seventh to the Fourteenth Century AD,' 94–118.

78 See the exhibition report at www.asia.si.edu/exhibitions/past and the pamphlet which accompanied it. On the historical background to this trade, see Ph.D. Curtin, *Cross-Cultural Trade in World History* (Cambridge, 1984), 90–108.

79 As noted above, Makdisi's theories are best considered in terms of the paradigm of 'influence'. The article discussed is to be found in R.G. Hovannisian and G. Sabagh (eds.), *Religion and Culture in Medieval Islam* (Cambridge, 1999), 3–23 (reviewed by D. Reisman, *Islamic Studies*, 39 [2000], 488–91; J.E. Montgomery, *JIS*, 12 [2001], 182–4; J. Meri, *JAOS*, 121 [2001], 718–19; L. Conrad, *Der Islam*, 80 [2003], 202–5). See further G. Makdisi, *The Rise of the Colleges* (as in n. 37); *The Rise of Humanism in Classical Islam and the Christian West with Special Reference to Scholasticism* (Edinburgh, 1990) (reviewed by R. Serjeant, *JIS*, 4 [1993], 242–4); and the articles conveniently collected in his *Religion, Law and Learning* (Aldershot, 1981). Further studies in which other scholars apply 'borrowing' as 'influence' are to be found in *Héritages et emprunts culturels au Moyen Âge: Islam, Byzance et Occident*, Colloque Château de Morigny, Étampes (Essonne) novembre 1986, a special number of *Revue des Études Islamiques* 55-57 (1987-89), 235–327.

80 Makdisi uses the term 'scholasticism' to denote these educational practices and values: see *Religion and Culture* (as in previous note), 4–8. In my opinion, he asks it to do too much.

81 *Religion and Culture* (as in n. 79), 7: 'the presence of institutions in a culture devoid of antecedents for them suggests their reception from another culture with requisite antecedents'. Makdisi's approach, then, holds a resolutely Boasian view of culture, be it in the shape of Robert Lowie's radical diffusionism or simply as an accidental, acquired and mutable congeries of borrowings. See generally A. Kuper, *Culture: the Anthropologists' Account* (Cambridge, Mass., 1999) (e.g. 61–3 for Lowie's 'radical diffusionism'; 98–9 for Geertz's vision of culture as 'an ordered system of meanings and symbols'). A fine example of a history of trade predicated upon a Boasian notion of culture as a series of borrowings is Curtin's *Cross-Cultural Trade* (as in n. 78).

82 Thus Garth Fowden, in his article in this volume and in his wonderful *Quṣayr ʿAmra* (as in note 59), considers what Greek artistic traditions and representations may have been interpreted to mean for the late Umayyad elite and for the Caliph al-Walīd ibn Yazīd. See also note 59 above.

83 *Religion and Culture* (as in n. 79), 9 and 21 respectively.

84 Williams, *Keywords* (as in n. 75), 87.

85 I. Hacking, *The Social Construction of What?* (Cambridge, Mass., 1997), 21–3 and passim. See also Kuper's excellent book *Culture* (as in n. 81); Brightman, 'Forget Culture' (as in n. 55), 509–46; T. Eagleton, After Theory (London, 2003), 55–73 (apologies for culture).

86 See J. Clifford, *The Predicament of Culture: Twentieth-Century Ethnography, Literature and Art* (Cambridge, Mass., 1988), 145–8 (collage) and 230–36 (collecting); R. Wagner, *The Invention of Culture* (Chicago, 1990) (culture as invention).

87 C. Lévi-Strauss: 'Diversity is less a function of the isolation of groups than of the relationships which unite them' (quoted from Kuper, *Culture* [as in n. 81], 243).

88 Clifford, *Predicament* (as in n. 86), 16–17.

89 The term 'group' may seem something of a misnomer for these scholars by no means present a unified vision, yet, like the cultures they studied and the contested meanings of culture which they promoted, they were united by the enormous theoretical and methodological differences that obtained between them as they converged in the contact zone of ethnography.

90 For succinct critiques of Clifford's approach, see P. Rabinow, 'Representations are Social Facts:

Modernity and Post-Modernity in Anthropology', in *Writing Culture* (as in n. 34), 234–61 (especially 242–7); Kuper, *Culture* (as in n. 81), 210–15.

91 See C. D'Ancona, 'The *Timaeus'* Model for Creation and Providence: an Example of Continuity and Adaptation in Early Arabic Philosophical Literature', in G.J. Reydams-Schils (ed.), *Plato's* Timaeus *as Cultural Icon* (Notre-Dame, Ind., 2003), 206–37. On the Arabic translation(s) of the *Timaeus* and of Galen's epitome of the *Timaeus*, see 211–12 and 228–9, notes 18 to 23, and the references provided by D'Ancona. The reception history of (complete) Platonic dialogues in Arabic translations is still obscure. From the discovery of David Reisman, it now seems almost irrefragable that Muslim scholars had access to a doxography, of considerable scholarly accomplishment, of at least excerpts of accurate translations, rather than abridgements or paraphrases, of sections of key Platonic works: F. Rosenthal, 'On the Knowledge of Plato's Philosophy in the Islamic World, with Addenda', *IC*, 15 (1940), 387–422 and 16 (1941), 396–8 (reprinted in his *Greek Philosophy in the Arab World: A Collection of Essays* [Aldershot, 1990]); F. Klein-Franke, 'Zur Überlieferung der platonischen Schriften im Islam', *IOS*, 3 (1973), 120–39; D. Gutas, 'Plato's *Symposion* in the Arabic Tradition', *Oriens*, 31 (1988), 36–60; idem, 'Galen's *Synopsis* of Plato's *Laws* and Fārābī's *Talḫīṣ*', in G. Endress and R. Kruk (eds.), *The Ancient Tradition in Christian and Islamic Hellenism* (Leiden, 1997), 101–19 (both reprinted in his *Greek Philosophers* [as in n. 2]); D.C. Reisman, 'Plato's *Republic* in Arabic: A Newly Discovered Passage', *ArScPh*, 14 (2004), 1–56.

92 For the intellectual and cultural move involved in the attribution of this work to Aristotle, see C. D'Ancona, 'Al-Kindī on the Subject-Matter of the First Philosophy. Direct and Indirect Sources of *al-Falsafa al-Ūlā*, Chapter One', *Miscellanea Mediaevalia*, 26 (1998), 841–55; 'Pseudo-*Theology of Aristotle*, Chapter 1: Structure and Composition', *Oriens*, 36 (2001), 78–112; and P. Adamson, *The Arabic Plotinus: a Philosophical Study of the* Theology of Aristotle (London, 2002). Franz Rosenthal's uncovering of the 'dicta of the Greek Sage' (passages of the Arabic Plotinus preserved in sources distinct from the *Theology*) made it possible for us to appreciate the intellectual and cultural specificity of this identification: F. Rosenthal, 'Aš-Šayḫ al-Yūnānī and the Arabic Plotinus Source', *Orientalia*, 21 (1952), 461–92; 22 (1953), 370–400; 23 (1954), 42–65 (reprinted in his *Greek Philosophy in the Arab World*). On the problems involved in understanding the transmission of the Arabic Plotinus, see M. Aouad, 'La *Théologie d'Aristote* et autres textes du *Plotinus Arabus*', in R. Goulet (ed.), *Dictionnaire des philosophes antiques*, i (Paris, 1989), 541–90.

93 The complexity of the chain of philosophical readings and re-readings does not end here. In an end-note, number 80, 237, she notes the remark of Marc Geoffroy 'that it was Themistius' paraphrase of Book *Lambda* that provided the patterns to interpret Aristotle's claim of the self-knowledge of the First Principle along the lines of the Neoplatonic doctrine of the mode of knowledge of the divine *nous*'. Note that D'Ancona herself refers to the 'transformations the Neoplatonist doctrine underwent in its Arabic adaptation' as 'a cross-pollination' (211).

94 London 1992. 'Transculturation' must not be understood as synonymous with the 'cross-cultural', for such studies are predicated upon cultural difference and the *crossing* of boundaries and frontiers. Thus, Constable (*Trade and Traders* [as in n. 14], xxiii) explains 'cross cultural' as 'used for trade across a multiple frontier of language, religion, cultural heritage, and ethnicity', declaring in a footnote the influence of Curtin's study (*Cross-cultural Trade* [as in n. 78]).

95 *Imperial Eyes* (as in previous note), 228.

96 *Imperial Eyes* (as in n. 94), 6 and 7.

97 I prefer 'contact zone' to 'frontier' which is predicated upon the idea of 'division' and which I find to be too slippery. So, for example, according to R.M. Eaton, *The Rise of Islam and the Bengal Frontier 1204–1760* (Berkeley, 1996), Bengal's historical experience is best viewed in terms of three frontiers: political, agrarian and cultural, each of which 'moved by its own dynamics' (xxiv). Such methodological intricacy occludes rather than reveals Bengal's character as a 'contact zone'. See further R.I. Burns, 'The Significance of the Frontier in the Middle Ages', in

R. Bartlett and A. MacKay (eds.), *Medieval Frontier Societies* (Oxford, 1989), 307–30. Eaton's conceptualising is fully in the tradition of Frederick Jackson Tuner whose West, according to Burns, 'became a more slippery concept, not only a place, or at times a condition, but especially a "process"' (308). Even when Turner's epigones recognise 'frontiers as contact-zones ... of intercultural contact' (Burns, 310) and are 'fascinated by the interaction of cultures, both by osmotic interchange and in the wake of violent conquest' (Burns, 315), the idea of the 'frontier' remains a methodological hindrance, despite Nora Berend's valiant efforts to salvage it: 'Medievalists and the Notion of Frontier', *The Medieval History Journal*, 2 (1999), 55–72.

98 J. Johns, 'The Language of Islamic Art', *Oxford Today* (Trinity Issue) (2005), 13–15; J. Johns, *Arabic Administration in Norman Sicily: the Royal* Dīwān (Cambridge, 2002), 4–5; A. Metcalfe, *Muslims and Christians in 'Norman' Sicily: Arabic-Speakers and the End of Islam* (Richmond, 2002). See also Menocal, *Arabic Role* (as in n. 45), 118–21, and C. Robinson, *In Praise of Song: the Making of Courtly Culture in al-Andalus and Provence 1065–1135 AD* (Leiden, 2002), 18–22 and the anecdote of the Frank garbed as a Muslim discussed on 355.

99 'Interculture' is an adaptation of the intersystem: Drummond, 'The Cultural Continuum' (as in n. 42), 352–74. According to M.M.J. Fischer, 'Ethnicity and the Post-Modern Arts of Memory', in *Writing Culture* (as in n. 34), 194–233 (at 201), 'it is the inter-references, the interweaving of cultural threads from different arenas, that give ethnicity its phoenix-like capacities for reinvigoration and reinspiration'.

100 See B. and D. Tedlock, 'Text and Textile: Language and Technology in the Arts of the Quiche Maya', *Journal of Anthropological Research*, 41 (1985), 121–46.

101 I am quite aware that by identifying such a thing as *the* contact zone, I am prone to the tendencies to homogenizing and essentialising which a number of critics have identified in applications of the concept of hybridity by theorists such as Homi Bhabha, tendencies which these concepts are intended to challenge: see A. Loomba, *Colonialism/Postcolonialism* (London, 1998), 173–83, esp. 179; B. Parry, 'Signs of Our Times: Discussion of Homi Bhabha's *The Location of Culture*', *Third Text*, 28–29 (1994), 5–24; J. Nederveen Pieterse, 'Hybridity, So What? The Anti-Hybridity Backlash and the Riddles of Recognition', in S. Lash and M. Featherstone (eds.), *Recognition and Difference* (London, 2002), 219–45. Writings such as the *Kitāb* of Ibn Faḍlān, for example, are, in and of themselves, a distinct textual contact zone located within a geographical contact zone, itself unique and distinct for its specific nuances and differentiated in terms of the ideological and institutional structures which inform it: see also Loomba, *Colonialism*, 180.

102 The methodological underpinnings of this approach are radically different from an approach which considers a specific chorography as a site of influences or borrowings. Thus Constable, *Trade and Traders* (as in n. 14), according to whom the entire Iberian peninsula was a frontier, 'a gateway between Christian and Muslim worlds' (1), differs from Cynthia Robinson who explores the dynamics of an early thirteenth century illustrated Arabic Andalusī manuscript in terms of the courtly culture of the Mediterranean: *Medieval Andalusian Courtly Culture in the Mediterranean:* Ḥadīth Bayāḍ wa Riyāḍ (London, 2007). This is a continuation of the project initiated in her monograph, *In Praise of Song*. Through the notion of a Mediterranean courtly culture, she seeks to offer an alternative to the Manichean dualism typical of the scholarly study of al-Andalus, between those who traditionally have valorised the originality of a 'Spanish Islam', thus rendering Spain's Muslim past acceptable to Spanish nationalism, (reinvigorated, in its present, comparativist transmogrification, as *convivencia*) and those who consider Islam merely as a thin veneer upon a perdurable tradition of Hispanic Christianity: see M. Marín, 'Introduction', *The Formation of al-Andalus. Part 1* (as in n. 41), xv-xxiv. For M. Arkoun, *Rethinking Islam: Common Questions, Uncommon Answers*, trans. and ed. R.D. Lee (Boulder, 1994), 123, the Mediterranean is a hermeneutic in which 'the dialectic of influence and residues, comparativism, creative tension between language, history and thought' and 'instructive tension between the rational and the imaginary' can profitably be understood, with a view to putting into perspective

'local Mediterranean cultures and universalist tendencies.' Arkoun tartly remarks that by 'Mediterranean' 'Europe' is usually meant (121): for him, 'the sociocultural bases of unity in the Mediterranean world' are: 'a severe code of honor that prescribes vendetta and maintains women in an unfavorable position, primitive tools, archaic agricultural techniques, an inflexible patriarchy, cities shaped by climate and the sea, a style of life and communication in which warm and spontaneous sociability takes precedence' (129). The post-classical, pre-Islamic Near East ('Late Antiquity') is another such contact zone, in which much useful research has been conducted. Such studies (of which Crone's study of Roman, provincial and Islamic law, discussed above 157–60, is one example) are characterised by their attempts properly to account for a shared cultural, social, religious and intellectual language (a *koinē*): see Montgomery, *The Empty Ḥijāz* (as in n. 60). The contact zones which emerge from a reading of the present collection of articles are the monastery (Key Fowden), Quṣayr Amra (Fowden), the Islamic hospital (Pormann), the court of Frederick II (Akasoy) and Venice (Howard).

103 I have singled out these Arabic writers (from the fourth/tenth, sixth/twelfth and eighth/fourteenth centuries) because in works by each of them, identities are improvised through jarring and disconcerting encounters, in the contact zone, with non-Muslims (the Rūs, the Franks, Normans, and Mongols, respectively), encounters which they try to contain through writing, a process which merely emphasises what Homi Bhabha describes in terms of a third space, a disjuncture between enunciator and enunciated. See H. Bhabha, 'How Newness Enters the World', in *The Location of Culture* (as in n. 5), 212–35. The notion of 'third space' is appropriated from Fredric Jameson.

104 On 'intersections' as theoretical contact zones: P. Childs and P. Williams, *An Introduction to Post-Colonial Theory* (Hemel Hempstead, 1997), 185–226; on *Tawḥīd* and *Falsafa*, see the excellent article in this volume by Ulrich Rudolph, 'The Presocratics in Arabic Philosophical Pseudepigrapha', 65–75; P. Adamson, 'Al-Kindī', in P. Adamson and R.C. Taylor (eds.), *The Cambridge Companion to Arabic Philosophy* (Cambridge, 2005), 32–51 (especially 34–9 and 46–9); C. D'Ancona, 'The Arabic Version of *Ennead* IV.7 [2] and its Greek Model', in: Montgomery (ed.), *Arabic Theology* (as in n. 60), 127–55; Atomism: A. Dhanani, '*Kalām* Atomism and Epicurean Minimal Parts', in ed. F.J. and S. Ragep, with S. Livesey (eds.), *Tradition, Transmission, Transformation: Proceedings of Two Conferences on pre-Modern Science Held at the University of Oklahoma* (Leiden, 1996), 157–72. A.I. Sabra has written a wonderful appreciation of *kalām* atomism: '*Kalām* Atomism as an Alternative Philosophy to Hellenizing *Falsafa*', in Montgomery (ed.), *Arabic Theology*, 198–272. A consideration of Rudolph's Arabic Presocratics, of D'Ancona's 'Theological Aristotle' and of Kevin van Bladel's *Hermes Arabicus* (Ph.D. dissertation, Yale University, 2004) reveals that these thinkers were contact zones whose cultural situations permitted a rich series of ideational intersections.

105 J.E. Montgomery, 'Al-Sindibād and Polyphemus, Reflections on the Genesis of an Archetype', in Neuwirth et al. (eds.) *Myths, Historical Archetypes and Symbolic Figures* (as in n. 8), 437–66. See also R. Simon, 'Sindbad the Survivor', in *Islam and Otherness* (Savaria, 2003), 373–95.

106 J. Sanders, *Adaptation and Appropriation* (London, 2006), 9.

107 I have attempted a 'soft' version, which is in part a study of 'impropriation', one which recognises the potential for 'polygenesis' but opts for 'a deliberate act of exclusion': J.E. Montgomery, 'Al-Jāḥiẓ's *Kitāb al-Bayān wa-al-Tabyīn*', in J. Bray (ed.), *Writing and Representation in Medieval Islam: Muslim Horizons* (London, 2006), 91–152. On 93, I discuss 'the impropriation of classical rhetoric as contributory to emergent intellectual and religious interests' and 'stress the electivity of third/ninth century Islamic religio-cultural autonomy.' Deborah Howard's subtle and nuanced contribution to the present volume, 'Memories of Egypt in Medieval Venice', 119–34, oscillates between a hard and a soft account of the Venetian appropriation of Alexandrian identity, wisely leaving room for the notions of diffusion and distillation in her analysis.

108 *History of Science*, 25 (1987), 223–43, repr. in F.J. Rageb et al. (eds.), *Tradition, Transmission, Transformation* (as in n. 104), a volume which contains a series of commentaries exploring the

implications of Sabra's thesis. Page references are to the numbering of the article in *Isis* followed by that of its reprint. See also A.I. Sabra, 'Situating Arabic Science: Locality versus Essence', *Isis*, 87 (1996), 654–70 (repr. in M.H. Shank [ed.], *The Scientific Enterprise in Antiquity and the Middle Ages* [Chicago, 2000], 215–31). Further important explorations of the possibilities and limitations of the appropriation paradigm are: G. Saliba, 'The Development of Astronomy in Medieval Islamic Society', *Arab Studies Quarterly*, 4 (1982), 211–25 (repr. in his *A History of Arabic Astronomy: Planetary Theories during the Golden Age of Islam* [New York, 1994], 51–65); R. Rashed, 'Greek into Arabic: Transmission and Translation', in Montgomery (ed.), *Arabic Theology* (as in n. 60), 157-96; Cheddadi, *Les Arabes et l'appropriation de l'histoire* (as in n. 8).

109 A.I. Sabra, 'Some Remarks on al-Kindi as a Founder of Arabic Science and Philosophy', in A.O. Al-Omar (ed.), *Dr Mohammed Abdulhādi Abū Ridah: Festschrift* (Kuwait, 1993), 607–601 (sic).

110 This phrase is appropriated from an article by Lorraine Daston, 'The Moral Economy of Science', *Osiris*, 10 (1995), 3–24: F.J. Ragep, 'Introduction', *Tradition, Transmission, Transformation* (as in n. 104), xv–xxxiv (xvii–xviii). In this extended commentary on the concept of 'appropriation', the editors identify five inflections to its applicability: 'appropriated transmission and traditions' (xix–xxi; 31–138); 'selective transmission and transformation', in which the accent is on 'expropriation' rather than 'appropriation' (xxi–xxiv; 139–200); 'transmission and linguistic transformations' (xxiv–xxvi; 201–62); 'naturalization and cultural acceptance' (xxv–xxvii; 263–368); 'naturalization and cultural resistance' (xxix–xxxii; 369–480).

111 D. Gutas, *Greek Thought, Arabic Culture: the Graeco-Arabic Translation Movement in Baghdad and Early ʿAbbāsid Society (2nd-4th / 8th-10th Centuries)* (London, 1998). See the reviews by R. Kruk, *Bibliotheca Orientalis*, 57 (2000), 742–4; L. Tuerlinckx, *Byzantion*, 69 (1999), 592–3; B.L. Bevan, *MW*, 90 (2000), 248–50; Ph.W. Rosemann, *Tijdschrift voor Filosofie*, 61 (1999), 369–71; H. Kamaly, *Iranian Studies*, 32 (1999), 575 8.

112 See also Rashed, 'Greek into Arabic' (as in n. 108), 162 and 164–5, for the importance of empire and Baghdad respectively. In making this point, Gutas is developing an argument made by his teacher Franz Rosenthal, *The Classical Heritage in Islam*, trans. E. and J. Marmorstein (London, 1992), 4: 'the ʿAbbāsids no longer stood in that cultural-political opposition to Hellenism which had been unavoidable for the Umayyads'.

113 I have tried to explore some of these implications in 'Al-Ǧāḥiẓ and Hellenizing Philosophy'; for the Arabic-speaking Christian milieu, see the studies of S.H. Griffith, *The Beginnings of Christian Theology* (as in n. 8).

114 *Adaptation* (as in n. 106), 60.

115 See pages 65–76.

116 See, for example, 'Pre-Plotinian Philosophy in Arabic (other than Platonism and Aristotelianism): A Review of the Sources', in W. Haase, and H. Temporini (eds.), *Aufstieg und Niedergang der Römischen Welt, Part II*, 36/7 (1994), 4939-73 (reprinted in Gutas, *Greek Philosophers* [as in n. 2]) (4948).

117 'The Graeco-Arabic translation movement was causally and directly related to the "first Byzantine humanism" and also, through the Arabic scientific tradition in the Islamic world which fostered it, to the renewal of the ancient sciences in Byzantium after the horrors of the '"dark age"' (*Greek Thought* [as in n. 111], 186).

118 151–4.

119 *Classical Heritage* (as in n. 112), 2.

120 See further F. Rosenthal, *Knowledge Triumphant: the Concept of Knowledge in Medieval Islam* (Leiden, 1970).

121 Consider the map of this same city which one might be constrained to draw from the material analysed subtly by Ulrich Rudolph in his article on the Presocratics in this volume, 65–76.

122 Leiden 1992. This edition contains, as supplement on 331–60, his article: 'Humanism in the Renaissance of Islam. A Preliminary Study', *JAOS*, 104 (1984), 135–64. See also the companion

volume, *Philosophy in the Renaissance of Islam: Abū Sulaymān al-Sijistānī and his Circle* (Leiden, 1986).

123 In *Philosophy in the Renaissance of Islam*, Kraemer speaks of 'problems generated by the assimilation of an alien pagan legacy into a society regulated by religious law' (x). It is clear that the extent of the Muslim achievement in the naturalisation of this legacy consists in the integration of a body of materials of refractory alterity. Remy Brague proposes two models of assimilation: 'inclusion' and 'digestion': 'L'entrée d'Aristote en Europe: l'intermédiaire arabe', in *Aristote, l'École de Chartres et la cathédrale*, Actes du colloque européen des 5 et 6 juillet 1997, Chartres, 1997, 73-9 (77-8). I should like to thank Anna Akasoy for providing me with a copy of this article. See further S. Stroumsa, *Freethinkers in Medieval Islam: Ibn al-Rāwandī, Abū Bakr al-Rāzī and their Impact on Islamic Thought* (Leiden, 1999), 218, note 20, and 219, note 9.

124 A. al-Azmeh, *Muslim Kingship: Power and the Sacred in Muslim, Christian and Pagan Polities* (London, 1997), 10.

125 Another example: S. Brock, 'From Antagonism to Assimilation: Syriac Attitudes to Greek Learning', in N. Garsoïan, T. Matthews and R. Thompson (eds.), *East of Byzantium: Syria and Armenia in the Formative Period* (Washington, D.C., 1980), 17–34.

126 Cambridge, 1983.

127 See also page 5, where we learn that 'to diffuse these exotic plants over a very large and, to varying degrees, hostile area was no mean feat.'

128 See the reviews by M. Morony, *MESA Bulletin*, 32 (1998), 185–6; H. Mukhia, *The Medieval History Journal*, 2 (1999), 169–72; E. Wieringa, *ZDMG*, 153 (2003), 209–10.

129 The *Riḥla*, Travel Book, of Ibn Baṭṭūṭa (d. 770/1368–8 or 779/1377) is a perfect example of the textualisation of this zone of human habitation and civilisation, from the Atlantic coast of North Africa to the China Sea.

130 Gutas, 'Pre-Plotinian Philosophy' (as in n. 116), 4945, footnote 7, traces the coinage of this phrase to P. Thillet, 'Sagesse grecque et philosophie musulmane', in *Les Mardis de Dar el Salam* (1955), 55-93 (at 60).

131 Leiden, 1977.

132 Versteegh's theory of influence is fully traditional. He refers, for example, to 'the Arabian conquest of the culturally superior civilization that was Hellenism' (13). Such influence, however, does not, in his opinion, preclude originality: see 18.

133 See for example, C.H.M. Versteegh, *Grammar and Qur'ānic Exegesis in Early Islam* (Leiden, 1993). The case for Arabic grammar as largely an indigenous development of Islamic law has been made repeatedly by M.G. Carter in various publications. See for example M.G. Carter, 'Les origines de la grammaire arabe', *REI*, 40 (1972), 69–97; 'Arabic Grammar', in *Religion, Learning and Science in the ʿAbbāsid Period* (The Cambridge History of Arabic Literature, 3; Cambridge, 1990), 118–38. Account should also be taken of C. Schöck, *Koranexegese, Grammatik und Logik: Zum Verhältnis von arabischer und aristotelischer Urteils-, Konsequenz-, und Schlusslehre* (Leiden, 2006).

134 For an example of the fancies inspired by an uncritical adoption of 'diffusionism', see J. Walbridge, *The Leaven of the Ancients: Suhrawardī and the Heritage of the Greeks* (Albany, 2000); reviewed by D. Gutas, *ArScPhil*, 13 (2003), 303–9; and J. Walbridge, *The Wisdom of the Mystic East: Suhrawardī and Platonic Orientalism* (Albany, 2001). Walbridge's central thesis is that certain philosophical systems are like fossils and thus able to transcend history, via a capacity for total revivification, with the result that textual persistence, in no matter how fragmentary a state, may enable a later philosopher, such as al-Suhrawardī, to reconstruct the system *in all its detail*. Or, as if we could reconstruct the pre-Socratic Heraclitus' complete system (presuming of course that he was a systematiser) from his gnomic utterances: see G.S. Kirk, J.E. Raven and M. Schofield, *The Presocratic Philosophers: a Critical History with a Selection of Texts* (Cambridge, 1999), 181–212; E. Hussey, 'Heraclitus', in A.A. Long (ed.), *The Cambridge Companion to Early Greek Philosophy*

(Cambridge, 1999), 88–112. Despite the egregious role which Walbridge allots to the intellectual capacities of an individual, illumined, philosopher (and thus the extreme idiosyncrasy of this heightened 'appropriation'), I read his work through the lens of diffusionism because of its annihilation of time.

135 The machineries of direct and indirect transmissions, and their complexities, are outlined by Gutas, 'The Life, Works and Sayings of Theophrastus in the Arabic Tradition', in W.W. Fortenbaugh, M. Huby and A.A. Long (eds.), *Theophrastus of Eresus: On his Life and Work* (New Brunswick, 1985), 64–7 (repr. in Gutas, *Greek Philosophers* [as in n. 2]).

136 On 'natural selection', see G. Beer, *Darwin's Plots: Evolutionary Narrative in Darwin, George Eliot and Nineteenth-Century Fiction* (Cambridge, 2000, first ed. 1983), 28; L. Otis, 'Introduction', in ead. (ed.), *Literature and Science in the Nineteenth Century: an Anthology* (Oxford, 2002), xxii; on 'facticity', see Beer, *Darwin's Plots*, 2, and especially the quotation from Barry Barnes on how 'a successful model in science frequently moves from the status of an "as if" theory to a "real description"'; Otis, *Literature and Science*, 9–15; Bloom, 'Criticism, Canon-Formation, and Prophecy', (as in n. 33). It is the agency of 'facticity', for example, which enables modern surgeons to talk unselfconsciously of organ 'transplants' and modern authors to speak unreflectingly of the 'plots' of their books. The imaginative economy boosted by this anthropomorphizing strategy becomes clear when we note that in certain nineteenth century thinkers the process was reversed, the notion of personal identity was introduced into the natural world and the body-machine analogy was valorised in conjunction with developments in industrialisation and technology. Take Herbert Spencer for example who, in *The Principles of Biology* (1864–7), explores 'the distinction between individual in its biological sense, and individual in its more general sense': Otis, *Literature and Science*, 285–9; see further 13–15; Otis, 'Introduction', xxv–vi.

137 Beer, *Darwin's Plots* (as in previous note), 33. See the representation of this 'tree' on page xxxiii; H.E. Gruber, 'Darwin's "Tree of Nature" and Other Images of Wide Scope', in J. Wechsler (ed.), *On Aesthetics in Science* (Cambridge, Mass., 1978), 121–40; St. Alter, *Darwinism and the Linguistic Image: Language, Race and Natural Theology in the Nineteenth Century* (Baltimore, 1999), 5–6, 108–45 ('on the contrast between branching and unilinear conceptions of the relationship among species linked through transmutation' [150]). Alter argues that 'for Darwin, nature's tree rooted wild proliferation in a basic unity; beneath the branching chaos, the common trunk secured a fundamental, indeed organic, integrity' (6). See generally P. Bowles, *Evolution: the History of an Idea* (Berkeley, 1984), 142-205.

138 Beer, *Darwin's Plots* (as in n. 136), xxiv–v; ead., *Open Fields: Science in Cultural Encounter* (Oxford, 1996), 95–114 ('Darwin and the Growth of Language Theory'); Alter, *Darwinism and the Linguistic Image* (as in previous note), argues that the 'emphasis on the similarities between linguistic change and biological transmutation ... supported Darwin's case for evolution as a whole' (6). His discussion entitled 'Ramifications in the Human Sciences' (140–45), afforced with a plethora of reproduced diagrams and schemata, is extremely informative. The classic formulation of the stemmatic method is P. Maas, *Textual Criticism*, trans. B. Flower (Oxford, 1958); on its merits and demerits, see L.D. Reynolds and N.G. Wilson, *Scribes and Scholars* (Oxford, 1991), 207–11; T. Whitmarsh, *Ancient Greek Literature* (Cambridge, 2004), 26–9 (who stresses the patriarchal aspect of controlling the genealogy of manuscripts); Montgomery, 'Introduction' (as in n. 6).

139 See the description of the method in Schoeler, *The Oral and the Written* (as in n. 6), 130–40.

140 *Languages of Nature: Critical Essays on Science and Literature* (London, 1986), 39. This complex of ideas was potently rich in the Victorian imaginative universe and it has been explored to great effect by (among many others): P. Morton, *The Vital Science: Biology and the Literary Imagination 1860–1900* (London, 1984) (an exploration of the literary transformations of the imaginative vitality of the life sciences); L. Otis, *Organic Memory: History and the Body in the Late Nineteenth and Early Twentieth Centuries* (Lincoln, 1984) (on the concurrences of nationalism, philology and evolutionary biology in the question of heredity: 'it was because of analogy that the organic

memory theory promised to unify all knowledge into a continuous system, and this aspect of the idea particularly appealed to lay thinkers writing on the outskirts of the scientific community' [19]'); ead., *Membranes: Metaphors of Invasion in Nineteenth-Century Literature, Science, and Politics* (Baltimore, 1999) (on the collusions of borders, bacteriology and imperialism). It is an interesting feature of Otis' works, especially *Membranes*, that she continues the tradition of the scientists she studies, by applying the lessons derived from her analyses of nineteenth century science as panaceas for contemporary international and social problems: 'to save ourselves from the twentieth century's viruses, we must abandon any such illusory divisions, directing our attention instead to the ways in which we are interrelated. If we continue to believe that connections to others diminish our sense of self, eventually our ideology will kill us' (179).

141 This is one of the sequence of seventeen 'procreation' sonnets (1–17), and the first to introduce the theme of poetic immortality, in the manner of Ovid and Horace: see the commentary by G. Blakemore Evans in W. Shakespeare, *The Sonnets* (Cambridge, 1999), 116 and 127–9.

142 Shakespeare's insight may be unique, but his passage is a Renaissance topos, commonplace also in Antiquity: H.S. Wilson, 'Nature and Art in *Winter's Tale*', *Shakespeare Association Bulletin*, 18 (July, 1943), 114–20. He here anticipates the circularity of Darwin's intellectual strategy in the phrase 'natural selection': nature is personified so as to act like a horticulturalist in tending nature itself and thus to reproduce and replicate nature. See also L.T. Evans, 'Darwin's Use of the Analogy between Artificial and Natural Selection', *Journal of the History of Biology*, 17 (1984), 113–40.

143 Translated by Channa Newman and Claude Doubinsky (Lincoln, 1997), ix: 'any text is a hypertext, grafting itself onto a hypotext, an earlier text that it imitates or transforms.' For Alan Watson, *Legal Transplants: an Approach to Comparative Law* (Edinburgh, 1974), the term 'transplant' is employed in its factitious sense: 'the moving of a rule or a system of law from one country to another, from one people to another' (21). On page 30, the value of any classification of the varieties of transplantation ('imposed reception, solicited imposition, penetration, infiltration, crypto-reception, inoculation and so on') *for its own sake* is rejected.

144 The archaeology of the notion of 'hybridity' has been written to great effect by Robert J.C. Young, *Colonial Desire: Hybridity in Theory, Culture and Race* (London, 1995), pursuing some of the points made in his *White Mythologies: Writing History and the West* (London, 1990), 141–56 ('The Ambivalence of Bhabha'). On the deep link between Darwin and Bhabha, see Beer, *Darwin's Plots* (as in n. 136), xxvi; see also D. Milne (ed.), *Modern Critical Thought: an Anthology of Theorists Writing on Theorists* (Oxford, 2003), 287. In addition to his perspicacious summary of Bhabha's location in late twentieth century theory (286–7), Milne provides a valuable bibliography of critical responses to Bhabha's work (288).

145 Edinburgh. See further my 'Preface' to this volume, vii.

146 If at times in this latter chapter Goodman leaves me wondering how much of Epicurean philosophy was known by al-Rāzī (and, if any, in what form it was made available to him, though see the article by A. Dhanani, '*Kalām* Atomism', as in n. 104), his comparisons are stimulating, judicious and informative. Such intimations of Epicureanism by Islamic thinkers may for the present be most profitably approached as instances of polygenesis, as I would tentatively propose, *in nuce* to be sure and without opportunity for adequate corroboration, for the Stoic presence in the first centuries of the *kalām*. Part of the problem is certainly sloppy terminology, for we ought to reserve the designation of 'Stoicism' for the complete system (its 'all-or-nothingness') and not for those approaches which may voice one or more Stoic inflections or accents: see A.A. Long, 'Stoicism in the Philosophical Tradition: Spinoza, Lipsius, Butler', in B. Inwood (ed.), *The Cambridge Companion to the Stoics* (Cambridge, 2003), 365–92. I think the same reserve ought to be applied to what is sometimes identified as 'Muʿtazilism' in aspects of the thought of al-Ghazālī (d. 505/1111), for example.

147 In Chapter Six, Spinoza's ideas on human freedom are used to elucidate those of Maimonides and these in turn are shown to shed light on the Aristotelian ethical notion of *akrasia*, impotence or incontinence, while in Chapter Five 'friendship' within the Judaic and Islamic tradition is examined. Chapter Four is devoted to the interactions between Maimonides and his Islamic philosophical predecessors.

148 See further N. Walterstorff, *Divine Discourse: Philosophical Reflections on the Claim that God Speaks* (Cambridge, 1995).

149 See D. Sedley, 'The Ideal of Godlikeness', in G. Fine (ed.), *Plato 2: Ethics, Politics, Religion and the Soul* (Oxford, 1999), 309–28.

150 *The Myth of the Eternal Return, Or, Cosmos and History* (Princeton, 1974), 102–12.

151 See, for example, J. Renard, *Understanding the Islamic Experience* (New York, 2002; previously published as *In the Footsteps of Muhammad*); G. Constable, *Three Studies in Medieval Religious and Social Thought* (Cambridge, 1995), 143–248 ('The Ideal of the Imitation of Christ').

152 I owe this realisation of the importance of 'the unused or uncontrolled elements' in metaphor for conceptualizing any methodology to the work done by Gillian Beer on Darwin's use of language: *Darwin's Plots* (as in n. 136), the quotations are taken from page 7. See also Otis, 'Introduction' (as in n. 136), xxi. Otis, *Literature and Society* (as in n. 136), 10, notes of Michael Faraday that he 'used the words "static" and "dynamic" "merely as names, without pretending to have a clear notion of the physical condition which they seem meaningly to imply".'

153 For a similar use of 'Islamic', see Gutas, 'Pre-Plotinian Philosophy' (as in n. 116), 4940: 'it must be emphasised that "Islamic civilisation" includes both the religious and secular culture that was generated not only by Muslims but by members of other religions as well, pagans, Jews, Christians, and Zoroastrians. In the expression "Islamic civilisation", therefore, the term 'Islamic' has more of a cultural than a religious connotation.'

154 Beer, *Darwin's Plots* (as in n. 136), 8.

155 From the sleeve-notes to Gidon Kremer, *Hommage à Piazzolla*, 1996.

Index